A Rose

FROM CHARLIE AND MARIE

A Rose
FROM CHARLIE AND MARIE

Dennis Frank Maček

CITI OF BOOKS

CITIOFBOOKS, INC.
3736 Eubank NE Suite A1
Albuquerque, NM 87111-3579
www.citiofbooks.com
Hotline: 1 (877) 389-2759
Fax: 1 (505) 930-7244

Ordering Information:
Quantity Sales. Special discounts are available on quantity purchases by corporations, associations, and others. For details, contact the publisher at the address above.

Printed in the United States of America.

ISBN-13   Paperback   978-1-960952-25-7
                 eBook   978-1-960952-26-4

Library of Congress Control Number: 2023909712

Table Of Contents

Everything this work represents is dedicated to dearest Judith Kay Wilson, of course, and I must mention Christine Gilbert of Austin, Texas, and John ("Joe") Kuykendall of Reno, Nevada, and Dr. Daigan Lee Matsunaga of the Eikyoji Temple in Hokkaido, simply because I'm awed by large souls.

D. F. M.

FOREWORD

Part 1

Usually when people get the chance they cater to their deepest desires, such as wanting someone to love or wishing to be consumed by some grand adventure, even when those desires are buried or denied. The deepest, most durable longings are inexplicable, such as the urge some people have to self-destruct. They're also irresistible.

Maybe this explains why I married Marie, and why she married me. Now understand, this is apart from simply caring for the other person, which is another matter entirely. We, Marie and I, fit together necessarily, and that only comes from some kind of design. Marie can explain this better.

FOREWORD

Part 2

Charlie is referring to a fact we can't explain: Everyone's life reflects a remembrance of lives past. Yes, I know: we can't possibly "remember" from one life to the next because our brains die. But neither can we "forget" what our real Selves have become. That's the point of having peak experiences.

On Earth, when we had finally come together, we gladly resumed cultivating the Selves we were before we could remember. This is really not a profound concept. For us, on Earth, the profound part was how we came to love each other more and more deeply, and how together we could do great things, beautiful things, things worth dying to accomplish—and things which made certain persons want us to die.

I am able to tell you this because some particulars—such as the image of meditative blue beaming from Charlie's eyes— we do carry into eternity. I can also recall an impression that somehow Charlie was out of place when we met, exactly as though he'd been living on a different planet.

Chapter 1

October 11, 1984
Tegucigalpa, Honduras

Ignoring hints of dysrhythmia and heartburn and promptings of curiosity about the city through which he had passed in a taxi, Hollis "Charlie" Grumbles arrived at the central post office and tried to mentally photograph the ambience before going inside. His inner voice reminded him: *Keep the ol' focus.* This "errand" he presumed to be a trial; bringing it to fruition was all that mattered now. Realizing this mindset caused him a twitch of smile. In a crisis he would be ready to adapt.

With strong strides, gripping a cheap brown briefcase, Charlie entered the stone-and-stucco building and felt another satisfaction when he heard his boot heels tap the clay-tiled floor. The regularity underscored his steady focus. And there he saw the counters perpendicular to a wall festooned with quaint official photographs, exactly as he was told he would, and there he saw a middle-aged man clutching a briefcase enter the lobby from another direction and look around. But the fellow's briefcase was black.

Charlie's mind leaped for solid ground: Maybe the guy had been unable to find a brown one; maybe the instruction was erroneous. Did the color really make any difference? *Don't blow it now after coming so far. Make the sweat in my shirt dry out.*

Charlie busied himself at a central counter by extracting dated magazines and newspapers from his briefcase. A-ha! The middle-aged fellow seemed to be doing likewise at the next counter. It was barely 8:30 a.m. local time; only one other patron was busy in the lobby, and she was on her way out.

"Senor, disculpa me," Charlie said just loud enough to attract the nearby fellow's attention. *"Hay olor a gas aqui?"* ("Excuse me, sir, do you smell gas here?") Charlie felt sure this replicated cheap fiction or scenes in old movies.

"Si usted huele gas por cierto, llame seguridad," the man replied peevishly. ("If you really smell gas, tell the security guard.")

A moment of fragile silence passed as Charlie strove to clear his mind. This was not the way things were supposed to work, in fiction and—especially—now. Slowly Charlie turned to assay the other man. He was middle aged and middle class; prominent grey in his hair and beard. That was per instructions. But he was supposed to carry a cheap brown briefcase identical to Charlie's.

Sh-i-i-t, Charlie said to himself. *How stupid of me.* Methodically he resumed scrutinizing covers of old periodicals he'd pulled from his briefcase, eventually to put them back. *I'm gonna do this no matter what.*

Soon afterward, the middle-aged fellow left the premises and Charlie did meet his contact, who indeed carried a brown briefcase and matched all the descriptors, although he looked much older and fatter than the man who had left. He and Charlie exchanged code sentences and briefcases (yes, the man had noticed a faint gas odor). Then Charlie left the building and promptly departed the country to resume his "errand."

On the prepaid flight back to Mexico City he felt grateful that his gaffe at the post office had only been heard by the man he'd addressed initially; probably he hadn't jeopardized his chance of getting another job like this. He folded his arms over the new briefcase, realizing he had no inkling of what it contained.

That afternoon in Miami, after passing quickly through customs during which he was handed a sealed white envelope, Charlie drove to the Sands motel near the airport in a rented car. There, per instructions, he picked up a swarthy otherwise nondescript man called Julio, who accompanied him to a large two-story brick house about three blocks from the edge of "Little Havana" where Julio tapped in a code to access the front gate.

Given the height of the enclosing wrought-iron fence and the number of outdoor TV cameras visible, the house was clearly a fortress. There were pit bulls outside and not-so-swarthy Hispanic men inside packing pistols and walkie-talkies. Charlie was introduced to a "Commander Raúl," a bemused-looking Latino who could have been taken to be the owner of an insurance agency. After an exchange of code sentences, Charlie handed over the briefcase and envelope to "Raúl" and was summarily escorted out. He returned to the airport where he checked in his rental car and entered the U.S. Customs office, his work almost done.

Debriefing went smoothly. Charlie had little to report aside from his expenses. Per instructions received in Austin, he refrained from asking any questions of his own. He was surprised by some questions his two handlers asked, such as whether he'd heard radio music inside the Honduran post office ("nary a note"), and whether "Commander Raúl's" mustache was grey ("it had some"). He decided they were testing his capacities for observation. They barely seemed concerned about Charlie's assigned small-talk with his contact in Honduras. Had he perceived anything amiss from it? No, he hadn't.

Perfunctorily the debriefers thanked Charlie and indicated that a white unsealed envelope laying along the edge of a desk was for him. He took it and opened it to glimpse inside: several greenbacks, as he'd hoped.

"You'll find ten one-hundreds and ten twenties," one handler said.

"Great! I guess I'm supposed to pay taxes on this, huh?"

No response of any kind. A few beats. Charlie remarked that this had been his first such errand. Again no response except for two nods from one head.

"Does either of you gentlemen have two tens for a twenty?" Charlie said. He felt heady, almost giddy. He understood why: he had something tangible he could actually offer to Marie. Evidently his life had changed drastically, and he didn't know if that was good or if he was sprinting toward catastrophe. He could only intuit he would stay in the current that had brought him to this strange place, whatever it was. Little more than 24 hours earlier he was not only impecunious, he hadn't the slightest hint of the experience he had since undergone.

****

October 10, 1984 (the previous day)
Austin, Texas

Raking oak-tree leaves in his parents' front yard, Charlie decided he couldn't long ignore the well-dressed man who had come to stand at the little fence and watch him work. A white man, early or middle forties, well kept, his car across the street and a door away, the fellow searched Charlie's face as Charlie approached him.

"Good afternoon, Dr. Grumbles," he said. "How's the job-hunting going? This is no idle inquiry; I really want to know."

Charlie saw no reason not to respond. "It's goin' all right, I suppose. There are jobs out there. Most of 'em seem to be scud work, though."

"Oh. Are you going to settle for one?"

"I guess I'm gonna have to. What is your business, sir? I believe I'm clear with the IRS."

"How 'bout I-N-S?" A little smile. "Just a joke."

But Charlie had betrayed a flash of alarm.

The fellow produced a wallet. "My name is Rick Denton. I work for various agencies within the Department of Defense."

He extracted a photo ID and held it high, face out.

Charlie pressed the fence to scrutinize the laminated card. It looked legitimate. Denton replaced it and promptly slid out a clutch of ID cards. One by one Rick Denton showed Charlie ID cards from the NSA, CIA, DIA, and at least three other intelligence agencies. "I have a few more of these yet," Denton said. He fumbled a bit putting the cards back in his wallet. As he slid the wallet into a breast pocket he declared his job title: "I'm Assistant Interagency Coordinator, Pacific Southwest Theater."

Charlie looked impassive. He strongly preferred to have never met this man.

"Actually," Denton commented, "there are only eight of us for the whole world, would you believe. Four of us are assistants; we have to do other kinds of work, too."

"What does an interagency coordinator coordinate?" Charlie asked, surprised that he had asked.

"Well, sometimes assistants like myself coordinate recruitment. Basically, our job is to preclude duplication and cut costs every way we can. I figured as a taxpayer, you would appreciate that. We're very cost-conscious for obvious reasons."

"Yeah? Like which reasons?"

"They're called agency budget cuts. Also Congressional oversight committees."

Charlie determined that despite the man's accommodating demeanor, he was not to be trifled with. Ohh-kaay. "And you're here to cut costs," Charlie said.

"Precisely."

"As a taxpayer, I'm delighted, of course. The more power to you, presuming all those agencies even need to exist, which I doubt. Now, what do you want from *me*?"

"We need your help. We think you need us."

Denton held up an open hand conveying a let-me-finish demand and went on: "We need you to help us by taking up some overload so we can do our jobs. I—we—try to hire on people, just like yourself, for what you might call piece-work. That's how we free up professional operatives in our agencies so they can go about their business and accomplish their various missions. Meanwhile the agencies get by with fewer full-time personnel. I'm sure you know, each permanent employee the government puts on costs a fortune in the long run. We want to keep our full-time operatives on their primary jobs and avert having to put on new ones, which would also entail training them up."

Denton paused for breath, Charlie remained impassive. "Right now we can't afford more professionals," Denton resumed. "You can help by filling a gap now and then. Do a little job here, a little job there; run some errands, do a few chores; all in your spare time. You'll be helping us keep our costs down, and you'll be sparing us grief."

Charlie's first response was a disdainful smile. Then: "You're barkin' at the wrong coon."

"*Au contraire.*" We know with whom we're dealing. That's why we need you." A barely perceptible pause. "And you need us to pay you and protect you."

"Protect me. How will you protect me?"

"*Why* is actually more appropriate."

Then The Unthinkable unfolded. Denton told Charlie exactly what he never wanted to hear from a U.S. government official: that he was technically a MIA but in fact a deserter, perhaps also a traitor. (The subject of why he was called "Charlie" came up.) Did Charlie remember a Corporal D.J. Burke from Boston? Not really. Well, he was the sentry posted in the tree who saw Charlie and one Captain Pat Fromholz being taken prisoner. Did the name Ervin Strait ring a bell? Charlie's mind flashed on a luminous nirvana land, a place known only in dreams—or some past life—but . . . no, sir. Well, one day long ago Charlie gave Pat's dog tags to Major Strait; that was when the major and another downed American flyer were retrieved in Cambodia after being assisted by Charlie and local guerrillas.

"Nah. You've got the wrong fella," Charlie said.

Denton flatly recited a number of facts about Charlie's past. Charlie's eyes widened as he heard thinly disguised ridicule of what he wrote on the first postcard he'd sent to his parents from Hong Kong, which he remembered doing at the urging of Mme. Picard whom he had accompanied to the colony. Recreations of how Charlie had sustained himself in Los Angeles sounded like plagiarisms of his own dreams about past lives.

"The second flyer, the blond-haired fellow," said Charlie. "What happened to him once he got back?"

"Oh, he died—actually got killed—in Tulsa or Kansas City, some place like that."

"And how is Madame Picard?"

"Very uncooperative. I talked to her myself."

Charlie smiled unvolitionally. His mind drifted backward in time, then abruptly returned. "Don't you fellas have better things to do?" he said.

"That's exactly my point! We sure do. That's why I'm here."

"Look, guy. I nearly lost my life over there a number of times. I saw some weird, horrible shit. —If you were in my skin you'd have a hard time sleepin' at night.— I've done my utmost best to avoid anything to do with that whole world you come crawlin' out of because it's, y' know, connected to all that." Charlie paused to regain his animus. "I wish I'd never, ever seen you. Does that tell you anything?"

"I bet we couldn't do better. Except . . . ." Here Denton smiled at Charlie.

"What?" said Charlie.

"Except," continued Denton, "for that well-educated lady friend of yours. Mary Overstreet."

"Marie?"

"Whatever. She's perfect. Actually you led us to her. We wouldn't have found her if it hadn't been for you."

Charlie felt his equanimity shaken. While he steadied himself he responded lamely about Marie being "certainly well trained." In the ensuing moment of space between him and Denton, he felt his mind begin to drift back in time again. He braked it by reminding himself of the truth of the axiom that the past will always persist in the present, in a welter of ways that give us only glimmerings.

****

January 7, 1970
Ahn Loc, South Vietnam

Hauling all his gear and two heavy textbooks, Corporal H. Grumbles, Medical Corpsman USMC, dashed over bare red earth to jam himself into the "Jolly Green Giant" before the rest of the detachment even reached the field. Experience had taught him to be inside a helicopter before the pilot climbed in—at least here—because instantaneously prop wash would turn his universe to red choking dust.

He made it handily and settled in, soon to be joined by two dozen Special-Forces personnel, most of whom were not as quick as he. A Green Beret captain sat next to him and stoically wiped dust from facial crevices and tunic. The huge chopper lifted off. After several minutes the captain regarded the blue-eyed medic at his shoulder with a kindly paternalism despite only about eight years age difference between them.

"You'll be our medic?" the captain said.

"Yes, sir," answered Corporal Grumbles, feeling everyone aboard glance at him. He was of medium size and build, clearly physically fit, facial features unprepossessing except for his serene gaze. The Anglo boy-man approaching age twenty.

The detachment was constituted of jungle fighters and technicians. They were en route to a secret base that happened to be on the other side of the Cambodia border.

"The name's Pat," said the captain, proffering his hand.

"Believe it or not, I go by Charlie," Grumbles said.

Everyone in earshot grinned. Charlie and Pat shook hands. Charlie nodded to men looking his way.

"How come we got us a Marine?" Pat said smiling.

"I happened to be available. I volunteered."

"So how long you been in country, jarhead?" Pat asked.

"Almost nine months," said Charlie.

"Ah! Time to be born again, huh?" Pat said.

"Oh, yes, sir." (A little grimace from Charlie; an exchange of wry smiles.) The captain eyed Charlie's name patch and said, "You're H. *Grumbles*?"

"Used to be a Czech name before it got changed," Charlie responded.

"So how come you go by 'Charlie'?"

Charlie thought through his answer before he spoke.

"I'm not interested in killing anyone. I make sure everybody knows that. But I'm a Marine. So my outfit named me Charlie, like I'm in sympathy with the Cong."

Pat regarded Charlie levelly before he asked, "Are you?"

"Hell, no. They're killers."

Some of the men nearby glanced at Charlie. He sat stoically looking inward, appearing to be quite sane and intelligent, which is actually how he regarded himself.

Charlie reckoned he had proof that he was right about himself. Back home everyone was bent out of shape, one way or another, by the war. But the war was here and they weren't. After he had put in two strife-riven semesters in pre-med at the University of Texas, Charlie joined up to find out what was really going on and to get a break from school. He had turned eighteen the month before he enlisted; his father publicly (and privately) avowed he was crazy. But now that Charlie had a clear idea of some of the realities involved in this war, he, at least, was not bent out of shape. To him the whole conflict was senseless. In all earnest, setting aside preconceptions and prejudices, it was utterly stupid with no hope of redemption. A lot of people were getting killed, or they were being maimed in different ways, for no justifiable reason. This was not to presume that any side—and there were a few "sides"—lacked sincerity or heroism or zeal. Those qualities were spread around to excess.

So what were they fighting about? To Charlie, nobody knew. Occasionally a reason was advanced by a general or a politician, but it could never be sustained; eventually it was allowed to evaporate. The U.S. had not even declared a state of war. There was no creditable purpose or goal for doing that. Charlie determined that probably the North Vietnamese knew what they were fighting for (and to him they were benighted if not mad or stupid), but their lackeys in the south knew less.

Thus for Charlie being in this war was an education in negativity. If he survived (and was mostly intact), he'd have a precious insight by which he could live effectively: Upon culling out the implausible and unreasonable and absurd elements from reality, anything remaining that's worthwhile should be sought out relentlessly and treasured.

Under the engine noise the captain's voice insinuated itself into Charlie's conscious: "Hey, Marine. How come you *volunteered* for this trip?"

Charlie was prepared for that question. "I'm tryin' to learn stuff," he said.

Pat chewed on that for almost half a minute. Finally he said, "Where we're going, I'm afraid you're going to learn that the locals are interesting, all right, but they just don't like Americans."

Charlie glanced at Pat with an expression which clearly asked, "So?"

Pat responded: "So, we'll probably kill a bunch of them."

*

February 2, 1970
Kandal Province, Cambodia

In a caul of comfort-causing sounds of afternoon rain outside his tent, Charlie pored over *Gray's Anatomy of the Human Body* and sipped a Coke. If he tried, he would not be able to recall being happier. The rainfall was a delight; at that very moment, if his experience served him true, sunlight beamed through breaks in the clouds nearby; in a little while the sky would be azure and probably a rainbow would arc the verdant valley to the east. Later he would go out to look across the valley and inhale fragrances subtle and unimaginable.

The worn, blue-covered anatomy textbook Charlie had bought on a whim at a used-books shop in San Francisco; he'd never regretted the tolls he paid for carrying that massive volume everywhere he'd gone in the last ten months. Now he found himself blessed with all the time he could want to read it.

So far, mission casualties were nil; land mines caused the main danger but this locale seemed to be spared of them. To Charlie, the wonderment was Uncle Sam actually paying him to be here.

Charlie's anatomy text, however enlightening, was but prelude to the main treats Charlie would give himself by dipping into a green-covered, old edition of *Chiropractic Principles and Technic* and working through some techniques and their effects. At Cam Ranh Bay a Navy officer who was about to ship home insisted on giving this book to Charlie, and now it was his treasure. A little later today he'd try applying the moves on Captain Pat or whomever he could. He wanted to get a sense of how skeletal manipulations felt and to synthesize what he was learning from both texts. Then, if there were no casualties from the day, he'd explore an area of forest where he had found a stream which apparently emptied into a partially hidden pond of indeterminate expanse. He loved creeks and ponds.

Abruptly Charlie raised his head and listened. Rain had stopped. For a moment he thought he had heard rapid footsteps nearby, exactly as if a person (or two) ran past his tent. He stuck his head out. *Nothing untoward going on.* The ambience emanated peace that seemed almost palpable.

Already golden light beamed on desultory spots of wet green. Charlie found his gaze transfixed by dripping foliage and clean sky. He could smell freshness and renewal rising like vapor all around him. He was sure he could flourish here forever. All he'd really need would be a girlfriend, a very close girlfriend, and much more knowledge of this environment which constantly disclosed surprises. A subliminal prompting made him decide to go talk to Captain Pat who was getting radio transmissions in the command post.

Charlie left his tent and slipped past wet fronds and branches, treading soundlessly on mulch and soft turf. Only the captain would be in HQ which was dug into a small rise about fifteen yards from Charlie's tent. Except for a Boston boy named DJ Burke pulling watch, the detachment was doing a sweep a few miles west. And there stood Captain Pat outside his command post, looking into the entry. Charlie took a couple steps, his mouth opening as he was about to utter a greeting.

Pat whirled around; he appeared distressed, disheveled, wet. He was pointing a pistol right at Charlie; his other hand gripped a grenade. Pat lowered his pistol and spoke to Charlie's eyes, his word like a whip.

"Run," he said.

Charlie braked, turned part-way around, and hesitated. He looked to Pat again.

"Get going!" said Pat. "Go!"

Charlie bolted, Pat busied himself with the grenade. Within twelve seconds the bunker imploded as Pat's grenade went off inside, destroying electronic equipment.

Charlie charged into the bush in a state of anxiety. For the next ten minutes he quietly worked his way through dense forest to circle the camp from perhaps two hundred yards away. Then he slipped back toward it, intending to observe it from cover at the edge of a tiny glade on the north perimeter. Supposedly the invisible sentry Burke was looking down from a tree at more or less that spot; maybe he could tell Charlie what was going on.

Charlie dropped onto his stomach to pull himself under cover of low branches to the edge of the small clearing. He felt sure he was doing everything right; if necessary he would stay hidden until the detachment returned. He finally peered through undergrowth to look across the open area, and realized he lay about eight feet from a pair of pajama-trousered legs and wet feet in sandals. They were motionless at first, then stepping toward him quite deliberately. Just above the moving ankles Charlie could see a rifle end casually pointed downward.

Wondering whether to lie still or spring at the rifle, Charlie abruptly realized that in weeds next to his left shoulder a second pair of feet had materialized, their owner motionless and waiting. Charlie tore a look upward. His gaze traversed the entire length of a rifle barrel before it met narrow dark eyes in a brown face grinning down at him.

Five or six of them marched him back to the ruined command post; some pointed rifles at him, some didn't bother. A few actually smiled his way, fleeting, abstracted smiles. To Charlie only one thing was clear: they had him. All told he saw nine or ten guerrillas, most of whom looked like pre-adolescents, although a couple appeared incongruously aged, almost ancient. Shockingly, two or three were females (he couldn't tell if they were girls or women, nor could he care either way). Charlie began to understand one thing more: he could not project his future because these people met all criteria for being called "irregulars."

Somehow it seemed appropriate to Charlie that when he and his captors reached the bunker, Captain Pat was sitting glumly but unharmed next to a tree. Charlie and Pat exchanged morose nods. A few guerrillas conferred briefly. Apparently an order issued from whatever they said. Someone jabbed Pat with a rifle barrel and he arose. Charlie found himself marshaled back toward the bush in a southerly direction. Everyone moved out quickly. Where in the hell was DJ Burke who was supposed to be on watch? Charlie never found out. In a few minutes, the base camp was back in some other world.

"I wonder where we're headed," Charlie said.

"Search me, pardner," Pat replied.

Sweat streamed from the two men's faces even as they sat resting. The guerrillas had hustled them south and then southwesterly, skirting Pat's Special-Forces detachment with a sure margin of safety. Charlie and Pat were given globs of brownish rice, chunks of some tuber vegetable, and a few strips of stringy jerked meat, exactly the same food (and portions) as their captors. They gladly wolfed down their rations.

"I hope this ain't dog," said Charlie. He tore off a bite of meat and chewed.

"These people don't eat dog," said Pat.

"Strangest Vietnamese I've ever seen," Charlie remarked. "They can't be Cong."

"Uh, I've got some weird news for you, jarhead."

That was when Charlie learned he was in Cambodia, a fact he had only suspected.

"Hope you don't mind too much," Pat concluded. "We might be here a while."

"I wish they'd have let me bring my med kit."

"They've got it. I saw one of them pull it out of your tent."

Charlie brightened. "How about my books?" he asked.

Pat shook his head. "Out here's where we learn to do without almost everything," he said.

Before dusk the guerrillas settled into a congenial spot about two hundred yards from a spring where they posted a lookout, setting up camp without actually making a camp. Thus they could vanish in a moment and leave barely a trace. Cooking was done with charcoal in little pits so smoke was negligible, although the aromas drove Charlie and Pat wild. Some highly emphatic gestures and expressions from the squad leader caused Charlie and Pat to understand their place was here, exclusively.

"They must want us for something specific," Pat declared.

Charlie figured they'd find that out soon enough; he didn't care anyway. These people were exotic, their setting was a paradise, the air and smells were unspeakably energizing. At that moment everyone there knew serenity in the midst of danger. Perhaps death for them all was merely waiting for nightfall. And perhaps the girls or women here knew things unimagined in Texas or California or even Matamoras. God knows what else was known in these parts.

"I can really get into this," Charlie said.

Pat gave Charlie an odd look but soon joined him in voicing observations about their captors and what was going on, the first being that the guerrillas didn't say much to each other. At some point Pat realized why this was so.

"You know, I think they're speaking different languages," Pat remarked.

"Sir?" Charlie said.

"Listen closely. I bet we're hearing at least two-three languages."

Before long Charlie concurred. During dinner—a communal, happy affair with the two Americans included—Pat's lingual observation was confirmed sufficiently to render it fact. Apparently there were two squad leaders; both tried to communicate with Charlie and Pat in languages that sounded different from those used in like attempts by one of the ancients and by Sun Hou, a prankster who looked like a pre-adolescent boy.

After post-prandial drinks and smokes (of strong, indigenously made stuff), Charlie's and Pat's new company exhausted their store of English words with what seemed to be "Americans," "Nixon," and "Mickey Mouse." Eventually the Americans were separated, an extra sentry was posted, and mosquito nets and small rugs were passed around. The band spent the night under stars and woke in a mist.

Immediately after a breakfast of leftovers with strong tea, the guerrillas rose as if to make a bathroom trip en mass, and to Charlie's mild surprise, marshaled Charlie and Pat into an easy-paced march through incredibly thick jungle for the next two hours. By Pat's reckoning they still headed southwest.

Abruptly the terrain rose. Multi-layered vegetation overhead obscured any view of summit. The band stopped to rest before climbing. Canteens and rice balls and pickled vegetables were passed around; per usual very little was said. One of the ancients lit a brown cigarette. With no warning of any kind, hard pops of rifle fire dropped two of the group and they were under attack by some invisible force that could only be described as vicious.

In about two minutes two more of Charlie's and Pat's company lay still, and the Americans found themselves suddenly deserted as the guerrillas melted into forest, carrying off one of their casualties. After the firing ended, Charlie and Pat lay prone for an excruciatingly long chain of moments before they got their first view of their assailants: small brown thugs—male and female—in black pajama uniforms.

"Oh-oh. Khmer Rouge," Pat warned quietly.

As if in response to what he'd said, one of them jabbed Pat's ribs with a rifle barrel. Another kicked Charlie. Further dialogue was quashed.

In short order the corpses were stripped of anything of value, all of which was dutifully collected and turned in to the leader, and the Americans were assayed by the leader and their hands were tied behind their backs with thin, sharp cords. They were also bound to each other's ankles with about six feet of leader between them. Silently and rudely Charlie and Pat were marched away by seven or eight guerrillas in black. They were never able to get a fix on exactly how many there were.

All that day Charlie and Pat were moved due west through untracked jungle. Only the next morning did they get any water; they were given no food until the second evening, and then only some rice. Any deviation from their behaving exactly like automatons was punished severely. Once during their first afternoon, Charlie, walking ahead of Pat, attempted to protest a beetle plainly gnawing on his neck. He was hit so hard in the shoulder with a rifle stock that he fell. Pat bent to protect and encourage him. Instantly three guerrillas clubbed and kicked Pat almost unconscious. With great difficulty Charlie and two Khmers got Pat back on his feet and stumbling forward. Shortly afterwards Charlie discerned that Pat's face was dominated by an abstracted, stoical mien, which Charlie felt compelled to adopt for himself. From then on, a kind of stoicism was the main part of his repertoire for coping with reality.

But even bone-deep impassivity could barely sustain the two Americans during their second morning with the Khmer Rouge. Exhaustion, pain, and acute discomfort had become intolerable when again they came to a stop where the terrain pitched upward.

Brief guerrilla confab; the band turned south. They had barely resumed marching when the green earth beneath the point man, about fifteen yards ahead of Charlie, spewed black for a loud instant; the man and his legs separated in mid-air and dropped. A land mine. Before anyone could react the rear-guard man fell lifeless, and the ambush was on.

Charlie and Pat dropped to the ground and slithered for cover, as much to hide from their captors as to avoid being hit. The Red guerrillas quickly formed a rapid-firing wedge and forged out of encirclement, disappearing into green forest and leaving behind their captives and corpses. A pair of grenade explosions seemed to propel them away.

Physically and psychically drained, Charlie lay face down while silent people surrounded and stood over him. He looked up warily and was greeted by familiar faces showing him tentative smiles. "Aahh-hah!" Charlie tried to shout, but his throat was too parched and his jaw wouldn't work.

Charlie's and Pat's previous hosts promptly cut Charlie's hands free but they did not cut the cords around Pat's wrists. When Charlie stood up he saw why: a grenade fragment was embedded in the captain's left temple; another had shredded the side of his neck. Pat lay utterly still, at peace with everything on Earth.

Reflexively Charlie sprang to feel for a sign of life and found none. Without thinking he grabbed onto a gray-clad Khmer shoulder and held on for a moment. A few comrades looked his way and shook their heads wordlessly.

There was no time to spare. Red guerrillas were nearby, probably aroused like hornets. One of the squad leaders removed Pat's dog tags and handed them to Charlie. Someone put an arm across Charlie's shoulders for a second. The guerrilla band receded into jungle taking Charlie along. He found out why they wanted him only two days later.

June 1, 1970

Houston, Texas

About quarter past midnight Mary Prather Overstreet managed to pull herself out of the Beckenworth Emergency Medical Clinic on the southeast edge of town after the worst day and night of her life. She had long disliked emergency-care facilities, but now she hated white cops and post-adolescent Mexican-American males much worse.

She was the one, not the damned cops, who had been afflicted that night. And that wasn't even considering that she had to butt her head against concrete walls of intentional ignorance and stupidity. And slam into figurative walls she and her fellow VISTA volunteers did every day. That was part of their mission and worth the price they paid for it, they told themselves and believed.

Fine. But lately the price had rocketed out of orbit. Just after 3:30 that past afternoon, shortly after she'd left the junior high school where she taught basic math, biology and language arts, while immersed in thought about teaching adult evening classes, Mary passed a clutch of adolescents sucking beer in front of a vacant shop preceding an alley. (Later she learned that beer was primarily used to mitigate after-effects of inhaling glue or paint- thinner fumes.) She'd seen plenty of retrograde kids in San Angelo, Texas, where she'd already put in two years at the state college. There she found the boys were mostly white and plain stupid, and she herself had done plenty of degenerate things. But these boys were utterly wasted, disgusting. She'd have some acid comments about this for parents she'd interface with that evening.

Mary felt the punks eye her blatantly as she strode past them. She returned their collective stare with a look of thinly veiled contempt. Sure enough: one of them uttered something insulting for her delectation. The others brayed laughter at her and all she represented on Earth. Immediately afterwards she couldn't recall what had been said to her or whether it was in English or Spanish. All she remembered was pausing and saying very clearly with gestures graphic and obscene: "I have seen little, tiny *gusanos en mierda* bigger than what you have, *chicos.*"

Probably the wrong thing to say. For sure, she'd picked the wrong place to say it with no safety buffer. There were five or six of them, and they were primed for any kind of distraction they could find. And she presented an ideal target: attractive Anglo female, barely older than they, alone and burdened by an armful of books.

They surrounded her and before she knew it she was cordoned into an abandoned trash area in the alley. There was nothing she could do—almost. She was pawed over and fingered; her slacks were undone; she was hit at least three times, once flush on the cheek, as she kicked with both feet and scratched with her free hand.

When their fun was finally over they left her gasping and sobbing against a concrete retainer wall. How she made her way back to her flat after that was a mystery to her. Later she recalled taking a very long shower and trimming three torn fingernails. Her right foot was deeply sore; she remembered with satisfaction that she'd felt pain there from kicking one of the punks. She had to halfway smile: if she hadn't been so badly outnumbered she would have held her own fairly well.

That evening, sustained by only a Stouffers turkey tetrazzini entree and a Snickers bar, Mary Overstreet assisted two certified specialists in their endeavors to teach older juvenile delinquents and overburdened adults the basics of math and biology. Mary always tried to do this in tandem with teaching elements of English usage and grammar. This evening she was on an adrenalin high. It helped her step more deeply into her own style of teaching, which had recently begun to emerge and grow. In a moment of reflection, despite her exhilaration, she realized that she would still have to learn more, a great deal more, about everything conceivable, and that included herself.

Shortly after she left the school building for her second walk home, Mary realized with a jolt that she would be learning a lot about herself very quickly, very soon.

She had passed (warily) the spot where she'd been pawed and punched the preceding afternoon and had turned onto Mendoza Street, putting her a block west of a well-lighted arterial street, when she knew she wasn't walking alone. About two seconds after that realization she felt a hand grasp her left arm from behind her; a second hand—belonging to surely another person behind her—clutched her jersey on the right side. She heard a voice: "Come on over here, baby."

"Shii-t!" Mary blurted, and she instantly twisted and lunged forward like a fullback, breaking both grips and gaining impetus. She let drop a textbook and notebook but she held on to her other school materials as she sprinted madly for the intersection ahead, with excited voices right behind her. After she'd gone several strides one of her assailants clutched her jersey again and pulled her to a stop. Mary abruptly turned to face him and tried to kick his groin but only managed to kick a shin. She heard a yelp and looked into the dark face of a very young man stepping back from her. The other man, chunky and also quite young, grabbed her clothing briefly but again she was twisting hard and lunging away. Both punks reeked of beer and cigarettes. Mary broke into a sprint and, to her surprise, got clear without another hand touching her.

When she had gone a few blocks farther Mary noticed her breathing was still rapid, partly because she was fuming. Dirty bastards! What business did they have imposing their grubby selves on her? Plus now she was sans her notebook and biology text. She'd look for them on her way back to school in the morning, which meant she'd have to get up earlier. Maybe she'd better call the police right away, she thought.

And then she was "home": a darkened duplex owned by a Mexican-American family named Villegas. She and two other VISTA volunteers, Carol Jo and Betty, shared half of it for the summer. Nobody was home in either half. She suddenly realized she couldn't call the police because her phone wasn't installed yet. She went inside and turned on lights and proceeded to intimidate a few mice and dozens of cockroaches.

Back in Merkel, Texas, where she'd been born and raised, and back in San Angelo where she lived off-campus, Mary had never even stepped inside a house as overrun with vermin as this one, and this was where she stayed! She shuddered as she spotted mouse turds and roach shit in unexpected places, such as on her cot in the living room. She heard a noise at the back door and wondered whether she'd written her name and address in the notebook she'd dropped. If so, no sweat, she decided; those turkeys who had tried to jump her couldn't figure out how to pour horse piss out of a boot, even with instructions printed on the heel. A noise at the front door: maybe Carol Jo and Betty were back.

Very distinctly, Mary heard herself say *shit* when she saw the semi-familiar young man stride into her living room, his eyes fixed on hers. He'd caught her flat-footed. A quick struggle and she was tackled. She got up but couldn't avoid the punch (along with, "Not this time you don't!") that nailed her head and put her down long enough for the back door to be opened from the kitchen, the other man to be let in, and lights to be turned off.

Only hints of illumination seeped into the room from a street light a couple of doors down. Mary heard a switchblade knife open. They ordered her to keep quiet or they'd use it. To reinforce this point, the man with the knife clutched Mary's hair, pulled her head sideways, and slashed at her face deftly. The steel was so sharp Mary hardly felt it slice across her left cheekbone. She didn't realize she'd actually been cut until she felt the intolerable sting, then her own warm blood spew out and drip on everything within twenty feet. She tried to scream but hands muffled her mouth and the laceration felt like an ember stuck on her skin. They quickly pulled her clothes off and made her lie across the cot on motes of roach droppings. Then they befouled the ambience, in various ways, as each climbed on her and pounded away to get release.

They lingered in the dark afterwards, relaxing and fondling her. Mary was sure they used the word *otro*, and that might have caused her to bunch up her energy for drastic action when she heard the Villegas family return home to their half of the duplex. Hurting and madly outraged, Mary suddenly jettisoned herself off the cot, snatched her jeans off the floor, whipped them at the face of the man who reached for her, and bolted out the front door. Clutching her pants, she charged to the Villegas' door and beat on it mightily as she yelled for help.

The police were hardly sympathetic, both at the Villegas' house and at the emergency-care clinic. Mary Overstreet was sure she'd seen at least one cop smile with amusement (or vicarious satisfaction) when he heard about her dishabille while she had pounded on her landlord's door that night. All four interviewing officers had eyed her up and down; then they refused to comprehend what she, a middle-class white girl, was doing in that part of town. And they were paid good money!

Could she identify her assailants if she saw them again? Damned straight she could. But had she seen both of them in full light? Not both, and one only briefly before he slugged her. *Right, ma'am.* Could she say for sure which one had cut her face? *Given the circumstances, not for sure.* It's gettin' late, ma'am. We've got things that need gettin' done.

At the emergency clinic, as the second pair of interviewing police were about to leave her to the tender ministrations of the swing-shift nurse who kept checking her watch, Mary heard herself address the officers with emphasis and vigor.

"Officer Tanner. Officer Posey!"

They stopped short of leaving and turned to regard her. She eyed them sternly.

"Thanks so much for all your fine assistance. Your helpfulness is just amazing."

They couldn't miss the irony but their only response was to nod to her and touch the brims of their hats. Before they could take a stride Mary continued.

"Would you tell Officers Boutwell and Harmon they'd better say their prayers tonight. They'd better pray their wives never go through what I've been through." Mary paused, then resumed: "And tell 'em to pray that *you* all never go through what I've been through tonight."

She sneered at them and turned away. As the police left they heard her mutter, "I want to be there if it happens."

*

Mary Overstreet felt lucky that her housemates had lent her a five-dollar bill to take a taxi home from the clinic. The drive home was short; instead of going there directly she caused the driver to cruise through the area where she'd been set upon twice in the last twelve hours. She wanted to get a good fix on those *fieros* who'd invaded her person this night, look them in the eyes and get a more defined picture of what she was going to do to them as soon as she possibly could. They weren't anywhere in sight but that was all right. She would be stronger the next time she'd see them. From then on they were hunted men whether or not they knew it. One way or another, she'd find them and repay them even if she had to rent a car for the sole purpose of driving them down.

To her satisfaction, Mary Overstreet never forgot this resolution although it was never fulfilled. In the years that followed she often recalled a different satisfaction in arriving at her flat that bleak early morning and sitting on her besmirched bed (really only a borrowed cot) to crystallize more important resolutions to be realized immediately.

First, to help herself smooth out her own splintered edges, she put some green crumbly substance (left by a visitor who'd been in Austin recently) into a tiny smoking pipe. She lit it and got two good inhalations from it. *Oh, thank God for this stuff!* Then she brushed out her wavy raven-black hair and thought about her sister and her mother back home. Now if only she had a Mars bar or Moon Pie . . . . She went hunting in the refrigerator and, lo and behold, she found Carol Jo's fudgy ice cream. She knew she would eat it all.

As Mary Overstreet ate the ice cream her black, bright eyes (derived from a distant forebear who was definitely not Caucasian) locked onto infinity. She knew she'd have to transcend her resolve for revenge. That meant she'd have to perform miracles within her own psyche as of that moment. *Fine.* Now for Miracle Number One: short of her own death, nothing could make her know defeat. *Ever.*

"Sounds good to me," she said aloud to the dark.

Miracle Number Two was actually overdue: Mary Prather Overstreet needed a personality alteration. *Nothing too drastic, of course.* That would be no problem: from now on she was Marie Prather Overstreet.

"All right!" she said audibly again.

If she had to withstand intolerable experiences—and rebound from them quickly—and if she had to be productive every day and not waste her time and psychic energy, she owed herself this indulgence. Come the dawn, Marie Overstreet would take on whatever came at her.

April 17, 1972

Stung Treng Province, Cambodia

Burdened by ordnance, *Chah-dree dah maydeek* (Charlie the medic) scouted a likely campsite for land mines and edible plants. He also kept an eye out for tigers and, far worse, those little bright-green snakes the Vietnamese called *Hanuman*. His guerrilla group was on a contact search: find 'em, hit 'em, run like hell in a direction away from (but not opposite to) a lush plateau overlooking the River San. If need be, make a stand. Anything to turn them away from home.

And who were "them"? Charlie thought about this every day. Who weren't they? Khmer Rouge, of course. Marauding North Vietnamese. Sometimes American Green Berets who'd call in supporting air strikes. Occasionally they'd see a whole battalion of Cambodian army regulars who always assumed they owned whatever they beheld. Worse were the undisciplined paramilitary brigands, including the Sihanouk loyalists. Once Charlie observed a large patrol of Laotian regulars moving resolutely across an area of forest he was sure was the frontier. Any day, he mused, he and his *compadres* probably would be shooting it out with Red Chinese and North (or maybe South) Koreans, then eventually Russians and—who knows?—maybe some Cubans or East Germans or Polish mercenaries.

What on Earth were all the warring elements doing here? What did they want, for God's sake? Charlie was sure they themselves did not know. Not really. Even if they did, to Charlie's people the issues involved would be irrelevant. All the warring contingents were simply invaders, including those Marxist guerrillas and regular Cambodian army troops who had been born and raised in this very province. To varying degrees, "invader" even applied to some of the people who lived in this delightful part of the land and fought (and often died) to protect it from outside domination.

And who were these denizens? Charlie felt awe whenever he regarded the answer to this question. They—his "comrades" now—were an amazing assortment of Cambodian men and women farmers, strange tribespeople (at least two different kinds), and some international free agents who happened by and settled in. These included Charlie and another American, a black man named Lewis; a few "Brits" (an Englishman, an Australian); a Burmese couple; an Indonesian sailor; a Filipino; a South Korean army deserter; plus five or six persons of indeterminate ethnic or national origin (and in two cases, sex).

They also had the sporadic services of a French nurse named Anouk who was part of the long-time planter family still hanging on in the row of beautiful colonial houses sequestered in a grove. Charlie learned that generations of French-family wealth financed the guerrilla operation. At one time the band even included two downed American fliers, but both had been killed the year before Charlie arrived. Notably absent from the militia ranks were any *Youn* (Vietnamese) and Thais, except for Lanh the carpenter who was half Thai.

They really were a militia, and they were incessantly on call. Every member was an integral part of the highland *kampong*; their mission was to defend it, their home, from invaders. That's what they were doing when they discovered and made off with Charlie and Captain Pat over two years before. Apparently they just presumed that Charlie would grow into their rural, Buddhistic life; thus he would be in their home guard. After a year or so, Charlie realized they were right.

Recently he had even assisted in the helicopter rescue of two fugitive American fliers who couldn't believe an American was helping them go back home, but he himself was irrevocably staying. At first Charlie surprised himself as well. But he rationalized that he was needed here and *couldn't* leave. (Down deep, he knew he wanted clarity in which to define his life and here he was finding it every day.) He could go back when his daily life turned humdrum.

And needed he surely was, although he was lucky to fill the need to an appreciable extent. After he had been recaptured from the *Khmer Krahom* (Pol Pot's Khmer Rouge), Charlie had been taken home—to the largest village of three villages overlooking the San. Evidently his captors intended to acculturate him first, but they needed his services urgently. But what could he do? He was just a medic; all he had was his medic's gear. Then he met Anouk Picard, the nurse, and he did the best he could, from treating land-mine maimings to adjusting dislocated shoulders. But his job was simply too difficult; he needed American stuff: drugs and anesthetic, hypos and scalpels and various instruments. Maybe he could get some of these things from supply store back at the secret base. In about two weeks the militiamen, who by then had reason to trust him, took him back to where they had first captured him.

Charlie was surprised at how quickly he and half-dozen comrades covered the ground between home and his former base camp. On their second afternoon out, he found himself peering into Pat's wrecked bunker. He could honestly say he didn't recognize it. Nor did he recognize the camp, for good cause. The site was in the center of a square, equivalent to a city block, of forest thoroughly cratered by bomb explosions. *For God's sake, why?* To Charlie it was inexplicable (like so many other things) and too absurd to think about. He poked about for corpses but found none, nor did he find equipment of any value. He found only some sports magazines sticking out of dirt near where his tent must have been. His *tent* . . . .

Charlie called for help and he and his comrades dug into a mound along the lip of a crater. Hah! They found his tent buried under three feet of soil and jungle debris, encasing his textbooks on chiropractic science and anatomy, his sewing kit, and an unopened Coke can. A driving rain had begun. In a few moments they were digging in a sea of mud. Charlie was sure that somewhere in this mess reposed letters from his parents, Hollis (Senior) and Marguerite. A call sounded: We *evacuate*. Charlie took up his books and, protecting them as best he could, carried them into the bush.

Now Charlie sat under a huge tree and waited, intending to learn from the monkeys who owned this forest. He would watch their earnest leisure for as long as pleased him, then fix his gaze on the freshly washed sky and just sit, enjoying the fragrance of mid-afternoon air without focusing on it. There was too much work to do in the world; any people confronted with the opportunity to enrich themselves by doing nothing had the mandate, the responsibility, to follow through on it. With this point of view Charlie felt very comfortable.

Along with his load of ordnance and medic supplies, Charlie carried a sack of sweet potatoes and some locally common vegetables. These would be used to garnish—his senses reared up at the thought—a few pre-roasted ducks stuffed with wheat and rice and pork. For appetizers the guerrilla group would roast filets of San River fish, pre-blackened and wrapped in banana leaves. They had clay canteens of homemade aperitifs, metal canteens of local brandy, and various delicacies (by Charlie's standards) to smoke with their drinks.

Along with his efforts to learn Khmer, today using some interesting propaganda leaflets left by Son Sann's troops also patrolling this area, Charlie had intriguing comrades he wanted to learn more about and perhaps interrelate with. On this trip a couple special ones loomed in his mind: their loose pants fit nicely across their rears when they moved vigorously; they smiled warmly into Charlie's eyes and seemed unattached to any men. The night could be especially interesting. Yes, there might be all manner of treats to enjoy before *s'iuf*.

Moving casually, Charlie's fellow guerrillas reappeared on the forest line to his left to set up camp for the night. This seemed a nice-enough spot with sources of fresh water nearby. Abruptly Charlie realized he was gazing at three tan-uniformed figures ahead to his right; they were not holding their rifles casually. Before he could react, several more uniformed figures appeared, all intent on something hostile. A half-dozen of Charlie's comrades stepped into the clearing, braked when they spotted the soldiers, and quickly reversed direction.

A cluster of rifle reports went off at Charlie's right. Shots answered from his left. Tan-uniformed men forged across the patch of clearing about thirty yards from where Charlie sat. One fell backwards and lay still. The rest pushed into the forest and suddenly reappeared (minus one or two) and vanished in the direction from which they'd come. Shooting of all kinds flared up directly in front of Charlie but out of his sight. His breath catching, Charlie stood and crouched, then bolted with his load of gear to join his fellows in the forest, shouting "hey-hey-hey-hey!" so they'd know who he was.

In dense jungle Charlie found himself in a pitched firefight, and he knew fear drilled into his core. From a hidden place just ahead he heard the *thunk* of a mortar shell dropped into a tube. In almost that same moment overhead came a —*whirrr*— then —*ba-looof!*— and earth exploded nearby, shrapnel tearing up foliage everywhere.

Charlie's gut heaved. His arms and hands went feeble. His legs seemed to work but he could barely direct them. Somehow he delivered the ordnance he carried. Again he heard it. *Thunk!* Then —*whirrr*— *Ba-looof!* To Charlie it felt like earth erupted almost under his feet. He scrambled for cover toward the monstrous base of an ancient fig tree which, he noticed later, rose from the edge of an overgrown ravine. At the same time he dragged along a supine comrade who twitched with life.

Plunging headfirst, Charlie slammed against the lumpy base of the tree, barking his bare head on the wood, jolting his neck and dropping his headband over his eyes. His legs splayed over the person he had dragged there. *Thunk!* —*whirrr*— This is it! Charlie thought. The shell was en route to dropping right on him. He was aware of a sudden gust of air. Something electric flickered up and down his body.

Ba-LOOOF!

Concussive impact burst into his every fiber. But the shell exploded in the ravine, shrapnel shredding one side of the tree base shielding Charlie's head, violating live wood.

"*Goddamned mortars!*" Charlie muttered as he realized, actually knew with a certainty, that he was alive through some miracle. *Miracles are real.* Abruptly something close to a miracle occurred: two perfectly rounded implosions forty or so yards away: grenades going off where hidden invaders had dealt out death. Then no more *thunks* and no more mortar rounds coming in. Now Charlie listened to rapid rifle fire and another grenade going off inside the curtain of jungle just ahead. His comrades must have been using the ordnance he'd brought to good effect. In half a minute firing trailed off. The men in tan did not have cause to fight hard. Whatever Son Sann had to offer could not have been worth laying down one's life to get.

Charlie felt something move under his lower legs. He reached back for the body he had dragged with him and felt an absurdly thin shoulder. He scrambled to see who it was. The sight of blood diverted him but he instantly forgot about it. Spitting a Khmer expletive, Charlie realized that his comrade's eyes were open and fixed on his. Then despite her pain a sweet smile spread across her face. Under a brown tunic—breasts rose and fell gently. Ah, yes, Charlie thought again, *miracles really happen.* Later that day, in a private moment, he resolved always to be receptive when they came.

*　　　　　*　　　　　*

Call me anything; of course I have no name. You can call me Ariel if you like.

I do not exist anywhere in the physical universe, but I do exist. Telling you how would be a futile exercise, but to a degree I can tell you why.

My purpose and my nature are one and the same: to help Charlie do those divine things he was—and is—designed to do, that is, when he needs help. Exactly what "divine things" depends on Charlie; the possibilities may be infinite. Consider his Life with Marie. Let me add that I am proud of the way Charlie synthesized what he learned in the moments of crisis you have read about. I had very little to do with that. Sometimes I have had to help Charlie avert a bad fall or else recover after taking one. A spectacular instance of the former would be the time Charlie's corporeal being would have been blasted off the surface of Cambodia if I hadn't suddenly become a stiff breeze that caused a sailing mortar shell to veer off course several yards before dropping and exploding in a gully. I have never gotten proper credit for that one.

Still, I am nothing close to being some kind of "angel," whatever that is. I just do my job. Once I even worked as a functional "person" (replete with a documented history) to give both Charlie and Marie a critical boost in their sideline occupation. When necessary I have been known to help Marie out, of course, because her well-being has been so crucial to Charlie's. Does Marie not have an "Ariel" of her own? I imagine she has. Some things I simply disdain to find out. I do know that Marie's purpose for existing on Earth, or anywhere else, is the same as Charlie's, which is essentially the same as yours and mine: to exercise our natures. We bring ourselves to fruition by doing what we are constructed to do.

Now if my "job" strikes you as being an impossibility, you are right more than you know, if only because those two—Charlie and Marie—have always been a little crazy even by my standards. I suppose this is one reason I love them.

*　　　　　*　　　　　*

May 5, 1975
Tuba City, Arizona

Marie Overstreet dreaded, perhaps feared, the bright charcoal-black eyeballs focused on her when they beamed fear or hurt or confusion or rage. She was afraid those flaring eyes reflected what was in her own. That, along with the children's odors, could weaken her root conviction of rightness in her mission and her manner of carrying it out.

She had little resolve to spare; the odds seemed to be growing against success in her métier, which was to motivate and enable those darling Navajo children to exploit their innate mental capacities. To this she was committed regardless of all resistance.

The hardest recalcitrance, of course, came from parents. Certainly they had reasons for resisting options and knowledge for their children, but never mind their goddamned reasons, Marie had thought often. Even espousing "progressive" ideology, parental reasons for maintaining ignorance or outright stupidity were irrelevant as far as she could see. And when parents resist education, she believed, they cause a kind of evil: Normal children who are not born to be stupid are *raised* to be stupid. And then life spits them out. Of course this was true all over the world, Marie knew; ask any front-line teacher anywhere. Long before Marie graduated from college she had heard incredible stories of intentional stupidity, all of them first hand. Thus she was sure her cynicism was realistic and healthy. Plus it gave her personality an edge that was useful.

Now she waited for little Tonia Chee to come out of the assistant principal's office. Bad enough that the girl disdained using restrooms; she had to show, actually flaunt, her *panocha* to certain boys. Worse, she seemed to think "books" was a four-letter word. (The kid had probably never done a lick of homework. *Ever*.) Marie had decided she would take on the whole Chee clan, if need be; present them with implacable facts and reasons to make definite changes in Tonia's life.

Ah-hah! Marie saw Mrs. and Mr. Chee stalking down the hall toward her, followed by two more adults. That's a lot of bodyweight moving in on me, Marie mused.

The principal's door opened. Tonia stepped out serenely.

"Mr. Perkins says you are picking on me," Tonia announced.

"You do what I tell you, and you will not be picked on," Marie said.

A lot of the kids were quite bright; even this one. Marie was satisfied of that despite her doubts about Tonia's young father who seemed to be minus something. Four parents began to crowd Marie as she ushered Tonia back to the homeroom.

They passed the girls' restroom. Marie stopped and pointed to it. "You will always go in there, from now on. Do you hear me?" she said to Tonia.

She waited for a response. None. The bunch tried sweeping past her to enter the homeroom. Nope: first she wanted a response from the girl.

Apparently everybody thought Marie was kidding. Meanwhile she could hear boys in her homeroom raising holy hell. The girl purportedly wanted to be in the room, which was what her parents and the principal wanted; the boys inside wanted to be out. The villain, to all concerned, was clearly the white witch who persisted in being witchy, despite being grossly outnumbered.

Marie reiterated her requirement and stood her ground as four adults stoically crowded her against the door to the homeroom. Lay a hand on me, you jerk, and I'll deck your ass, her eyes said to both fathers. They summarily laid plenty of hands on her, and breathed on her. The worst was happening. She felt edges of panic cut into her.

Thank God, Marie thought as she spotted fellow teacher Gary McWilliams striding down the hall toward them. *Reinforcement*! She called to him tersely as he approached, and he glanced at Marie over the knot of humanity surrounding her.

"Afternoon, Ms. Overstreet," he muttered and strode on.

Inside a minute, the wild-eyed shouting and shoving began, and built quickly.

Per her own expectations, Marie acquitted herself well that day, although she came close to being physically bowled over and walked on. And few observers would have guessed how perilously close she came to being undone from within. But she made her stand, then went on to perform effectively through two full class periods.

In her cottage that evening, as she smoked a cigarette (the contents of which had been transformed by blending in some green-gold particles and repacking it), she reflected that mental acuity and strength can be a tough handicap to live with sometimes. Here on the reservation—as everywhere else— ignorance prevailed with a kind of perverse pride in upholding it. (A futile attempt at contrast would be trying to tell white people in the suburbs that those big vans they drove were actually a waste of metal and they should get rid of most of their guns.) Yet she would never allow herself to dismiss any class or group of humans as worthless.

"Sheez," she said exhaling smoke. Talk about stupidity: here she was ingesting two kinds of drugs, plus cigarette- paper smoke. Well, now she felt smoothed out. There were people to be loved here, especially the Navajo children. She could appreciate them better when she felt good. And she could appreciate their stark, beautiful land better when she unburdened herself of anger. Thus maybe she could empathize a little with the children's parents, whose tiny nation was stuck like an embolism within her country, which had gotten very sick during the last ten or fifteen years. Both countries could die together.

Despite these grim reflections Marie realized she was feeling refreshed. Good. She needed to revitalize and feel strong. There was much work for her to do, here and elsewhere. Her pride and ego demanded she keep doing it, and that might help her realize the ultimate objective: investing her life with real meaning. She acknowledged that she might be deluded about life—anyone's life—being potentially Meaningful (spelled with a capital "M"); yet this was her commitment, and she affirmed it daily.

Wind moaned outside the glass panes, cleaning off the mesa as it always had. Marie tried to peer through solid wall. Nearby, she envisioned, a coyote was scrambling to run down a jetting gray rabbit. And gaining on it. She wondered how she would fare teaching in a big-city ambience up north and decided she would try that next.

July 29, 1975
En route to the Mekong, Cambodia

This whole situation may have evolved naturally, but it was surely perverse, Charlie thought. Here he was in brown rice-paddy water up to his knees, wearing a conical woven-grass farmer's hat (and French sunglasses brought all the way from Hong Kong), and he was armed to kill: a U.S. M-16 in his hands, an old Japanese semi-automatic pistol in his homemade shoulder holster, and three percussion grenades clipped to his belt, plus a hunting knife. Only God could track the gravitational skeins by which these armaments had slid from points of origin all the way into Charlie's hands in the secluded Kampong they called Prasat. Except for a crude first-aid kit, Charlie the medic carried no medical gear; his tyro apprentice, named Pich Yon, carried some.

The second half of this situation was more perverse: Charlie was leading this militia band, and they were on a deadly hunt. They had ranged farther than usual and Charlie feared getting lost, but they were focused on stalking a swiftly moving seven-man patrol of *akhmau* (Pol Pot's soldiers) who might have penetrated the secret existence of Kampong Prasat, the sanctuary sequestered serenely atop a well-shaded plateau. The few scattered villages and half-dozen hamlets of the kampong, with their attendant fields and orchards of diversified crops, had been a tacit fact in the countryside since long before independence. Now the inhabitants had to preclude *all* outside knowledge of their revered sanctuary. Especially now. Among Charlie's people and comrades an understanding had evolved regarding how to deal with Khmer Krahom: whenever any appeared they had to be killed. Thus Charlie's mission was simple: annihilate that damned patrol.

This was semi-swampy country, flat and green with tangled stands of banyan and fig. Here and there people worked paddies on reclaimed land; Charlie and his band almost always waved or nodded to them, sometimes pausing to ask them about the topography or, say, a passing squad of soldiers. Whether Charlie and his comrades were known here was unlikely since their home plateau had receded far to the east.

Charlie was possibly unrecognizable as an American. His clothing was rural Khmer. He wore a headband under his farmer's hat to hold back sweat from washing off smears of dark brown stain applied to his nose and cheeks as sunscreen and camouflage. Only his short, light-brown beard was a noticeable indicator of Caucasoid stock.

God! What am I doing? Charlie caught himself thinking for perhaps the fiftieth time. Again he had to block out images of his mission's ultimate success. Just do it, don't think about it, he told himself. Absolutely killing seven soldiers seemed to be an unthinkable objective; but failure to do it could be catastrophic. They had to succeed. Charlie forged ahead of the rest of his twelve-person troop. Push through these paddies; get ahead of that bunch of *angkar* thugs; envelope and ambush their asses before they reach a market town called Seng which was nearby on the Mekong. Do or die.

With his Marine-Corps training and constant tenure in the militia, Charlie was better qualified than most fighters living on the plateau to lead a band of guerrillas, although he lacked Khmer-language fluency and the birthright of a native. (Even the Picards, who were all from France, had deeper roots in this land than Charlie.) Regardless, everyone in the kampong knew Charlie was delighted with their country and fascinated by the graceful souls who understood, because of their natures, how to enjoy it. They knew he loved them.

When Charlie used Khmer he spoke it with blunt, humorous authority. He had managed to learn key words and phrases in a few of the languages spoken by groups of locals who were not Khmers. Strangely enough, Charlie found (by chance) that his comrades responded nicely when he'd use an occasional Spanish word or even full sentence. "*Adelante!*" he had said calmly with a wave when it was time to set after the Red patrol, and his troop followed him as one.

Charlie had had little choice but to lead. When the "mayor" Mr. Hop pointed to him, and the elders of one of the neighboring villages concurred, Charlie was It. The two senior militia commanders (both former officers in the Royal Army, one a Cambodian, the other perhaps a Cham) were fiercely ill. Two bands of the militia were already engaged elsewhere, one of them including that other American, the angry black fellow who called himself Lewis. Drought combined with the necessities of harvesting and planting had claimed other likely squad leaders.

Protecting home was becoming increasingly more difficult. Since April things were changing in the countryside. Except for dispirited stragglers, enemies to harass and divert from this lovely plot of forest and farmland had dwindled to one, but that was the angkar of Pol Pot and company, the dreaded Khmer Krahom. Such an enemy could not be harassed and diverted; they had to be killed or completely avoided. Kampong Prasat had become a tightly secured, completely hidden, secret place, to whatever degrees were humanly possible to avoid the death of a holy way of life at the hands of true maniacs.

Charlie had presumed he would actually kill to preserve his kampong, for Life to him now encompassed more than living on the land and knowing its people (and, truly, they were of the land). It embraced harmony and therefore serenity. And great pleasures, be they aesthetic and sublime or outright organic.

Charlie had acknowledged to himself that the magical nights of his still-new Life had set hooks deep into his fiber. The commune food always drove him wild when it was being cooked (and it always satisfied). People depended on him and their respect was unconditional. Of course he was enthralled by the delightful bodies and manners and smiles of vibrant, estrogen-packed women he had come to know, and the incredibly dear children who were ever present, and the intriguing variety of trees and foliage which often hid artifacts (even whole disintegrating buildings) abandoned in antiquity. Immersed in such a Life, Charlie had learned that an entire season could pass on a breeze. Splashing through a paddy, Charlie mused about some of the kampong kids, then he visualized some flirtatious quirks and habits of three or four women who had returned his attentions in recent months. Stepping onto dry turf, Charlie realized he was smiling broadly. He was holding the grin as he turned to regard Pich Chhoun stepping alongside him. A delightful young woman, Pich Chhoun beamed right back at him and emitted a soft, feminine vocable.

"Hi," said Charlie, and he knew he looked foolish.

"Hi," said Chhoun and gave a wry little smile.

Focus, Charlie told himself. He reckoned that if they headed northwesterly about two kilometers and cut back south quickly enough, they'd run right into their quarry. Already he had spotted their distant movements. But if he miscalculated or if the enemy changed course, he'd have to know. He decided to send Chhoun and Ly Nou, both of them quick and smart, on a looping sweep in the opposite direction. They could track the situation and block any *angkar* escaping the trap Charlie envisaged.

Split off they did, and as Charlie and his troop descended a wooded hill and bore right, they could see their enemy traversing another line of paddies perhaps half a kilometer ahead. Charlie's heart started racing. Do or die! Some kind of creature, small and thick, bit into his calf and attached itself there, but there was no time to remove it.

*

Charlie's objective was to cut off and ambush the patrol of black uniforms before they reached Seng. His troop would bury them in the jungle. If the *akhmau* were to reach the town, Charlie envisaged going right after them and shooting them on the streets. If need be, he would do that. In all events, they had to overwhelm the bastards very soon.

Twenty minutes later these thoughts were uppermost in Charlie's mind until he realized somebody was shooting at him. Tops of buffalo grass and weeds flew off on both sides of him. Those hard pops and rattle noises were fired rounds! Without another thought Charlie plunged headfirst toward a banyan stump, sans his M-16. His headlong drop was triggered by a bullet having torn through his left thigh; another had nicked his left wrist and smashed the rifle from his grip.

Flat on his belly, Charlie took all of a minute to understand what had happened and to assess the damage.

"Holy shit," he finally said, and looked around. Everyone in his troop was likewise flat; he couldn't tell who else was hit; a few were trying to return fire. Charlie must have raised his head too much because rounds tore through his hat and knocked it askew. He knew he might die here, but he managed to scootch a few yards to his left to find better cover.

Charlie sensed another burst of rounds zip close overhead. Through patches of tall grass and foliage just beyond him, he discerned where they might have originated: a slightly elevated ridge of tree-covered ground, like a levee, barely twenty yards ahead.

"Oh, you dirty bastards," Charlie muttered.

With a gasp, he tried to focus while he still could. He extricated two grenades and drew his World War II-vintage Japanese pistol which he set before himself.

"You're supposed to die," Charlie informed the enemy. He tried not to realize how precipitous a step he was taking as he yanked the pin from a grenade. Heavy load of death churning in his curled hand, he poked himself up, braced himself for a second on his left arm and throbbing wrist, and flung the grenade with strength and skill summoned by extreme urgency. Even as he let it fly his pitch felt true.

Charlie dropped face down and reached for his pistol. About twenty yards away earth erupted with a pah-*loom!* spewing dirt and debris into air. His arms splayed out, shock overtaking him, Charlie still grasped the pistol butt in his right hand, sighted down the barrel toward the area of grenade impact, and used both hands to squeeze off rounds in case anybody there was vulnerable now.

As if trying to fulfill Charlie's intention, a black figure rose into view precisely at that spot, bending and pulling something heavy. Instantly the black uniform pitched backwards and fell out of sight. What the soldier had been dragging was black: a wounded comrade who crawled into cover.

Charlie was aware of small-arms fire to his left and right; grenades exploded ahead. He squeezed off two more rounds into the patch of bush he had fired at before—and watched in horrified astonishment as the scene replayed: two black-clad figures simultaneously materialized on the run; to Charlie's eyes they had hurtled themselves directly into his line of fire. One dropped like a mannequin chopped off at the base. The other dove out of sight, possibly hit.

Yells of *Ki* flared up from Charlie's comrades as they charged the low ridge. Without actually thinking anymore, Charlie sat up and used pressure to stanch the flow of his blood. He watched as his troop overwhelmed and cut down the remaining *akhmau*. They quickly stripped off and bundled seven black uniforms which they would take away to burn. The band had suffered only one other casualty besides Charlie, a man with a bullet hole through the base of his rib cage. He and Charlie were lifted on makeshift stretchers and borne off into the forest.

Charlie could only lie back, his brain tumbling, and wonder why they were headed the way the way they went. He was in shock: until now he had never been engaged as a combatant; he had never killed before; this was the first time he'd been wounded. He began to presume he would die. Then a jolt deepened his shock.

Led by two scouts searching for additional *angkar*, the band had reached a clearing. There they saw, quite prominently, Pich Chhoun and Ly Nou hanging by their necks high above the ground. Nou had two crimson stains on his tunic; his face showed he had died in pain. Chhoun merely hung there looking calm and barely distressed, incongruously dead. To Charlie's eyes, the two bodies wavered slightly. The next day he knew he had dreamt of them relentlessly, but he could not recall a single dream.

*   *   *

That was the first of two blood-chilling images that would haunt Charlie into eternity: the body of his comrade, a projected lover, hanging utterly violated way up in the foliage, perhaps swinging a little. (In time, Marie would likewise be haunted by images derived from Charlie's sketchy but horrified accounts of this.) Charlie would encounter the second trauma-causing sight many years later back on his native soil.

You might ask, given my job, what I was doing when Charlie got ambushed. Why did I not help him avoid getting wounded? Did I perhaps enhance his aim and strong right arm when he pitched death at the enemy in the bush? Had I pushed those *yothea* into his line of fire?

Two answers are no and no. Another is this: Some things just happen . . . the way they do.

But let me tell you that I always fulfill my role, even if that involves my being on the opposite side of the globe from Charlie, perhaps helping Marie prepare for the relationship she and he would have together some day. From now on you can presume this about me.

*   *   *

Chapter 2

September 15, 1977
Amsterdam, The Netherlands

As though miraculously, as yet incongruously, some lights had already come on around the university quarter of this city, and hints of rose-red and peach danced off patches of canal surface exposed to western sky. Constantly engaged, Marie sat at her sidewalk table and happily took in all manner of relaxed urban activity.

Dear old Jed (short for Jennifer Esther Davis), Marie's best friend since a year ago, would be delighted to see Marie's current circumstances and condition. And someday she would hear of them in vivid detail. Ah, this means Marie must be truly pleased with herself, Marie thought as she observed herself from a distance. *Right*, she responded internally. This moment could be assayed as perfect were she to analyze it. She only wished that her father—dead since she was ten—could see her now.

Part of Marie's exultation was that her whole day had encapsulated a number of secret fantasies. Rene—ah, dear, sweet Rene—had caused her an incredible wake-up orgasm and a luxurious second sleep afterwards; later she had swum, done stretches, and bathed; she had eaten and drunk wondrously that afternoon while doing a bit of sight-seeing; she had even gotten in some reading, some time for contemplation, and a couple pithy exchanges with Rene's associates on why adults might choose to learn subjects not immediately relevant to their lives.

Marie affirmed her notion that she had actually earned all this, which thus vested her existence with a kind of meaning that transcended mere time and the laws of matter and motion.

And no one could seriously begrudge her the joy she was experiencing now. To have reached this state she'd had to live and work by all the rules the world imposed on her, while breaking as many as she could without self-destructing. But mainly she had made risky, creative thrusts at the boundaries of reality (for instance, when she was teaching back in Arizona and then Chicago, routinely setting up her ego as a target in the classroom during every class every day, week after week after week). She realized that she had also been highly fortunate in many ways, so she showed her appreciation of her good fortune by going with it full bore.

A delightfully modulated, Gallic-accented voice sliced through Marie's musing.

"A penny for your thoughts," it said.

Marie's inward gaze shifted out across the table. Rene Mouly smiled directly into it. Notions of "wry," "jovial," "indulgent" caressed Marie's ken.

"Only a penny?" she said.

"I could never afford to pay full price!"

"I was thinking how lucky I am, and how lucky I have been."

"I, too, am lucky. Very lucky," Rene Mouly said. He reached across the table to place a hand lightly on Marie's left hand and wrist.

With her, Rene had never been other than sincere, although Marie knew that he could easily have beguiled her, even exploited her nature and naivete. She had realized this upon living with him for a few months. Marie felt astounded to learn how trusting and deeply needful she was; Rene probably perceived that in her as readily as he would spot first-morning sunbeams on a daffodil. Thus he had always tried to boost Marie's self-expectations. A thoroughly dear man, Marie thought, and she smiled fondly into his brown-liquid eyes, then admired the handsome head as it lowered to regard her fingers.

After a moment Rene looked up at her thoughtfully and said, "Let us get something to munch, as you would say. We can get a good dinner after my conference, at our leisure. They have some fine vegetarian restaurants here. You might like that."

Great; that would give her more space, Marie thought. She would have time to stroll and explore while Rene attended his university conference on how to best recycle scarce metals. Then they'd eat a light dinner after which Rene would suggest all sorts of activities. Perhaps.

Despite his taking good care of himself during his fifty-plus years (and two marriages), Rene often fell into bed well before Marie was ready to do likewise. The man was, after all, immersed in his science and teaching and his business interests, which together afforded him great satisfactions and considerable income. (For months Marie had been astonished by the fact that someone as high-powered and affluent as Rene could act, and actually be, so unpresumptuous and . . . Marie loved this trope . . . laid back.)

"You know, I envy you," Marie said unexpectedly as she and Rene scanned the menu board.

A tiny laugh. "Why is that?"

"I haven't done any real work since May; you are engaged in all kinds of projects. What you do is important within objective reality, not just only for you. Yet you seem to take everything casually; it's never a big deal."

Rene shrugged. "Sometimes it is no big deal, what I do. Maybe all of it. But, as you know, I work hard, sometimes maybe too hard."

For a few moments Marie sat nodding abstractedly.

"Do you want to return to your work?" Rene said this with perceptible deference.

"No. Not yet."

"Good. You have been developing standards."

"Standards?"

An assured little smile, direct into Marie's eyes. "In lovers. In men. From now on, never will you tolerate having less than the best. The very best."

That seemed axiomatic to both.

*

Much later that evening, in their hotel suite, Rene was his usual attentive self toward Marie. Then after they were settled in bed, he gracefully began to emanate an urgent need that truly surprised her, especially in light of their long day.

For years, Marie had presumed that a man possessed of real animus would show her sharp, maybe rough edges. Despite those edges and partly—yes—because of them, she would eventually scream for fruition, for utter release. And when she achieved that state she would shudder and scream even harder and roundly lubricate the spot on which it happened. Now she was experiencing a man whose edges were smooth and strong, and she almost did scream with a shudder. Finally she loosened soft noises which startled Rene and surprised even her.

Hooh! she thought afterwards, nothing like developing high standards.

"Wow, Rene, I've never felt so good!"

"*Bien entendu.*"

He lay back spent, quite happy.

Now Marie was the one to use the words *mon cher* as she prepared to lie close to Rene and dive into delicious sleep. Too bad they had to arise early; they would have to be at the airport by 9:00 a.m. to catch connecting flights home to Aix-en-Provence. "Mr. Europa" planned to conduct two of his senior engineering seminars at the university after lunch.

Later tomorrow Marie and Rene had all sorts of fine activities pending. Even some business would accompany their pleasure: At dinner they would learn from one of Rene's favorite associates how much richer Rene had gotten in the last several days from his investments; indeed, he probably made good money while he'd been making love to Marie tonight. Musing on the bidet for the second time in less than twenty-four hours, Marie hit upon a conclusion much like one-plus-one-equals-two: Life can be just fine.

Returning to the bedroom where Rene lay stretched out casually watching her move about, Marie reminded herself of a premise she'd long considered crystallized: One day she'd live up to all her options and personal gifts. She would fulfill the role or roles for which she was designed. Thanks to Rene and her own growing wisdom, surely she'd do a better job of it than she had done so far.

Once again Marie made herself comfortable for the night next to Rene. In the dark, during their remaining minute or so of wakefulness they addressed immediate concerns. ("Did you tell the desk to call us at seven?" "Did you set out the blue vial?" Et cetera.) They held hands. Marie tried to recall intimations of that interior surge she had felt sometimes when she knew she was thrusting at reality with her entire being. Yes. She would be ready for that again fairly soon.

Seemingly apropos of nothing Marie said, "I owe you a lot, Rene. I always will."

After a moment came Rene's response: "I think I see."

September 15, 1977
Hong Kong Colony

"Very old French wisdom," Madeline Picard, matriarch of all Picards in the Far East, said to Charlie: "The more things change, the more they stay the same. This applies to many, many things. Truly." She paused, then added, "In your world and mine."

"We have different worlds?" said Charlie. Because Mdm. Picard had selected him to help her conduct business in Hong Kong, Charlie resolved to be astute. But often he'd find himself distracted by Mdm. Picard's charming accent and mannerisms, especially her occasional winks.

"Oh, we come from different worlds. But, yes, now we share one. Lucky for us both," Madeline said and winked.

The subject which evoked ancient wisdom was one in which the French have recent knowledge: revolution. Mdm. Picard's point: someday Norodom Sihanouk would be back in charge, if not he himself then his son; to some degree he was still in charge despite seven years of exile. All the Khmer

Rouge would eventually recede into hiding. Then things in Cambodia would be as they had been before 1967; some things still were as before, and would be later. Now the problem was to overcome anomalies, such as foreigners, especially French old-line colonialists, being considered criminals.

By Jeep and helicopter, plane and airliner Charlie and Mdm. Picard had come all the way from their highland sanctuary, crossing practically the breadth of Cambodia, then traversing all of Thailand, to fly to this exotically European city. To Charlie, doing this at first seemed unimaginable, but to Mdm. Picard—"please call me Madeline, Sharles"—this kind of trip was fairly routine. Certain business had to be conducted sometimes.

For Charlie to help out, he needed to look bourgeois and travel with a French passport. Madeline had arranged for both (with some amusement). Still, an American missionary priest whom they'd met on the flight from Bangkok insisted on relating to Charlie in English and treating him as . . . well, an American. Father Jay—"it's really Bobby Jay, but who can stand being called that"—gave Madeline the impression of being psychically depleted. Charlie found his company—and his penetrating green-eyed gaze over the rims of his dark glasses— disconcerting. This was a counterproductive situation.

Charlie needed to keep his wits about him because he carried large amounts of yen, francs, Deutschmarks and dollars all over his person. In Hong Kong he toted around a dirty, old duffle bag stuffed with clothes and cash. Madeline's and Charlie's chief objectives: buy guns, munitions, and other ordnance (after he'd inspected them); ensure that all the materiel got shipped off safely to Bangkok. Their scenario entailed catching up with their shipment in Thailand and taking the materiel on to Cambodia.

Usually Madeline dealt with representatives of underground cartels, a situation that gave Charlie good reasons to feel anxious. Worse, here there was no forest or bush into which he could disappear and fight if he had to. At every lunch and dinner he felt markedly out of place. After a few days he was more than eager to return home on the lovely, green plateau.

Madeline and Charlie spent the better part of five days into the evenings involved in intense shopping, negotiating, and administering. Tangentially they purchased medical equipment and supplies, which they also shipped by air to Bangkok. Then Madeline had to make arrangements to maintain her family's financial well-being; this included bank visits and numerous consultations with fund managers, also with a firm of solicitors. For all this she wanted Charlie's presence because she often physically transferred piles of cash from a bank to a money manager or vise-versa.

Sometimes a banker—always a German—would muse aloud: Did the Picards have more assets to sell or invest if they needed to? Madeline's indirect answer: But of course. Interest had piled up in various funds and accounts. If need be, the Picards could tap their equity in revenue-producing holdings in Malaysia and France. As far as rubber or coffee from Cambodia, however, the answer was direct: "*Notre stock est epuise, mein Herr.*" (Not right now, good sir.)

But someday that last fact would naturally retrogress, Madeline reminded Charlie on a few occasions. "It is but a matter of holding out, winning some time; then winning more time if necessary," Madeline said. She had heard that already the *Angkar Krahom* was devouring itself. "For something sacred, you must be willing to give all," she added. "If you hold back even a little bit, you deserve to lose everything."

Charlie asked, "What if it costs everything the Picards have for us to keep holding out the way we've been doin'; would you spend it all?"

Madeline answered, "Of course."

At dusk during their final evening in Hong Kong, while he was lounging on the bed in his hotel room with a view of lights coming on all around Causeway Bay, Charlie listened to Madeline outline dinner options. She was physically in his room with him, which was most unusual. For the last week of nights they had retired to their separate rooms and vistas. Sometimes they watched Hong Kong television for a while; usually they simply bathed and dropped off.

This evening began to feel festive. Their work here was virtually done. The day had been relatively easy, with a fine late-afternoon lunch at a Thai restaurant. Tomorrow they would finish up and pack. Madeline was animated. Charlie felt energized. Despite constant anxiety, tedium, and exhaustion, the last few days had given Charlie the thrill of fulfilling grave responsibility: he felt confident that ordnance and medical supplies were well chosen. And he had safely escorted Madeline into dark corners and secret rooms scattered over an alien place. He knew she appreciated this, which pleased him.

Madeline broke off her practical considerings and her dark eyes took in Charlie for a brimming instant. Abruptly she seated herself on the bed close to his reposed left arm. Already she had surprised him by knocking at his door perhaps an hour early and pressing herself inside, following him as he nonchalantly returned to the bed upon which he'd been lying to gaze out the window. Except for bath zoris he wore only the powder-blue silk undershorts Madeline had bought for him as part of a wardrobe to see him through the week.

"We should have some wine," Madeline announced.

Charlie presumed she wanted to celebrate their work being well done.

"Sure," he said, only mildly interested.

Madeline took up the phone and called room service. She requested a white, dry French wine, "one which is only a little fruity," chilled, with two glasses, also white French cheese, a loaf of bread (French), and strawberries and peaches. Post-haste.

"One's first consideration should be total comfort with no distractions," she declared. "Next is *l' ambiance*."

With that, Madeline rose to open drapes wide, turn off the television, turn on a distant lamp. The radio was next: 1940's American dance music.

Meanwhile Charlie watched Madeline with burgeoning wonder. She moved quickly, strongly, seemingly effortlessly.

My goodness, she's at least twice my age and she moves better than I do, Charlie exclaimed inwardly. He was also surprised by her leanness which he hadn't actually registered before; in fact, he had never been cognizant of her physique. The satiny pants-suit she was wearing now (with black high-heel boots) revealed things about her. Surely, Charlie thought, she'd had kids, husbands . . . .

Madeline sat again near Charlie's left arm. "Let me tell you a little bit about myself, Sharles." And she breezed through an autobiographical survey of careers, marriages, sons, a daughter, and primary aspirations. She said she wished principally to experience Life on the highest levels attainable by a human being, moment to moment to moment. For more moments, totalled, than anyone in history. As a coda she mentioned that by American standards she would be considered "a man's woman."

The colombard, cheese and fruit arrived and were dispatched with gusto. Dinner could wait, forever if that pleased them. Mdm. Picard and Charlie inexplicably discovered all manner of trivia to talk about, such as how Charlie had managed to get his leg back into shape once the bullet hole had healed. He said it was a careful combination of isometrics and stretches, in tandem with having to use it rigorously. She maintained that his youth helped him more than he realized. Her point: Surely youth is wasted on the young; French people were saying that long before anyone else, except for possibly some aged Buddhist or Vedantist monks. Again with widening wonder, Charlie realized he was becoming captivated by the fragrance Madeline wore, by her dangling gold earrings, by the tiny lines at the corners of her eyes and mouth. *My goodness.*

As Charlie mindlessly focused on a fairly long, deep line etched into Madeline's right cheek, Madeline scrutinized the bullet-entry and -exit scars on Charlie's left thigh. Conversation flickered out. Far down and away the bay had turned blue-black and glittery. To Charlie, this evening was clearly special in ways still unrevealed.

With no word, Madeline casually began rubbing the bullet-entry scar punched into the front curve of Charlie's thigh. At first she barely brushed it with her fingertips. After six or eight seconds the movements segued into a minor massage. Charlie's mind redirected itself to his own body. He thought he felt fit, lean, dynamic. Good. A sigh escaped him as he responded to gentle changes in his self-awareness. Soon one change was alarmingly apparent, and it became more and more so with each half second.

Madeline moved her focus to the exit scar behind Charlie's thigh, sliding her fingertips over to it.

"Is it stiff?" she said.

"The scar isn't!"

"Ah."

Madeline abruptly rose from the bed, removing her suit jacket. "I will show you something," she said and proceeded to completely unbutton her plum-purple blouse, the hem of which she pulled loose from her waistband. As she sat on the bed again she winked and added, "The places I am not wearing what you call 'underwear.'"

"Ah!"

The hand back on Charlie's thigh. Then both hands, the fingernails lacquered in reddish purple. Charlie glanced at two bejeweled finger rings glittering on lean flesh.

"Men respond so fully to a woman's suggestion, even just little tiny hints," Madeline remarked looking positively gleeful.

The thought occurred to Charlie: he actually loved her!

"I'll bet you know many things about men," Charlie said.

"I am thinking, I will show you some things I know," Madeline replied, and she undid her satiny slacks, pulling them loose but not dropping them. "So much depends on good presentation. Enticing presentation."

"I see."

"Do you know how old I am?" Madeline asked.

Charlie nodded he didn't. "It makes no difference," he said, meaning it.

"That's good! It shows you have intelligence; also you are aroused, hot. Now I will show you how to best please a woman such as this; a real woman, not some ooh-la-la little girl." An arch smile full of fun beamed upon Charlie. "Get ready!"

The next morning, under Madeline's urging, Charlie bought a picture postcard and addressed it to his parents in Austin, Texas. He simply presumed they were both alive to read it. On the front he wrote all that he could think to say: "Doing fine, time sure flies! I'll write first chance I get. Take care, God bless.

Love, Hollie"

*   *   *

As you can well imagine, if Charlie had still harbored attractions to "ooh-la-la" young women before that evening in Hong Kong, his episode with Mme. Picard drastically altered that proclivity. Call the event a "young-adult-male fantasy" (or, conversely, a "middle-aged-female fantasy"); yet fantasies can become reality. Charlie and Marie would verify this readily.

Only humans can fantasize, and therefore I cannot. This is one more thing I envy you because fantasy is the prime context for magic. To Charlie, the mere existence of brainy, buxom women with wide shoulders was proof that magic is a gift so wondrous that nobody can realistically aspire to receive it. And that really is true. Therefore when something magical happens, all you can do is accept it.

Who would quarrel with this?

*   *   *

January 2, 1979
Manhattan, New York City

Marie had always thought that self-inflicted damage was an outrage; causing it by ingesting too much alcohol was stupidity beyond comprehension. Yet this was her second consecutive morning of having to recover from precisely that stupidity, gross as it was. Worse, she'd aggravated it by ingesting some "recreational drugs" that she was long unaccustomed to using despite her history of enjoying them.

Oh, God, if she could leave her entire body in a dumpster and get away from it, she would. (Just removing her head would help a lot.) The fact that she'd always disdained celebrating New Year's, coupled with the fact that she was now worse off than most of the bourgeois morons who made a big deal of it, actually caused her depression.

Her best friend Jed, on the other hand, lay on the floor with an ice pack wedged into the juncture of her thighs and might never have been happier. She moaned anyway and gazed piteously at the ceiling. Marie thought Jed's physique and manner of curling up made her look like a bull snake with arms.

A wristwatch ticked maddeningly. Well past noon, this day was gutted.

"If you're going to pay for your sins, you might as well enjoy it," Jed declared when she realized Marie hadn't spoken in over a half hour.

Marie made her mouth work and they tersely reviewed curative measures they hadn't taken. They had yet to take a walk in the fresh air, and maybe a pizza would do them good. Outdoors the temperature was below zero with audible blasts of arctic air knifing down the streets. (The sky was cloudy, but only a few pitiful snow particles survived to reach pavement.) Jed and Marie considered actually taking a walk if they could work up the fortitude. From Jed's windows the streets looked almost deserted even though commerce marched on. Likely they wouldn't get mugged or even approached by panhandlers because muggers and beggars wouldn't be stupid enough to be outdoors on a day like this.

Eventually they opted to send out for Chinese food, which worked out miraculously. By the time they'd finished eating they each remarked (with almost no trace of irony) that this latest development exemplified the kind of vision, insight, and ability to sort through and synthesize data that so empowered them as great teachers.

"Y know, maybe I ought to try your ice-pack thing," Marie said as she and Jed lazily recounted how they'd made fools of themselves recently.

After Marie had returned stateside, her surviving Christmas in New York could have been traumatic without a lot of help. She missed Provence; she was sure she missed Rene whom she had come to regard partly as a father figure. Equally straitening, she had become "an orphan" since her mother had gotten what she seemed to implicitly wish for and died, while Marie was in the middle of touring Central Europe preparatory to going back home. (Marie didn't go back to Texas because the funeral was already taking place about the time she first learned of it.) Fortunately she had Jed's friendship and company (and fine studio couch) to help her over the rough spots; for this she was more than grateful.

Conversely, Jed was delighted to have her friend back. She and Marie had maybe thousands of details to share, a barrage of perceptions and insights to exchange, and vital mutual support to convey. The two women promptly enhanced each other's Life immeasurably. Their bond was broadened by joint efforts to install Marie in the professional and social networks to which Jed subscribed. In short order Marie was either offered or about to be offered good jobs in all the boroughs. This situation helped brighten her mood day to day.

At the same time, Marie realized that she was often irritable, edgy. Mental images of all manner of sexual activity frequently preoccupied her. The reason was patent: she was sex-starved.

God! I'm bereft, deprived, dry, she told herself. One can exist this way for a long time before going crazy, she thought, but *why* for heaven's sake? Maybe some people really couldn't. Men have been known to kill for sex, a fact with which she was learning to empathize. Ah, but thank heaven for holidays and Jed's horny male friends.

Thus Marie's aberrant life style had come to a screeching stop on New Year's Eve and New Year's night, and she was feeling effects similar to Jed's, a result of unabashed excess. Both women considered this turn of events completely natural. Lately they seemed to constantly find themselves in propinquity with attractive, unattached men. Jed decided this was the start of a phase in which she'd try to make up for the deprivations she'd undergone as a master classroom teacher in the New York public-school system. Her professional life had become almost a hell; it had used her up day after day, week after week. "Finally I said, 'Jed, time to get real again,'" she had told Marie. ("Believe me, Tex, getting the old horns shaved off really is the pits, especially when you realize you don't *care* anymore.")

On New Year's Eve Marie and Jed had twice gotten mildly drunk and then high in two different apartments (both times among friends and good acquaintances). At the second place, feeling a definite rapport with a man named Mike or Randy whom she'd met a few times previously (but whose name she could never get a retainable fix on), Marie, by then in unspeakably libidinous straits, managed to spend some very intense time with Mike or Randy in a specially designated bedroom where they found the bed done in black rubber sheets. To Marie, losing her unintended celibacy seemed like a murky, delightful dream, devoid of time and space. The release it gave her felt so good that she imagined herself physically glowing and grinning for about twelve hours afterwards. The following evening she was primed for a pyrotechnic explosion all over again, only this time she'd stay closer to sober so she could enjoy it better.

*

And did she ever.

"Wow, you're luscious!" the fellow named Jeff remarked when Marie pulled off her sweater, then turned and pointed her half-bared rear at him.

Jeff was sprawled bare-chested on Jed's opened studio couch, watching Marie by warm candle light. Jed was inside the lone bedroom with Jeff's companion, a robust man named Andy. All sorts of unseemly noises seeped through the closed door, so Marie had bent forward (wickedly) to turn up the radio volume. Funky neo-bop; F-M, round-about-midnight New-York-kind-of-jazz; subtly thrusting even when swinging. *Perfect*. Marie ensured optimal volume and, still bending at the waist, peeled down her scarlet bikini panties.

Jeff made an appreciative sound. It melded with the music. Turning campy, Marie snatched up a black silk scarf that she tied with deliberation about her hips. She gestured at Jeff's trousered legs.

"You'd better take those off," she said.

In three seconds Jeff, a fit, agile fellow, was totally naked. He lay back with an urbane smile and Marie congratulated herself on picking what had to be a good one.

"What? You don't have fish-net stockings?" Jeff said wryly.

"My last pair's at the dry cleaners."

"Oh."

Marie climbed aboard and casually straddled Jeff on her knees, spreading her *panocha* wide and rubbing it on one of his pectoral muscles, then the other. For half a minute she alternated rubbing spots. Little high-pitched vocables started escaping her. Jeff moaned from his depths, eyes intent on the tower of treats looming inches from his nose. Marie reached a hand behind herself to check the size of their pending connection. *Wooh*. Again Jeff moaned, louder than before.

"Come again?" Marie said.

"Shit, I haven't come the first time!"

Whap! Marie cuffed him on the shoulder.

"Any dirty talk around here, I'll do it," she said.

Marie could feel drugs at work. Grass and coke do not serve any "creative" function, she thought, but they sure *stimulate* creativity. Right now, though, she could be a lot more creative if she had a double-cheese slice of pizza. *Pizza? Saturated fat, cholesterol: a kind of alcohol, right?*

Slowly, she rubbed her lower set of lips a few more firm strokes. She bent and bit between deepening breaths. Jeff's fingers and palms explored and tickled expertly.
Audibles—one voice high and soft, the other voice deep with building urgency.

"Push your butt down here," Jeff whispered after a few more seconds, each of his hands cupping a white globe.

Whap!

"Hee-hee-hee!"

"Hee-*heeh*!"

A different man's voice maybe ten feet away: "*Peee-tsah!*"

Marie's heart clenched into a gigantic fist, Jeff's legs rigidified. Two breaths petrified.

The voice had originated barely beyond Jeff's foot soles. Marie's body and scarf dominated Jeff's vision, but her torso twisted sharply as Marie tore a look at whoever—or whatever—was behind her. Jeff's head snapped up for a glimpse.

There stood a swarthy man wearing a suit and topcoat and bearing a large, flat, white box. "Hi," he said, his eyes widening. He was still buttoned for the cold.

Quickly the man said, "Oh, I thought you were Jed. Sorry." He paused, reflected, then added: "You must be Tex . . . Maria. Jed told me about you. I thought Jed looked a little . . . large . . . compared to the last time I saw her.

"Who are you?" Marie said over her shoulder.

"Looks like Kary," Jeff said below.

"*Yo soy* Kareem Kameen," the dark man said. He was glancing about for a surface on which to lay the pizza box.

"How'd you get in?" Marie demanded.

"Jed gave me a key, long time ago. I'm out on the Island now. Just thought I'd stop by and give Jed her Christmas present. Besides the pizza, I mean."

Marie dismounted Jeff and stepped to the floor, eyeing Kareem, who was putting the pizza on top a stack of magazines on Jed's credenza.

"Hey, I'm sorry to have interrupted," Kareem said. "Where is Jed, Maria?"

"Hi, Kary," Jeff said.

"Hiya."

Kareem—Kary—glanced at the closed bedroom door. Stone quiet in there. Two beats transpired. "Looks like my timing's just great," Kary said dejectedly. He turned toward the front door and started walking.

Marie surprised herself. Distinctly she heard herself announce: "I'm not gonna waste the opportunity, Kary. When there's pizza, I *eat* it." Kareem stopped and looked back. Marie made smiling eye contact with him as she added, "Take off your coat, make yourself comfortable." She ascertained he was short and compact and strongly built, and definitely a different breed. Within a moment he had placed his elegant top coat over Marie's outstretched hands and she draped it over her bare shoulders.

Jed had a good microwave oven and a six-pack of cold beer on hand; the pizza was extra-large and well laden with bad stuff. They saved a few slices on a plate that Jeff put on top a stool and pushed into the bedroom for Jed and Andy.

"Let the air be sweet," Jeff said, closing the door firmly.

"Oh, great," said Kary, I'm going to reek of pizza right into next week. Put a real crimp on my sex life." He winked at Marie. "Unless I can meet some Italians."

"I know what you mean by a crimp," Jeff said to Kary, taking up a condom with his fingertips. "Excuse me," he said to Marie and (with an urgent look) to Kary and padded away, his naked backside quickly receding into the bathroom.

"I'm out of here," Kary said to Marie with a smile. In liquid movements he scooped up his coat and switched off a lamp to put the room in candle light again. In a moment he was gone and Jeff reappeared and, yes, it was time to re-open the box of expensive chocolates Jeff and Andy had brought when they'd arrived.

In a little while Jeff smiled at Marie and it was his turn to adjust the radio volume to get the overall intensity level just right. For a moment Marie felt charmed by the notion that her mind and body together were beautifully analogous to a tuning fork, and it was humming like its ancient prototype. Quickly she made for the bed and scootched onto it, pulling the covers over herself. She peered out at Jeff and said levelly, "You mind gettin' your buns in here."

And even in retrospect everything worked out better than Marie would have expected. Over the years afterwards she would look back fondly at her days and nights with Jed and Jeff, while Kary's status evolved to his becoming her second-most intimate friend.

"My forebears weren't all camel jockeys and elephant hunters," he once told her. "They were mostly traders, procurers, exploiters. They gave to United Way."

When Marie asked him the obvious he replied, "Oh, I'm equal parts Arab and Afro. Hard to stereotype, huh?"

"How'd you get all those muscles?" Jed said to him one day as though she was wondering aloud. "Lots of pushups?"

"Just grew 'em," Kary said, smiling. "I'm a nurturing type."

After a few weeks of chaste companionship with Kary, Marie confided to him that she wanted to know how hard his bare stomach and butt felt to her touch; she wanted to feel some muscles. Kary responded that he would like to find out if Marie was real, not some illusion. At the moment they were in a shop looking at books together.

Mutual wishes were fulfilled that same evening in Kary's loft apartment. "Oh, god, you are a wondrous piece!" Kary exulted after he had gotten the chance to fondle Marie's salient parts. "*Gee*-zus!" he said, and quickly showed Marie he liked to use his tongue and nose a lot. Marie had been happily stroking and caressing masses of dark brawn in various, delightful places, and she found herself astonished by the delicious way Kary did things she loved, using even his thick hair to build a beautiful Gestalt of arousal which—well, which grew like one of those newsreel atomic-mushroom clouds. "Oh, my god!" Marie said after a while, and lost herself to an unstoppable wave of shocking softness that seemed to wash completely over and through her, from soles to scalp.

In the weeks that followed, any time Marie wanted to forget that she was on Earth, Kary was there for her, energetically using little points on her body to build *Gestalts* of intolerable excitement that he would always bring to fruition. Of course he enjoyed his rewards. "I tell you, Maria, after I've been with you, I usually swear I'll never want to screw again," he said happily more than a few times. To which Marie would respond: "I'm moved."

One late afternoon while she was alone in Jed's apartment Marie acceded to herself that she was flattered by the way men in New York City were responding to her. These were accomplished, creative men who weren't necessarily on her wave-length (as Jeff and Kary seemed to be). She liked the drive they possessed to succeed here, the sharp edges to which their personalities had been honed, their testosterone barely under control. She was ready to bet she could smell high concentrations of testosterone in almost any locus in Manhattan, regardless of divergent sexual designs.

But . . . . But what? The men Marie had met here, the single, heterosexual men, never reminded her of— That's it! They weren't anything like laid-back Texans (so many possessed of a touch of the poet that she'd taken that trait for granted). Well, so what? Well, the hard, sharpened edges she saw displayed by men in New York didn't render the men all that sexy or civilized. They seemed to be either acquisitive or just coping with the exigencies of big-city survival. They surely weren't anything like Rene. *Ah, Mon Rene Soigne.* He'd been right of course: Marie had developed high standards in what she expected of men, mostly apropos of how they would try to Live well on a daily basis.

God! I could be in Provence right now, she told herself, knowing that if she were there she'd be treated very well by a man who was fully developed. (A pang somewhere in her core.) Of course, Marie acknowledged, she had realized all along that if she were going to fulfill her various potentials she'd have to pay dearly. That was a fact of life.

Marie sighed as she lay down to nap before she and Jed would go off to engorge themselves with Caribbean food and take a brisk walk in the cold. As Marie's Self drifted into pleasant suspension on theta waves, reality gently exposed a few of its aspects: I bet I could do maybe as well back in Merkle, Texas; even some places in Oklahoma or New Mexico might be all right. Yes, this seemed unassailable. A final tenuous notion: whatever Marie decided to do elsewhere, some day Jed would join her.

January 31, 1979
Stung Treng Province, Cambodia

Bearing his personal gear and two heavy books but sans ordnance, Charlie began picking his way along a sparsely wooded ridge, then stopped. He turned to look back for a final image and found it unremarkable. About twenty paces back perhaps nine of his comrades-in-arms, all of them thin and bedraggled, stood in various postures amid the foliage of their land and impassively watched him. Now they were ex-comrades. Charlie nodded to them and one of his hands rose a few inches and dropped. Reciprocal gestures, tiny smiles. Charlie turned forward and resumed his leaving.

Lewis, Charlie's sole countryman, an irascible Black man from Florida, was not there to see Charlie off. About fifty yards inside the forest Lewis brooded in camp and guarded the guerrillas' gear, including Charlie's scantily supplied medical kit. Almost certainly, Charlie was right: there was simply no reason to go on. But for Lewis, there also seemed no place else to go.

"You can go back; I can't," he had said to Charlie during their final campfire discussion. "What would I go back to?"

Charlie replied that he didn't really know.

"But I do know this," said Charlie. "I'm not good for anything if I'm dead, or if I'm missing my hands or legs."

Speaking for himself Lewis almost said, "Eh, so what?" but merely thought this, glaring into embers.

By now, life was changing in the countryside. The Vietnamese army had invaded and overrun Cambodia. Khmer Krahom resistance still flared up in spots, often on the edges of Stung Treng Province, but *angkar* soldiers were usually steamrolled when they stood in the way of the Vietnamese. —Thank God! Charlie and Lewis had thought quite often.— Logically, the militia to which Charlie and Lewis belonged would have enlisted in the *angkar* to resist the invaders. Actually, they would have much sooner joined the Vietnamese to help root out the Khmer Rouge. But either course would have been self-defeating. Could they have allied themselves with Prince Sihanouk or Son Sann or some other warlord? That would have been pointless and very dangerous.

For Charlie, life had become a senseless struggle to survive in a swamp rife with hidden, lethal dangers. Monsoons attacked his world with abandoned ferocity. Malaria was another threat to which he and his comrades were exposed when they left the plateau. Besides being starved every day—willing even to shoot and eat Hanuman, the divine monkey—Charlie felt deprived of the Life he had come to love (heightened each day by unabashed but gentle women, adorable children, and all sorts of outrageous excuses for throwing a *bon*). In the second-largest village on the plateau actually flourished a tiny *wat*, where, despite his non-fluency in Khmer, Charlie had gotten occasional (and infinitely patient) instruction in the rudiments of Buddhistic philosophy from the three monks or the two nuns in residence. All that could no longer be defended because the primary fact of life to Charlie and his recent comrades was that of course the Vietnamese had found and invaded Kampong Prasat. In fact, they had begun to use it as an outpost.

When Vietnamese columns first cut through Stung Treng Province, Charlie's militia outdid itself trying to divert the *Youn*. Yet every strategy wilted under overwhelming numbers and firepower. In short order the militia took demoralizing casualties no matter what it tried to do. Suddenly one day, entire companies of Vietnamese forged up onto the plateau. They promptly reopened and repaired the two roads to and fro, set up a police station and some communications equipment, then (after prevailing upon monks from the *wat* to conduct thanksgiving rites) marched on. The war was definitely *finie*.

And what of Madeline Picard and Anouk Picard (the stoical nurse) and various unattached women of the commune, and Charlie's favorite militia comrades, and Mr. Pech and Mr. Ny (the village mayors), and an orphan boy called Peou who had taken to Charlie as a kind of surrogate son. It deeply grieved Charlie to wonder about their well-being, with no way of knowing if they still lived and were free.

Aside from Charlie and Lewis and two Khmer men who rarely spoke, Charlie's guerrilla band was reduced to a handful of mountain tribesmen and a few other foreign tribal people who had lived on the plateau but apparently feared returning to it. They were warriors adrift. Finally Charlie had announced in Khmer that he must go home. Precisely for what, Charlie didn't know; he knew only that he must go. Thus he looked back at his remaining comrades for the last time.

****

"Sharles, I'm so glad to see you. I am preparing your favorite stew."

"Madame Picard, I have just come out of the forest. I have avoided Vietnamese checkpoints. Don't tell me you knew I was coming."

"Very well. But if I had not known sooner you were coming, I would have baked a cake, as they say in America. Hoohk! You stink. I will hug you later."

And hug him later Madeline Picard certainly did, although not with the strength and urgency Charlie had expected. In recent months life had been hard on her. Whole companies of Vietnamese soldiers had trooped through her houses. (For a while she considered herself their prisoner.) Except for her cousin Alain who lived in the fourth house, Madeline was the last Picard remaining on the plateau; even Anouk had gone off to Malaysia with no intention of returning.

Many people of the kampong had been wasted serving in the militia as it twisted like a wounded snake trying to fend off the Vietnamese. For several days Madeline was sure Charlie had been one of them until she heard possibly otherwise from Mr. Pech. Some neighbors with whom she'd been close had recently died of typhus, and four promising young persons in whom she took a parental kind of pride had gone off to Phnom Penh with the Vietnamese.

Surely someone of Madeline's age (Charlie had reckoned it was between fifty-five and sixty) required a period of restoration now and then; Madeline must have determined this was the time for hers. And perhaps it would best be accomplished in her family's home back in Burgundy. (Many times previously she had told Charlie about the sprawling ancestral house rising from a limestone plateau—as would be expected—looming over a stretch of river named the Saone.) As Charlie ate, he perceived that her mind was drifting there, and he tried to imagine the scene.

"We should leave this place and go home," Madeline said abruptly. "At least for a little while."

Charlie felt something palpable being shoved inside his viscera and upwards into his brain. Life, he was sure, had been accruing things for him to accomplish. Whatever those things were, they were out there. A person would be wise to fulfill his dharma. But Charlie couldn't feature himself permanently away from Kampong Prasat, although the name for this plateau now seemed inappropriate given Vietnamese occupation. And if he left, could he simply go back to America? His connections to America felt tenuous.

"Where is Peou?" Charlie asked, referring to the boy.

Madeline didn't know. Nor did she know the fates and whereabouts of most of the unattached women and the handful of long-time comrades Charlie asked her about. Now Charlie knew why he had felt a current of sadness imbuing the atmosphere from the moment he stole back onto the plateau.

"Khmer Krahom—where have they gone?" Charlie mused aloud, referring to Pol Pot's murderous Khmer Rouge recently displaced by Vietnam's army.

Madeline responded, "Mostly Thailand I think."

"Will they be able to return?"

"Who can say? Maybe someday."

Futility. Dreadful, dreadful waste. All compounded, over and over and over. No guarantees against more horrifying absurdities; maybe soon. For a long moment Charlie fixed on these realities. They could crush, absolutely crush, the vision he harbored for himself of someday fulfilling his powers and capacities until he would know divine contentment.

"You're right. We should leave," Charlie said.

Madeline merely nodded.

"Will the Vietnamese let us go?" Charlie asked.

"But of course. Provided certain conditions are met."

Madeline displayed her endearing wink. She could arrange to have any "conditions" met, no doubt.

Charlie recalled tense moments during his one experience of vis-à-vis contact with Vietnamese soldiers. About two weeks before, he helped carry two Khmers with most or all of their legs blown off—right into a recently installed Vietnamese outpost incorporating a small town on the San River. (Charlie simply could not avoid exposing himself.) Distinctively foreign-looking soldiers manning a checkpoint (and appearing lightly armed) scrutinized the litters and perfunctorily allowed Charlie and his companions to enter. The *Youn* soldiers made no effort to detain Charlie, although they surely paid him cognizance.

Nor did those he encountered in the town interfere with him; some appeared willing to help. After he left the wounded at an aid station run by a Russian doctor, Charlie was simply allowed to return to the forest. How does one deal with invaders such as that?

"What 'conditions' do they want?" Charlie asked.

"Oh, what you call 'the usual.' What all people want."

Charlie regarded Madeline quizzically. She resumed: "Aside from love, which is exceptional, why does anybody do anything? For money and sex, of course."

"Oh, really. I didn't know people are so simple," Charlie said. "Since when has all this been true?"

"Always, the root of all action is money and sex. Unless love is the reason." Madeline paused to consider her conviction, then resumed strongly: "Many times it is yet more simple, because money is used mainly to *get* sex, one way or another."

She smiled knowingly. Charlie failed to find a comment.

"Sometimes there are substitutions," Madeline added, "but they are not primary. A person sometimes acts because of hate, or desire for revenge; people act on pride. Ah, but always, underneath those reasons, once again—money and sex. This, what our philosophers say, is universal. Also it is natural."

And Charlie found himself beholding a truth about human nature that would resolve a great number of mysteries in his Life from that moment on. He was surprised he hadn't recognized it before. Maybe he had actually known it all along. Didn't the *apsaras*, those ancient, beautiful stone females in jungle temples, tell him this? Still, he intuited that yet another primary human motive existed, maybe the preeminent one, and he felt determined to learn what it is.

"What will you pay the *Youn*?" Charlie asked, now awed by the obviousness of the connection between money and sex and perhaps all the rest of human conduct.

"We will give them what they want. I will find out."

*

Two weeks later, over lunch in the restaurant of a fine Hong Kong hotel, Charlie reaffirmed his notion that he was one of the most fortunate people in the world. (*Easily* one of the most fortunate.) He understood this to be true even as Mme. Picard told him that she couldn't buy him a French passport of high-enough quality to pass INS scrutiny upon his re-entering the United States. Maybe, she offered, he could buy an acceptable passport of some other country, or maybe he could just contrive to smuggle himself back into his homeland. Mme. Picard and Charlie had posited that he would do everything necessary to preclude arrest as a military deserter.

In all events, Madeline said, she would leave for France with her brother on the next day. "Fernie," the brother, was pulling up family stakes in Malaysia to ensure Madeline's return to "civilization." ("He is what you call a troll, but a sweet troll," she remarked.) Charlie would be left to his own devices although Madeline would "loan" him some money and help him contact underground refugee networks in the Colony.

Charlie thanked Madeline Picard for her many favors, he hoped with the sincerity and simplicity he knew she admired. He added that someday, somehow, he would earn the good things that came his way. Madeline responded that she had no doubt he would. Then her lean, lined face and black-liquid eyes appeared abstracted.

"It's good that we're both going back," Charlie said after a moment.

Silence. Notions gestated, crystallized. Soon Madeline declared, "You must always be careful, Sharles." She spoke with gathering strength: "You must never allow yourself to become wasted. All countries have machinery that wastes people. All countries, all the time. Birth is therefore made absurd. It is all so stupid!"

That afternoon, at Madeline's insistence as before, Charlie sent off his second postcard to his parents: "Sure am looking forward to seeing you. Can't really say when, hopefully within the year. I'll be in touch! Love, Hollie," he wrote. "P.S. Take good care of yourself."

Early the next day Charlie met Fernie (indeed a troll) and saw Madeline for the last time. In the first shafts of sunlight to penetrate morning bay mist she looked unexpectedly radiant. She took Charlie's arm as they walked from the lobby to the semi-circular driveway outside.

As Madeline prepared to duck into the limousine bound for the airport she smiled into Charlie's eyes and said, "There is splendor in the world, Sharles. You have proved it, as I have. We have Lived." A wink. "Bye."

With that, Charlie knew he would be trying to stand on tiptoe and stretch his entire being, from this moment on for the rest of his Life . . . straight into the heart of Eternity.

*

June 6, 1979
Waters off west-coast USA

A derelict tanker of Dutch origin, bearing one of those typical names the Dutch put on ships, plied the California Current just west of Santa Barbara, bound for the Port Of Los Angeles all the way from Hong Kong. It would load up in port and head back for Hong Kong but this time sans one esteemed member of its on-board company.

Anomalously, the old tanker veered portside and bore rectilinearly toward the California shore. Soon vehicular traffic on a coastal highway was readily visible to hands on deck. They didn't know this was more or less the spot from which a surfaced Japanese submarine had quixotically shelled the U S of A thirty-seven years before.

Almost casually the pilot turned the ship west to regain course, and—very anomalously—cut off the engines. To the captain and first mate this action was worth two thousand Hong Kong dollars for them to divide as they wished, prepaid in strict confidence. Shouts of farewells sounded on deck. Something splashed off the starboard, followed by more shouts. The old tanker drifted for several minutes before the engines coughed back on. By then a castaway in a lifejacket and clutching a plastic bundle to a surfboard was clear of prop pull, and kicking with the waves to make for gray beach.

Little more than an hour later, walking along the shoulder of Highway One swinging his oilskin bundle, Charlie felt his whole being energized by his swim to shore; to his core he felt he could cope with everything. He was also grateful to forces beyond himself that he'd been foresighted enough to carry new running shoes and clean underwear and a toothbrush in his waterproof book bag. He stopped to open the bundle, enjoying hints of smells of times past, and put on his shoes.

In less than a week Charlie had found his way to central Los Angeles where he submerged himself in American subcultures and eventually acquired a social security card with his old number on it. After a month at the Salvation Army he felt ready to write to his parents to say he was stateside, in good health, and wanted them to come get him. He needed to be home, he acknowledged, and he sure missed them.

*   *   *

So far everything here is prologue, but all of it is important to Charlie's and Marie's story. Bear with me now, for I know of what I speak.

I hope you understand that I am implicit to this story, so you can expect me to interpose like this occasionally, although doing this is only one aspect of my job, which I described to you before and which entailed my doing things that you would consider impossible. For instance in a moment's notice I can—and have—become a Malaysian taxicab driver with a good safety record (as you will see), or a German sailor with proven investment expertise and a philosophical bent.

Does this tell you anything special about the nature of reality? If not, that would be understandable because probably you lack distance. Many of the things you do all the time, things you consider necessary and natural, are really impossible. Thus I am able to communicate with you.

One thing more, and I bring this up because of its relevance. Remember: I never lie to you. I might tweak you sometimes, or inadvertently convey something inaccurate or invalid, but never do I lie. I never have, never will.

*   *   *

Chapter 3

August 22, 1979
Austin, Texas

Feeling clammy, sticky, and (she was sure) smelling funky, Marie stood naked in front of her six-foot-tall mirror and critically assessed what she saw, actually the product of all her activities and some of her knowledge. First arms akimbo, then arms at her sides; then one lateral view, then the other. *Not bad, not bad . . . actually, really good.* A body most women would kill to have, she thought, despite too much time sitting in classrooms and working at a desk and typewriter and, most recently, a computer.

Perfunctorily Marie did a few stretching exercises while scrutinizing the image before her. Nothing wrong with me that a few weeks of concentrated working out won't cure, Marie concluded. She thought she might cut out drinking beer for a while, too. Slowly, carefully, she stretched her quadriceps, then her lower torso muscles. Oh-ho! Thank goodness for this full-length mirror and her balance scale; best investments she'd ever made.

Marie did a few serious stretches prior to taking a shower, all the while reflecting on the day she had experienced up to about an hour before, when her productive energies had been directed to her Ph.D. work at The University of Texas. She would tell Jed in a letter she projected writing that her work in curriculum design and language-arts teaching methods was good. Some of it might even be real, in contradistinction to theoretical propositions or academic gamesmanship. Whether it would lead to anything that would ultimately *mean* something—well, the jury would be out on that for some time.

Out of the shower, Marie cut a sharp sigh as she toweled herself dry. What she really needed at once was some high-quality time for her most central Self. "Oh, lord!" she said audibly, and reality abruptly opened its petals to reveal a glimpse of truth: high-quality time with a thirty-year-old "stud," even a well-trained one, could not satisfy this woman now.

"Gee, *whiz*," Marie muttered exactly as she had thousands of times since she was six years old. "Enough of this stuff."

Marie went to her efficiency kitchen and ate two small bowls of leftover rice and a corn tortilla rolled over a carpet of chunky peanut butter and raw honey. Most of a Coke washed it all down. As she ate she pulled on cotton panties, an athletic bra, and loose outer clothes. Then she brushed her teeth, snatched up her karate ghee which she bundled and tied with her black belt, and bolted from her flat. Advanced class would begin at 6:30 p.m.

Beads of two people's sweat flying in air shimmering with heat, Bobby Hatch slipped Marie's punch and showed his cocky smile; instantly he blocked her follow-up kick to his midsection, the smile even more prominent. He never saw the foot flying at his face as Marie's bodyweight shifted abruptly before him. Without actual thought Marie decided: *wipe it off*. She let the ball of her right foot go all the way into her target.

Boof! Solid impact—bone on cartilage.

"A-a-a-*gkh!*" Bobby saw a spark in black velvet and felt instant pain.

"Shit!" said Marie, seeing a gout of the kid's blood and feeling instant regret.

Everyone who'd observed her sparring with Bobby Hatch agreed: that was one hell of a fine hit. Too bad she hadn't pulled it sufficiently short of breaking Bobby's nose. The instructor of the evening, Jeff Hatch, Bobby's older brother, obliged Marie to drive Bobby to a nearby emergency clinic.

"Next time don't be so stupid," Jeff told Bobby before he left with Marie. "A red belt should be able to handle a combination like that." He turned to Marie: "Killer combo; good kick. Don't do that in here again."

"Don't do what?" Marie said.

"Try to change somebody's attitude."

Marie just nodded and moved on. Pussy! she thought. She didn't know which brother she'd meant that for. A pleasant-looking fellow whose name Marie didn't know unexpectedly accompanied Marie and Bobby out of the dojo, volunteering his pickup truck to drive Bobby to the clinic.

"I can just spray the blood out with a hose, "he said. A wink at Bobby.

In short order they took care of business, leaving Bobby to get his broken nose treated. On their way out of the clinic the man suggested they go directly to a live theatre downtown called Capitol City Playhouse. With luck they could be there by curtain time.

"They're doing *Steambath* by Bruce Jay Friedman," the fellow said. "An American classic if ever there was one. Besides *Streetcar and Salesman*, of course." He gave a pleasant chortle.

Marie cut him one of her assessment glances. He looked nondescript but refined. Something about the way he handled things reminded her of Kary back in New York.

"We've been working out. I'm too funky," Marie said.

"In this town, who isn't?"

He stood waiting. He'd presented a most interesting option, but Marie took her leave and went home (a course of action she would always regret). She simply felt defeated, somehow, and irritable.

Late that same night Marie decided to subvert her budget and do something she actually needed to do: she telephoned Jed back in Manhattan, waking her, to tell her that she'd been meaning to write to her—and she definitely would soon—and lately she'd been vaguely troubled and was turning into some kind of ogre. Bobby Hatch's newly altered appearance, for instance, bore this out.

Jed needed a few minutes to grasp the import of this telephone call. Marie simply talked. There was no one else with whom she could share things that mattered to her.

"You're lonely!" Jed blurted after a few minutes of interchange. "You need real companionship, that's all."

And there it was. The missing key ingredient, the core element absent from Marie's Life: Real companionship, at all levels. It had to satisfy most of her needs; it had to embrace ecstasy. Jed didn't have that, either; she was always "making do," filling parts of the gap in various ways.

Marie's immediate problem, Jed and Marie determined between them, was her being too busy even to "make do." She'd be lucky to find time and energy just to rope a decent "stud." For companionship beyond that—well, she could only pray for a miracle. But they were optimists and true romantics, the women concluded, and they knew that miracles do happen. Receptivity would have to be their watchword.

"I'm glad I called you," Marie said in closure, and Jed croaked a final *bon mot* and threw her a kiss.

August 23, 1979
Los Angeles, California

Even at one hundred yards looking across a busy street (congested by milling vagabonds on both sides), the man's bearing and walk unmistakably belonged to Hollis Grumbles the senior. Charlie barely caught a glimpse of his father to apprehend that. At his vantage point atop a retaining wall across the street from the Sally, Charlie sat transfixed in hazy sunlight by the image of a compact, vigorous, thick-shouldered body with a uniquely rounded head (and, Charlie realized later, looking shockingly older at close range). *So that is what I sprang from!*

Charlie waved futilely. Even if he were spotted, the man likely wouldn't have recognized him for his lined, stubbled face (colored almost iodine by too much sun), his shaggy hair turned partly rufous, and his whipcord physique. (Only his eyes had not changed with the years.) Charlie jumped onto pavement and hurried across the street to intercept his father before he strode into the Salvation Army dormitory in search of his son. En route Charlie shrieked "*Eee-i-i-i-hee-hee-hee-heeh!*" from a crazy joy some passersby clearly noted.

*

For the life of him, Charlie couldn't recall afterwards just how he and his father physically acted when they met outside the Sally. Had they embraced? Leaped and pirouetted? Did they shake hands? Charlie could only remember shouting some banal sentences, perhaps not in English. Had his father recognized Charlie at once or was there a time-delay? Charlie had no recollection.

"Hungry?" his father had asked. Charlie did remember that, along with Hollis saying, "Let's get us some Chinese food."

Only after gorging themselves on Oriental-style fast food did Hollis Sr. broach one of his main concerns.

"Your mother's waitin' for you and she's pissed," he said over his sticky plastic plate. "You can imagine why."

"Hunh," was all Charlie could respond. He had expected this for years but didn't know how to best ameliorate it.

"We'd better head out," his dad said.

They retrieved Charlie's books and his few (very few) personal belongings and took a taxi to the airport. Hollis had booked two seats on Southwest Airlines for Austin, Texas, due for departure the next morning.

"First we need to get us a *mo*-tel room with a shower," said Hollis Sr.

That evening after some more Asian-style food, Charlie and Hollis drank dark Beck's beer in their motel room near the airport and discussed with gusto Charlie's announced decision to become a chiropractor.

Responding to his father's attempt to ask tactful questions, Charlie declared that he intended to earn his living by doing something that would generate real benefits for a lot of people. He mistrusted the American medical establishment. Chiropractic was an effective alternative. He had already developed chiropractic skill without benefit of formal training. He hoped, once he got a degree, to make enough money to buy a good car and experiment with planting various types of trees.

"Oh, a real dreamer, huh?" Hollis said, fearing he'd expose prematurely his utter pride and delight.

"I don't know, sir. May *be*."

"I can tell you a fact that might put a little crease in your picture," Hollis said. "So pay attention."

Charlie paid attention.

"I hope you realize you're considered 'missing in action,' and there's a little matter of where you've been and what you did, and with whom, all the time you've been 'missing.' We're not just talking about several months here, either."

"Yeah, I realize that. But I don't care."

"How's that? . . . I must be missin' something."

"I don't care what anybody's gripe is. People living in this country can't complain about me or anything I've done. If some people working for the government have a bitch, to hell with 'em. I just don't care."

"Well, those same people might see things differently."

"They might not see anything at all, at least as far as I'm concerned. For all they know—or care—I'm dead! I'll just play it like that. In the future, though, I'll pay my taxes and everyone can just go on living."

Hollis mulled over Charlie's vision. If Charlie were mistaken, they probably wouldn't take him away in handcuffs. And if they did— Hell, he could claim to have all sorts of personality defects and mental problems and probably get awarded remedial scholarships and collect disability benefits.

Charlie tuned into his father's thoughts.

"They've got nothing on me, Daddy. Nothing they can prove."

"Maybe they don't have to 'prove' anything."

To Charlie the whole issue lacked merit, although he realized he might be naive. But his potential adversaries were so difficult to underestimate. "They couldn't pour piss out of a boot with directions printed on the heel," Charlie remarked.

"That's quite a figure of speech."

"I got it from you, sir. Long time ago." Charlie regrouped his thoughts. "I might be wrong about the CID, but not those civilian . . . ." Charlie couldn't find a metaphor except for absurd-sounding ones (such as "drunken monkeys").

"White shirts?" Hollis suggested.

"Yeah. Those civilian white shirts jerk off in bunches, as we know. And their right hand doesn't know what their left hand's doin', so to speak."

Hollis responded calmly, "Do you have any real basis for any of this?"

Charlie let a few moments pass while his mind ranged over dimming scenarios in Viet Nam, then to Captain Pat's bombed-out base camp and a Vietnamese-Russian field hospital on the River San. Charlie surprised himself by answering in a dialect he'd abandoned before he'd graduated from high school: "Ah seen thangs wudda made yer *blhud* run cold." (I've seen things that would have made your blood run cold.)

Redundantly Hollis tried to feature some implications. "Just remember, boy," he concluded, "if all you know about is what you've seen, you'll always be in deep squat."

Again Charlie realized he might be underestimating potential adversaries, never a wise course. Still, audacity is often wisest. His were the last words on this irksome subject: "Well, we'll see."

After a late, fat-laden breakfast the next morning, Charlie surprised himself by initiating something he'd considered beyond his capacities. Before he and Hollis departed the motel for home, Charlie simply called his mother to say he couldn't wait to see her—which was true—and he and his father would be home directly. His mother was patently happy to hear this. For Charlie this was a big step toward setting things right. A simple act, he thought, can easily cause magic as well as *karma*.

Hollis was surprised that Charlie had made the call and remarked as much.

"After the stuff I've seen, sometimes it's hard to do even little things that are what you'd call . . . 'normal,'" Charlie said. "It's kind of hard to explain."

"Here in the real world, pretty often nobody cares what you've seen," Hollis said.

Charlie had other things to think about. Rising excitement caused by realizing that he would return home imminently—actually, in time for supper!—made him feel almost nauseous and faint. While they waited to board their flight he tried to focus on something compelling; thus he told Hollis about some interchanges that had occurred between himself and a crew mate, "Dieter the Deutscher," aboard the Dutch freighter from Hong Kong. Dieter, a handsome German national a few years older than Charlie and of radically different sexual design, had been Charlie's apprentice-assistant as the crew's medic. Dieter overtly appreciated Charlie's sharing details from his past, as Charlie often did so he could remember them better. But this Deutscher disdained unconnected visions.

"At least a dozen times," Charlie told Hollis, "Dieter the peter—that's what I called him—pressed me with questions about why I was going back to the United States. 'Vhy do you vish tsu go back, baby cakes?' he'd say."

"Yeah? So what'd you answer?"

"Let's say I tried to answer him. He was real critical. He'd say there's all kinds of neat things to do in the world if a person can stay free of life-constricting patterns. But anything I said I wanted to do would put me into some kind of pattern."

Hollis nodded affirmation. "So why *did* you come back?"

"I'd better accomplish my dharma. Or else. Here I can do it best."

Charlie pondered before he spoke again: "One day I told him I didn't want my life to be just a *schnort* in the night. You know? I could've said 'snort,' but I used *schnort* because it sounds like it could be German. I think I was actually hinting, like, maybe his way of, uhm, existing, might be amounting to that, just a snort somewhere in the dark. I'm referring to universal dark."

"I understand. So what did he say?"

"He said, 'Charlie, you're such a bitch'—with that twinkle in his eyes."

Charlie fell silent as he recalled images of his shipboard friend, then resumed, "That same day he told me, 'You vill find, baby cakes, in real life, ecstasy ist rare. Better you avoid such life, so called.'"

Hollis nodded and commented, "He's right, you know. Sooner or later you're gonna have to pay bills every damned month; every day you're gonna have some kind of family obligations; and finding job satisfaction, that might never happen, unless you've got the right luck. It can be a real grind."

"How do you get around that?" Charlie asked.

"For openers, work for yourself. That's one reason I'm so glad you want to be a chiropractor."

After Charlie and Hollis boarded their flight and got seated, Charlie related to his father Dieter's parting words before Charlie jumped ship: "Charlie Brown, I wish you very much ecstasy. At the very least!" Then Charlie added: "It's the goddamned partings I want to stop, Daddy, from now on."

For several minutes after takeoff, as Charlie faced again the reality of his returning home, he found himself longing ineffably for the food he had known for so long: charcoal-broiled fish with peppers, roasted duck or wild hog, occasional sauteed beef, brown rice with vegetables and fish stew, exquisitely sweet little bananas baked with lemon sauce, among other dishes. (Dreams of eating such food or smelling it cooking used to wake him up in Hong Kong as readily as his nightmares.) A skein of mental associations reprised the thrills he'd felt those few times he'd spotted a tiger—a *real, live tiger, actually in the wild*. Once he had even run after one (armed with only his "gat," the old Japanese pistol) to get a better look, which he was only half successful in accomplishing, thank God.

Hollis brought him back by declaring: "When we get home you're gonna find it's not as congenial and nice as it used to be, mainly because people with money have been colluding with people with bigger money, mostly yankees, and they and their flunkies do everything they can to get rich, which usually involves buildin' and sellin' stuff that nobody really needs. I bet they do that so they won't miss having real lives."

"Yeah?" Charlie said, vaguely interested.

"Yeah, really. Making money is a stop gap. I suspect your European friend would agree with me on this: almost invariably, people use it primarily to get better sex, or else to compensate for lack of it. Blood simple."

"Y' know, I believe I've heard that before," Charlie said.

"It's a truism about human living, sort of like that old saying about death and taxes. Just about everything we do comes down to getting money and pussy, uh, depending on whether you're a man or woman, of course. That's what's really going on, all the time. Very few exceptions."

"How 'bout people doin' things, or making sacrifices or whatever—out of love? That does happen sometimes."

"Yeah, well, that's exceptional. Doin' somethin' out of pride: that's another one." Hollis delved into his subconscious knowledge for a moment, then added: "I believe there's one more exception. It's kind of a mainspring motivation that might be more basic—and widespread—than I've realized."

"Sir?" Charlie said.

"Well," Hollis declared, "unless I'm mistaken, nobody wants his Life to be just a schnort in the cosmic night."

*　　　　　*　　　　　*

There you have it: Charlie's primary motivation for the years ahead, provided his past did not explode in his face. He did project that could happen, but he posited he could deal with it if he didn't find it too irritating. (He fancied himself as having grown a bit cranky.) Did I take some pride in Charlie's development at this stage in his Life? You could say I matched Hollis Senior.

Once Charlie returned home my job was temporarily finished. I resumed it briefly to help him meet Marie at the University of Texas in early spring of 1980. This was in a lounge used by graduate students. Marie was the graduate student; Charlie had followed her there in hopes of talking to her after having spotted her a few times on campus and in other contexts. Charlie was taking undergraduate courses preparatory to attending chiropractic college.

Marie actually recognized him from previous sightings. This time she looked at him closely because he reminded her of rodeo bronc riders she had seen when she was a girl in West Texas. I had to prompt him to look up at her, then smile into her eyes. And I had to prompt *her* to say something friendly to him, which she did although it was soon forgotten by both.

Yet each made an impact on the other; each registered the impact. Period. During the rest of that spring they definitely noticed each other on campus or at the river, and sometimes they nodded or even waved to each other. Eventually Charlie went off to chiropractic college in Portland, Oregon. Marie pursued her Ph.D. until she finished it.

After Charlie earned his chiropractic degree he married a Seattle woman named Beverly, a serious sculptor. They had little affinity for each other, although they did produce a son named Brent. In less than two years they divorced and Beverly managed to get custody of the boy along with a wealth of sculpture tools paid for with Charlie's credit cards. An EMS helicopter pilot where Charlie moonlighted suggested that Charlie set up a checking account for little Brent's welfare and ride a Greyhound back to Texas, which is exactly what Charlie did.

During those same four years Marie fared a little better than Charlie, but her destiny was the same. She worked at two high-level positions, but evidently her experiences dampened her enthusiasm for jobs. I learned that she married a man named Don because he was virile and he needed her help to live as an adult. That union lasted only about as long as the contemporaneous war over the Falkland Islands.

One night in September of 1984 in Tempe, Arizona, Marie determined that she needed more "magic" in her Life. And for this I give her much credit. She resigned her position with the state, liquidated everything, and went off to northern New Mexico for two weeks. Then she segued into Austin, Texas, where she remembered that "magic" can be palpable, and where a person seeking inspiration or wholeness—barely to mention excitement—can (if she is receptive) feel those very forces emanating from the trees and river and creeks. "I'm *home!*" Marie announced to the cosmos when she crossed the city limits.

Evidently for humans, real inner strength sometimes requires a wounding and healing, and loss might be the worst kind of wound to endure. But only humans can grow stronger from that. A strong person is best able to dare things that are dangerous, and the danger, along with daring, carries all kinds of rewards.

*   *   *

Chapter 4

September 26, 1984
Austin, Texas

Striding onto familiar turf, Marie entered the University of Texas campus and declined to stop at a mobile espresso stand near the fountain. She needed to save every dollar she could, but mainly she needed to keep her focus on investigating a pair of job openings to which she'd been referred.

Gentle strains of acoustic guitar music—a hidden duo playing nearby—captured her ken. *Ah* . . . . This was cutoffs-and-Frisbee weather. Mid-morning air held a hint of tang; autumn en route! Days like this beggared any philosophical inquiries. Even better days lay ahead . . . .

"Take one of these flyers, missy."

The words had come from a person sitting behind a card table she was passing. A chubby hand proffered a sheet of paper.

Marie glanced at a sign on the table. It said, "SOTA (Students Older than Average)." A white-bearded, white-haired man with very black eyes leaned forward extending an arm toward her. Marie noticed he wore blue-denim work clothes and was soft-bodied. She took his flyer; he sat back in his chair shaded by a live oak bough.

"You'd better read that and show up there," came the voice again. "You look older than average." A half-smile directed at Marie's eyes.

Marie half-smiled in return. "Thanks, I think," she said.

Marie moved on briskly but scanned the flyer. That very morning, it read, SOTA would meet for forty-five minutes in the graduate-student lounge in Calhoun Hall. Plenty of free coffee. Well, all right, Marie thought. She would be walking right past that building. Instead she could walk through it and help herself to a cup of coffee and revisit all two or three pleasant experiences she'd enjoyed as a graduate student.

Within early-morning mist along the River San, despite having just come down from the plateau with a stomach full of breakfast, a man can find himself stepping into a world totally unknown, replete (perhaps) even with real tigers. Air feels thick and soft there, enhanced by an aromatic fragrance of decomposing vegetation. Utter strangeness and familiar sensations can work wonders in a man's brain, triggering release of all sorts of chemicals inside him. Spongy bottom land cushions feet in sandals as a man presses on, pursuing eternal mysteries. Something unknowable that has always been out there might—just might—suddenly reveal itself to him, if only because he happens to be there, pausing in a clearing between banks of mist. The trick—yes, the trick—was to be alert.

But on a day like this, being somewhere other than here, now, would be woefully self-depriving, Charlie realized with a soft jolt. He found himself entranced by a rotunda of azure interrupted only by tree lines and red-tiled roofs of the University of Texas. Mockingbirds worked through their repertoires as though they were trying to merge themselves with everything they saw. Young men in cut-off shorts chased Frisbees in open spaces. Oh, God! Charlie thought. Yes, I'm grateful.

For now, the macro-scene was too much to take in at once. Charlie glanced at a small white sign attached to a collapsible table he was passing. The table, tended by a chubby man with white hair and a white beard, belonged to a campus organization called SOTA (Students Older Than Average). The man seated at the table took pains to make eye contact with Charlie.

"Hi, guy," the fellow said. "Take one of these."

He handed Charlie a printed flyer, which Charlie scanned mindlessly as he stepped forward. Uttered words made Charlie pause and look back.

"Hey, don't miss it, bubba! You don't want to not go." The man was talking to Charlie.

"Huh?" said Charlie.

The fellow repeated himself, adding: "Trust me on this."

"Sure," Charlie said. He scrutinized the man's face for a second and looked into luminous black eyes.

"You seem to be familiar somehow," Charlie remarked. "Do I know you?"

The fellow laughed easily. "Not in this life," he said. "Even though we seem to dress pretty much the same."

Charlie ignored the latter assertion since he himself wore a form-fitting T-shirt and running shorts, although, he realized later, he often did wear blue denims. "It's the attitude I emanate," the man remarked. "We're kindred souls. Hey, make sure you show up at this. Starts in ten minutes. [Beat.] Free coffee."

With a hint of smile and a nod, Charlie moved on. He said "thanks" over his shoulder to the fellow and got a little wave in return.

Well, what the heck, Charlie thought. He was on campus to look up kinesthesiology instructors who were performing a study and needed physically fit subjects older-than-average-student age. Charlie was curious about the thrust of their work and he needed every dollar he could get. Coffee would hit the spot at the moment, and he could score a free cup in the lounge in Calhoun Hall and be out of there before the meeting started. And he could scan the faces of people who'd be there because, somehow, he felt he needed to do that.

****

Marie stood along a wall, close to an exit, sipping from a Styrofoam cup and casually observing others in the lounge. A few graduate students were relaxing there, but no meeting seemed imminent. Charlie walked in, turned her way, and their eyes met.

Instant mutual recognition, a fact that both registered.

Charlie smiled at Marie as though he'd known her for years.

"I'll be ding-danged," Marie said to herself very precisely. She felt short of breath as she watched Charlie busy himself at the big aluminum coffee urn, then, wearing a vague little smile, walk directly to her and stand alongside her.

Too much Life had passed since the last time they had met here. Too many redundancies had been generated. This was not the time for subtlety or even good sense. Charlie and Marie regarded each other evenly.

"Hi," Marie said, and extended her hand.

"Hi." Charlie took her hand and held it firmly for a moment. "My name is Hollis Grumbles. Call me Charlie. Who are you?"

"Mary Prather Overstreet. Call me Marie."

Quietly but portentously Charlie said: "Me Charlie; you Marie."

Marie tittered. She took a sip from her white little cup. Charlie did likewise. The stuff was incredibly hot.

"What kind of name is Grumbles?" Marie said, keeping her voice low.

"Used to be Czech. I don't remember how it sounded, you know, originally. Actually I never really knew."

Marie gestured with her head: the door. They moved toward it. As they stepped outside, Marie heard herself remark, "I had an uncle once named Bill Sauer."

****

That morning they strolled together on campus with no apparent purpose other than to catch up. They were smart enough to focus on the most recent years.

"Remember when we met before?" Charlie said. He knew that she did.

"Oh, I remember. Afterwards I used to wave when I saw you, you know, here and there. I think for several months."

"Unh." Charlie was flashing on occasions he could recall when he had waved to her. "Time does fly," he said.

"The last time I saw you back in that lounge was in March of '80," Marie declared. "Thank God, I had my dissertation outlined by then. I finished it that summer."

Somehow Charlie found it appropriate to say with conviction: "I'm proud of you."

Somehow Marie understood why he'd said that.

Charlie decided to recap his recent past to bring that topic to closure.

Marie did the same, trying not to sound too formidable. "No kids, though," she added. "Not yet."

"Didn't you like marriage?" Charlie said. "Blood simple, it seems so necessary."

"I don't regret getting married," Marie said, "except as a waste of energy."

"I don't either. Especially when I think about the first time I saw my son."

"Ah."

In short order other baggage was opened, aired, and put away indefinitely. Charlie averred that his ex-wife had expected him to make her happy. Of course he couldn't possibly meet that expectation. Their sex life had soured, and he crumpled psychically. End of story. Marie declared that her ex-husband's needs sapped all her capacities. She couldn't serve him sufficiently and still live. She couldn't serve him sufficiently, period. Her only option: get out.

Both were amazed—stunned—by their own recollections.

"Marriage is a calling. If a person isn't able to do it right, she or he shouldn't do it," Marie asserted. "It really takes some kind of specialized training, which even I didn't have, and that's despite having my Ph.D. Even if you live alone, life is complicated."

"Live and let live, for God's sake," Charlie commented. "I think that's the essence of doing it right, along with helping your partner out every way you can."

"I'll buy that," Marie responded, then added: "Is this all we've learned?"

"Well, I've learned not to settle for second-rate sex," Charlie rejoined. "Otherwise, I'm easy."

"I bet you are."

Marie elected to see how "easy" Charlie was by inviting him to join her in a yoga class she would attend the following day.

"What time?" he asked.

They did attend the class together, after which Charlie regaled Marie with stories of his funnier adventures in Los Angeles and a few in Vietnam. To Marie's credit, he thought, she asked him few questions about his past. At about this time they came to posit—individually and jointly, implicitly and explicitly—that anything they could do together would be more fruitful for both than if they did it separately. Within a few days this became axiomatic.

*   *   *

In case you wanted magic, there it is. But this is magic in a minor mode compared to magic you will see later. Trust me on this.

Also on this: I have no desire to fix you or make you a better person. Even if that were my job, I could never presume to know what my objectives would be. My vision is simply too limited.

That being said, I must point out that to Charlie's and Marie's everlasting credit, each comprehended a notion that is more difficult to grasp than most humans realize: The main impediment to loving or, believe it or not, learning to be loved is the damned ego. It seems almost impossible to subordinate. Usually it preempts healthy self-esteem and deflects fruitful actions and knowledge. It diminishes a person's worth more than you might think.

Ego can subvert every kind of love story of which I am aware, and, believe me, I know some love stories beyond any imaginable on Earth. Being human entails bearing an affliction that I will not abide.

*   *   *

"What it comes down to is, a married couple has got to have enough magic and money," Marie said apropos of the discussion she and Charlie had been having about the prerequisites for a real marriage. Charlie readily concurred. To his mind, he was enjoying a foretaste of magic just by being with Marie; the issue was how to ensure that she got her share.

Marie declared, "All we've got to do is figure out how to pay the bills so that we'll be *able* to make our kind of magic."

"I've also got to make sure my son Brent gets whatever he needs," Charlie said.

They contemplated these verities for a moment. Then Marie averred, "Sometimes, you know, I think I can understand how a person might be willing to kill to get money. Having to scramble for money just to survive is so . . . debilitating."

"Hey, tell me about it," Charlie said. Then — "Do you think you could kill anyone?"

Marie said she doubted that she could, although sometimes what she'd seen as a teacher had caused her to actually desire the death of certain individuals she referred to as "life-suckers in positions of authority and respect."

"I guess we have to look for good jobs," Charlie declared.

"Assuming they even exist . . . ."

It was about time for Charlie to leave Marie's apartment. He rose and walked to the door and Marie followed him. At the door Charlie turned and paused to kiss Marie's forehead and cheek. He held her lightly as had become his habit in the six

88

evenings they had spent together. This time he held her longer, and less lightly, than previously. And that felt right.

"Something you want? Something you need?" Marie said. She fairly well knew what the reality was.

"I'd really like it if we could take off all your clothes for a while."

"Well . . . I'm going to have to take them off anyway pretty soon. You can help."

"Oh, god, I'd love to!"

They subtly removed themselves from the door. "I'll help you, too," Marie said.

And help each other they did. Slowly at first.

"Oh, lord!" Charlie said in a little while. He had pulled off the last article of Marie's clothing and was utterly busy enjoying newly uncovered places. By now he, too, was naked.

Soon a wondrous, arousing scent rose like steam from the two of them. It was really a blend of smells, a synergy. Stretched out on a rug, Marie noticed it just as her neck arched and mouth opened. Charlie had ceased to notice it; he had begun shouting non-words.

"Oh, god!" Marie started to say but her own feminine-pitched moan took over, and got deeper and deeper until it broke into a long, thin scream as the wave of something unspeakable rolled from the tops of her feet all the way up her body.

Some time later they lay next to each other holding hands on the floor, their heads and knees supported by overstuffed cushions that Marie liked to collect.

"Boy, that was really something," Charlie said, still in a kind of shock. "I almost don't believe it." Eyes wide, he simply gazed at the ceiling.

"Just a harbinger of things to come. —So to speak."

Marie rolled onto her side to be closer to Charlie; she put her face against his shoulder and upper arm. Yes, he smelled good. To her, this really was contentment, and her eyes softly closed. Her final thought of the evening was to acknowledge the truism that some people are simply fortunate.

****

October 10, 1984 (before the "errand" to Tegucigalpa, Honduras)

As Rick Denton stood confronting Charlie over his parents' front-yard fence, he felt comfortable in his assessment of Charlie's personality and character. (Collaterally he realized he should not be as confident about what he knew of Marie.) Denton perceived that he'd caused Charlie to feel unbalanced, so he decided to help: "Look, you need money, right?" he said to Charlie. "We can pay you pretty well. Also you need our protection."

"How well would you pay me?"

"Oh, in the neighborhood of a thousand per day. Plus we handle all normal expenses."

Charlie stood expressionless; his unfocused eyes widened.

"Sir?" he said after a while.

Denton apprehended the new problem. "About a thousand per day, when you actually work. Plus we cover normal expenses."

"It sounds appealing."

"We thought it might."

"Uh, let me ask again, how do you all protect me?"

"We allow certain things—that is, we cause things—to just slide. We try to ensure you won't be prosecuted or hassled. It's not easy to do; you're hardcore A-W-O-L, as I presume you realize."

"What kind of guarantees can you make?"

"No guarantees. But we'll do our best. I guess I can guarantee that."

"When would I start?" Charlie said.

The answer rocked him: "Tonight."

That same afternoon, in a nondescript office downtown, Charlie, Denton, and another representative of Charlie's new employer, a Mr. Rugowski, clarified most details and issues: No passport and immunizations? Arrangements were being made to nullify those facts. ("Reality in these matters might be superseded," Rugowski declared, "and we can implement a form of reality that is more congenial, if you get my drift. In the meantime, don't drink the water when you're out of country.") Executing the job itself? A piece of cake, as people say. The "errand" Charlie was to undertake struck him as so simple he equated it with the job done by a "mule" in narcotics trafficking. No, he was informed, it was easier than that. And the most important thing he was to understand about any "errand" he'd carry out? To do exactly what his future "instructors" told him to do; neither more nor less. One thing was crucial: *nothing* was to escape his attention. He was to see, hear, smell — *notice* — everything in his ken within the context of a job. "Focusing on whole welters of details eventually gets to be second nature," Rugowski assured him. Would Charlie get more work if this job went well? Who could say?

Of course the essence of any job Charlie would do, from its inception, would be secrecy. When they requested that he pledge secrecy he did, categorically, as they knew he would. They were pleased to note that he asked no irrelevant questions but one: whether his "potential fiancee" could be told of what he was about to do. Well, what did *he* think? (Issue closed.) But the question gave Denton pause.

"Uh, what do you mean by 'potential fiancee'?" he asked Charlie.

"I can honestly say I don't know whether she is my fiancee," Charlie responded. He regarded Denton and Rugowski levelly. Then: "What do *you* fellas know?"

A beat. Denton spoke: "According to our profiles, you two complement each other up and down, from end to end."

Thus in that very same office in the evening of that very same day, Rick Denton should not have been surprised, after Marie had asked him and Rugowski "How secret is all this supposed to be?" and after they had responded, to hear her say, "Charlie's my sweetheart. You think I'm going to keep things from him? That's crazy." She smiled after she said this but they felt the sting of ridicule.

"We know we have to be real," Denton said. "Okay, so we'll try to be flexible."

"We can live within the parameters of reasonable compromise," Rugowski contributed. "So long as they're not breached, if you get my drift. My agency has a lot at stake in our missions, regardless of how mundane or nebulous they might appear."

Marie caused herself to simply wait silently, impassively, as Charlie would.

In a moment she heard: "So, all right, you can tell Charlie the basic details of what you've done after you get back. But *Charlie only.*"

That concluded Denton's and Rugowski's preface to a part-time, temporary-job offer which Marie had to find irresistible, especially if she preferred not to carry on a postal-service romance with a federal-prison inmate, since military desertion and possible treason were bona-fide crimes and long-standing facts in Charlie's life that he had never revealed. Several times during this evening, even as Denton determined that Marie was possessed of a hidden arrogance probably stemming from self-confidence well founded, Marie silently conceded that Charlie did a magnificent job of covering up his past.

October 11, 1984

On a prepaid Continental Airlines flight back to Texas, Charlie felt eerily energized. Throughout this trip he'd had good cause for anxiety (such as the jolt he'd felt in the taxi on his way out of Honduras as he passed columns of government soldiers moving toward the airport). Now it was all behind him, and everything he'd been promised had materialized, for him a rare experience since his graduation from Western States Chiropractic College. A lot of things he'd done in the last twenty hours could have gone wrong, but here he sat in comfort, elated at earning, actually earning in a most facile way, an outsized reward.

Marie's image had constantly played on his mind that day. Now he could fix on it. He had something tangible he could offer to her. Somehow she and his newly gotten gains were connected. His karma must have been right.

Except for one thing, which he'd taken some pains to identify for himself. At his debriefing, in reference to "Commander Raúl" and his thugs in Miami, he would have liked to have asked, "What kind of sleaze-bag operation did you put me into, anyway?" Of course they wouldn't have answered that, but now he regretted not having asked it. Maybe he would have discerned a clue instead of only suspecting that he'd been face to face with a Nicaraguan *Contra* leader. He and "Raúl" had nodded to each other and exchanged perhaps ten words. If he had indeed aided the *Contras*, to Charlie his payment was bloody. That would be a blot on the job he had run, which disturbed him. Worse, when he got home he was unable to contact Marie no matter what he tried.

October 12, 1984
Alajuela, Costa Rica

After flight delays, cancelled flights, and rocky flights (low-level turbulence having caused those Mexican pilots to *use* their flight training to get down to Oaxaca safely), Marie felt put-upon. She only wanted to earn needed dollars and, ostensibly, help ensure that Charlie would be left alone by the U.S. Justice Department. She rambled in these thoughts as she gazed about the *mercado central*, looking for a middle-aged gringo who would know of her and give her certain things.

Boof! She felt jarred internally by the realization that an American man she'd been inadvertently admiring suddenly made eye contact with her and held it as he began to stride directly toward her. Her breath caught in her thorax. *Now what the hell.* The fellow was tall, angular, handsome, with thick salt-

and-pepper hair brushed straight back; he reminded her of "Dirty Harry" Callahan, the movie police detective portrayed by Clint Eastwood. As he approached her he smiled. His mouth opened.

"Marie Overstreet?" he said musically, and his open right hand came out to her.

Marie managed to inhale. "Right you are," she said.

"Sam Wallaby," said the man.

They shook hands cursorily. She could tell he was a lot livelier than Dirty Harry. He explained with an easy grace that he had spotted her while he was out of sight between some vendors and he'd guessed who she was. He didn't mention that he'd been admiring her vitality and off-beat good looks for a solid minute before he thought, *god, she's my contact*! Right after that, Sam the Professional made himself visible so he would be noticed by Marie before he approached her.

For several minutes Sam and Marie toured the open-air market, with Sam pointing out favorite stalls while overtly swinging a tote bag inconspicuously attached to his wrist and belt by a plastic-encased cable. At one point he showed Marie an actual little lock under his wrist.

"I know this isn't exactly covert," he remarked when they stopped next to a delightful fountain. "But, hey, we're among real people; this is *La Vida*. I can't help being, you know, ex officio."

Marie could only shrug. This fellow was DIA Area Field Chief; he likely knew what he was doing. As they ambled among stalls and tables and racks of merchandise Sam casually gave her instructions regarding what to do next, much as though he were arranging an after-work soiree.

"Look, when you get to S-S and go to the Paradise Hotel downtown, across the street is Fortunato's Cantina. That's where you'll go at four o'clock today," he told her. There, at the back end of the bar, Marie would be asked about her children "David and Lisa," her friend "Joanna McClintock," and whether she'd be going to New Orleans. She would hear a terse report on "neighborhood conditions." Sam could only say the contact would be an Hispanic male; Sam couldn't say what he would look like or which language he'd use. ("He's the one you'll give this bag to, but don't even start to give it to him until he gives you, actually puts in your hand, a white envelope—standard-sized white envelope—which should be sealed.") Most of this Marie already knew from her briefing.

Marie and Sam stopped next to some painted boulders marking a corner of the market square. "Here," Sam said, and handed over his tote bag to Marie as though it had belonged to her all along. He helped her secure it to her wrist and belt.

"Well, there you are. You know what to do with it."

"I hope so," Marie said. "Thanks very much."

"Ah, my pleasure, dear lady."

As Sam turned to leave he sub-vocalized the words, "Wow, lady, you are beau-ti-*ful*! And truly nice to be with."

"Good luck to you!" Marie said after him.

Sam looked over his shoulder at Marie, as much to get a final fix on her as to respond with a smile and little wave. He already knew he'd feel light-hearted the rest of that day. And some day he would see a lot more of that vibrant woman.

*

Feeling a little heady from her meeting with Sam Wallaby, Marie left the country on a prepaid shuttle flight from San Jose to San Salvador, where things happened pretty much as she was told they would. But even after she'd arrived in El Salvador, her chest felt as though she'd exerted herself with a tough workout that afternoon.

When Marie found her contact in Fortunato's bar she was surprised that "Daniel," a scruffy, light-complected Latino, looked too young to be involved in high-level machinations such as this probably was. Then she had a brief conflict with "Daniel" over who would hand over what, first. Hoping she was doing right, Marie compromised Sam Wallaby's dictate to not turn over the tote bag until a white envelope was in her hand. She let loose the bag and placed it within Daniel's reach even though his fingers still pinched the envelope. She did this because he appeared to be considering pulling a gun on her to get what he wanted. He looked edgy, heated up; she was sure he carried a pistol under his rumpled sport jacket. Marie wanted to perform this "errand" smoothly so she had to avert drawing attention to herself, one of Mr. Rugowski's main principles.

Things went well enough after that. Daniel even gave Marie a quick smile when he heard her interested responses to the five sentences he related about his *barrio*—the intermittent water, power lines having come down, heavy vehicular traffic, et cetera. Marie perceived she had gained Daniels's confidence, which made her feel she was doing the job well. Her business concluded, she went back home via New Orleans.

In New Orleans Marie had to leave the airport and take a taxi to the Federal Building to complete her errand, an absurd imposition she would not countenance in the future. Plus she had to pay cab fare with her own money because they'd provided her with only twenty dollars in U.S. currency. (Fur *would* fly.) In a CIA office two men who looked like academics interrogated her relentlessly for about a half hour. Marie was surprised by how mundane most of their questions were. She adhered to Rick Denton's counsel to not ask questions; what they wanted her to know, they would have told her.

During her debriefing Marie volunteered no information or observations about Sam Wallaby other than he was "a nice guy." She had plenty to relate about the hot-head in San Salvador who seemed totally willing to compromise her errand if he didn't like the direction the breeze took outside. She saw the two heads in front of her nod concurrence to each other and she wondered what they knew; then she decided not to care.

After reporting expenses and returning *colones y pesos* she hadn't used, Marie was summarily handed a white envelope, this one unsealed and holding $1,200. Someone was quickly found to drive her back after she complained acidly about the imposition of having to taxi into downtown from the airport. Before long she was on a Delta flight home, mission completed, richer than she'd ever thought possible for one day's work and feeling a steady current of some kind of power coursing inside her.

At the same time, Marie was seeing a recurrent phantasm of Charlie's face and upper body. They'd enjoy that money together. Plus she had done Charlie a good turn, ostensibly. Denton and Rugowski probably would do whatever they could to forestall Justice Department proceedings that might jeopardize Charlie's freedom. Marie definitely needed Charlie to be free.

This prompted Marie to worry about what she had actually accomplished by executing her mission. Did it wholesomely affect people's lives and the world in which they lived? Down deep she was sure it didn't. If her errand had accomplished anything, she determined, it was likely not for the better, given the U.S. history in Central America.

But there was Sam Wallaby. Charming, intelligent, patently good-hearted. He looked too much like a college professor of law enforcement to be involved in dirty business. *Of course! Americans are notorious suckers for image.* Ah, but the image that Charlie presented was genuine. What you saw in him, what he projected, was real. (Marie was mildly surprised to realize that her libido had risen during the last stages of this trip.) A phantasm of Charlie came up again, and Marie framed it and tried to sharpen the details: his boyish round face, the sharply defined deltoid and pectoral muscles. Yes, she was committed to his well-being, to his Life, and before long he would know this.

****

October 13-14, 1984
Tai-pei, Taiwan

After a long afternoon of briefings in which he articulated his and his superiors' projected strategy for defending their designated corner of the Republic Of China against attack by undoubtedly hundreds of mainland aircraft, Chang K'ung was almost sure his efforts were wasted. The gerontocracy and their claques, his target audiences that day, understood only how to use rifles and howitzers; plus they were lucky to still be awake until evening. Chang empathized with that last point: he himself craved a quiet place to just sit for five or six minutes and succumb to an urge to sleep.

The fatigue of unsatisfying, tedious work was overwhelming. Chang excused himself from his meeting, slipped into a restroom reserved for generals, took a corner stall, and simply perched on a commode with his eyes closed.

Was this weariness worth enduring? Yes. Chang was poised on high ground to become the youngest major general in modern Chinese history. Before long that would probably be one of his rewards for defending his country with distinction, and that was how he defined his life. Decades ago he had decided to stop conjecturing whether he even had a "Life." He did not. From top to bottom, inside and out, he was a "creation" of the organization which he served with unqualified dedication. Given his technological and tactical talents and his personal strengths, Chang decided that he could reasonably aspire to do—or be—whatever he might imagine within his context.

And what he had been imagining with growing intensity for so many years now—a fearsome shudder overwhelmed him. He decided to go with it and let his chin drop almost to his chest . . . .

Oh-ho! Through the trees he spotted the frontal attack coming at his command center from three directions. Now he saw them clearly, approaching in thick, stupid waves, formidable from the weight of their numbers.

Alone Chang confronted the point of the nearest, largest wedge of shock troops, all identical in dingy gray, and he unlimbered that old machine gun he'd learned how to use before officer-training college. He was fortunate to have several olive-drab cases of ammunition scattered near his feet.

That old gun worked! All he had to do was hold it and point it accurately, and they fell in segments of four or five abreast. They kept coming but he got ahead; they had to climb over the corpses to advance, and he kept adding to the heaps and clutter of corpses. Finally only a knot of nine or ten of them remained standing, unable to advance or fall back. Some fired at him fecklessly. He considered allowing them to retreat into the woods but that would be contra his code of performing his job to the limit. With gut-clutching distaste he watched tracers from his .50-caliber gun slam into them, knocking them down and leaving gaping holes. He annihilated them as quickly as he could.

Chang snatched up the old machine gun and as many green cases as he could carry, cursing his not having more limbs and hands. Weighed down, he bolted through brush and between trees to meet another invading wedge of "them," and just in time. He immediately fired point-blank and they fell in a line, from left to right, almost at his feet. Amazed and gasping, Chang managed to keep firing. He dropped another line of gray corpses, then another. At last he had a minute in which to set up his gun properly on a soft knoll, then he resumed firing almost point-blank, mowing down a wide wave of bodies moments before they overran his position on this edge of forest clearing. Methodically, frenetically, Chang fired at a new wave. He couldn't believe he was doing this!

The old machine gun stopped working. Good. His right hand and forearm were fatigued beyond feeling. He snatched up the M-16 he'd providentially set against a tree there and had to fire from the hip as he strode at them. From his far left to his far right, the line of soldiers halted, then receded back to the tree line, many of the faces showing abject terror. But any one of them had the means to kill him in an instant. Again he had to finish the job. His ammunition was running low. Chang cursed in English, raised the automatic rifle to his shoulder and tried to make each round count. He thought he cut down every man standing although a few might have reached the woods and disappeared. Then he bolted through a field, gasping and sweating, barely able to go on.

There was yet another incursion, and he wouldn't shirk destroying it. They were coming over a rise when he caught them. Again he fired accurately from the shoulder until the clip was gone. At least he'd blunted the advance. He drew his Beretta and walked toward them, firing carefully and quickly, dropping perhaps eight more. Some fired back. Chang was sure he'd been hit at least twice but he didn't feel the wounds and he could still function. He threw his empty pistol at them, reached behind his left shoulder, and drew the samurai sword strapped to his back. He kept advancing on them and they melted back. Somehow his sword turned out to be a cutlass, much like an eighteenth-century European pirate's weapon. He would use it anyway, but painful fatigue in his right arm and hand caused him to hesitate. Not for long. Some of the vermin had slipped away, but at least a half dozen were blocked by an ancient stone wall. He approached them quickly, before they too could get away, and loosening a deep yell of chi began his slashing and thrusting, killing methodically but none too efficiently. Some died very hard, screaming and grimacing. They seemed to be of all kinds, ages. Although he felt appalled, even sickened, Chang's job was to kill them all. His hands were now sticky and he felt burning hot spots where they'd been freshly spattered. His strength was almost gone. Without feeling a warning he went down on one knee. With a loud gasp he dropped onto his other knee, the boney cap hitting amazingly hard tile.

A shock wakened him. Chang moaned as he opened his eyes. The incongruity of himself on his knees in a commode stall, coupled with his boundless relief at realizing that he'd merely been dreaming (and that it was over!), made him bray out a laugh. He rose to his feet quickly and looked outside the stall. More relief: no one there.

"*Gee*-zuz!" he blurted, parodying the exclamation he'd heard on his first day at Fort Benning in the United States. He gazed momentarily at the knuckles of his right hand, the fingers tensely curling under. "I can't make a fist!" he said to himself in English with a wry little smile, recalling a similar remark made in a frothy American movie he'd seen near Fort Benning.

Chang realized he'd undergone a stress-charged experience; he let himself savor his relief from its passing. And as he washed his face and doused his eyes, he realized that he'd been profoundly tested; and he had passed the test without reservation. The trick now, he told himself, would be to benefit from the experience. A superior man evolves to higher levels of ability by integrating—and using—all that he undergoes.

Chang had always believed he could accomplish whatever he thought was important, and this afternoon's dream had both confirmed and exercised his powers of resolve. But something else had occurred as well, something subliminal. Chang had to acknowledge that his secret, deepest desire was asserting itself.

Since adolescence he had been aware that his most primary aspiration animated his entire career; yet he could never divulge it to anyone. Basically, Chang wanted to start his own country. He had long harbored the conviction that someday he would actuate, then guide to fruition, a true revolution that would make a difference in people's lives and affect many millions of lives far into the future, maybe for all time. In short, he envisioned creating the quintessential Chinese state, but a Chinese state free of excess baggage from the past and modern economic fetters. (He could almost see it glittering on the Strait of Taiwan: a city-state separate and aloof from the so-called Republic Of China, with access to two coastlines.) Oh, to be thoroughly able to *be* Chinese while living free of artificial limitations: the potential for good was infinite, unimaginable. Founding an actual country based on that vision would give him a Life. It might even justify his numbing existence.

Now was probably a better time than most to make a decision about that, Chang thought, so he made one. *New T'aip'ing Revolution*. This is what he would call it. Then a much more important decision: The "New T'aip'ing Revolution" was now underway. As of this very moment, it had begun.

But might this whole notion be only a whimsy, the fevered musings of an egomaniac? No matter. It demanded to be done, Chang determined, and he was the person to do it. It might never happen, even inefficaciously, unless he took the initiative, regardless of Taiwan's unforgiving Sedition Acts and the fate that befell the nineteenth-century namesake of Chang's "new" revolution.

*

One perquisite of being part of the Kuomintang which ran the Republic Of China (in exile) was exclusive access to some well-appointed, rarely used facilities. Before he left the restroom, General Chang sat impassively in a leather-covered armchair beneath a long, rectangular woodcut of a dragon and took up a cigarette lighter. His first problem in advancing the New T'aip'ing Revolution, he had just determined, was to remember at every moment that a great enterprise must never be hastened or its greatness will be undermined. "Every large undertaking requires the fullness of time in which to ripen," he told himself in English, frowning at the lame metaphors.

To reinforce the point, Chang activated the cigarette lighter and touched the short flame directly on a callused knuckle of his left hand, then suppressed the urge to cry out while smoke rose before he cut off the flame. The burn spot would serve as a prominent reminder. By the time that heals, he thought, the principle of avoiding haste will have become a habit of mind. And he would have the scar to remind himself further.

Chapter 5

October 13, 1984

Despite nagging grogginess, Charlie bounded out of his parents' car as soon as he parked it and dashed to the concrete stairway ascending the east flank of Mt. Bonnell, Austin's highest landmark. The day had already been gutted; soon the sun would set behind the Western Hills. Marie stood waiting, looking none-too-chipper herself. When she saw Charlie coming she jetted toward him, and they physically charged at each other and came together with an impact. They clutched and kissed each other with abandon.

"Whoa-*ho*! Have I missed you!" Charlie said when he could talk. Then—"Where have you been?"

"You might not believe where I've been when I tell you," Marie said breathlessly.

That struck Charlie as odd. He knew he would learn what she meant, so he declined to pursue it. They held onto each other for a while, each thinking: Ah, this is where I belong!

A little later, as they simply held hands, Marie said, "You know, I can't really imagine the places where you've been."

"Come again?" Charlie said, aware of a little alarm going off somewhere.

"Let's go on up," Marie said and started up the stairway built into the small mountain.

Perhaps fifteen minutes later, as they strolled along the summit ledge overlooking the Colorado River—which always mesmerized Charlie when he could gaze at it—Marie disclosed some facts she'd recently learned about Charlie, most of which he was neither ashamed of nor hiding from her. She knew, now, that he was a MIA and evidently a deserter from the U.S.

Marine Corps, that he'd lived overseas illegally, possibly as a traitor, and had returned illegally, and that a day ago he'd "run an errand" for some agency (or agencies) in the Defense Department. She'd even been told his mission had taken him to Honduras. Rick Denton's name was mentioned a few times.

"I wanted to come up here," Marie said, waving an arm about and casting a glance at the spreading roseate light, "so we won't be, uh, 'overheard' by the wrong people."

"I wasn't trying to hide anything about myself," Charlie responded evenly. "I surely would have told you everything, once it got to be . . . you know, relevant or worth knowing. — You know?"

"You don't have to tell me anything," Marie said. "Although I sure wish you'd tell me everything."

"I'll tell you whatever I can think of, whenever I can."

"That'll be fine."

Marie then told Charlie about the errand she had run, using broad strokes to avoid boring details. She added that Mr. Denton had approved her telling Charlie all this. And she was now $1,200 richer, just like that.

"No one approved my telling anything to anybody," Charlie said. "I made a promise. My lips are sealed. Um, I've got about $1,200, too."

That made $2,400 between them, minus deductions to pay a few pressing debts and indulge in a few rewards for both.

"So we've got about two thousand dollars," Marie said.

"Cool! Do you know what we can do with a chunk of change like that?"

"I shudder to think."

"I think for openers we should get together this weekend," Charlie said. "My folks would love to meet us for dinner at Threadgill's. Maybe for once I get to pick up the tab."

Before Charlie and Marie descended Mt. Bonnell, they recalled Rick Denton's declaring to each that someone with a name like "Eleanor Gilchrest" had contacted him. He had said that portentously, as though the name would be significant to them, which it wasn't. That sort of thing, Charlie and Marie acceded, sharpened their awareness of the lesser, vague anxieties they would incur by getting involved in doing "errands."

October 14, 1984

As Charlie helped Marie cut up an array of foods to stir-fry after each had undergone a stiff workout that afternoon, Marie's telephone rang and although Marie wasn't expecting a call, she answered it. Audibly and distinctly she repeated the name announced on the other end: "Eleanor Gilchrest."

"Yes?" was all Marie could respond.

Ms. Gilchrest prefaced her message by saying that Rick Denton had referred Marie to her; and she thought she could contact Charlie with this same telephone call. (At this point Marie found herself feeling a bit strange.) Basically, Ms. Gilchrest was calling to inquire whether Marie and Charlie would prefer to run *joint* errands. Sometimes they (whoever "they" might be) had need of two temporary operatives to handle a particular situation. The pay wouldn't be any less. Indeed, it should really be higher because joint "errands" called for people who had unique backgrounds and personal qualities.

"That's us!" Marie said, adding that she would consult Charlie, and she promptly did so without bothering to muffle the mouthpiece.

He was all for the idea, as Ms. Gilchrest said she thought he would be. And Marie? To her it was a fine idea. She'd be able to keep track of Charlie better.

Charlie interposed loudly: "Who is Eleanor Gilchrest? Who does she work for?"

Marie repeated the question into the phone.

Ms. Gilchrest was apologetic, for she thought they knew. Her job title was "Interagency Operations Coordinator," and she worked for E-Systems Corporation, a private surveillance-equipment manufacturer located outside Dallas. She really couldn't tell them any more except that she would contact Rick Denton and Ray Rugowski at once. ("Usually they're very receptive to my suggestions," she said.) They would get in touch with Marie and Charlie. Of course, even E-Systems couldn't guarantee the availability of joint missions. They'd materialize when they materialized.

Marie thanked her caller with terse grace and got a like response. After she hung up she felt a vague sense of having communicated with a different world, or maybe a different order of being. She glanced at Charlie and saw he was gazing at the juncture of kitchen wall and ceiling.

"Strange things do happen," he said bemusedly.

*   *   *

Consider how emphatically Charlie and Marie would have felt about "strange things" happening if they had known the truth about "Eleanor Gilchrest": She actually did not exist. No more than I do. And no less.

Now to me, there is nothing especially strange about becoming someone who had not existed previously; even someone with a history. You can disregard my notion here as fanciful, but what do you really know that invalidates it? Facility in using your PC or other electronic gadgets will not help you at all when it comes to dealing with matters like this.

But even by my standards, what General Chang K'ung resolved to set in process several thousand miles west of Charlie's and Marie's scene of delight that evening is bizarre. Yet if Charlie and Marie could have somehow learned of General Chang's resolution, they likely would have dismissed it as just another instance of egoism and power lust gone extreme. They might have even considered it completely natural. Could I be wrong to call it bizarre? There is so much about humankind I cannot begin to understand, including how you can do things that are so good—sometimes.

*   *   *

October 16, 1984
Austin, Texas

Charlie and Marie arrived at Marie's apartment after food shopping together. Each had been job searching during most of that afternoon. The telephone was ringing; Marie answered it while Charlie brought in groceries.

"That was Rick Denton," Marie told Charlie with a smile after she'd concluded a brief conversation that Charlie had tried not to monitor. "He wants to know if we'd care to take a short trip to Canada, together."

"Really? All right! Like when?"

"He said he can't say for certain. Probably next week; Wednesday's a likelihood."

"What did you tell him?"

"I told him *'sure.'*"

"Ah, right. Did Denton say anything else?" Charlie asked.

"Only that jobs like this pay the same as we'd get if we both went on individual errands. He wishes we had more experience at this, but he's sure we'll do all right."

"Of course we'll do all right."

"Looks like we're going to be partners," Marie said.

They each had some points to earnestly express about that.

After a few minutes Charlie realized that he was on the verge of taking a giant step into uncharted territory. Therefore this was an excellent time to be thoughtful instead of impulsive. Tentativeness might also help.

"If you ask me," said Charlie, "I think it would be wonderful—really, really wonderful—if we were married. — You know, to each other."

Marie contemplated that briefly. "Is that a marriage proposal?" she said quietly.

"It's a thought. An idea. I think it's a real good one. So, well, I don't know if the timing is quite right, but I would be honored—totally pleased—if you would marry me, dearest. I'd call this a proposal."

Marie's head felt as though it were lifting into space. Her legs felt strangely absent. She took hold of the back of a chair with one hand—trying to make the action appear casual—and resolved to enjoy the moment.

"Wow. I guess it is," Marie said. "Are you really serious, man?"

"Am I serious? I've never been more serious in my life. Of course I'm serious! I want to do things for you. You're all I care about, really. I don't want to live unless we're together."

Charlie thought he should back off slightly. After a moment he said, "Give it some thought, dear lady. If you'd like, I'll get you any kind of ring you want."

"How about a big dinner to celebrate the occasion?"

"That, too."

"And a trip to Costa Rica, or some place that's romantic?"

"Whoa! I'm looking for something to take notes on."

Marie saw him taking up a pen.

"Are we gonna have kids?" Marie asked.

"I hope so. Didn't you say you want to have kids?"

"Well, yes, but I hardly know you."

"You will. I promise. I always keep my promises."

Marie threw her arms over Charlie's shoulders and kissed his left cheek. She spoke into his eyes: "Now try to understand, dear man, I don't want to live without you, either. *Of course* I accept."

"You do?"

"I do."

And Charlie knew that his Life was peaking. And Marie was sure that she'd never been happier.

"Oh, boy!" said Charlie.

"Oh, yes!" said Marie.

October 21, 1984

"We might have planned this a little more thoroughly," Marie said as she and Charlie walked hand-in-hand on the compacted-gravel trail next to the river in downtown Austin.

"Oh, we've done okay," Charlie replied. "Like your list of expectations. I'd say it was fairly detailed and extensive, to put it mildly."

"Well, yours was just the opposite, to put it mildly."

"I wanted to leave room to improve it," Charlie said, momentarily slipping ahead of Marie to face a phalanx of joggers heading in the opposite direction. "The only big expectation I have is that we get used to backing each other up. All the time; never holding back."

"Well, we're almost like one person—not two people anymore—so that shouldn't be much of a problem."

"You would think, but don't count on that! Believe me."

"Listen, I'm completely committed to you, and your well-being, and everything about you," Marie averred. "Being your main support in Life, that'll be like breathing."

"I believe I can say exactly the same thing," Charlie responded.

"Well, then, we're almost married," Marie said.

Charlie stole a look at Marie's face near his left shoulder. He thought he saw joy inlaid with pensiveness.

"Are you sure you're ready for this?" Charlie asked, thinking that maybe he should feel more anxious himself.

Marie's answer was no less than strongly affirmative, and both allowed themselves to fix on sun-dappled ripples of river surface rushing by only two yards away. Mid-afternoon sunlight was slightly diffused by a barely perceptible overcast. Horizons appeared as pure azure. A dazzling day!

Still holding hands, they stopped at a spot where they felt unlikely to be disturbed in the next few minutes. For a while they merely stared at the water. Marie sighed very softly, an expression of peace, contentment, a blending with everything.

Charlie spoke first. "I promise you, I will be committed to you from this moment on, forever," he said.

"I keep forgetting you're kind of a Buddhist. You don't think death can part us, do you?" Marie said.

"It won't part us."

"I promise to be committed to you," Marie said. "Forever."

"We won't ever be parted," said Charlie. "Not really."

"I'll make sure we won't be," said Marie.

"I'll make sure, too."

For several moments, Marie and Charlie, holding hands, stared at the river lying before them.

"I believe we're married!" Charlie said.

"It sure seems that way," Marie said. "But if we're not, I marry myself to you as of this moment."

"And I marry myself to you," Charlie said.

Together they gazed at the river a little more.

"That should just about do it," Charlie said.

"This'll be just great!" Marie enthused. "Together we'll be much more . . . *effective* . . . fruitful. I mean at living. Together—we'll be great personalities!"

Charlie turned to look into her dancing dark eyes. The rest of the world receded.

"You *are* a 'great personality,'" was all he could say.

"We should celebrate," Marie declared as she and Charlie strolled happily to her car about ten minutes later. And after they went to the Travis County Courthouse to sign a form, and contacted Charlie's parents and Marie's sister to inform them of what they had done, they celebrated for three days and three nights in every way they could think of, shamelessly depleting their recent $2,000 windfall. They hoped to celebrate further on a trip to Canada at government expense, but that errand did not materialize for about two years. Instead, each got called to be hired for a regular job, Charlie at a clinic and Marie at a privately funded education-research "laboratory."

As each secretly expected, when Living gets complicated, the degree of complication immediately ratchets upward a few levels, which was exactly what happened when they received a telephone call from Rick Denton whose professional honor, along with Ms. Gilchrest's honor (Denton averred), depended on their prompt action. In effect, Mr. Denton told them they would indeed be taking a honeymoon trip at taxpayers' expense, but any warm clothing they packed would be unnecessary.

October 28, 1984
Oaxaca, Mexico

An American graduate student named Michael and a Mexican worker named Ramon, who drove the Ford pickup in which they all traveled, met Dr. Overstreet at the airport terminal and took her to San Cristobal de las Casas, a small colonial city about sixty kilometers to the south. Marie found both men to be genial and helpful, but the personal lens through which each viewed his milieu in San Cristobal gave them biased images of life there. Ostensibly on site to evaluate and assist in two American-sponsored education projects for rural Mayas, Marie determined that her best sources of insight to this context would be her own eyes and ears and intuition. Thus she ascertained that San Cristobal was an attractive town with an interesting ethnic mix, but the whole place, including surrounding ranches and forest and farms, writhed from interrelated tensions. As they drove to the central plaza, seeing several truckloads of armed soldiers riding through the town gave her cause for apprehension.

After following routine procedures at a primary school and two municipal buildings, and following an obligatory stop at the American project director's *casita*, Marie induced Ramon to take her to a clinic about five kilometers outside of town. There she was introduced to an American medical "professor" of chiropractic . . . one Dr. Grumbles. For a moment, an objective onlooker would have said that both doctors seemed inordinately pleased to meet each other.

"Haven't we met somewhere before?" Dr. Grumbles said happily as he pumped Marie's right arm.

"If we had, I'm sure I'd remember," Marie said a little breathlessly, her eyes wide and beaming.

"Well, come on, Dr. Overstreet. Let me show you what they're tryin' to do here. We can probably use your input."

And show her around Charlie did (while constantly resisting the urge to wrap his arm around her). Marie was appalled by the primitive medical situation she saw, although she tried not to show it.

"It's beautiful here, but a person can sure die in a hurry from all kinds of things," Marie remarked, her head shaking unvolitionally.

"That's for sure," said Charlie. "Here. You'd better take this drawing. And this little cachet bag or whatever it is. Gifts to you from the local people, via me."

He handed to Marie a portrait drawing on cardboard made by a child and a tiny hand-woven bag with drawstrings and embroidery on it. Both had been tendered as payment for services he'd performed.

"Please, take them," Charlie said.

"Wow! Thanks; I will."

In return, Marie passed to Charlie a manual-sized compendium of grant sources and a recent edition of *Mother Jones*.

"Here. You might be able to use these," she said.

Covertly, they also exchanged tiny cameras and recorders, one set blank, one not, that each would pass on to associates such as Michael back in town. They did that as they strolled outside the clinic beyond anyone's earshot.

At one point Marie said evenly, "My uncle or brother or father named Sam."

Overtly Charlie registered those words.

"Ah. Red band Thursday night, Cantina San Miguel," Charlie said carefully.

Marie nodded. She got it.

Back at the clinic entrance, Charlie and Marie shook hands and said the usual things people say before parting, but they uttered "take care" and "be careful" earnestly.

"If you see any soldiers on the road, for God's sake give 'em a wide berth," Charlie added.

"Stay clear of *anybody* with guns out here," Marie responded, then urged quietly: "Promise me!"

Charlie promised. By now both he and Marie could feel menace so thickly textured it was almost palpable everywhere. They knew that if they had to, they couldn't live in such an oppressive circumstance. Maybe, each hoped, they were helping in some way to improve the situation here by accomplishing their errand.

Fully a day passed before they saw each other again, and then only briefly in a secluded town named Zipolite where they were debriefed separately. The straightforward errand was thus culminated; all that remained for them to do was meet someplace, ostensibly in Oaxaca, and return home. Since they were so far south, they followed up on a recommendation Charlie had read about and reunited in Puerto Angel, a primitive seaside hamlet where accommodations were cheap and congenial, and where they totally relaxed for two days, hoping this would cause Marie to become extremely fruitful.

"Has this been an interesting time for us, or what?" Marie said while she and Charlie were enduring the long bus ride back to Oaxaca.

"Oh, yeah," Charlie said. "But we've got t' remember, we could have gotten ourselves shot to pieces for nothing by some *Federales* or maybe Zapata wannabees aiming to bag at least one gringo. Or some irate ranchers, or whatever they've got down there that corresponds to rednecks, might have decided to take out *indio*-lovin' *yanquis*."

Marie allowed as that could have happened. Still she felt some reluctance to go "back to reality," she said, referring mainly to herself and Charlie starting their new jobs. "I guess our next big challenge is to keep that edge we felt down in Chiapas and that blaze we experienced, you know, moment to moment down in Puerto Angel," she declared. "That would really enhance our Lives."

And a few days later reality of a different nature tinted their Lives as they read news reports of officially sanctioned mistreatment of Indians in the Mexican state of Chiapas. A particularly vicious episode near San Cristobal de las Casas prompted Marie to telephone Michael the alleged student (who was no longer there) to find out how bad it had actually been. One thing she learned by telephone was that Ramon had been hacked to death by insurgents after they'd knocked his truck into a ravine in retaliation for putatively working as a driver for American agents in the employ of big ranchers.

"Were we being used for dirty tricks against so-called *communistas*?" Charlie wondered aloud.

"If that's what was going on, all we did was help to maintain the status quo," Marie commented. "Boy, talk about a diabolical situation."

For a few moments they pondered the ramifications of that. They also recalled that during and after their "errand" they had been subtly led to presume that they'd been involved in an extra-legal U.S. drug-interdiction effort that ostensibly justified any kind of chicanery.

"Y' know, I think 'brother-uncle-father-Sam'—remember that code sentence?—actually referred to some cleric, a priest named Sam who's got a Spanish surname," Charlie declared. "Just lately I've seen his name in the paper a couple times. Apparently the fella's been kicking up dust for the Mayas down there."

Marie snorted in disgust. "That means the business we were into wasn't strictly for Uncle Sam."

"Well, what do we know?" Charlie said. "I'm a chiropractor; I adjust things. If I had time I'd plant trees here and there. You adjust people's attitudes and teach 'em things. When we have time, we need to read and work out. We've got a Life. We're just not into the . . . machinery of foreign affairs. Whenever we do one of those errands, it's not our job to question why. If we did, they probably wouldn't tell us."

"I know it. But maybe we've helped a bunch of droogs stick it to Mayan Indians who've been getting whacked in the neck for the last several centuries. How can we live with that?" Marie paused only for air. "For all we know, that priest is a marked man now, and we helped mark him. That stinks."

"Oh, it smells okay," Charlie said. With a peremptory gesture he pointed to the ceiling while he held an open hand behind his right ear. His fingers jabbed toward the door: *we go outside.*

A minute later, Charlie and Marie walked hand-in-hand down the sidewalk away from their apartment and any electronic listening devices. A principle was quickly established between them: they wanted to mitigate damage caused by their "errands."

"You know, first we'll have to make sure we know which way the wind's blowin' before we go peeing on the posies," Charlie said. "We've got ourselves to worry about."

Marie nodded, then smiled assuringly. "You do the peeing, I'll do our thinking."

With little further discussion, they returned home determined to thwart pernicious errands whenever they could. They had only to divine how to do that safely.

November 7, 1984
T'ai-pei, Taiwan

Now the youngest major general in modern Chinese history, Chang K'ung had gone home for an afternoon respite from learning his new duties as missile-defense commandant for the northeast quadrant. He needed to refresh his perspective.

The recent promotion was causing Chang to balance imponderable elements: his new military role and the exigencies of national defense, the roles he was expected to fill in current and future national affairs, and the role (or roles) he envisioned for *himself* in the future. The *Gestalt*, as they would call it elsewhere, mandated contemplation. "Always, philosophy blooms first," Chang reminded himself, "then comes rice planting."

Gazing at a callused, black-tinted knuckle on his left hand, Chang made a decision: now was the best time to begin implementing a strategy that had recently become viable. Less than two weeks before in Manila, at a major electronics-industry exposition, Chang had been introduced to a Mainlander who held cabinet rank in the Communist government. Chang paid him special interest partly because the man was said to have stated publicly that he felt disaffected by his corrupt and shabby country.

Chang found himself drawn to the Mainlander as soon as they'd been introduced. Later Chang felt pleased when the grayish, bureaucratic Communist singled him out for conversation. Perhaps the gray man sensed they harbored a common interest. Lin Piao, First Assistant Minister of Foreign Trade for the People's Republic of China, appeared self-effacing and staid, but he was also rumored to have underground connections in the military and science establishments of the Soviet Union. (How he had made them was a matter of wild conjecture.) On the same day that he and Chang met, Minister Lin hinted to Chang that he indeed had those connections. As with all unlikely rumors, Chang believed, the hearsay about this man was probably true.

As Chang got to know Lin Piao a little better during meetings and a few clandestine conversations over the course of two days, Chang got the distinct impression that his new Mainland acquaintance was animated by a desire to do something definitely extraordinary. He had uttered the words "plutonium 239" and "beryllium," with and without benefit of a translator, in at least two contexts. To Chang the implications were clear: this man not only had access to quintessential contraband, he wanted to "deal," as Americans liked to say. Chang reciprocated with his own implication: he was interested in acquiring such material (although in actuality he didn't yet know what for).

Before leaving Manila, Chang made arrangements with Lin Piao to ensure they'd be able to contact each other by telephone on a secure line after they'd returned to their homelands. (This turned out to be unexpectedly easy to do.) Chang understood that he would have to take the initiative to make that happen, and he looked forward to it with some pleasure.

In his "secret office" at home Chang seated himself in a straight-backed armchair and contemplated: Thus far, his relationship with the high-level Mainlander was anomalous and tenuous at best. Yet it was real. But for what purpose can such a rapport be utilized? Possibly acquiring what I will need to fulfill my destiny of fathering a Chinese country based on pure Chinese values. But how will I do that? I know only that I need to amass irresistible power to gain protection for my state—and whatever wealth is required to launch it—from The People's Republic and the United States and, I think, Japan.

In short, when I demand something from the governing apparatus of those countries, especially the United States, which I will need to shield me from reprisals by the Taipei government, they must give it to me. I need international "clout." And how does one acquire that? Through fear, I suppose. Yes, fear. *Mental images are beginning to cohere—*

Chang bounded from his chair. More contemplation would have been counterproductive. He knew what he had to do, and this was the right time of day in which to do it. Despite his wearing soft clothes, Chang left his house and drove straight to his office to make an unofficial telephone call. That was the way to do it.

As Chang gripped the phone waiting for the connections he'd activated, horrific images from that dream he'd had in the commode stall flickered before his mind's eye. Then a telephone on the other end was buzzing intermittently, calling someone who inhabited a world much different from his to answer it. Only one person in that world should pick it up and speak.

His breath catching, Chang felt the familiar foreboding that quickened his soul sometimes when he projected himself doing very difficult things that he had to do. *But would a sane man actually resort to terrorism?*

Chang's initial telephone conversation with the Honorable Minister Lin turned out to be a surprisingly pleasant and fruitful experience despite the predictably vague level of their talk (mandated by the fact that what they were doing was considered seditious by their respective governments). The Mainlander's manner was expansive and good-natured, as though he was dealing with a cousin or brother with whom he'd been out of touch for a long time. The words "beryllium" and "cesium" were actually bruited about, in tandem with references to a "material" they wouldn't explicitly name. *Of course* Lin could gain access to those materials, given sufficient time and money. What a question!

Necessarily their conversation was vague for another reason: Lin knew only a little Mandarin although he could understand it somewhat. Chang could muster only vague memories of the China he fled with his family in 1949; what little Cantonese he knew he had learned in the army after returning to the Republic from his years of training in the U.S. Often both men resorted to English words to convey a point.

As a compliment and bonding gesture, Chang referred to Lin Piao as "Mo Tzu," a fabled Chinese general of millennia ago, and Lin happily accepted his new "code name." Chang K'ung and "Mo Tzu" were about to become figurative bedfellows.

During the course of all this, Chang blithely subsumed a truth about his vision and objectives (and himself) that he had not really confronted: Yes, he would use whatever means were most effective to gain international "clout." Yes, he would resort even to the most naked form of terrorism if that would mean success.

After exchanging a few remarks with Lin about deriving power from real fear, Chang caused his contact's eyebrows to rise unvolitionally by making a promise: Chang would deposit three hundred thousand U.S. dollars in the Central Bank of Malaysia and ensure Lin Piao's access to it, by the next day. This was not to be construed as a mere demonstration of earnestness. The deposit would be made to facilitate "Mo Tzu's" beginning the process of acquiring "materials," real materials, which would work. Mo Tzu could name his own rewards whenever he chose.

"Challenge is sufficient reward," Mo Tzu remarked. "After my performance, we will discuss additional compensation, if that is desirable and necessary."

So, thought Chang, Mo Tzu could be uncomplicated as he was being complicated. Within several minutes after hanging up Chang arranged for a deposit of 350,000 U.S. dollars to an account in Singapore. He promptly telephoned Mo Tzu again to inform him of how to access the money. Gracefully, Mo Tzu thanked him for his courtesies and reiterated his promise to take effective action.

Chang indeed cared that his money would be used effectively. His wealth, derived from an array of family holdings, was considerable. But he would waste nothing. The New T'aip'ing Revolution had begun, and he had just taken the first step in advancing it. Any waste of resources, whether money, time, or energy, would be a dereliction adverse to the Cause.

So there it is. But now I am sapped of energy. Even my knees tremble.

"Taro-san! We leave now," Chang ordered his driver over the phone. He always employed a personal driver of Japanese origin even though the army made drivers available.

Today Chang owed himself a reward for his many recent decisions and energy expenditures. He would cause himself to be driven into the hills and mountains; later, en route back, he'd dine at a favorite inn he hadn't been to for years. And, yes, he would order along his civilian adjunct, a snobby Taiwanese crab (in spite of her femininity and fine legs) named Wu Hsiu-fen, and he would oblige her to relax and enjoy herself. That might help him to maintain her loyalty in the weeks and months ahead, when he would have to depend on her, implicitly, in ways she would never imagine now.

And by late afternoon, while being driven through the outskirts of Lo-tung and heading south with the beauteous Ms. Wu seated beside him, Chang almost whimsically reached one more decision. He was thinking about a female American intelligence operative who seemed patently attracted to him during the few times they had met. She should be used as a window to American counterintelligence. Of course she should! And he had better do that if he valued his duty to his Cause.

Summarily he turned to Wu Hsiu-fen and requested that she learn more about the American agent, such as her name, which Chang had forgotten despite at least two introductions to her.

November 8, 1984
Austin, Texas

Marie met Charlie atop Mount Bonnell on the west side of Austin overlooking the Colorado River as it swept into town. The park-like peak was always a fine place to view a sunset. The higher, fresher air, Marie said, helped her clear her mind. Meeting there likely gave her and Charlie the additional benefit of being able to talk immune from electronic eavesdropping.

"Maybe we ought to blow off running any more errands," Marie said to Charlie as they gazed over the Western Hills after a fairly arduous day on their jobs. "Have you read what's been going down in Chiapas since we've been there? It's murderous."

"Yuhh, I've heard. You know, I bet they don't manufacture M-16's anywhere in Mexico. Yet all the army kids I saw are packing 'em. The fucking kids are lucky to be able to read and write their names, yet every one of 'em carries an automatic rifle, along with orders to shoot *communistas*, courtesy of Uncle Sam."

"By the way, d' you hear about Father Sam getting busted again down in San Cristobal?"

"I've heard. Y' know, if we'd known what the hell we were doin' there, maybe we could have averted some of the consequences we might've helped cause."

"When we do an errand, maybe we can change the outcome somehow," Marie said. "We've talked about that."

"It's possible you're talkin' treason," Charlie said.

"Yeah, I know. But, heck, maybe we should try it."

"Well, maybe we could just try to put a different spin on things once in a while."

"Yeah, let's do it, then," Marie said in a tone of voice turned authoritative.

Something was now established. Marie had implicitly taken up the challenge: As of this moment, she would be looking for ways to effectively alter the outcomes of errands that struck her as being directed at nefarious objectives. Of course, she acceded, this might be a fool's mission, but for now it was her own affair of honor.

"I want to do at least a couple more errands," Charlie said apropos of nothing.

"Well," Marie declared, "I want to make a difference, a meaningful difference, in the context of overall reality, so to speak. What I'm talking about subsumes eternity."

"Ah."

Charlie did understand Marie's abstractions and concerns, and with some pride, for he apprehended a little of his own influence there. As they sat gazing west, his heart felt a yank that made him actually grimace as he glimpsed a phantasm of the little wat sheltered by banyan boughs on the edge of Kampong Prasat. He saw Madeline's lovely, serene face turn to him with a smile of appreciation. Memories of shipboard conversations with Dieter flickered through his mind. The past was too large to carry into the present except as a subconscious foundation, Charlie told himself; he'd best focus on the present and try to look ahead when he could.

Marie meanwhile entertained ghosts of her own: her father, dead but having loved her; her mother, still needing her to be strong, vital; and dear, old Rene, trusting that she would do what was best for all the world. These weren't ghosts. (Even now Rene might be awaiting her overdue state-of-her-Life message.) And there was Jed with whom she intended to share some of her Life someday; that Life had better not be diminished.

"I guess if they don't kill us," Marie said, "those errands might put a real edge on our Life. But we've gotta do them right."

"Um, what do you mean by 'do them right,' I'd like to know."

"Oh. Well, we don't want to hurt anybody or kill anybody; right? Isn't that why we talked about altering outcomes, or maybe 'putting a different spin' on things?"

"Yuhh . . . . So?"

"So for openers," Marie said, "how about if when I see an errand's headed in the wrong direction—say I can see that in the end it's going to cause real harm—I'll say, 'A-one.' Okay? *A-1*. We'll take that to mean, abort the entire mission any way we can. And then we try to abort it without getting caught. How about that?"

Abstracted gaze, desultory little nods: Charlie gave it some thought. "Um, what if I see that it should be aborted, as you call it?"

"Well, then you say 'A-1,' and we'll try to blow it."

"Oh. All right."

"We've got to be real careful and . . . subtle . . . about how we call our signals," Marie said. "We don't want to give ourselves away."

"*Signals*?"

"Like 'A-1.' That's only for openers. If we're pretty sure the errand should go according to the way it's been set up, one of us might say, 'Z-1.' Then we don't mess with it. We do it as assigned."

Charlie gave that some thought, too. Then he said, "Uh, what if you say 'A-1' and I say 'Z-1'? What do we do then; flip a coin?"

"No. We listen to me. I'll call the shots." Marie added, "Someone's got to be the final arbiter."

"Well, all right. Maybe you can devise some more signals."

Marie appreciated the mandate and trust. "You really are adorable," she said to Charlie when they got home. And a little later Charlie was heard to exult, "Sometimes I can't be-lieve my good luck!"

Thanksgiving (in the U.S.), 1984
Jakarta, Indonesia

Monsoons give warning when half the sky darkens in patches and wind comes in gusts, and then the sky partly clears before dark clouds return and wind gets stronger bringing the fresh smell of rain to mask smells of the city. Charlie recalled that these warnings can cause apprehension mixed with a secret feeling of delight, but now the sky and wind made him feel edgy. He consciously wished that Marie would not be alarmed by the monsoon coming. They would have to be lucky to get out of Indonesia before the storm hit, Charlie thought, and for the first time found himself seriously wondering whether he and Marie were underpaid.

Such negative notions were properly dispelled by the intelligent good looks and capable demeanor of a U.S.-Embassy staffer who expedited Charlie's passage through customs. When she and Charlie had gotten clear, as Charlie was replacing his passport in his jacket pocket, Debbie Kassenbaum shifted her black-liquid eyes from the darkening sky and pleasantly turned them on Charlie's soul.

"You have something for me?" she said musically.

"'Deed I do," Charlie drawled, preoccupied by the woman's attractions. God, you look barely twenty-two, you must do a lot of aerobics, he thought as he handed her the envelope he'd brought all the way from the New Orleans Federal Building.

"Thanks," Debbie said. "We'll take a cab. I'm supposed to tell you what you'll be doing in Irian Jaya. I believe you'll be assisting a medical mission there. I believe you know someone there." She made the last two statements sound like questions.

"Right," Charlie said. And with a perfunctory glance he ascertained that she was in her early or mid thirties.

The taxi ride mercifully skirted outlying slums of Jakarta. In less than three-quarters of an hour they arrived at an Indonesian-government airfield. En route, Debbie briefed Charlie as much as she could, given that his errand was basic and she'd never been to Irian Jaya, which lay in the opposite direction of the impending storm.

I bet CIA, Charlie decided about Debbie during their desultory conversation. She simply didn't look like State-Department material. Without pressing, he learned that she'd been with "the agency" for a little over ten years, beginning a year or so after she'd graduated from a small college in Ohio (where a very prominent blue-eyed movie star was also an alumnus, she said). With quiet pride she told him that she'd earned an M.A. at George Washington University while she worked full time at her career. (She didn't say what field her degrees were in, Charlie noted, nor did she mention the movie star's name.) She also told him that she had a condo near Falls Church, Virginia; she rarely spent any time there; she loved SCUBA diving and she loved to dance.

Intentionally low-profiled, Charlie decided. And somehow different. Charlie realized that although he had a mild interest in seeing how this woman looked completely undressed, she held no sexual attraction for him at all.

At the airfield Debbie accompanied Charlie as he was led to a two-engine commuter aircraft being loaded with medical supplies. Abruptly Debbie pulled a thick, orange, letter-sized envelope from her handbag and thrust it at Charlie's free hand. Although he'd been expecting to receive something from her, he had no idea of what the envelope contained.

"You'll need this, of course," she said. "Take care."

Charlie noted that she hovered near the hatch until it closed and the engines accelerated. *A real pro. With a hard edge to her.*

Later Charlie learned that his flight experience to New Guinea was virtually identical to Marie's: boring despite three refueling stops. The four other passengers on Charlie's (as on Marie's) flight were military officers, all imperious, taciturn, and evidently unlearned in English. Could such men shoot little kids if they thought that was part of their job? *In a heartbeat.* In days and years ahead, Charlie and Marie jointly maintained that all "people" who support themselves by relying on force and institutional authority instead of living by their own brains and brawn and character, are no more than shit.

After a full day of getting shuttled from one "community" school to another along the edge of very thick jungle, Dr. Marie Overstreet, an education consultant for the U.S. AID, felt much more concerned about the ever-darkening sky to the south than the feasibility of someone in her role trying to provide concrete assistance to anyone.

By late afternoon she obliged her Land Cruiser driver to take her to a specially located compound which served as a clinic and makeshift hospital for an ethnically diversified rural area. She'd been instructed to get an idea of what other services the huge U.S. mining company Freeport-McMoRan was providing to people outside Jayapura. Her heart leapt into her throat when she heard one word from a very familiar voice inside the main cinder-block building.

"Next!" Charlie called out as a dazed-looking Amungme farmer dropped off Charlie's adjusting table and, half smiling, made for the door to the main room. A minute later, as Charlie was preparing to adjust the neck of a Komoro woman, Marie strode into his adjusting room with apologies for interrupting.

"Dr. Grumbles, I believe you have something for me?" Dr. Overstreet said with a wry look. "My name is Marie Overstreet. I'm with the AID."

The two doctors regarded each other with relief at the other's safety as they shook hands warmly.

"Oh, ho! I sure do have something for you," Charlie responded and handed to Marie the envelope Debbie had given to him back in Jakarta. "You know where this goes, I presume."

"Sure. And this is for you." Marie gave to Charlie a plastic-covered book a bit larger and thicker than a deck of cards. It was a recently compiled glossary of local idioms, with a little extra. Part of Charlie's commission was to take it to New Orleans without fail. Subsequently, he and Marie jointly inferred that the glossary included code sentences for the edification of some agency's operations office. (Marie was sure she'd spotted a few of those sentences.) As for the identity of the code sender, Marie guessed he or she was one of several functionaries working in the mining company's administrative offices. Likely he or she was the recipient of the envelope which Charlie brought and Marie dead-dropped later, as instructed. This was the closest they came to knowing what they'd accomplished by this errand.

"Perhaps we'll meet again, maybe this evening in Timika. I've heard it's a real interesting place," Dr. Overstreet said to Dr. Grumbles as he pocketed the little book.

"It might rain like crazy tonight," Charlie responded. "If it does, maybe I'll see you at Freeport, in the dining hall."

"I'm pleased to have met you," Marie responded as she and Charlie shook hands again. As they did, Marie tugged Charlie into a corner of his clinic room and whispered to him urgently.

"Be real careful, okay?" she said. "I've been hearing rumbles about a revolt or something fixin' to blow up here. If it happens, we'll be right in the middle of it."

"Oh, great," Charlie said, "and all I've been worried about is a damned typhoon."

"A *typhoon*? Really?"

"Well, maybe just a heavy storm. A monsoon."

"Oh, well, be careful of that too," Marie said as she left.

No storm made landfall that night and the next morning, although clearly one was close. Charlie and Marie barely glimpsed each other at breakfast in the company's main compound. All the while, tension dripped from the ambience of the mining operations. Roots of unrest had sent out shoots and tendrils from the mountains through the rain forest. Rumors flew of insurrection, by whom (exactly) and against whom (precisely) nobody could say. Yet it seemed inevitable. Reports of desultory gunfire after midnight were easily confirmed. A security guard was missing, having left behind his right hand and a quantity of blood.

Marie finally managed to meet Charlie at the motor pool. Abruptly she declared, "We really shouldn't be separated like this, you know. Job or no job." And Charlie could only nod grimly.

Marie had arranged for herself and Charlie to be shown around a network of veritable reservations inhabited by people called Amungme and Komoro, both groups native to this beautiful island for untold generations. In "civilization" near the base of the mountain being mined, indigenous tribespeople were confined to spaces impinged on by tracts of ramshackle housing for several thousand "transmigrating" workers and their families. Outside the company compound, squalor seemed de rigueur. Not the most edifying of tours, the outing was extended to view more interesting things.

The guide and driver named Dave was an American geologist employed by the mining company and evidently of senior status. (He disdained a Jeep and appropriated use of an air-conditioned Ford Bronco.) Dave made every effort to show and explain the mining operations, which were gigantic despite not having been in place long. Marie, meanwhile, missed no opportunity to comment on the ecological and social effects of that mining. Charlie mostly kept to himself, preoccupied by something.

Clouds had closed in and wind velocity had picked up. It was time to head back down the mountain to the central compound. But first they all paused on a ridge overlooking a tributary of the Ajkwa River. The height on which they stood enabled them to view the tributary-river confluence, which looked unnaturally gray except for clay stains. The river beyond appeared somehow lifeless, that quality accentuated by the incredibly wide swath of hills and intervale (on both sides) having been denuded of trees and undergrowth. Tree trunks still stood near the river, but they looked dead and coated with slate-gray mud. By now Charlie was both shocked and appalled: How do people manage to justify such gross violations of nature? Abruptly Charlie remarked:

"Y' know, I try to plant trees whenever I can. Here, there seems to be a big effort underway to just kill 'em. There's some kind of *discrepancy* goin' on that I don't quite understand."

For the moment, Marie decided to change the focus. "How come that river looks so dead?" she asked Dave.

"The water is perfectly safe," Dave said. "At worst, it meets U.S. drinking-water standards. Most of 'em anyway. That's only crushed rock making its way into the river."

Charlie interposed: "Looks like the whole thing's been altered; the current, the level, you name it."

"Doesn't that cause a big build-up of silt all the way downstream?" Marie asked.

"Yeah, but we're working on it," Dave said. "The whole ecosystem is constantly being monitored so we can preclude permanent degradation. You know what they say about 'an ounce of prevention.' So far, the quality of the river itself isn't much different than it's always been."

At that moment Charlie threw exaggerated looks down around his own ankles and feet. Dave and Marie had to notice.

"Oh, excuse me," Charlie said. "I'm lookin' out for that politician's dog my daddy keeps tellin' me about. Every time it wets on somebody's feet, the politician says, 'Oh, that's all right. It's just a little rain.' People believe him!"

The point was lost on the company geologist.

"We've been cutting back on the volume of tailings being released to the water," Dave said, and as he dismissed the problem—the storm hit.

"Looks like you got more than your feet wet," Marie said to Charlie when they were back inside the Bronco.

Dave had been getting messages on his short-wave radio while he lurched their vehicle back onto the road. "Some kind of emergency going on in a few places," he announced. "Keep an eye out for groups of Papua—native people."

About a mile from the company compound Charlie was sure he heard gun shots through the storm. Nearing the compound gate they were met by a half-dozen Indonesian-army jeeps moving deliberately, two abreast. Marie counted at least four nervous-looking machine gunners in back seats. The Bronco was an unlikely target, but who was to say it *wasn't* a target, Marie thought.

As they approached the compound entrance, Charlie and Marie spotted two corpses of natives dropped near the edge of the road. A rifle lay near one.

Two gun shots clearly sounded from off the road nearby. Dave accelerated sharply the rest of the way to the gate. After a number of delays getting into the compound and then into the business offices, Charlie approached a mine executive and identified himself and said, "We need to get back to Jakarta as soon as the storm's over."

"Fine," said the fellow. "Who is *we*?"

Only then did Charlie realize that he and Marie had become separated again. All of a sudden the entire ambience shuddered. All office lights went out as the earth quaked again. Charlie heard the executive's assurance that everything was really quite normal.

Only with a lot of patience and arm twisting did Marie manage to get on a flight to Jakarta the next morning. It took that whole day and well into the night before she finally arrived there in the middle of a serious cloudburst. She was bringing her errand partially to term by meeting with a U.S.-Embassy staffer named Debbie Kassenbaum whom she had met briefly two days before.

Both women were discommoded by this late-night meeting at a military facility. In an open boarding area they exchanged handshakes, half-smiles, and letter-sized envelopes. With an earnest expression Debbie told Marie, "Minimal overrides; our allowance is sufficient." Marie responded, "Fine," then each proceeded on her way in separate taxis, the one for Marie having been dutifully provided by Debbie.

I wonder if she's CIA, Marie thought after a final wave to Debbie.

At that very moment Debbie was wondering how Marie usually spent her days. She wondered also about the strength of Marie's arms and about other matters relating to various parts of Marie's anatomy. Such musings would ease her back to sleep on a sticky monsoon night.

At the Jakarta International Airport, Marie made her way through a customs checkpoint, showing her own passport and visa, and hurried to board a TWA flight to Hawaii. En route she glanced through a bank of windows and noticed outside in a loading area a well-dressed American man and a man who looked like a priest talking intently to . . . *Charlie*. Charlie was supposed to have already left for Hawaii on an Australian airliner. Marie invoked the hope that she and Charlie would meet in Hawaii and go home together, which of course did not happen.

*

"You've got to wonder just what in the world we accomplished with all our globe-trotting," Charlie said as he and Marie sat in the Dallas-Fort Worth Airport almost exactly thirty-six hours after they'd last seen each other. They had just reunited with tearful hugs and strong kisses, then had promptly dropped onto a padded bench to await their commuter flight to home. Both wore rumpled clothing and smelled musty. Their hair was matted. Each was appalled by the other's haggard look.

Marie tried responding to Charlie's comment by saying she didn't care, except for one thing: "Did you get paid all right?" she asked Charlie.

"Yup. They made it an even four grand. How 'bout for you?"

"The same. We made some long dough between us. I'd hate to pay taxes on it."

"Well, let 'em try to prove we made it. By the way, we've still gotta go to work, like in about four hours."

"I'll be a zombie when I get to the lab."

"Yeah, I know," Charlie said. "Maybe we can sneak into a closet or someplace and take a nap." [Beat.] "As perverse as this sounds, we need the jobs! They're more important to us than . . . globe trotting."

For a minute they stared at the wide window across the waiting room.

"Geezus, what a Thanksgiving," Marie said with a sigh.

"No one would believe it if we told 'em," Charlie said. "I don't believe it." Charlie tried to ignore his fatigue; he found himself recalling his separations from Marie in places congenial to neither. He added, "I'm just about ready to swear off doin' 'errands.' Maybe they're no good for us."

Marie nodded. She mused audibly: "I don't see how that errand accomplished any good for anybody. It just seems like a lot of sound and fury signifying nothing."

Charlie remarked that the Defense Department probably needed some intelligence regarding Irian Jaya developments; he and Marie had been the conduits. Marie wondered aloud whether she and Charlie had abetted "a situation where people get whacked."

Charlie knew her concern. In his mind's eye he, too, could see the rain-drenched corpses fallen by the side of the road. "So, what's a few tribes of people and a rain forest and a river more or less?" he said.

"We could be negating our very Lives."

"I know you're onto something, but it's tenuous. I hope."

Charlie and Marie simply stared into space. Time passed.

"You know what I want?" Marie said.

"Name it."

"Pizza!"

"*Pizza?*"

"Yeah, with double extra cheese, and mushrooms and onions."

"Hmmm. Let's see what we can do. I'm gettin' hungry myself. Also I'm getting—"

Charlie paused in wonderment. He twisted into his seat.

"What's that?" Marie asked.

"Horny! I believe I'm gettin' horny. Must be all that Asian food."

Marie twisted likewise. "Well, let's see what we can do," she said, her eyes glittering the way Charlie loved to see them.

****

Marie clasped her right palm over the telephone mouthpiece and muttered across the dinner table to Charlie: "It's like she was reading my mind!" Instantly Marie switched to talking into the phone in normal tones: "Eleanor Gilchrest, I'm delighted to be hearing from you. Would you believe—"

Interposed from the other end of the line: "Yes, I'll bet you and your husband were just getting ready to start talking about me!"

In fact, during Marie's and Charlie's post-prandial conversation (their first in over a week) Marie had been preparing to raise the subject of E-Systems' connection to Defense Department officers such as Rick Denton.

"Actually," Marie responded, "we didn't know *you* knew we're married now."

"Oh, I know everything. I thought you knew!" Ms. Gilchrest said cheerfully. "Anyway, I'm calling to say I've heard, just incidentally now, I've heard by sheer happenstance that you and your soul-mate did a bang-up good job over Thanksgiving weekend. Under very trying circumstances from what I understand. I'm actually quite proud of you, both of you."

Thrilled, Marie promptly relayed the compliment to Charlie, who smiled.

"I'll bet you're finding anxiety to be a little bit addicting," Ms. Gilchrest remarked.

"Uh, not yet," Marie replied.

Eleanor Gilchrest laughed softly before she made an odd request: Would Charlie pick up an extension phone. This lady from E-Systems had something personal to say to both of them. Of course Charlie complied.

"You probably won't be hearing from me anymore," Ms. Gilchrest began. "I'm retiring. For good! Before I do, I want to make sure you understand a few things about what you've been doing, all right? [Beat.] If you're going to do more undercover work, be it overseas or domestic, even if it's only on a contractual basis as you've been doing it, you must bear in mind at all times these points that I'm about to tell you:

The first one is that you must always act ingenuous, and never ask for why's. This you already know; I'm just reinforcing it, okay? Now for the hard part: When you do undercover work for anybody, for any agency, you must display no hint of moral crisis. If you do, you're finished. Do you copy?"

Charlie and Marie said they thought they understood her.

"One last point, then," Ms. Gilchrest said, "and it's this: Never—I must repeat, never—scrutinize that face you see when you look into a mirror."

"I guess the jobs we do had better be *worth* doing, then, huh?" Marie uttered.

"I guess you'd be wise to think that way," Ms. Gilchrest responded.

"Well, thanks very much," said Charlie.

"Thank you," Marie said quietly.

"Oh, it's been my duty, and my pleasure," responded Ms. Gilchrest, who then said her goodbye and hung up.

Chapter 6

December 7, 1984
Austin, Texas

Charlie pulled on oars and wished he were back inside. Insouciantly Marie munched a banana. This was lunch time and they were in a rented rowboat on Town Lake, and chilly wind gusts rendered the situation less than pleasant. But the air was fresh, the exercise used up calories (for Charlie), and most likely Charlie's and Marie's discussion could not be overheard by anyone, accidentally or electronically. "Sometimes I get the feeling we're being monitored by someone no matter where we are or what we're doing," Marie had commented a few times previously, to which Charlie concurred.

"Look at it this way," Marie said to Charlie as he rowed them farther away from shore. "Paranoia can be a virtue. It's called prudence. But we have to practice it with some regularity, even ruthlessly. Do you remember our plan?"

"What plan?"

"A-1. Z-1."

"Oh. Yeah, of course."

"Well, I've come up with some more signals; you know, for responding to different scenarios," Marie said. "Sometimes we *shouldn't be* just 'conduits.'"

Charlie knew she was tacitly alluding to the phone conversation they'd had the previous evening. The one they'd had with Ms. . . . .

As Charlie rowed, then let the boat drift, Marie briefed him on six alternative courses of carrying out—or intentionally not carrying out—an "errand." A-1 and Z-1, the original signals, now carried permutations to meet different contingencies. Charlie tried to form an acronym from the central or initial letters of the various tactics. Finally he uttered,"ACABEDIMAZ!"

"It doesn't make much sense, but I guess we can remember that," Marie said.

"Maybe we should print it on a matchpad or the backside of a car bumper or something," Charlie offered. "Just in case."

"Not necessary. A wise person knows when to be paranoiac."

Before Charlie rowed them back, he and Marie reinforced their resolve to preclude adverse effects caused by their "errands," when and if they perceived such effects. From now on, their watchwords would be prudence and flexibility; their first priority, of course, would be never to be *suspected* of "adjusting" or intentionally "miscarrying" any of their missions. The entire prospect caused them each a frisson.

"Wooh!" said Charlie. "D' you think maybe we're cruisin' for a bruisin'?"

"That might be part of the charm!" Marie replied.

Again each felt a frisson, the start of a series of thrills that would extend over more than ten years.

Agana, Guam

At about that same moment, Area Lead Agent Debbie Kassenbaum felt a frisson of her own as she projected what her new job entailed. Unlikely as this once seemed, she had been named the Agency's new station chief for the Southern Rim, a recognition that truly gratified her. Plus she would operate from Taiwan, a duty post she desired. Her secret thrill came from realizing that she would be in a position to utilize the privileged information she had learned about certain members of the Kuomintang. That claque of militarists still ruled Taiwan, a real country regardless of how external political leaders classified it. Debbie had gathered arcane information about all the primary and most of the secondary members of the Kuomintang, with the possible exception of General Chang K'ung. Aside from Chang's impressive dossier and the fact that he maintained an austere life style despite inherited wealth, Debbie knew only one underground fact about him. But it was critical and might give her real clout in his eyes.

Debbie had learned that, for reasons best regarded as mysteries, Chang had recently been in contact with Undersecretary Lin Piao of the People's Republic. Contacts between high-level officers of the "two Chinas" were unusual but sometimes normal, especially in trade matters. Nothing about this one computed, though; the content of both calls seemed anomalous. Debbie was sure that something totally unsanctioned was going on. She would bet that if Chang and Undersecretary Lin were to learn that someone else knew of their association, they would exert themselves to obliterate the fact. Fortunately for Chang (Debbie would advise him), only a few NSA and DIA functionaries knew of his contact with Lin, and Debbie could probably obscure that intelligence. Chang would be wise to take her into his confidence, a prospect that Debbie found utterly thrilling.

As far as Debbie could recall, Chang was the only living person she had ever actually admired since she'd turned, say, twenty-one years old. She wasn't sure why. Perhaps it was because she intuited that he harbored grand dreams, but, again, she didn't know why she believed that. Maybe that was the crux of her attraction to him: She wanted to learn, in depth, all there was to know about a person so enigmatic, so intriguing. This desire, Debbie now realized, had become an obsession, and it was pleasing to dwell upon.

From the neck down, was Chang constructed from strands of elevator cable, as he appeared to be? She wouldn't be surprised if he were. What really motivated Chang to excel as he did and, Debbie believed likely, configure great aspirations? Where did those motivations originate? Was the cause merely a giant ego? Or was it wider and richer than that? Did K'ang love anyone in particular? If so, of what sex was his beloved? (*Ah, now the really interesting issues.*) Did Chang get erections like other men?

If he did, how did he like to relieve them? Did he have normal digestive processes, or were his special? Debbie was shocked by the noticeably moist lubrication of her own arousal, caused by, of all things, a man—who was not even present.

Consciously, Debbie changed her focus: better to fantasize about that womanly creature she'd met in Jakarta, the robust, dark-haired courier, that Dr. Overstreet. *Ahhh.* Maybe someday she would land in Taiwan and they would meet again, and Debbie would be ready for her.

As she had so many times over the last two decades, Debbie reflected that life was basically a pointless exercise full of senseless horror, although she herself had been spared the horrors (so far). But now she could construe a hazy reason for her tenure on Earth: life was interesting, undeniably so. And sometimes—yes, sometimes—it could be vibratingly exciting.

Leningrad, Russia, U.S.S.R.

At about this same time also, in their apartment still cluttered by unpacked belongings, Senior Physicist Andrei Platonov vaguely mumbled something to the back of his wife's head as she sat reading. Without a trace of interaction he shuffled past her chair and headed for their bedroom simply to escape the coils of consciousness.

Tatyana Ivanovna Platonov called to Andrei's back, "Goodnight, dearest!" for which she received no response, exactly as she'd expected. For her to follow him would have been utterly self-defeating; she knew that too well. Thus Tatyana bent to her astronomy book, stared at a page of illustrations for several moments, realized her strength was deserting her, and simply let go and wept bitterly. If Andrei heard her, he gave no sign of it.

"God damn everything!" Tatyana shouted clearly. She threw her book at the floor with real force to punctuate her attitude.

Andrei, being smart, would not come out to her now. If only those others, all those witless, cruel functionaries who were causing dear Andrei and herself so much grief, would appear! She would alter their sexual equipment right there and now. If they even had any. Fantasies of violence didn't cause Tatyana to feel better; they merely enabled her to summon her resolve.

She could not live as she had been, nor would she. For the last two years her "life" had been subverted until it was next to nonexistent. Her deep inner light was all that remained, and it had been submerged, buried, almost extinguished. Andrei surely loved her deeply—how could that be otherwise?—but no longer could she prove that. Had he shown her any affection in the last two years? She couldn't recall.

(Indeed! Andrei himself is surely partly to blame, she thought. But she didn't care about that point.)

For at least the last twelve years Tatyana had been shuttled all over the Soviet Union as wife to a prominent physicist in deepening disgrace. By some miracle they'd wound up back in Leningrad, her beloved home city. However, two days ago Andrei learned that he'd already been reassigned (again) to Kazakhstan, a turn of events so unabashedly absurd as to be obscene. Setting aside issues of wasted expertise and talent, a home for them had ceased to be even a dream. They were convinced they would have been better off had they been banished to Gorky.

Perhaps incredibly, these were Tatyana's secondary concerns. Her primary concern was Andrei's health—physical, mental, emotional, and professional. And it was failing. Badly.

Yet her Andrei was arguably the brightest physicist in the whole Soviet Union and a bona-fide expert in allied fields. A man of wide-ranging interests, in the West they would call him a "Renaissance man." Unfortunately for his career (and thus for Tatyana's life), one of Andrei's "deeper interests" had turned into an obsession: fostering the natural, inalienable right of all individuals to do and think as they thought best for themselves and their families and countries (unless a person was fairly adjudged to be a real and immediate danger to others). Such an obsession carried a correlate: deep and abiding disdain for—

and outright opposition to—all those who would curtail that right.

Thus Andrei constantly found himself standing athwart all lines of authority within his milieu. No person of any authority could surpass Andrei's intellect and character, and the frequent contrasts were jarring. "I fear that I am beset by mean, little people," he often remarked. (Tatyana preferred to call them "essentially worthless micro-organisms.") The mean, worthless viruses vastly outnumbered whatever support Andrei could muster. Once his career began to slip, anything he undertook they ultimately blocked. They not only prevailed, they brought him down. Even his dearest, staunchest friends receded from him.

Thus Tatyana found herself with a shell of a husband, two estranged offspring (a daughter and son), increasingly inferior medical care, and no home nor friends. Utterly committed to Andrei and to his well-being, she could bear this no longer.

"God damn all this!" Tatyana uttered at the ceiling. All right, she determined: they would go, apparently docilely, to Kazakhstan, the less-than-secured backside of Soviet nuclear-missile-development programs. Andrei's access to fissionable materials was still intact. They would use that access to plutonium, to recent nuclear-technology information, possibly even to nuclear weapons.

The steps after that would be tricky, but as of this moment Tatyana felt equal to them: she would contact whoever was willing to pay well for the weapon components; collaterally, using Andrei's access to them, she would acquire those materials. Then she would sell them to whoever paid the most (after factoring in potential buyers' quotients for discretion). Her penultimate objective: enable Andrei and herself to leave the country, ultimately so they could live. Yes, she would need a lot of help; eventually she'd be paying certain people to assist her in accomplishing the stages of each of her steps.

Tatyana thought, I will generate my own Five-Year Plan to recoup some of my losses. And if the process should require, say, ten years to accomplish? She would give it ten years.

Desperation—that she had. Now she also had a challenging *raison d' etre*.

The hour was still early enough for Tatyana to telephone her cousin Marina and arrange to borrow a manual of Arabic idioms and one of Cantonese idioms. As soon as feasible she'd also acquire grammar texts in case she needed to learn either language in depth. For her, great luck would be finding a well-funded, very discreet French terrorist.

January 5, 1985
Austin, Texas

Shockingly, Hollis the senior had finished off two overstuffed fajitas with a proper salad and was now working on his second dark beer, a British ale, and this was only lunch.

"You can't eat like this all the time; don't even think about tryin' most days of the week," he remarked for his son's benefit. "Even I don't, and I've got the metabolism of a hummingbird. [Beat.] I've got a metabolism like . . . like Jack Palance had when he was playin' an Apache or a crook."

Charlie nodded acknowledgement of the remarks and sipped his only brew of the afternoon, this being a work day. His mother sat next to his father at the small pub table, serenely enjoying a wine cooler despite chilly weather. Marie was at her job or else "power lunching."

Charlie's mind drifted to the complex of offices in the privately-funded education "laboratory" at which Marie worked; it fixed on Marie for a moment, then swung over to Honolulu and all the way over to Quezon City in the Philippines. Unself-consciously Charlie grinned as he recalled standing outdoors at the Manila International Airport and hearing Marie say "Not recently" without having missed a beat.

*

On New Year's Day in the U.S. Charlie had delivered four boxes of "medical supplies" to St. Jude's Clinic, a Catholic

Church-sponsored medical-care facility in Quezon City. Marie was in Manila working at the Central Bank of the Philippines, assembling copies of key accounts for the International Monetary Fund. Of course, Charlie's supplies actually were not "medical," and Marie ensured that some of the materials she handled went to Honolulu by courier, as mandated by a particular U.S. intelligence agency.

(Of course it didn't *rain* while they were there; instead, veritable sheets of water dropped from the sky almost in waves. Worse, they were able to meet only once during those three days, and only briefly in the Manila Ritz Hotel dining room.)

The most singular aspect of the errand was Charlie's discovery that he had brought crude satchel charges into the country, along with two .38 revolvers and a box of cartridges. He and Marie determined that Charlie's "supplies" were to be somehow involved in—probably used against—Corey Aquino's bid for the presidency of the Philippines. St. Jude's Clinic was located barely a mile from her campaign headquarters.

"A-1," Marie told Charlie as they strolled the Ritz dining room. "Abort." Instead Charlie opted for "A-2" (abort; advise local authorities), a stratagem he and Marie had presumed they'd probably never use. Marie's task was to warn the Quezon City police chief of "terrorist activity" at St. Jude's, which she did without implicating herself.

An odd aspect of the errand was Charlie's meeting the director of the clinic in Quezon: a burly, fit-looking man, prematurely bald, with striking eyes the color of young green olives. When they met he was wearing a sodden tee-shirt over which lay the black Roman collar of his calling.

"You know, I've seen you before," Charlie declared as they shook hands.

"Of course. That was in Jakarta, at the airport. I was there with the assistant U.S. envoy; remember? I'm Father Bobby Jay Nobles. Father Jay."

"Oh, of course," said Charlie. "I was thinking we'd met someplace before that, a long time ago."

"No, I think not."

But Charlie had felt some kind of association with Hong Kong, as though he'd been there recently in a dream. He remembered making that same connection at the Jakarta airport. It came to him that, yes, in a different Life—Mme. Picard looming close by—Charlie heard that same husky voice coming from a priest who wore sunglasses and had a lot more hair.

Charlie never got the chance to mention his recollection to Father Jay. Two days later, at the airport before departing Manila with Marie, he was about to relate his memory of meeting that priest to Marie when they were distracted by finding two .38 revolvers—probably the same pieces he'd brought in—with most of a box of cartridges—in Charlie's flight bag. Before they could leave the country they had to dispose of the pistols (into Manila Bay from the shuttle helicopter en route to Clark Air Base), which prompted Marie to remark that everything they'd done on this errand took place in a murky context.

"Sometimes you know you're being confronted by intentional wrong-doing," she added, "but you can't tell, really, if it makes a damn bit of difference."

Charlie understood that.

"This whole thing's been weird," said Marie. "Then, again, what isn't?"

Charlie nodded empathically.

Marie declared: "Intentional wrong-doing in our context might even turn—"

Charlie cut her off: "Y' ever screwed in a helicopter?"

"Not recently," she replied.

"Hollie, your mother says you look a little peaked today. Did you and your bride overdo it this New Year's, or what? If you did overdo it, for god's sake tell me how."

Charlie knew that conviviality aside, his father suspected him of some kind of deception. His mother sat nodding serenely. Yes, she suspected something, too. Charlie felt nonplussed; conflicting notions buzzed and collided. He reached a resolution as he realized his mother was rising and excusing herself to leave for a short time.

"Well, sir," Charlie said after a few beats, "would you believe I've been—actually, Marie and I have been—doin' a little side job. At least for the time being we've got us some extra work that pays real good and it covers all kinds of expenses. That's why we've been out of touch sometimes."

"What kind of work y' all doin'?"

"Uhm, you might say we perform errands. Usually we have to go to other countries. You know, like those 'south-of-the-border' trips we've mentioned. The only reason we could afford 'em is that we get all our expenses covered."

"I see. If you don't mind my asking, who do you do 'errands' for? The U.S. government?"

"Uh, correct."

"Yeah, bull shit."

"No! What I'm telling you is true. We really do run errands, so to speak, for certain agencies of the government. It's nothing Earth-shaking, but it's highly beneficial."

"Surely you jest, Hollie. First you say you 'run errands' to other countries, you and your wife go zipping off to other lands at someone else's expense; then you say you're doin' it for Big Brother. And then you say it's beneficial to someone. The plausibility is overwhelming."

"Look, Daddy, I've been known to maybe embellish facts a little bit now and then, you know, to get a desired effect. But what I tell you is true. [Beat.] You can tell Ma if you want to, but I kind of wish you wouldn't. No one's supposed to know."

Hollis pondered briefly before he spoke: "What next? My son, renowned expert at gettin' laid and crunching spines and hangin' out in jungles for maybe a decade at a time. He's got him a treasure of a wife, to say the least. And he and she just happen to be workin' for Big Brother on the sly."

"Well, it's just an extra little job on the side. We don't know how long it'll last."

"Or whether it'll *kill* you."

"I know that's possible. We're often in jets or taxis."

"And when you get there maybe the natives aren't altogether friendly."

"Maybe. They're not friendly here, either. They know about my past, Daddy."

With a grunt and a sharp look at Charlie, Hollis turned the subject over in his mind a few times. It didn't look half-bad, really. But it made him fearful.

"Livin' outside the pale: it's kind of *addicting*, huh?" Hollis asked Charlie.

"It might be. It's got strong fringe benefits, for sure. I believe now I can start up a trust for Brent up in Seattle."

Abstracted, Hollis Senior fixed on a space in the crowded pub through which Marguerite, his wife and soul-mate, was soon to return. Abruptly he told his son, "Well, so long as it doesn't kill you. Or Marie. That would be a horrendous waste! More than we can imagine."

Charlie concurred; Hollis added, "And so long as you don't get greedy."

"Um, what's wrong with a little greed, sir?"

"A little is okay. It's natural. It helps you get important stuff if you don't already have it. After that, it only causes the wrong priorities, plus a lot of grief sooner or later."

"You know I know that. So does Marie. I just want to set things up for Brent if I can. Y' know Marie wants me to start my own practice a little ways down the road."

"So do it. I wish you the best fortune possible."

"Thanks. Uh, you can tell Ma if you see fit. I don't think she'll be tellin' anyone. The trouble is, I shouldn't have told you any of this. If Marie finds out, I'm in trouble."

"Uhn! Damned if I know what t' tell your mother."

January 21, 1985
U.S.S.R., the backside of it

For a while Andrei Platonov had thought his beloved wife to be insane, or worse.

Out of earshot of anybody that bleak Kazakhstan afternoon in Alma-Ata, Tatyana had led him about on the snowy, desolate lanes within sight of the walls and windows in the Soviet People's Institute of Science when she made her request in exactly the same manner as when she directed him to buy her new boots or wait in line at the butcher's shop. She simply wanted him to build a prototype of a very small nuclear bomb, strictly for her. A model? No, a real one, one that would be eminently effective, easily portable, and readily replicated. *Fin*. Request completed.

"You must be insane, or maybe worse!" he did manage to say, but no, she noted that she was only "crazy as a fox" (as people liked to say in the West).

What would she think of next?

She then proceeded to aver the incredible: If he accomplished what she wanted, eventually he would regain his health. Then, of course, he and his beloved would know such bliss as they had known in years gone by, although perhaps not as copiously.

Indeed! Real happiness requires health, and how would he, Platonov the disfavored physicist, *find* health? Regaining health requires wealth, a mere fact of life.

Wealth comes in various forms, Tatyana responded, and with a valuable product to sell to eager buyers she would obtain the most effective kind: hard foreign currency which they would use in foreign climes and in foreign medical facilities. That was not a dream now; it was her focal point.

Andrei's mind reeled. After some moments he managed to ask why she would want nuclear-fission explosives. Was she already in the service of foreign adventurers? No, was her calm reply, but she surely intended to acquire a large sum of their money.

*

Since that bleak but remarkably luminous afternoon just after the turn of the new year, Andrei found himself

145

subconsciously, then consciously, energized. Within the course of perhaps a week he managed to surprise not only his colleagues but himself with his renewed vigor. His daily objective became finding time and mental space in which to think about a secret project, do some research related to it, and (as soon as feasible) begin "tinkering." At the Institute, if a directive from above or a personality conflict impinged on his time or energy, Andrei simply gave it short shrift.

During these first weeks of the new year, whenever Andrei noticed that his will or physical reserves were sputtering, Tatyana abruptly (and very discreetly) repeated her promises of renewed health for him and recaptured bliss for them both, based on her acquiring foreign cash. *Trust me,* she exhorted him perhaps twice, although both knew that to be a redundancy. With tentative satisfaction Tatyana and Andrei each noted that the effect of this new dimension to their Life was no less than synergistic.

The problem, the real problem, Andrei determined, was precisely what kind of fissile material to use. Over time he might have access to any existing form. Initially he leaned toward weapons-grade uranium because it emits minimal radioactivity; it might be perfect for what Tatyana had in mind to sell abroad. Ah, those sweet-looking little steel canisters of powdered plutonium oxide were almost irresistible to try working with, and they only weighed about two kilos each. God help me, I am tempted to take one home under my coat to show it to Tatyana!

In their secretive conversations, Tatyana stressed that with Andrei's assistance, *she* would be primarily responsible for acquiring the fissionable materials to be used in replicating Andrei's prototype. On that hallowed day somewhere in the future, she would have the key element—*money*—with which to induce people (under her precise direction) to supply her with everything she needed. Mainly what she would need from Andrei in this connection was a list of names of key Institute personnel, along with his defining the accounting and safeguarding procedures for radioactive substances in Kazakhstan.

What a team, Andrei concluded: he would design and build a set of unnamable devices; Tatyana (with some assistance from him) would acquire raw materials and sell the finished products. For someone not associated with an institute, she was sophisticated about how Soviet laboratories worked. An important bit of lore she had long understood was that parts of shipments of plutonium, uranium, cesium, and other substances were routinely but covertly held back during initial inventory procedures. (For what purposes, nobody could say for sure.) Thus the bits and pieces were not on any official inventory; they were simply excess, absorbed by private caches that had grown and multiplied.

Ah, Life in Kazakhstan. Stultifying, yes, but relatively simple. Simplicity could be a real gift. Andrei found himself thinking this every day lately. Here some mundane stresses were necessarily absent from a person's life. A man could make time to think, to tinker with things, to restore himself if he so chose. Likely as a consequence of that simplicity, Andrei began taking longer, more vigorous walks through snowy fields; whenever he could, he put in long hours refurbishing his wife's and his dismal apartment. Normally fastidious, this meant he bathed even more often, causing him to be in their wretched little bathroom (which he resolved to remodel) quite often, which enabled him to watch Tatyana in all degrees of undress. Things were definitely beginning to happen again. Tatyana, of course, noticed. He knew that she noticed because her smiles were approving, or else inviting. The lilt in her voice became more noticeable. One day only about a month after their arrival, Andrei declared to the cosmos: "I love Kazakhstan!"

January 23, 1985
Austin, Texas

Shortly after nightfall Charlie lay spent next to Marie who lay prone and naked except for her black garter belt and gold necklace with the tiny mother-of-pearl teardrop. Perfumed votive candles bathed their bedroom in warm light. Marie stretched lazily; in a voice that fairly glowed she asked Charlie to rub her back. This he proceeded to do with deliberation and strength, working his way up to her back starting above the knees to enable him to admire the rounded fullness of her. Marie gave him encouragement by emitting soft, appreciative vocables. For both, the elapsed day and abbreviated evening had been more than enough. Soon Charlie would pull on loose-fitting boxer shorts, cover Marie with a sheet, and blow out the candles.

Unexpectedly Marie uttered, "We did good; didn't we?"

Charlie was surprised by the grammatical error until he realized she meant "good" was what they'd accomplished by calling down authorities and actually helping to destroy dangerous contraband during their recent errand in the Philippines. "Let's hope so," he said. "It took me until last week to recover from that goddamned episode."

"I noticed. I was sapped long after we got back," Marie said.

"At this rate, it'll take a miracle to get you pregnant."

"Who knows; maybe we're better off for the delay," Marie remarked. Her mind switched to another track. "Kind of inspires us to get into shape and stay in shape, huh?"

"Don't think I'm not concerned about that," Charlie said, adding that he'd been doing roadwork most days despite his malaise. He overlooked divulging that he'd signed up for membership at the Hyde Park Gym, a well-equipped weightlifting establishment. He hoped the yoga class he and Marie took would offset his muscle tightness.

In a little while Charlie verged on sleep. Marie abruptly rolled onto her back and began talking in a casual tone: "Do Buddhists believe that sooner or later things'll get turned around, and we'll see a kind of synthesis of minds, and ultimately we'll have peace and justice on Spaceship Earth?"

After a beat, Charlie responded, "Some Buddhists, I'm sure."

Soon Marie said, "Wherever we turn, people are dying for nothing. You know what I mean: prematurely, violently, or maybe their existence is the same thing as death, or worse. Usually that's a direct result of premeditated action by jerks, by assholes, who know they're doing wrong but they do it anyway."

"Yeah, I know it. My dad's afraid we might get ourselves killed for nothing. It really is 'a jungle' out there."

"Ah."

Thus Marie learned that Charlie had told his father about their doing "errands." She knew Hollis well enough to expect that he wouldn't ask to be told a lot of specific details, which she and Charlie were honor-bound to never divulge.

Now Charlie began speaking levelly, deliberately: "Death, dying, I can't say I actually mind. It's natural enough. It's part of the whole deal; you know? The separations are what I fear. Mainly the premature separations, especially from you."

"You fear that?"

"Yes. I sure do."

Charlie took Marie's hand firmly in his. "I'll tell you this," he said, "if anything harmful happened to you, if I couldn't be with you every day, I'd sooner not live."

"Are you willing to take the chance that could happen?"

"If you are. But only if you are."

Marie turned onto her side, facing her man.

"You're wonderful, d' you know that?" she said.

"I've often suspected as much."

"I've feared those separations, too, but now I fear them worse," Marie said.

For a while they lay quietly. Marie broke the silence in measured tones:

"If we're smart, from now on we'll plan things better, try to anticipate all the contingencies."

Charlie made large gestures toward the walls and ceiling. He pointed to his ears, then to the walls again. Marie nodded.

"We need to take us a little break out in the boondocks," she declared.

*

The following Sunday, Marie and Charlie hummed contentedly after a good barbecue lunch as they headed south from Kerrville, Texas. Charlie drove a rented Mazda which responded to his demands remarkably well. He and Marie owned only one car, Marie's old Honda Accord. It could have been "bugged," hence the rental car.

"I wonder how far it is from here to the Mexico border," Charlie said.

"Oh, maybe two hundred miles, if you go direct, on horseback."

"I try not to go anyplace on horseback."

Small talk completed, they reviewed the eight new coded options Marie had formulated for miscarrying and not miscarrying errands. These would supplement the eight they had previously formulated. Some code designations they might combine under certain conditions.

All the options were permutations of the initial two basic strategies: abort or complete the errand. Most refinements were responses to contingencies, the main one being the degree of risk they would likely encounter if they altered the mission outcome. (No reckless action would be tolerated.) As they had decided before, Marie would usually call the signal. Charlie contributed some cunning strategies, such as "abort the errand by supplying partial information after disposing of essential information." ("A-P-6, ducky.") Marie came up with the most unlikely one: "abort *after* completion by taking the bastard out." ("A-C-8, bully.") Despite their combined brain power Charlie and Marie required most of two days to spell out, integrate and internalize all their scenarios.

"I feel a certain urgency about all this," Marie said a few times that weekend, to which Charlie would declare, "Now remember, we don't ever get caught doin' things our way. If it looks like we're fixin' t' shoot ourselves in the foot, I say or you say—'C-N-R,' which means 'cut and run.' All right?"

During one of these exchanges Marie got distracted by the countryside along the winding highway south of Kerrville.

"Boy! If we had money I'd like to have a place out here," Marie said after a few minutes of silence. "Kind of a getaway."

Charlie peered at the odometer. "Yeah, but how on Earth could we take care of it? We must be at least a hundred and fifty miles from Austin."

"Well, first comes the vision. You manage to work things out accordingly when you've clarified the vision," Marie declared as she would say one-plus-one-equals-two."

"That's good, sweetie. I surely wouldn't disagree."

A moment later Charlie added, "I think I can appreciate all the things you do, and all those good things I perceive inside you, maybe a little better every day."

Marie touched Charlie's upper arm with affection.

"I suspect that's essentially what love is," she said. "I sure hope I can do a good-enough job of returning it."

Charlie turned briefly to Marie and their eyes met. Each gave a little smile hinting of the dawn that glowed within.

*   *   *

Here I can save you some time by relating that they actually needed about a year of sporadic innovating and revising and committing signal-codes to memory before they crystallized a comprehensive system of actions they could apply to errands they might carry out abroad. And over the next five years they executed, on average, about one per month in many parts of the world, sometimes landing in places the natures of which elude even my comprehension. Guinea-Bissau, Brunei, Belize, El Salvador, Burkina Faso, even Luxembourg: we know they exist as ostensible countries; but the question is why.

Rarely did Charlie and Marie undertake two errands per month (and only once did Marie do a third, on a weekend when Charlie was immersed in a shoulder-adjustments workshop

151

out of state). Probably their most memorable jobs occurred in Mexico (a few times), Canada (twice), Malaysia, Holland, Belize, and Turkey. They went to a host of places they wanted to visit, such as Denmark and Greece, but they simply arrived, accomplished their jobs, and left, as was congruent with the nature of "errands." Unhappily, they never got to Ireland. Happily to both, except for a trip to Amman, Jordan, they were spared from operating in Israel and its immediate neighbors. (They never learned why.) This saved them from making very difficult choices that probably would have been mandated by their joint code of honor.

One reason some assignments were especially memorable was that they were simply done, period. Marie and Charlie decided to do them exactly as directed, without perceiving a need to delete a digit in a code they were passing on, or to withhold data going in or coming out, or to destroy portions of information entrusted to them, which sometimes they felt they had to do. Lightheartedness seems to be important to people.

All this required astute management because most errands took place in mid-week rather than on weekends. That meant Charlie and Marie had to be their own boss. Thus Charlie launched his own practice in a converted house in central Austin as soon as he possibly could. Marie did likewise, consulting for school districts and private schools and teaching part-time at both the community college and The University of Texas to keep her skills sharp and maintain an income. Eventually Marie operated out of a garage office installed behind a second house she and Charlie bought for investment. After a few years Charlie moved his practice four blocks to a nicer, larger converted house.

And of course they had the double issue of whether Marie wanted to get pregnant, but then her not getting pregnant despite their best efforts to conceive. They resolved all this in their own way, first by adopting an infant they named Lisa, and then by Marie finally getting pregnant but miscarrying, and two years later giving birth to little Julia.

You should know that from them, from Charlie and Marie jointly coping with Life issues, I learned that humans can deal with things much better when they exercise gusto and panache, along with adhering to a basic principle: To really Live, a person needs to be dedicated to a significant cause *beyond* his or her little desires and needs.

Of course I did my best to help out when my prompting would have made a difference. I sharpened their perceptions when they were in danger of getting caught sabotaging an errand. Sometimes I even gave them practical assistance when they wanted to miscarry a mission. The best example of that was in Houston, Texas, in the fall of 1988 just before Charlie and Marie were to leave for Guatemala City on a quick round trip.

Normally I disdain direct intervention; my role lies beyond that. But in this case I induced Charlie to open the package he and Marie were supposed to carry out of country and see what was inside. (Doing this sort of thing was absolutely prohibited, of course, but the package was loosely taped, and ignorance breeds grief.) The content turned out to be a two- or three-pound loaf of some yellow-orange substance; to Charlie it felt tough and malleable, as though made from plastic. Abruptly Charlie jerked his hand off it, his mind having frozen out all the feeling in his fingertips.

"Oh-oh! I think we've got us some plastic explosives," he told Marie.

She gave it a look.

"What do *I* know," she said. "I've heard of some stuff called, oddly enough, 'Semtex.' X-rays don't show it as being anything. It's not metal but it's lethal. Maybe that's what we've got here."

"I wonder how they'd detonate this."

"I don't remember what I read about it."

If what they had was indeed an explosive, they wondered, who was the intended target and why, for heaven's sake? They were deeply appalled; also fearful. Later they learned they'd had good reason to be fearful: Semtex was precisely what they were meant to carry into Guatemala. And somewhere down the road—Ka-blaaf! Heads and limbs were meant to fly. And guess who would have helped make that possible.

What to do? They considered their few options. All were infeasible. Then I interjected the idea: Substitute something harmless, and get rid of this stuff. Could they even pull that off, let alone with impunity? I led them to The Home Depot where, sure enough, a clerk showed them an epoxy putty into which they decided to try mixing sawdust (which they could get right there). And it worked, once they added paint thinner and petroleum jelly. After some mixing and kneading in the bathroom of their motel room, they had a mound of stuff which felt just about right.

Then all they had to do was buy the right-colored vegetable dyes at a Safeway and mix and apply them to their creation. *Voila*! Here is something with which you can blow up your enemy's cathedral, *señor*. Courtesy of the U.S. of A. Indeed, side by side the two loaves looked nearly identical.

"Hee-hee-hee-hee!" Charlie gloated even before he and Marie finished with it."All *right*," Marie said as she admired the match. "Let's go with it."

So they did (after they had dropped the real Semtex into a bayou). In Guatemala City they found their contacts at an outdoor market and passed on the faux plastique wrapped in butcher's paper and a special edition of the *Tampa Post*. Charlie and Marie both felt a stab of anxiety when the pair of thugs promptly cut open the wrapping to look inside. No problem here! They proceeded to complete their errand and flew back to Houston for a quick debrief and $2,400 cash between them.

At Hobby Airport, just prior to boarding their flight home Charlie abruptly said, "*Whooh*! Are we cool, or what?"

"Or . . . maybe just crazy," Marie said quietly.

During the next few weeks they waited to hear of any upshot from their ruse in Guatemala, but nothing ensued. After about a month they banished the episode from memory.

A year later, almost to the day, they were back in Houston and staying at the same motel prior to a briefing. Ray Rugowski surprised them by coming to their room with a thick, compact package and a faux-leather folder. He briefed them without prelude and they were dispatched to, of all places, the northernmost edge of Vermont, where they would cross into Canada as a pair of trysting lovers on a camping trip. They would take the package and folder which, in due course, were destined for the hands of parties they would meet in Canada. Aside from the errand duration being too brief, they saw no problem with the job.

Except Marie was disturbed by one detail which Rugowski revealed perhaps inadvertently: the name Headley. Later, during a stroll outside with Charlie, Marie brought it up. She had read some good poems by an Irish writer with that name; *something else* was significant about it, though. Marie wracked her memory.

"Well maybe there's some old-timey beer or some Irish politician named Headley," Charlie offered. "Maybe there's some notorious--" He was about to say "Irish bomb-thrower" when Marie cut him off.

"IRA! Sinn Fein!" she said. "No, no, no, no. Wait. Headley and his mob are the guys who terrorize the IRA. You know, the Irish terrorists."

"Hold it," Charlie said. "You think these are counter-terrorists?"

"No; they're just terrorists. Period. They're on the side opposite the other terrorists in Northern Ireland."

"Oh." After a moment Charlie said, "What if we're wrong? What if they're actually IRA terrorists?"

"What difference would that make?"

"I see your point."

Charlie proposed opening the package but then declared, "Ehh, to hell with it."

"Yeah, I'm afraid to take sides on this one and jeopardize our own interests," Marie said, and they simply proceeded to accomplish their errand. They felt perverse about doing it, but they did as they were directed. Were they right? I would never presume to say. Sometimes human reality is too bizarre even for me to comprehend.

*　　　　*　　　　*

Chapter 7

New Year's Day (in the U.S.), 1990
Taipei, Taiwan

Harried by her involvement in grand causes and bureaucratic mandates, Debbie Kassenbaum found herself hurrying through the international airport terminal to find two Dutch "tourists" expecting to meet her. She and they had quiet business to conduct for the U.S. government on behalf of the Nationalist Chinese government, which Debbie still equated with the Kuomintang, which she considered a claque of fascists.

"Well, howdy-doo!" Debbie said when she spotted Marie, then Charlie, waiting outside ROC Customs. Despite five years having passed since they had last met, Debbie kept a vivid memory-image of Marie. (Thus she vaguely remembered Charlie.) In fact she had inquired after Marie perhaps twice each year. Suddenly, there she was!

After an exchange of greetings and code sentences (with an incongruously warm smile bestowed on Marie), the threesome set out to make another exchange, this time in a taxi cab en route to downtown. This was a special taxi that came flying around a curve outside the terminal when Debbie stepped out; the driver was introduced as a consulate staffer. Inside the cab everyone could talk freely while Charlie and Marie gave Debbie sealed packets. In return she passed to each a tan letter-sized envelope.

"How long will you be in Taipei?" Debbie asked Marie.

"Just through tonight," Marie answered.

"Somehow I was under the impression that you're not expected back in Tokyo until the day after tomorrow."

"The sooner we get back, the better," Charlie interjected.

"We're in no rush," said Marie, "but Charlie's right. He's a little . . . under the weather, so we're gonna finish up and leave as soon as we can."

"You're ill?" Debbie asked Charlie.

"A little," said Charlie. "I'll live."

"U-hh," was all Debbie could say.

Of course this guy is a dip, Debbie thought. And of course he's ill. To Debbie, all American and Japanese men were "dips" (as she called them). And all men were either ill or horny. A mental neon sign flashed: Let's leave him in your hotel room tonight!

"What sort of dinner plans do you have?" Debbie asked, looking evenly into Marie's eyes.

"Say, y' know, that's a good question," Marie responded.

"How 'bout if we call you later this afternoon when we're finished here?" Charlie said. "You can take us to your favorite place, our treat. I'll just stick to rice or something. For Marie—if they can harvest it or catch it, she'll eat it."

"Ha-ha!"

Marie glowered out the window, lips compressed.

The driver turned to Debbie. "To the consulate, Ms. Kass?"

Debbie told him to drop her off there. Charlie and Marie were expected at the open-air market near downtown Taipei, to which they should be taken directly. And, yes, they could call her later at one of the numbers on the card she gave to Marie.

Before she exited the cab, Debbie uncharacteristically put a vigorous hug on both Marie and Charlie. In the process she slipped a tiny transmitter into Marie's jacket pocket. For good measure she attached a second one to the side of Charlie's suit coat just beneath the armpit. She used these electronic spy devices routinely on her job.

About an hour later she listened intently as Marie's throaty voice uttered, "*3-B.*"

****

On their way to the Taipei central market neither Marie nor Charlie could decide what to do about the next part of their errand. Fulfill it or abort it? They might also implement degrees of either course. They simply didn't know enough about the mission.

When the driver delivered them to the market on this sunny, cool afternoon, he told them he would wait for them a half block south on this same street, which formed the east boundary of the market grid. Good enough. They entered the marketplace and proceeded to stroll absently while they searched out a stall at which to buy quilted Chinese jackets. They needed two, one for Marie and one for Jed. They also expected to meet a contact there and consummate ostensibly urgent business.

How urgent? Marie wondered. What was actually going on? She had only bits of information. Apparently someone had infiltrated a shadowy cult which opposed the Nationalist oligarchy running Taiwan, and that agent needed the help she and Charlie might be bringing. Well, that was real solid. So how crucial to U.S. interests could their mission be? Not very. Maybe one of the two envelopes from Debbie might be susceptible to being opened; it might disclose something. But no such luck. Of course the darling Ms. Kassenbaum would have sealed her envelopes securely.

In his suit coat Charlie carried a flat, thick packet that he (or Marie) was to pass on. Doing that was the major priority of this errand. *Could it be opened?* Only by flagrantly violating major rules. Marie caused Charlie to stop in a lane between rows of stalls. Somehow she had already taken the leap.

"Let's see what we've got," she said, indicating the inside of Charlie's coat.

Charlie pulled out the packet, and he and Marie checked to see that it was secure. A razor-blade slit in the accordion folds at the bottom might not be noticeable. Charlie usually carried a pocket razor blade for opening medicines or snacks. Marie usually carried scotch tape in her purse. Both objects were handy. Would they try something as tacky as to use them? Well, if someone had infiltrated an organization, he was intending to betray people. Here in Taiwan, anyone seriously opposed to the Kuomintang—or its offspring party—wasn't worth a damn; alleged sedition would render a life forfeit.

"I think we might be helping out the wrong people," Marie said. "We'd better do something drastic or we might regret it."

Because of some kind of atmospheric static only Charlie heard that. But someone besides Charlie was able to hear Marie say, "3-B, ducky. *3-B.*"

Marie had signaled to physically diminish the "product" they were to pass on, a most unappealing course of action. They'd have the hassle of opening the packet, removing only some materials, and resealing the package as best they could— in less than congenial circumstances. (They stood in a narrow, unpaved lane passing behind two rows of stalls, their presence having been silently marked by at least one urinating merchant, possibly two or three.) Worse, by tampering with the "product" they'd be susceptible to potentially dire consequences.

"Shii-it," Charlie said as he felt for his pocket razor and struggled to focus.

At the same moment Marie knew real doubt and stress. Still, they worked quickly and effectively in the circumstance. Charlie's razor left a fine, straight slit in the folds at the bottom of the plastic packet. They fished out sheets of paper with coded sentences and call letters, two floppy disks, a pair of airline tickets, and a passport. They removed three sheets and an airline ticket (the carrier's name they promptly forgot). Everything else they slid back inside the packet. Marie's tape, a 3-M brand for office use, was next to invisible over the slit. She resisted the impulse to use a second strip for reinforcement: more likely to be noticeable.

Perhaps a head glancing at them from forty yards away, perhaps some other kind of movement near the end of the passageway caught Charlie's eye while they worked.

"I wonder if we're being watched," Charlie remarked.

"Don't say that."

"Something made that cross my mind."

"Don't even think it."

After a lapse of about three minutes in the fetid lane behind rows of stalls, Marie and Charlie resumed their strolling to look at merchandise. They arrived at a jacket seller's place, and a weasel of a man arrived there as well. They had never seen him before this, but he spoke to them.

"Ah, toulists, I see."

Marie responded, "We need winter coats."

"My wife ahrso," said the man. "She tohr me yestahlday!"

Before Marie and Charlie surveyed the stacks of red and black quilted jackets, Charlie slipped the packet he'd carried into the man's hands. Quickly and covertly the fellow passed an envelope to Marie. Then he simply walked away.

Apparently, so far so good. They'd might as well buy jackets. Charlie stiffened.

"I think someone is watching us," he muttered.

Alarmed, Marie said, "S-P, R-B" (split up, return to base). Without another word she and Charlie walked off in opposite directions.

Alarmed as well, Debbie strained to hear more, but unable to see Marie making a throw-away motion, all she got was Marie's enjoinder, "Product—away!"

Charlie had to postpone looking for a safe way to dispose of the papers and ticket they'd pilfered, for he was sure that two Chinese men in Western-style suits had been shadowing him and Marie. He quickly crossed a street in a diagonal line and waited for a moment and, sure enough, they were after him.

They would have to move a lot faster, though. At the edge of the market Charlie slipped across the street, found an alley down which he sprinted, and strode to his left onto a commercial street. He hailed a taxi cab and slid into it, getting low behind the driver. Pointing east urgently, Charlie induced the driver to get the cab going. By gesturing, limning, and displaying a ten-dollar bill, Charlie caused the cab driver to skirt the market.

When they got to the spot where the red Toyota taxi cab from the consulate was supposed to be, it was gone. Ostensibly Marie had gotten into it and left. What was the rush, for gosh sakes? Nonplussed, Charlie sat back and let the driver just drive for a few moments. Whoa—there were the two guys who'd been after him. One was eating something; the other stood about.

"Might as well go to the Imperial Hotel," Charlie said.

"You got it," said the driver (barely a trace of accent).

Twelve minutes later Charlie found himself absently gazing out the cab window at a familiar feminine figure plainly waiting for someone. The cab in which he rode approached the hotel curbside and pulled almost even with Marie before it came to a stop. Charlie told the driver to wait; when he stepped out Marie didn't seem at all surprised to see him. Given the circumstances of their departure from the market, she told Charlie, the consulate driver had "insisted" on taking her and their two flight bags to the hotel, where they had reservations for the night.

"You know, some guys really were tailing us," Charlie said. "Two of 'em."

"I know; I saw them," Marie said. "After we split up I spotted the pair of suits takin' out after you. I couldn't tell if there were more of 'em somewhere on the sidelines, so when I got into the cab we went looking for you. We thought we could, y' know, pick you up."

"Great! When I got to where the cab was supposed to be, no cab."

Cul de sac.

They packed their bags next to the driver and got into the taxi in which Charlie had arrived. A major part of their errand was still to be accomplished. "Take us to the central prison, Military Prison Number One," Charlie told the driver.

The drive took about a half hour as the ambience changed markedly: from relative openness to menace-induced claustrophobia. They couldn't recall seeing any transitions. At the prison entrance, Charlie and Marie announced themselves and presented a business card to a pair of guards. In a few minutes they were admitted and escorted down a dismal corridor to the commandant's office where they met a smiling colonel who declared that he was there on a temporary assignment (as Charlie and Marie had been told he would). Colonel Fang, who knew (and used) some Dutch words, also mentioned that his primary superior officer was General Chang K'ung, a name that carried some cachet even to Europeans. Yes, Marie and Charlie knew something about him.

Happily, English was the language of the moment provided it was kept basic. Marie and Charlie each stated the names of two Americans (for whatever reasons), Colonel Fang made some quick notes for himself, and Charlie and Marie each passed on to the colonel a sealed envelope; Marie gave him a hardcover book (containing a large sum of American cash, they'd been told). Colonel Fang handed an envelope to each.

That was it. Errand completed. Would they be going home directly? They gave it some thought. Ms. Kassenbaum was expecting their company, but a flight out was available within the hour. Charlie's gut still felt queasy. If they wanted, they would be driven right to the airport. The opportunity looked too good to decline.

"Let's go for it," Marie declared.

Charlie nodded to the colonel, who said something to an aide, who promptly hurried off. In a few minutes Hsiu-fen Wu appeared. Colonel Fang explained that she had just dropped off and picked up paperwork for General Chang, and she had one of Chang's cars. Would she have time to lift these guests to the airport, Fang asked her. She responded that she would take the time, which, much to Charlie's pleasure, she did.

Marie regarded this beautiful Taiwanese woman with respect and curiosity. There was no telling what really motivated this woman or what she aspired to; probably she possessed deep capacities. One thing for sure, Marie and Charlie tacitly agreed, this was one hell of a woman. Her petite, angular features and what seemed to be a wry attitude about everything in her ken only enhanced that impression.

As they stepped outside into a plaza where the car was parked, Hsiu-fen Wu displayed a hint of a smile. "You can call me 'Suzie Wu,'" she said.

At the International Airport, while they finished validating their tickets and checking their baggage with Japanese Airlines, Marie waited for an opportunity to not be overheard, even by "Suzie Wu" who waited nearby.

"I think we're under surveillance again," Marie said to Charlie.

"Yeah? —Where?"

"By the JAL sign, next to that big post."

Marie barely tilted her head toward the spot. Charlie cut a look that way. Oh, no; two familiar-looking men in suits gazed intently at infinity.

"Those are the 'suits' that were after us before," Charlie said. "I wonder who's sending those guys . . . ."

"I think Suzie Wu spotted 'em. I don't know . . . ."

"Oh, shit," Charlie said, patting his suit coat pocket.

"What's the matter?"

"I've still got those papers and ticket we copped, at the market."

"*Really*?" Marie said. "Get rid of the stuff! We can't take it with us. Don't go near customs with it."

They had no idea of what they'd pilfered earlier that day and still carried in Charlie's pocket. As soon as he could, his carry-on tote bag in hand, Charlie headed for a men's restroom to dispose of the contraband. He felt lucky that he spotted one of his stalkers slip into the restroom well ahead of him; he thought he'd glimpsed the other slip behind a pillar. This was not a good time to disregard potential foes.

Charlie abruptly veered away from his apparent destination and bulled his way into a throng of travelers forging up the concourse. Marie hung back twenty or thirty yards. Hsiu-fen Wu seemed nowhere in sight.

As the phalanx of travelers, including Charlie, swept past a trash receptacle, Charlie jammed his contraband into the container almost without breaking stride. Some distance ahead he paused at a gate to allow Marie to catch up with him. Again he thought he'd glimpsed one of the suits. He nodded to Marie: all okay. Hsiu-fen Wu rejoined them a moment later.

"Pardon me," Charlie said with a glance at both Marie's and the Taiwanese woman's eyes. "I thought I saw a man I used to know; long, long time ago. I wanted to catch him."

"No problem," said Suzie Wu. A wry half-smile. "Was he the one?"

"I'm pretty sure not."

They walked to their designated gate, and Hsiu-fen Wu waited until Charlie and Marie boarded JAL flight 1024. During the time they were with her, Hsiu-fen Wu showed herself to be serene but charming company, likely a perfect host. And—whooh!—under harsh airport-terminal light, ultra-feminine and truly lovely, Charlie thought when he looked into her eyes a final time and shook her hand farewell. As they boarded the plane Marie thought word-for-word: Small wonder women like that are such threats to American women. And off they went to Naha and Haneda Airports in Japan, the "bugs" on their persons rendered useless.

But Debbie had heard Charlie's and Marie's tense exchange at the ticket counter. She wondered who was responsible for the tailers. She wondered what Charlie was referring to when he mentioned "those papers and ticket," and copping them (at the market yet). She wondered to such a degree that she replayed her recording of Charlie's and Marie's voices several times. Their words were unmistakable. Her only conclusion was implausible: They're helping the New Taiping Revolution, for gods' sakes!

As Debbie sat in wonder about what she had just heard, Hsiu-fen Wu tore off the top of the trash receptacle into which Charlie had jammed the partial "product" he and Marie had pilfered. She was sure he had done that surreptitiously; her intuitions told her to learn more. What she found was not entirely cryptic: on three sheets of typing paper she identified likely references to army missile-defense bases, FAX numbers, phone numbers, and possible references to General Chang's most trusted associates.

Did all this relate to her employer's mysterious enterprise? She intuited that it did, but she could only wonder how. And what was Chang doing that caused some kind of covert scrutiny? Those Americans were undercover operatives. They were assisting her government; that is, they were assisting the Nationalist government which controlled her people and country. Did that mean General Chang was definitely opposed to the Nationalists? That was highly unlikely and she knew of nothing seditious he could have done. *Regardless*. Something irregular was going on: she was almost certain that she had seen two men surveilling Charlie and Marie. Of course she wondered about the origin of the stalkers, as she wondered whether Charlie was connected to Marie on a personal level, and whether Charlie had found Hsiu-fen Wu to be very attractive.

And about four hours later, alone and tired in his spartanly furnished home (his inherited opulence having been ruthlessly stripped down), General Chang himself wondered what was going on in his "own front yard," as Americans liked to say. From his ally Ms. Kassenbaum he had received a report of unlikely occurrences. Could the American couple he was told about be crypto-T'aip'ings? He couldn't imagine how. But from Hsiu-fen Wu he learned that they had likely thwarted (or blunted) infiltration of his Cause. The information she'd retrieved from the airport trash could have been damaging to him. (Thus Chang presumed the government was aware of the existence of the New T'aip'ing Revolution, and he had to eliminate security leaks and identify at least one "mole," problems he could now confront because he was aware of them.) I am truly lucky, he told himself in English.

Chang was convinced that an unfathomable intelligence and welter of powers governed the universe (he was averse to using the word "god"); somehow it originated and organized all that exists, including itself. Conceivably that same welter of powers could direct individual people's lives. Chang would never believe that it did, yet he had to feel grateful to *something* for all the fortune he had known, such as the help from those two Americans. *Gifts . . . a superior man accepts simply.*

Perhaps, then, with assistance from his strange American acolyte Kassenbaum Deborah and his Mainland ally Mo Tzu and now the enigmatic American couple, Chang and his cadre of cobras, as he called his fellow revolutionists, might be enabled to utilize the upheavals in the crumbled U.S.S.R. for his special purposes, which were surely illegal and would likely be judged immoral (by some people's standards) but which he could justify in one stroke: Any means was valid if it helped him fulfill his vision of a New Chinese Nation. That was his true destiny, Chang thought. Would he shirk it? *Never.*

"D' you think maybe we were a little bit stupid?" Marie said to Charlie above the clouds in a Boeing 747 on their way to Japan.

"Well, possibly," Charlie said, for earlier that day in the market back in Taipei, when they jeopardized their lucrative sideline they might have rendered themselves liable to harsh consequences. Still, they knew that raiding the package before turning it over to that weasel of a man near the quilted-jacket stall was a bold attempt to do what they thought they should do as whole human beings. And now they saw each other smile, the same type of smile. They realized they felt a bit smug because each was enjoying a brief shimmering of utter satisfaction.

****

April 1, 1990
Near downtown Manila, Philippine Islands

Inside the suite of offices occupied by Pacific Enterprises, Incorporated (also known as "CIA West" by many delivery persons, taxi drivers, and other knowledgeable Filipinos and probably all their kin) Charlie and Marie finished receiving a lengthy briefing directed by H. Dean Hess (of the CIA, no less).

The impending "trip" into China was going to be tricky. Too many CIA operatives were on vacation or sick leave, and Chinese counterintelligence seemed to know all the rest. In-country agents were under intense pressure and needed some relief. With that as background, the job Charlie and Marie were about to undertake would be more complex than usual.

They had already been "on the clock" for two days, which caused Charlie some anxiety because he worried about his practice at home. His friend and new associate, Joel Wilson, took care of patients for Charlie while he was gone, but Joel had his own patients. Then there was the dual matter of Julia's and Lisa's well being . . . .

A clean-cut, well-kept, obviously American white man was admitted to the briefing room. He hewed to the wall and tried to not interrupt.

Dean Hess perorated: "Now bear in mind these Chinese are incredibly smart, as smart as the Japanese in some ways, although in some ways not. At the very least, never forget they're as clever as we are. Do not deviate from the procedures we've established here. And take no unnecessary risks; our situation is dicey enough. You shouldn't have any insurmountable problems. If you need good luck, good luck."

Charlie turned partway in his chair to gaze upon the new arrival at this meeting. With an overt nod he made eye contact.

"Sir!" said Charlie. "Are you with the FBI?"

"Yes. Yes, I am," he said.

All eyes in the room turned on the man, who appeared momentarily nonplussed. Then he smiled genially.

During this moment Charlie's body swiveled to his right, then around to his left. Again he looked at the FBI man and gave him a perfunctory smile.

"Oh, I was just testing my guessing abilities," Charlie announced.

"Ah," said the FBI man, then he declared: "Actually we have a permanent office here; we've got maybe eight or ten other foreign stations. I'm here on TDY."

"Ah," said Charlie, and Marie wondered why he'd raised the point even though it was mildly interesting.

"If something's going on that affects Americans at home," the fellow added, "we want to know about it."

Polite murmurs of concurrence throughout the room. Briefing terminated, except for one ritualistic procedure: Charlie took a final glance at a set of photos on the desk before him, showed each to Marie, and overtly crumpled and torched them in a large metal bowl. (These were paper photocopies of real photos.) He and Marie deliberately scanned a fact sheet one last time, each pausing occasionally to reinforce memory of certain entries, and Charlie burned it likewise. Everyone stood up and filed out. Any conversation was terse and related to immediate matters, such as whether someone would hail taxis. Neither Charlie nor Marie saw fit to talk to anyone. Three minutes later they settled into a cab outside.

As each was about to complain about the perpetually thick air in Manila, they wordlessly gazed through the glass at a charismatic-looking priest and two nuns briskly entering the same doorway they had just egressed. (*We can't avoid that guy. Oh; now they've got nuns working there.*) Shortly after the taxi got going, Charlie silently, furtively showed Marie something he'd been barely able to restrain himself from showing her sooner: one of the photocopied pictures from the briefing. For a photocopy, the resolution looked very clear.

When she saw it Marie inhaled sharply. Charlie smiled satisfiedly and put it back in his suit pocket. They might need it to help them miscarry their mission or some part of it. Both minds replayed the name belonging to the face in the picture:

Zhang Yimou, legendary head of Public Security for Shaanxi Province. Both minds wondered briefly whether they weren't being foolish or downright stupid.

April 2, 1990
Shaanxi Province, People's Republic of China

In China everyone has something to do, all the time. Life is hard; its most essential elements dominate daily reality. Thus generally Life is simple.

"Have you noticed how many people in here were watching us before, but now they don't even bother?" Charlie said.

"Good thing; it was getting on my nerves," Marie said.

In fact, certain fellow passengers and two conductors in this and the adjoining train car had blatantly tracked everything Charlie and Marie did. That included crowding after them in the unisex toilet compartment. As soon as it was time to break out the lunches, though, everyone's attention turned elsewhere.

"Boy, this is some good stuff," Marie commented through her full mouth. "I wonder what it is." She was using chopsticks with authority.

Charlie only nodded, his cheeks distended. Sporadically his brain registered faint resonances of Life on a kinetic plateau looming beside a green river.

All told, for about six hours the two vacationing U.S. State Department staffers gazed across endless, flat fields of early wheat. Afternoon sunlight began to ripen into gold. Charlie and Marie went awe-struck as the steam-engine locomotive abruptly adjusted course and plunged into an opening in a massive wall, pulling its train through. On the other side: the ancient city of Xian, a popular destination for in-country tourists. Barely eleven months since the Tiananmen Square debacle, this city was also purportedly a haven for key political fugitives.

About a half hour after they entered the city Charlie and Marie were greeted at the train station by an earnest-looking, English-speaking young man who represented the Garden Hotel. Oddly, they went to the hotel by taxi, their fare covered by the hotel. The young man who spoke English was most attentive and alert; nothing escaped his cognizance, including attempts at confidential remarks to each other by Marie or Charlie. From that day on they referred to internal security in China as "liquefied graphite": pour it anyplace and it gets into everything.

Charlie in his haircut and expensive suit (which he wore even on the train, and managed to keep afterwards) and Marie in her black bolero hat and tweed jacket with padded shoulders (she kept her outfit, too) looked every inch ... Covert Intelligence Agents. As a fillip, Charlie sported skier's sunglasses and Marie wore wicked suede boots. They were actually in costume for their role: CIA operatives using the guise of U.S. State Department officers on holiday.

Overtly, Charlie and Marie had come to Xian on covert business. This would, of course, be readily perceived by anyone. Thus they would be recognized as a diversion. Something else must be going on, so they would be left alone (although never totally ignored). Then, of course, they would execute their subversive acts and scuttle home.

But Chinese counter-intelligence would anticipate such a ploy and take measures to thwart it. Thus Charlie and Marie were, in fact, diversions from activities being executed by professional U.S. operatives (and their agents) in Xian; their real mission was to play their role.

"Uh, basically. That is, mostly," Mr. Hess had told them.

"What do you mean, 'basically, mostly'?" Marie had said.

Their mission would harbor one little exception. While they diverted attention and resources from important rescue operations (they were told), they would also deliver a set of codes to an agent. These were important codes. This complication Charlie and Marie found slightly unsettling. More disturbing was their perception that too much of this errand was complicated beyond their ability to control what might happen.

"Y' know, I feel as though we're maybe letting ourselves get sucked into some kind of trap," Marie had remarked to Charlie. "And we're going to be the bait."

"We're definitely *bait*," Charlie said. "We can pull it off, though."

"Damned straight, we'll pull it off."

The assignment had sounded intriguing; plus they'd needed a vacation at the same time that little Lisa's presence was desired in Merkel, Texas. Meanwhile Grandma and Grandpa Grumbles were delighted to have baby Julia's company for a while. This "errand" was also a unique opportunity for personal enrichment, all round. But now it felt nebulous, perhaps menace-ridden.

After they had settled into the back seat of the Toyota taxi, Marie said evenly: "I don't want us separated while we're here." Then she said flatly, "Period."

Over years, the word "separation" had evolved ominous connotations. Moreover, Charlie always equated that word with "death."

"I hate it when I go to work and I don't see you for lunch," Charlie said.

Their mood lightened considerably once they got checked in at The Garden, a new Western-style hotel. Everything seemed charming or pleasing or amusing. And something else began emanating into their ken: Marie's criterion for a good time—*magic*. They felt it even before they'd cleared the lobby; it became almost palpable.

"Is this nice, or what?" Charlie said when they entered their room on the fourth floor accompanied by ministrations of an incredibly small and cute woman and a very bird-like dorky young man who fell all over themselves serving up tea and sweet wine and little cakes in the process of doing all kinds of make-yourself-comfy things before they left in a flutter (refusing attempts at tipping).

"Yes, it sure is nice here," Marie remarked, her eyes casting about at obvious places for microphone plants. Oh, to hell with it, she thought.

Marie and Charlie made audible, clear references to the U.S. Secretary of State and to their so-called "bosses" stationed at the Beijing Embassy. In the process, Charlie helped Marie out of her jacket and they undressed. Underclothes were vaguely damp. Marie went to take a shower ("Hey, there's a bidet in here!"); Charlie hung up their coats, then munched on complimentary snacks while he placed bedclothes over a few possible camera-lens ports as a gesture to propriety.

Soon Marie and Charlie switched places. When Charlie finished in the bathroom they discussed hiring a translator and taking tours of the city. There was a lot to see here, Charlie concluded as he sat naked except for a towel draped over the back of his neck in a faux-leather-covered armchair next to the bed. There was no sense in lying down now if they wanted to see some of the city before dark; Marie declared this while she sipped from a little glass of thick wine and proceeded to straddle Charlie's thighs, facing him.

"I'm sure you're right," Charlie said. Then: "Oh, wow!"

Marie hunkered down over Charlie's lap. She was in fine physical condition; she could hold that position and still make continuous undulating movements from the waist down. Charlie's palms gave support to each of her lower cheeks, facilitating her action.

"There's something in the ambience here. Have you noticed?" Marie said.

"Oh-ho, have I! —*Ohhh*!"

Marie had fit herself onto Charlie and come all the way down. A soft, totally feminine sound escaped her throat as she felt Charlie penetrate her all the way up, and Charlie loosened a low-register sound that was barely human. For an instant he lost all his breath. He gasped, his little movements sending electric ripples through Marie's insides.

"Ooh!" she shouted and took hold of his shoulders.

"What a luscious piece you are!" Charlie managed to say just before he and Marie started moving with each other, sometimes in unison, sometimes contrapuntally, quicker and quicker. Marie had no more words, but she made little noises which Charlie loved to hear, when he could hear them between his own.

At a point beyond tolerability, Marie's chest and throat and mouth cut loose an indescribable scream of pleasure starting at her very core. Charlie just kept moving wordlessly, harder and stronger than before, until again Marie could stand no more and released herself in a shuddering burst; and again, and again, and again this happened, with Charlie finally exploding with her, then a few minutes later working up to yet a deep quake when Marie had finished and could help him.

For a few minutes they simply hung on to each other, and the atmosphere went quiet. Charlie took measures to make sure that Marie knew she was appreciated.

"Seeing you all excited like that would've made my panties wet," Marie murmured. "It's still gonna do that later!"

"That's something to think about."

They hugged and laughed and caressed. Marie massaged Charlie's trapezes muscles. By reaching around her, Charlie manipulated some of Marie's vertebrae.

Ah, bliss.

Might they have been overheard through all this? Well, that couldn't have been helped. The plausibility of their roles required their being overheard some of the time. At least Charlie felt satisfied that he'd blocked most camera views from taking them in. Privacy for them would have to be a luxury because their job here still prevailed.

"We'd better get going. They've already begun serving dinner," Marie said.

"I just need fifteen or twenty," Charlie said, falling atop the bed and rolling into the center to leave room for Marie.

They made it downstairs in time for dinner, which was delicious local cuisine with few concessions to foreign tastes. Their enjoyment was interrupted by Charlie briskly slipping away between courses to use a lobby phone. Per instructions, he dialed a phone number he'd memorized, allowed four rings on the line, and hung up. He repeated this. If someone were to answer he was to say very distinctly, "I am so sorry. I have the wrong number," and hang up. Then he was to take it from the top again. Feeling glad no one answered, he hurried to rejoin Marie who would do the same thing using a different telephone number later that evening.

Had Charlie been observed attempting to make that "call"? Almost certainly. Had the number he'd dialed been recorded somewhere? More than likely it was. Whom had he telephoned, and for what? He and Marie hadn't the slightest idea, which was as it should be, they were sure.

After dinner they went directly to the lobby desk and arranged to hire two translators for the duration of their stay. As if this were a standard occurrence, Quing Yu and Lo Shiu Hong seemed to materialize from an alternate reality. A pair of attractive university students who had probably learned all their English from books, Quing and Lo Shiu purported to be happy to translate at all hours of day and night, plus serve as guides.

Charlie and Marie wasted no time in utilizing the services of these two young people, who for the first few hours appeared to be like sticks in mud, then for the next two days seemed to be constantly flirting with each other. (Both Charlie and Marie were almost sure that darling Quing had made some flirtatious gestures in Charlie's direction as well.) First they all went on a walking tour of the immediate environs. Then there was socializing in the hotel lounge with a number of apparently upper-middle-class Chinese couples who were most gracious but reserved toward these American tourists. Marie and Charlie also arranged to join organized tours of the city beginning the next day.

Immediately after their informal (but informational) walking tour, Marie broke off to use the same lobby phone that Charlie had, with the same result except this event was duly observed by Quing. Later Charlie excused himself from the lounge to go upstairs to their room for something; before returning he couldn't help being seen slipping into the men's restroom with a thin black briefcase. When he rejoined Marie and the translators and fellow guests in the lounge, he was empty handed. Some time afterwards, Lo Shiu impassively presented Charlie with the same briefcase and the explanation that someone "found it" in the lavatory. Of course the contents had been riffled.

All in all, things had gone well, Marie and Charlie later concluded as they sat in their darkened room at a window giving onto an arterial street four stories down, and they let themselves become hypnotized by ancient outre buildings, incongruous little gardens, and all manner of night-time activity outside.

*

Xian on a spring morning, Marie observed as she patted her butt, felt like an injection of vitamin B complex. Charlie, who'd been enjoying himself hugely over their champagne breakfast, had to concur. It was a fine day for a tour. One was available at mid-morning, so they joined it and partook of the sights and sounds and smells which this multifaceted city offered to anyone willing to go there. But even a spring day in Xian can be bent, as when the tour paused at the old-city wall on which was posted this exhortation: "Be disciplined and obey the law." Upon hearing it translated Marie shuddered inwardly. She didn't need a glance at Charlie to know he was revolted.

After a rather elaborate lunch, some duties had to be accomplished: Charlie mindlessly dropped a chewing-gum wrapper outside the restaurant door (then had to chew and dispose of the damned gum); Marie inconspicuously left an envelope on the tour-bus seat (it miraculously disappeared and later reappeared on the same seat); together they briefly slipped away from the tour and their translators, then acted as though they hadn't left. During a mid-afternoon stop at a communal tavern, Marie appeared to receive a note adhering to the bottom of a beer bottle. (Pulling off this ruse had required a little drama.) The afternoon passed quickly and left time for a nap before dinner back at the hotel.

"Mission more or less accomplished," Marie whispered close to Charlie's ear as they stretched out on the big bed.

*

Dinner that evening was rife with luscious sauces, and Charlie decided to wash his sticky hands and chin before dessert.

"Don't run away," he told Marie and left the table to stride across the double banquet room en route to the lobby restroom (in which, he said, they had "the best toilets in the whole republic"). Despite a feeling of well-being and satiation, Charlie couldn't shake the sense that he was being shadowed . . . from two directions. When he reached the lobby, he abruptly wheeled around. He saw only hotel-restaurant workers going about their business some forty yards behind him. *Humph.*

But two paces ahead had materialized a stereotypical working-class man in a dark-blue pajama "suit," and he was looking directly into Charlie's eyes. Charlie knew the man hadn't been anywhere in sight until now. He and the man each took a step forward, and Charlie almost collided against the flat, gift-wrapped object held out to him.

"Excuse me," said Charlie as he turned left sharply to skirt the man in his path.

"Pa-*reez*!" the fellow said.

Charlie dismissed what he'd heard, but when he glanced at the stranger they made sure eye contact. Charlie had to pause, for the fellow looked both resolute and desperate as he poked the gift-wrapped object at Charlie.

Charlie took it, even though he knew that doing so could drastically alter the course of his—and Marie's—Life.

"Thanks," he said, realizing he had spoken to the stranger's back. The man was walking away in a hurry.

Charlie proceeded into the restroom wondering what he should do with his "present." (*A bomb, some kind of contraband?*) Ka-*pop*! A pistol shot right outside the door. Then: footfalls past the door, rapid ones, two pairs or more.

Shi-it. Charlie slipped into a stall. Nobody else came into the restroom. Without really thinking about it, Charlie lifted the commode tank cover and jammed the "present" inside. It rested on a tube barely above water level. A little while later, his hands still wet, Charlie opened the restroom door and peered out cautiously before exiting.

Not to his surprise, several people including Marie were nearby in the lobby, all looking perplexed.

What in the world had happened? Marie was relieved to see that Charlie was unaffected by the shooting; at least it hadn't apparently involved him. She and he—and their translators—inquired around. In a few minutes they pieced together a scenario of four (or more) people briefly struggling, pair against pair, in a hallway just around the corner from the restroom door. Two had dashed off down the hallway; two more had disappeared around the corner of the other hallway. Apparently they were all still in the building. A lobby column showed a fresh patch of exposed plaster. Which pair had fired the shot? Nobody knew.

Abruptly a trio of hotel "staff" shoved past Charlie and entered the restroom, a minute later to emerge empty-handed. (Charlie had lingered to see that.) Patently empty-handed himself, Charlie accompanied Marie back to their table with hotel "staffers" eyeing them. For effect Charlie uttered maybe for the third time, "What in the world was *that* all about?!"

After dinner they took a brisk walk, soon leaving Quing and Lo Shiu to giggle at each other in their wake. That was Charlie's only chance to safely tell Marie about the determined-looking local man and the "present" likely still in the commode tank.

"Maybe you can get it later," Marie said.

"Oh, I don't know, babe. Big Brother is watching everywhere. We've still got us a job to do here."

"I know it. Maybe we can put one over on B B."

At about a half hour before midnight, first Charlie then Marie slipped out of their hotel suite. They went in opposite directions down the hall and took different stairways to the main floor, moving quickly without running. Their alleged purpose (if anyone asked them): to meet in the lounge for a good old-fashioned nightcap.

Where they actually met was outside the men's restroom in the lobby. Charlie had gone in for a minute; he swung the door open wide and exited just after Marie had arrived. They were barely together a moment before they went off in opposite directions again, this time to meet back in their hotel suite. Incongruously, Marie wore her dressed-for-success travel jacket as though she'd been intending to go outside, yet she didn't carry a purse. When she and Charlie separated in the lobby, both were empty-handed, a fact that wasn't lost on a large-sized hotel worker in uniform-green coveralls standing just off the lobby among three staffers.

In fact Charlie had passed that clutch of workers as he approached the men's restroom; he'd even nodded to them. (The features of one of them had fetched his eye, but he promptly dismissed the fact.) After Charlie had come out of the restroom and met Marie outside the door, the four hotel workers were close enough to hear Marie's pleasant "Hey, I'll see you in a little while, okay?" and Charlie's assured "You bet."

When they went off in opposite directions, Marie was the one to pass the little gathering of workers, one of whom definitely caught her attention, perhaps because he was bigger than the others. As she realized there was something familiar about the man, she realized also that he had been furtively scrutinizing her. For a nano-second, their eyes met.

Back upstairs in their room, Marie wrote Charlie a little note: "Let's see that snapshot you lifted in Manila." When he produced it from inside his toilet kit and they looked at it under a lamp, there was a moment of silent acknowledgement: the face in the photo definitely matched the face of the large-sized worker downstairs. They had been warned that Zhang Yimou, Minister of Public Security for Shaanxi Province, was formidable and zealous; now they knew him also to be a man of guises.

Charlie silently mouthed the words, "Big Yim." Marie nodded. She and Charlie proceeded to exchange a series of short notes by which they agreed to not open the "present" Charlie had gotten and retrieved—and which Marie still held clamped in her armpit inside her jacket—until they were out of China. For the time being they would keep it in Charlie's personal-sundries bag.

Finally it was time to get comfortable and shed the weight of a long day. Their only light came from two paper lanterns; they also burned incense and tried out the stereo system by inserting one of several unlabeled cassettes into it. Surprise! They found themselves inhaling an indescribable fragrance they had never experienced before. And they realized they were hearing graceful throbbing, the bass line and drums dancing off in a helix while a piano romped, then comped funky-edged for a muscular tenor sax seemingly trying to ejaculate.

"What are we *hearing*?!" Charlie said, delighted.

"Sounds to me like vintage Horace Silver. We used to hear stuff like this all the time in New York, on little FM stations."

"All *right*! That means it's time we tried ... *this*," and Charlie displayed a little brown paper bag holding a very expensive (by Chinese standards) homeopathic powder that Westerners are routinely urged never to partake of.

They mixed the powder with a strange-tasting local liquor provided by the hotel. Charlie had ensured their having Chinese beer and rice wine on hand in case they needed to wash down the liquor, but the mixture tasted pleasantly of fruit and wood smoke. Luckily, too, they had plenty of snacks handy because in no time oral gratification became mandatory for both.

"I wonder if they'd have hired us if they knew we did stuff like this," Marie said.

"Did somebody hire us?"

"Well, yeah. For this job!"

"Who? For what job?"

"Ha-ha-ha-ha!"

In the next moment Marie said, "Look out this window!" and Charlie joined her in gazing out a window they had ignored and kept draped until this moment. Down below, hotel lights and one strategically placed outdoor lamp illumined a lovely pond surrounding a tiny island on which two swans nested. Something broke the water surface and splashed, leaving concentric ripples.

"A-h-h-h . . . do you feel a kind of balance?" Charlie declaimed.

"Yes! D' you feel the magic?"

*   *   *

I doubt you would bother to ask: so what happened next between Marie and Charlie, up there in that night? Am I right? If so, then the animus informing this entire narration is coming through.

For both Charlie and Marie the time they spent together that night (actually it was already early morning) transcended all forms of "good." It must have, because two days later they decided to return to Xian in the foreseeable future, preferably as real tourists. Within a short time their decision became an unspoken intention.

181

Charlie would recall that intention frequently when some years later he almost returned to Xian, but alone. I tell you this reluctantly, and only to state a vital reality: The potential for sadness is prerequisite to joy; and real joy can engender its exact opposite.

This is not exactly profound, you might think, and I would concur. Now I ask, why bother to experience joy and sadness? What are they for? What is *all* your experiencing for?

Yes, in your deepest Self you know the answers, although putting them into words is next to impossible. I am posing the questions merely because I am supposed to.

*   *   *

April 4, 1990

At precisely 9:20 a.m. (Xian time) Marie swung open their hotel-room door to go to breakfast and nearly hit a hotel maid passing by in the corridor. The staffer, a very slender woman, moved at a slow, erratic pace while carrying a canvas bag stuffed with damp towels. Coincidentally Marie was wiping her hands in a bunched-up towel. She glanced at the bag, then glanced at the maid's eyes. Noncommittal but alert; the face unexpectedly quite young. That latter fact tugged at Marie's heart, and she resolved to make an effort she knew would make her heart race. But first things first: she stepped out the doorway and thrust the towel at the bag.

"Here. Please take this," Marie said very carefully.

Wordlessly, the maid took it, nodded, and moved on while jamming the towel deep into her canvas bag. A slip of paper was wadded into that towel; so much for the dead-drop part of their assignment. The mission was completed.

Abruptly Marie reached back and pulled Charlie from inside the doorway out to the corridor. Marie said, "Come on!" and she and Charlie overtook the maid at once.

The poor woman looked petrified as she peered into two white faces looming above her. Marie smiled at her reassuringly, used gestures to marshal her back to the room doorway, then told Charlie to produce the photo he wasn't supposed to have, which he did. They showed the photo to the maid and ensured she got a good look at it.

"Zhang Yimou!" Marie whispered firmly to the maid, the smile gone. With a large gesture using both arms, Marie added two Cantonese words which basically meant, *"here."* The alert almond-shaped eyes expressed acknowledgement, perhaps gratitude.

The women smiled at each other with curt nods. Charlie replaced the photo copy and closed the door to their room. He and Marie moved along briskly, passing the maid on her tasks.

In the elevator going down to the dining room, Marie said quietly, "Well, maybe we've accomplished some thing." A shrug. "If we did, it's better than nothing."

Charlie considered that for a moment. "Probably you're right; on the other hand it might have been a futile exercise," he said, and stopped himself from saying more.

"We do our best; avoid regrets," Marie commented, having stated one of their long-established principles, perhaps to justify her having taken an unnecessary risk.

Several minutes later at breakfast, with Quing and Lo Shiu enjoying themselves hugely at the table next to theirs, Charlie quietly remarked about feeling under constant scrutiny. Possibly, probably, every member of the hotel staff had a second function.

Marie digested that. She commented that she wouldn't be surprised if their room was being cleaned—and searched at the same time—even as they spoke.

Their chopsticks stopped in mid-air.

"Searched?" said Charlie.

"Searched!" Marie said.

They disdained to rise from the table gracefully. They bolted from the dining room and caught an elevator just before the operator closed the doors. At the fourth floor they got off in a trot and charged into their suite.

Sure enough. Hotel staffers were at work, two of them searching it, two actually cleaning.

"Excuse *us!*" Charlie said. He and Marie stood watching them stonily.

Two maids went about their routines, but two other "staffers" flapped about for a long moment before they fell all over themselves going out the door.

"*Sheeze!*" Charlie said.

Marie went for Charlie's personal-sundries bag, which might or might not have been searched. With no attempt at secrecy she removed the unopened "gift" they'd retrieved the night before. "Let's go," she said.

Clasping the wrapped object casually, Marie went out the door again. Charlie shrugged and went with her. They returned to breakfast with the "present" overtly in their possession.

After a little while Charlie said, "Y' know, when we came back in here I think I saw someone taking a picture of us."

Marie glanced at the "present" laying on the table. "This is not a good idea," she remarked. She took up the little package once more and rose from her chair. "I want to dispose of this thing," she said. "We don't want any trouble if we can avoid it."

"Okay by me."

Marie walked off to the restroom carrying the "present" and didn't return for over ten minutes. When she did, she was patently empty-handed.

Charlie noticed that Marie promptly swilled all their tea; she even drank down most of a bowl of cold soup.

"How'd everything go?" he said, searching her face.

"Well, I got rid of that damned thing."

In the next little while Marie explained that the "present" had been mostly a prop. Inside all the wrappings was some kind of message to (she guessed) Chinese exchange students in Los Angeles and Michigan. The message was in duplicate; she kept one copy. ("It's in four folded-up pieces.") She also kept a slip with the addressees' names, a microfilm, and a newspaper clipping. The clipping was in a blouse pocket.

"Where's the 'message' you said you kept?"

"Oh. Remember back in college, what we used to do with dope if it looked like we were gonna get busted with it? Let's say I've got about 20 hours; catch it or lose it."

"Uh, what about that slip, and the microfiche?"

"In a body cavity."

After breakfast Charlie, Marie, Quing, and Lo Shiu took a taxi drive to a few landmarks outside the Old City. Before lunch they strolled around the hotel for a last look at things. It was a fine, fine day.

Quing and Lo Shiu went on ahead to the Garden Hotel where they would all meet for a final lunch. Marie remarked that her stomach felt fine despite extra baggage. As they strolled past an opening in a wall of tall shrubbery Charlie realized he was looking at a friendly—and familiar—face: the fellow who had given him the troublesome "present."

"Oh, no," said Charlie.

"What's the mat— Is that the guy from last night?" said Marie.

"*Yup*. What do you want, sir?"

In Cantonese Marie asked the man if he knew English. He said some things in his native tongue. Marie tried to pick up words and put together utterances. She had come to Xian knowing almost no Chinese.

After a few moments Marie told Charlie that she thought the fellow wanted to wish them luck and thank them for something. *Ah*. Smiles all round, a little bowing. To Charlie and Marie the man appeared to be very, very young. Also ill-fed. Both noticed a fresh, angry abrasion above his left eye. Then with a gesture and big grin he uttered his own name (Yao Wenyuan). *Ah*. Introductions all round, handshakes, cursory bowing. Marie tried to extend her and Charlie's best wishes to

Mr. Yao. Then with fare-thee-well smiles, Charlie and Marie took each other's hand and proceeded on.

But Charlie was seized by an impulse. He stopped walking, and he and Marie backtracked a few paces. "Let's get rid of the snapshot," he explained.

Vis-à-vis again with Yao Wenyuan, Charlie produced the picture he'd been carrying in his jacket pocket and handed it to him.

"Zhang Yimou," Charlie said slowly, with great disdain.

Wide-eyed, Yao beheld the picture. Then he took it.

Marie extracted a Tom Clancy novel from her oversized purse; she jammed a clutch of Chinese currency amid the pages. Looking into Yao's eyes she uttered the Cantonese word for "gift" and, with a wink, gave him the book. Yao accepted gladly.

With final smiles again, Marie and Charlie resumed their walk. The hotel was a long city block away. Lunch beckoned. Charlie noted two men in gray pajama suits rapidly striding toward them from the direction of the hotel. The men were about forty yards ahead on the busy sidewalk. They forged along, walking abreast, absolutely focused on something—or somebodies.

"Come on," Charlie said, and he took Marie by the hand and abruptly marshaled her across the wide street, through streams of bicycle traffic in both directions.

"What's going on?!" Marie protested. She went along despite the perils.

Charlie saw the two men also crossing the street.

"Shit," Charlie said when they'd reached the far sidewalk, "we're gettin' busted. The two guys in gray, they're comin' after *us*."

Marie looked beyond immediate sidewalk traffic and saw them easily. "They can't bust me!" she said. "My pussy hurts. —The plastic and paper!"

"We go back to the hotel," Charlie declared. "*Now*."

Clearly the two men forging toward them had other intentions. In a moment they blocked Charlie's and Marie's way. One raised his hand as a peremptory sign to stop.

"I don't know these goons!" Charlie said to Marie. He set to walking right over them.

The second gray man reached for Charlie's left arm. Charlie stepped directly at the guy and gave him his left arm as though it was a piston. The pit of the man's stomach stopped Charlie's left fist; the man's gaping mouth released a sharp, sick noise. Reflexively Charlie hit him in the midsection again, a little higher, with a hard right. The guy's knees buckled, but Charlie was astonished to see him stay on his feet.

Marie directly confronted the other gray man, whose eyes widened at seeing his partner's physical impairment. The second man couldn't have been taller than Marie; his whole body was narrower. But suddenly he turned ferocious and came at Marie with both hands. Marie did a little sideways skip to meet him, her right knee pulled high and her torso turning away. In the same instant—*whuup!*—her right leg thrust her foot into the guy's upper gut, heel first. It was a smooth side kick with a lot of hip power behind it. The man gasped and bent double.

Both gray men stood grimacing, their activity postponed. Marie's victim appeared trying to extract something from inside his jacket, so for good measure she used the heel of her other foot on one of his shins and the instep to trigger a sharp yell. Passers-by gawked; some froze.

Wordlessly Charlie and Marie strode around the gray men and headed for their hotel. Ahead of them, uniforms on bicycles materialized amid foot traffic. Shrill whistles trilled. Some uniforms came toward them along the curb, followed by a black automobile sedan emitting a loud *goo-wah-goo-wah!* noise.

"Uh-oh," Charlie said, resonating in his mind's ear Captain Pat's voice in a different lifetime uttering a prelude to the words "Khmer Rouge."

"Cops, police, everywhere!" Marie said as she beheld uniforms closing in.

"We've got diplomatic immunity," Charlie said, and he and Marie stood still.

Marie's mind was on her daughters as she concluded words between them: "They've got guns. Clubs. Be careful now."

In the next moments they were swarmed over, and each was summarily yanked to a different black sedan. Unceremoniously, even without handcuffs, they were shoved into the cars and spirited to a downtown district of Xian, where they were led into separate institutional-looking brick buildings. But before they'd been forced into the cars, each noted with gratification that Wenyuan Yao was nowhere in sight. At least they could hope that he was free with his friends. Both felt pangs about probably not seeing Quing Yu and Lo Shiu Hong a final time, and they worried they would miss their train. However trivial those concerns, they superseded major concerns too nebulous and anxiety-producing to consider fruitfully.

Charlie and Marie indeed were lucky to have USA diplomatic passports. Were they spying? Most definitely not. They were on vacation. Could they prove they were not spying? If necessary, yes they could. Were they married? Indeed they were. How is it they had different names? Et cetera, ad nauseum. Their experiences were anything but pleasant, but they could have been much worse.

Interrogations were rigorous and maddeningly contentious. Everything was said through pairs of interpreters; these interpreters bore no resemblance (at all) to Quing and Lo Shiu. Worse, the process was protracted for no apparent reason. Neither was strip-searched, but each was shaken down, patted, and frisked at least a few times. Of course Charlie felt profoundly grateful to forces beyond himself for prompting him to dispose of Zhang Yimou's photo, the fact of which gave Marie great relief also.

Underneath all this, both Charlie and Marie felt the double anxiety that Shaanxi Internal Security "knew" things of which they weren't even aware, and that they might have been designated by the CIA (or whomever) to take the blame for something Internal Security "knew." They realized they were expendable regardless of assurances routinely accorded them as part of their errands. And if they were to be imprisoned, they'd eventually be released provided they weren't killed by accident or disease. . . . But paranoia is a form of madness. Both had often postulated the necessity of ignoring paranoia every time it raises its head, even when its existence looks justified.

*

After interrogation Marie had been led from the ground floor of one nondescript governmental office building to another. Four security persons marshaled her into a suite of offices, each with opaque glass windows, giving onto a common waiting room. She sensed Charlie's presence as another group of people barged into the waiting room, but she was bustled into one of the offices where someone put her into a chair before a large, G-I desk. Behind the desk, immobile, sat . . . Zhang Yimou, "Big Yim"—in the flesh. Marie recognized the face but gazed at him impassively, revealing only minor irritation.

The motionless man abruptly stood up and came around his desk to glower down at her for several seconds before he methodically peeled off the usual questions through a translator. He was pretty good-sized for a Chinese man, Marie thought; probably northern stock. He usually preceded his questions with a statement; his slanted eyes were always piercing. When Marie assayed using some Cantonese, he ignored it.

"Big Yim" had grounds for this arrest: recorded coded phone messages, a dead-drop of some kind of code, sighted contacts with a known subversive (out came pictures of Wenyuan Yao). He showed Marie a very recent photo of herself holding a small parcel. He tapped the photo a few times with an index finger. "Chineess plessahn," he said. ("Chinese present.") Those were his first English words. The translator immediately added, "Where is it?"

Marie alleged disposing of the "present" in the hotel-lobby women's restroom. A brief interchange ensued between her and Big Yim, with Marie answering his questions apparently to no desired effect. Finally Zhang gave her a look of disdain, loosened a little wave of dismissal in her direction, and went back to his desk chair. Two uniformed police caused Marie to rise from her chair. Before she was led out the office, Yim leaned back against his desk, gazed at her evenly, and she distinctly heard him say in English:

"Go home, Miz Ly-kaht." [Reichert, the surname on Marie's passport.] Zhang wagged an index finger at her. "Do not evah come back heahl. Undahstan?"

"Bye," said Marie with a tiny nod.

Charlie was waiting outside the office, surrounded by law enforcement personnel. He had seen Marie enter the office; when she came out Charlie thought she looked mildly dazed. He was led into that same office and immediately saw why.

Big Yim regarded Charlie levelly. The interview that followed essentially replicated Marie's session, sans closing remarks. When it terminated Charlie was advised through a translator that Zhang would consult with his "expert on American spies." He and Marie were to wait on opposite sides of the common room outside the office.

This they did, wordlessly, for about fifteen minutes, one occasionally glancing at the other, both wishing they were alone with each other somewhere else, most preferably at home.

They never laid eyes on Yim's "expert," but when Zhang had them called back into his office he finished studying notes on his desk before he simply dismissed them with another stern warning not to return (done through a translator). Marie and Charlie nodded to Zhang as they rose to leave his office again. Secretly they wanted to know what his "expert" had revealed about them. Could they really be considered spies; did the expert even exist? But prudence decried pressing any issue.

As they went out the door their eyes widened when they heard Zhang's voice distinctly say, "*Chaahree*! Not so fast."

"Sir?" Charlie said and returned partway.

Marie stepped outside the office and the door closed behind her, but she tried to hear the colloquy inside. Had Zhang really said "Charlie"? As far as she knew, the given name on Charlie's passport was "Mark."

Again addressing Charlie as "Charlie," Big Yim asserted that Xian was his own "Shangri-La" (using exactly that trope). Charlie at that moment was preoccupied by Big Yim's using what sounded like urban Black-American dialect:

"Don't you *ev*-ah be comin' back heahl, man," Zhang told Charlie. "Yo ass *will be* mine if ah see it again. Ca-peesh?"

Charlie had flashed on Richard Pryor, the Black-American stand-up comic, telling his story about an anomalous mellow moment between him and the vicious dog next door. Then very clearly Charlie saw a stronger analogy: campfire conversations in the Cambodian forest with his comrade Lewis, the man who said he had nowhere else to go.

"I hear you," Charlie said firmly to Zhang Yimou, who nodded dismissal.

On his way out again, Charlie heard behind him: "Pass on th' word to th' C-I-A, keep th' brankety-brank *away!*"

"Okay!" Charlie said over his shoulder.

In a taxi en route back to the Garden Hotel Marie heard Charlie muse audibly: "The world might be *a lot* smaller than we can imagine."

*

Marie had a few problems retrieving the four folded parts of the "present" she'd smuggled out of Xian, but after she did that she made copies of the whole. Written in columns of ideographs, the message fairly thrummed with urgency. Playing with the sounds that she could discern in the columns, Marie felt sure that names, probably of fugitives, were included in the message, and she felt grateful to forces beyond her for causing her to take such rigorous measures in getting the thing out of China. After she and Charlie returned home they telephoned the designated parties in California and Michigan and sent to each a copy of the message, along with a copy of the newspaper clipping and the original microfiche. And that was enough of that.

"I think we've done our bit for the cause of freedom in China," Marie remarked to Charlie during a walk on the river trail with their daughters. "Getting that stuff out, et cetera, has been a royal pain south of the butt. I mean that literally."

"We did our best, especially you."

"That's right! There's got to be some meaning in that. It counts for *some*thing."

Charlie gave Marie a pat on her behind, then put an arm around her. The girls saw this and fetched their parents' attention. To Charlie and Marie, of course, those little bodies and all they encapsulated were of much more significance than the entire population of China.

Chapter 8

April 23, 1990
Alma-Ata, Kazakhstan

It might have been the effect of estrogen-replacement therapy (now, shockingly, available to her out here in the wastelands). Possibly the cause was dear Andrushka's attentions to her despite his chronic physical infirmities. Whatever the reasons, Tatyana fairly glowed even when she slept. In fact, she and Andrei recently wondered whether she might be pregnant, a distinct impossibility.

One other element might have enhanced Tatyana's sense of well being—in ways so subtle that she couldn't define them except as energizers. After four years of making discreet inquiries and dropping hints to all sorts of unsavory types outside the scientific community, Tatyana had at last made contact with and, twenty hours earlier, had actually met with a Chinese "businessman" who represented himself as a potential mid-level buyer of the "small explosive devices" Tatyana had made known to be "available." Moreover, even in translation, the fellow came across as thoroughly trustworthy. The fact of his being Chinese made him especially estimable. Those people have a tradition of integrity, she'd told herself. Even the man's translator, a Singaporean lady sworn to secrecy, looked solidly trustworthy.

From now on, Tatyana determined, her mission revolved on keeping Andrei focused. As far as she knew, he hadn't decided for sure how he would detonate small nuclear devices (once they were actually built), nor had he physically tested a device similar to the model he had made at her behest a few years back. Producing a substantial number of the devices would entail several problems, presuming Tatyana obtained the requisite fissionable materials. Now was the time to finish the project.

Tatyana reminded herself that her part was not that difficult; it was merely dangerous. Already she had arranged for over twelve kilos of weapons-grade plutonium 239 to be diverted directly to Andrei's laboratory, contingent upon one thing: providing sufficient Deutsche marks or dollars to her contacts. Conditions for daily life were changing so drastically in what had suddenly become the former Soviet Union that only one constant remained: hard currency could accomplish anything.

Soon Tatyana would know just how sincere that saturnine Chinese "businessman" was: either he would provide her with the start-up cash they'd agreed upon or he wouldn't. If he did, other things, incredible things, would start falling into place, perhaps quickly. (For a stupefying moment steel fingers grasped Tatyana's stomach and intestines, then squeezed. It was fear, raw and mindless, that she quelled habitually.) Therefore, Tatyana resolved, everything required of her she would do in steps, simple, careful steps. And she *would* prevail.

At this very same time, Mo Tzu (the preferred and secret *nom de guerre* of Lin Piao, the sitting First Assistant Minister of Foreign Trade for the People's Republic of China) returned to Beijing from a trade conference in Moscow. As on all other such occasions, his arrival caused him no joy.

At home and his job every day was thoroughly boring. Worse, his job served institutionalized stupidity. His main challenge lay in skirting treachery, yes, outright treachery lurking at every turn. (Of course I am paranoiac, he would sometimes tell himself, but that does not mean my superiors, my underlings, my wife, my sons, and Internal Security are not wishing to undo me!) Withal, the "Republic" was a dreary sham, most of his considerable abilities lay fallow and atrophied (his high-level position just a ridiculous cul-de-sac), and (worse yet) he had had no sex with a woman in over four years despite being married. Small wonder I contemplate defection, he had been telling himself for uncounted months.

Less of a wonder, then, was Mo Tzu's flirtation with veritable treason. Since their first exploratory telephone discussion, on three occasions he had actually met vis-à-vis with the Enemy personified: the arrogant Mandarin bastard who would never consider regarding Taiwan as merely a "wayward province," General Chang K'ung.

Mo Tzu had wanted to hate the general (whom he'd called "a Hong Kong-style parody of Chiang Kai-shek") but he'd had little success. Aside from actually liking and admiring him and secretly taking pride in believing the feeling was mutual, "Mo Tzu" would never have existed if Chang hadn't created him. "Do you mind that I call you 'Mo Tzu,'" Chang had said earnestly, and at that moment Lin Piao's existence was invested with a purpose. Suddenly the possibility for acquiring wealth—and thus being able to opt effectively for a free life—existed. Feeling excitement every day was now a part of that.

In fact, a sweet Russian lady with whom Mo Tzu had met two times (with great pleasure) outside Moscow was willing to sell bona-fide nuclear bombs precisely of the type desired by General Chang. Her initial asking price was not too high: for forty thousand American dollars each, she would provide as many of the devices as Chang wanted. But for her to bring the process to fruition would require a capital investment, which would also demonstrate Mo Tzu's and Chang's good faith. Would Chang K'ung agree to that?

The most important job Mo Tzu could possibly have in the world now was to present all this to Chang. For the time being, his existence would be defined by his serving a function: he would be the linch pin in dealings between the Russian lady and Chang. With some luck, in the process Mo Tzu might be able to spend face-to-face time with the general's very desirable civilian aide, a Taiwanese lady who knew how to take good care of herself.

*

Although events in Formosa of February 28, 1947 predated her birth by almost eight years, Hsiu-fen Wu knew those events influenced her life in subtle and multiple ways. Historically, "2-28" and its context comprised a treacherous, crass milieu fraught with dishonor generated by hundreds of prominent Taiwanese, her family among them. (Her large extended family owned mercantile interests in Taipei and down in Peitou, plus they owned spin-off businesses such as inns and a taxi company in both places.) The upshot of "2-28": Taiwan being dominated by Chiang Kai-shek's Nationalists when they were expelled from China proper. And now Hsiu-fen Wu had to live up to the advantages her family had arrogated—and do her part to atone for the treachery that accounted for much of their good fortune.

Her situation was perhaps impossible: as senior aide to General Chang K'ung, she actually worked for the Nationalists and thus owed the government her loyalty. Yet Chang, her boss, had revealed to her (in piecemeal fashion) his actually subversive intentions regarding the status quo of Taiwan. In the foreseeable future the government in Taipei would be much less Chinese, Chang had told her several times; it would be constituted of many more representatives of pre-1949 Taiwan families. He expected to help make that happen. Whether or not she believed him, she was his primary assistant upon whom he depended implicitly.

On top of all this, "Suzie Wu" simply wanted to fulfill her potential as a person. Starting when she was in the provincial university, she envisioned that earning a Ph.D. at an American university would be an excellent starting point. (In what field? It made little difference, so long as she would excel.) She had not yet seen her way clear to pursuing a Ph.D. only because she'd been preoccupied by her extended family and her privileged position as a military staffer. She felt fortunate to have captured enough time to develop skill in autoeroticism, an activity she considered underrated and essential to a healthy person's psyche.

One other aspiration motivated Hsiu-fen despite herself: Yes, she was truly a "nationalist," a Taiwan nationalist. She believed that Taiwanese people were not meant to live under Chinese domination, *any* Chinese domination. The general knew this about her; he explicitly concurred with it (confidentially, of course). That was the main reason she thought he would be good for Taiwan and perhaps for the world if he were to succeed in forming a purely Chinese state autonomous from most of Taiwan. She felt only mildly troubled by not knowing *how* Chang intended to finance the founding of his state and how he would defend it.

Hints she'd gotten of Chang's strategy, such as when he'd met with that Mainlander in Singapore and Manila to discuss purchasing nuclear armaments, did not compute, so to speak. Moreover the quality of officers General Chang had already attracted to his Cause was simply too sterling to abet something heinous or stupid. But if Hsiu-fen was mistaken in her loyalty to her boss, she postulated, at least she was well paid and she led an interesting life worthy of pride.

*

If Charlie was considered something of an eccentric by those who knew and loved him, Marie was regarded as enigmatic to about the same degree. When she chose to do professional work (after attending to her family's and her own well-being), she worked with great intensity, but nobody knew for sure what Marie did from day to day except that sporadically she earned substantial fees by providing curriculum plans or solving curriculum problems for school districts all over the state. She also taught at least one course per semester at UT or some other local university because she truly loved teaching. Occasionally she wrote and helped edit education-journal monographs.

But Marie also wrote things closer to her heart, which might or might not have been presented to anyone outside the writers' support group to which she belonged: poems, essays, stories, at least one television-drama script and some short radio plays. Nobody knew how she had learned how to write these things. People simply presumed Marie had learned in depth whatever she needed to know.

Unlike Charlie's "tragically low-tech" approach to work and living, Marie found herself relying more and more heavily on electronic technology. Her besetting problem was finding time to practice Tae Kwon-do while she learned the intricacies demanded of high-tech users, on top of accomplishing all her professional work. Striking an effective balance was a constant, devilishly difficult struggle. Happily, by using, say, E-mail or the Internet, Marie could best perform high-powered tasks even while she cooked chicken or taught Lisa and Julia how to write sentences and tie their shoes.

Clandestinely Marie also used the Internet to exercise her personality while maintaining her anonymity. She would fire off broadsides to various cyberspace chat rooms and web pages and deal only with responses that interested her. Then she would write to the local press and various national publications, using her own name, and cite specific Web interchanges as the basis for her commentary letter. People who saw through her ploys and identified her often encouraged her to greater efforts, especially in her obsessing about "that alien fact of life": If something is physical it *has to have* limits.

The subjects Marie confronted this way might have been numerous, but she focused on topics closest to her heart. The right to abortion, she believed in. ("Don't even try to tell me that cluster of cells is a human being." "Lighten up! My husband, a Buddhist, is probably right: Life goes on forever; you can't really destroy it. But you sure as hell can destroy the environment and overall quality of life.") Too many parents were "intentionally stupid," and they've raised their kids to be stupid. ("The poor kids aren't born that way. Somebody must be training them to ignore realities. You want proof?") The U.S. economy will eventually succumb to so-called "entitlements." ("The very notion is an obscene fallacy, and whole generations plug into it as though it makes sense!" Her usual conclusion: "Nobody's really 'entitled' to anything except a reasonable return on what he's invested. This includes, by the way, all social-security recipients and all federal and military retirees.") In Central Texas, "people have to be immoral and crass and intentionally stupid if they think they've got a God-given right to ruin the Edwards Aquifer. Doesn't anybody remember what happened to Comanche Springs?" *Race* in 1990's America "might be some people's 'obsession,' but some people—validly so—do not give a damn about it one way or another. Sorry, but it's true." (A frequent peroration: "Members of all races are doing a bang-up job of depleting the Earth's resources and raising their kids to be stupid and do things that are downright evil.")

Usually Marie's on-line and epistlatory manner was abrasive or scornful (but not solely because she loved "twisting tail," she told Charlie and Jed). Her objective was to affect minds, and her methods were roughness and derision because they worked. "People need to get roughed up sometimes; they ought to feel pain. When you laugh at them publicly they hate it, so maybe they change their ways," she said many, many times.

*

After he and Marie had returned from Xian, Charlie found his role in Life abruptly changed: on a sweet April morning Hollis the senior completed a hard run along the river, waved to some acquaintances, and likely was dead before he finished collapsing on the grass from a ruptured brain aneurism. Thus the bottom dropped out of Marguerite Grumbles' Life.

Between Charlie and his mother lay a huge pool of grief and unfinished business. (The last time Charlie had talked with his father, Hollis jovially addressed him as an "old subversive" over the telephone.) Abnormally often during several weeks after that April morning, Charlie would catch his mind drifting to scattered villages and hamlets in the unlikely sanctuary poised above kinetic forest. Now reality held but diluted richness.

Over time, as Charlie strove to fill the gap caused by his father's parting, he felt awed by the connection he knew he shared with Hollis, self-described as "the world's most literate refrigeration mechanic." And they would be connected forever, as far as Charlie could see, because he had no doubt that the essence of his father would never cease to exist. What could possibly extinguish or destroy something like that?

Collaterally Charlie watched his mother, who had a great deal more recovering to do than Charlie, start to actually Live again, with increasing vigor. Charlie was awed. At the same time he felt dazzled day to day by Marie and Julia and Lisa simply being *themselves*. Thus Charlie crystallized a conviction that he eventually shared with Marie: When Lives and personalities function naturally, Life has to be dazzling. Marie responded, "I love hearing that from you."

May 5, 1991
Taipei, Taiwan

Despite his aversion to traveling without Marie, who was staying at home to take Lisa and Julia to appointments and parties (et cetera, et cetera), Charlie felt a kind of joy in accepting this errand and he didn't know why. Maybe he simply needed to get away by himself, or maybe he felt an attraction to Taiwan.

After some hassles at the airport, Dr. Grumbles arrived and checked in at the U.S.-government-sponsored medical mission on the south side of Taipei. His only problems had stemmed from bringing four boxes of fragile equipment ostensibly needed immediately at the clinic, which in actuality was a small, high-level hospital equipped mostly via private donations. He felt no surprise in seeing Debbie Kassenbaum, officially a member of the U.S. Consulate, come in to meet him.

They exchanged code sentences as they shook hands.

"Good to see you," Charlie added, and he meant it despite a strangeness he saw.

"Got your hands full on this one, huh?" was her response.

As far as Charlie knew, she hadn't seen the boxes he'd brought, two of them compact and heavy, the other two light and large and awkward to handle. They had been pre-cleared (once he presented various documents) through ROC Customs.

Debbie proceeded to explain that the first two parts of his errand—bringing in the "medical equipment" and making certain contacts—would be completed simultaneously when he met with Cheng Tsai-jing and turned the equipment over to him. That would also result in possibly taking home whatever Mr. Cheng gave to him.

And who was this Cheng Tsai-jing? According to Debbie, he co-owned a highly prominent machine-manufacturing company and was the premier benefactor of this medical-mission hospital. That squared with the limited information Charlie had been given, along with a principle he was supposed to believe which Debbie alleged as true: this was in furtherance of U.S. economic interests, a notion Charlie considered moot.

"By the way, there's a little twist in your job here that you might enjoy," Debbie said with a half-smile. "Mr. Cheng wants you to dine with him, this evening. I hope you don't mind my having taken the liberty to accept on your behalf."

"That depends," Charlie said. "Who's paying?"

"Ha-ha!"

Debbie handed him a card emblazoned with the name of a restaurant (but with no address or phone number); on the back inscribed in blue ink, 19:00. Drivers for the Guardian taxi company would know where the place was located.

"Aloha," she said. "Be there."

Charlie and Debbie exchanged little waves, and away she went to apprise Colonel Fang—and thereby his boss and supra-leader, General Chang K'ung—that the scenario they envisioned was about to become reality.

"Think solely with your ears, lady highly born; now time exists ripening," Debbie said into the telephone using what she thought was flawless Minnan Chinese.

"We're on it. Thank you, Ms. Kassenbaum," Colonel Fang responded, and Debbie marveled at how she'd forgotten that he spoke English better than General Chang.

"Please tell 'Cobra' hello from me," Debbie said and hung up. A little later she thought she might feel some compunction for what was likely to befall Charlie, but her priorities superseded wrinkles such as that.

Upon arriving at "The Golden Room" (according to the taxi driver's translation), Charlie had been greeted at the curb by three trim, serious-looking young men (all in dark suits), one of whom briskly went into the restaurant and momentarily returned beside a man of about Charlie's age. The man smiled at Charlie, evidently told one of his aides (or bodyguards) to pay the taxi fare, and extended a hand. Charlie took it with some pleasure. By now he had perceived the man's military deportment.

"I am Tsai-jing Cheng," the man said. "Welcome to Taiwan. I am told you have medical equipment we need."

"Yes," said Charlie, "That's all of it right here. Shall we take it inside?"

"We will get it."

Mr. Cheng uncoiled a command. Within a few seconds Charlie's boxes were removed from the curb and taken into the restaurant, thus completing the transfer. As Mr. Cheng and Charlie turned to go inside, the three young men—joined by a fourth—reassembled outside, clearly on alert. Mr. Cheng mentioned that a "secure car" would soon arrive for the boxes. Charlie didn't know what to make of all this, plus he felt preoccupied: on this narrow back street already devoid of traffic this evening, Charlie was almost certain he had caught a glimpse of men in Western-style suits surveilling the exchange that had taken place between him and Mr. Cheng's "aides." And he was quite sure that he had spotted—or felt he had spotted—a slender, well-dressed woman casually observing his business from the opposite direction down the street. He had to tell himself to focus; just do the job.

*

Over a variety of grilled seafood in a private room (simply but richly appointed) Charlie and Mr. Cheng talked briefly about several matters, all of which ultimately pointed to a common subject: the government of Taiwan was progressive but anachronistic. And its evolution was confined to narrow parameters in a dead-ended channel. That meant its economic potential was severely limited, Charlie gathered (with which his host concurred), and this prompted Charlie to think that maybe the objective of his errand was to provide industrial intelligence to an ally.

Cheng offered a vexing ultra-conclusion: "We need a new beginning—'from scratch' as you say in America. That is no problem if we have sufficient wealth. And that is no problem— no real problem—if we have complete freedom, uh— [Here Charlie helped him to use the word "autonomy."] And even that is no problem if we can acquire great power—or get help from countries that have great power."

"Sir, what kind of 'power' are we talking about?"

Cheng said that he meant military and economic strength and therefore great technological capacity as well. "We will start by using one thing we have that is special."

So far, Charlie was enjoying this. "And what is that?" he asked.

"The ability to cause great fear. Fear of consequences that are certain if conditions are not met, if behavior is not . . . acceptable to us."

"Ah." Charlie didn't know what else to respond.

In fact Cheng had been expressing precepts per General Chang K'ung. In his mind Cheng was even hearing replayed (in Minnan) his general's exact words as they had been uttered by General Chang himself. His voice—always confident, irresistibly rich in timbre. And the source of that voice— seemingly unassailable. One could not reasonably deny the general's limitless capacities and strength. Had he been in Chiang Kai-shek's position during the Red Upheavals, the name Mao Zedong would only be in footnotes.

Charlie spoke up: "Sounds to me like you're talking about terrorism."

"Use of terror can be a legitimate tool," Cheng responded at once.

"Only in the boxing ring. Maybe on the basketball court." Charlie pondered then added, "We've got laws against that, even on a person-to-person level. I bet you do, too."

"Perhaps I have misunderstood your position," Cheng said after a moment. His manner turned almost conspiratorial. "Tell me, Dr. Grumbles, do you understand the main principle of our New T'aip'ing Revolution?"

The question surprised Charlie, but (to his own amazement) he recalled the train ride to Xian and some remarks Marie had made about the T'aip'ing Rebellion which had taken place—and ended badly—in nineteenth-century China. "Of course I believe in revolution if people require it to be self-governing," he responded, hoping to sound at once knowledgeable and sympathetic, also noncommittal. But he didn't know what to make of the word "New," so he chose to overlook it.

Mr. Cheng spent a few moments pondering that omnibus response, during which he chewed absently and poked at his dinner. Charlie simply focused his attention on the well-prepared food; to him the issues at hand seemed academic.

Presently Cheng declared (more or less parroting General Chang): "Sometimes a revolution must . . . suspend rule of law—all laws—simply to win. In America you would call that 'opening a window of opportunity.'" Cheng paused and, much like his mentor, smiled disarmingly. "Surely, not the best of all worlds," he added, "but, hey, what are revolutions for?"

Charlie found himself transfixed by the logic and the command of American idioms integral to his host's assertions. "I'll be damned," he said abstractedly. Over his suspended chopsticks he regarded Cheng levelly. "Small wonder you're one hell of an industrialist," Charlie declared, recalling Debbie's assay of Cheng's reputation.

"Oh, I am more than a businessman," Cheng responded.

What Cheng meant by that was manifold, although he felt obliged to tell Charlie only that he was a devoted father of three and he considered himself something of a philosopher. In fact, Colonel Tian was a fine senior officer, a core component of the New T'aip'ing Revolution, and apparently a capable actor. Only Debbie Kassenbaum and General Chang knew that Colonel Tian was representing himself to Charlie as industrialist Cheng Tsai-jing, an actual person who happened to be out of country, probably in Malaysia, at this very moment.

While on her job, Debbie had covertly tracked the real Mr. Cheng's departure abroad. But more importantly, by having caused certain electronic communications to be erased, she had ensured that he couldn't have learned of his titular role as liaison between certain members of the U.S. National Security Council and his own government. Most importantly—from Debbie's standpoint—no record existed of the DIA Agent-In-Charge intervening here. She had ensured that any uncovering of "electronic footprints" would only absolve her of dereliction.

Colonel Tian was performing his role in order to divert the "medical equipment" Charlie had brought from Los Angeles for the Nationalist government of Taiwan, which badly wanted that materiel for its arsenal: two complete guidance units which control the flight of M-11 ballistic missiles. Acquiring the missiles themselves would pose no problem; and even without a prototype they might be manufactured locally. But the guidance units were unique, so unique that the U.S. Congress had outlawed any exporting of them. Now the Taipings had them, thanks to Ms. Kassenbaum's innovativeness and self-ascribed chutzpah.

*

Once she had seen Charlie going off with the "equipment" to meet Colonel Tian, Debbie knew a thrill of satisfaction lasting into the next day. More than once General Chang had averred (in strict confidence) that he would be delighted to have those missile controls for purposes entirely apart from his job of defending Taiwan militarily. He would have to be pleased with Debbie for arranging for them to be simply handed over to his adjutant, Colonel Tian. On top of that, Debbie hoped, she might soon find access to Marie Overstreet's attentions, now that the main obstacle to those attentions was about to be eliminated. Likely Marie would be coming to Taipei in a couple days to identify and claim Charlie's body.

At the old military-police headquarters in downtown Taipei ex-General Lau and his staff of counterintelligence operatives faced an urgent reality: two anonymous telephone calls (one a FAX), allegedly coming from the U.S. Consulate, both warning of advanced missile-system controls possibly being captured by members of a seditious plot against the Nationalist government which these former Kuomintang officers were sworn to defend. What was actually being perpetrated, and who was plotting? If they valued their jobs, they'd get the answers.

The existence of a clandestine, cult-like movement directed and funded by a person or persons very highly placed in the military hierarchy of Taiwan was widely suspected. Even the American CIA and DIA establishments posited the possibility of that. But despite the arc of those suspicions extending beyond the last two years, nothing was actually known about the movement, if in fact one existed. No leads had ever been substantiated or else they had proven to be ridiculous. Perhaps the plot evidently occurring now was connected to the mysterious one to which they had long been vigilant.

After he'd gotten those anonymous tips, Director Lau received confirmation that M-11 missile-guidance units had indeed arrived in Taiwan, but they had yet to be turned over to Cheng Tsai-jing (and thus the military). Nor would they be turned over to proper authorities because according to his investigators, about an hour earlier those missile controls had been turned over to someone else—exactly as Lau had been warned.

A pair of photos accompanying the field report showed an American man—one ostensibly connected to an American-sponsored hospital in Taiwan—apparently involved in that transfer, also as Lau had been warned. One photo clearly showed Charlie standing next to a taxi outside The Golden Room, evidently about to be assisted by young Chinese men. On top of all this, Lau had learned that this same American had physically brought those missile-guidance controls into Taiwan as part of a secret deal between governments. Thus he was flagrantly breaching good faith in two directions, on a high plane.

"Let's get that scum bag," one of Lau's lieutenants said in English, and Lau explained that city police were already dispatched to the restaurant to pick up Charlie for interrogation concerning probable subversive activities. And maybe, at last, that chimerical cult-like conspiracy would be proven to exist. Fifteen minutes later, though, a call from the Taipei Police Central Office informed everyone present that Charlie and the company he'd kept that evening had departed the restaurant before the police arrived.

Hsiu-fen Wu, meanwhile, had been exultant. Acting intuitively, on her own initiative she had gone to "possibly assist" Colonel Tian make contact with the American courier bringing in some kind of contraband for General Chang. She'd actually suspected that Charlie was involved. For years she had harbored hopes of someday meeting Charlie on a person-to-person level and crystallizing the rapport that she was sure existed between them (regardless of any relationship he might have in progress, for it could always be subject to revision). Discreet, oblique questioning of Colonel Tian over the last few days confirmed that Dr. Grumbles might very well be that courier, and he was!

Ah, but something didn't compute here: Unless he was operating outside the law, on a special agenda, Charlie wouldn't turn over American equipment—which he'd brought all the way over here—to a colonel at a restaurant. U.S. operations wouldn't be so chicane. Yet she had seen him turn over something to Tian, something she knew the colonel regarded as vital, probably dangerous to handle. What's more, the transaction had been tracked by two men Hsiu-fen Wu didn't begin to recognize.

A latent but startling conclusion about Charlie blossomed in Hsiu-fen Wu's mind: He really had a different agenda. "He must work for Chang now!" she said audibly in Taiwanese. Then in English: "I am darned!" She would definitely have to find out—and only from the source himself—how it happened that Charlie and she were comrades under a clandestine banner alien to them both.

But now she had to act quickly. Somebody was intruding on this scenario, and those two observers she'd seen had disappeared. No longer acting casually, Hsiu-fen Wu approached Tian's soldiers (all of whom knew of her), and soon she privately told Tian himself about the untoward surveillance. No problem, he said; the equipment had already been removed by his men. (Had he been observed? No way of telling.) He thanked her profusely and returned to his table to cut short his dinner with Charlie, which he did with grace and dispatch.

This left Charlie at loose ends on the east side of Taipei with his mission virtually completed. He had brought his flight bag with him and had no reason to return this evening to the clinic where he had checked in with "medical equipment" meant for Mr. Cheng. A room had been reserved for him at the Roma Hotel, so he decided to go there directly. Now he needed to find a taxi and perhaps get some advice from the driver about how to spend the next hour or two, if the driver spoke English.

A fire-engine-red BMW careened around a nearby corner and sped down the street to where Charlie stood. Even before it lurched to a stop beside him, he was aware of it being driven by a chic youngish woman, who stepped out of the driver's side and spoke to him across the top of her car.

"Doc-tah! Hed-*droe*!" Hsiu-fen said and gave a little wave.

Charlie felt a bolt of electro-kinesis drill through him as he understood why he'd felt that constant pull to Taiwan. The force it exerted on him didn't emanate merely from a synergy of beautiful coastal scenery and ancient, arcane vibrations.

"Oh-*ho*. Ms. Wu! Am I delighted to see you."

"I said you can call me 'Suzi' if you want."

Thus Charlie departed the locus about five minutes before state counterintelligence agents downtown got a call from Taipei police notifying them that Charlie wasn't in custody.

*

"How on Earth did you know I was here?" Charlie asked Suzi Wu when they were underway, headed to the Roma Hotel through a network of narrow streets.

"Oh, it is my job to know things." Her smile was radiant even when she was being wry.

"A-w-w-l-l-righty. Then perhaps you can tell me how I can spend the next two hours."

"Gladly. And you can tell me things."

First Charlie had to overtly appreciate his automotive surroundings, a new edition of those smaller-model "Beamers," very nimble and peppy. "This is quite some car you've got," he said. [*Of course she would have a convertible.*] "Back Stateside this little number would cost you about forty thau."

"Here you would pay almost double that amount."

Charlie whistled admiration. He glanced at Hsiu-fen Wu.

She caught the glance. "I get paid by the army to work for General Chang. General Chang also pays me." She laughed lightly. "I get many offers for dinner, also lunch. 'Dates' you call them. So for me food is small expense." [Beat.] "I exercise with wives at the Officers' Club, free."

"I see!"

For a long moment each was aware that the other was smiling absently out the windshield.

"You know General Chang?" asked Suzi Wu.

"Of course. Well, I know of him," Charlie said.

209

"He will be most grateful for what you have done."

Charlie had no idea of what she meant. Maybe General Chang was simply grateful for any kind of help rendered to Taiwan. Charlie had no suspicion that he'd been dealing with someone other than the designated Tsai-jing Cheng. Likewise, Suzi Wu was unaware of the ruse that Colonel Tian had perpetrated (despite the disclosure that Charlie would be bringing over military contraband). Neither she nor Charlie had reason to think events were not what they seemed. At the moment, moreover, reality seemed very pleasant.

For about the next hour they simply toured parts of Taipei and talked. The talk flowed freely, touching on many things. Apparently Charlie and Suzi Wu utilized exclusively the same length of brain wave. Consequently, although several mentions were made of Charlie's "wife" and "daughters," their names were never uttered. (Charlie considered this unintentional, but he knew that was only half true.) As Hsiu-fen recapped events in her life, Charlie distinctly heard the word "Taiping" used twice, and it almost gave him pause, but the subject slipped away in the stream of interaction.

When they finally arrived at the Roma Hotel, Hsiu-fen simply went in to accompany Charlie during check-in. On the counter she could see a handwritten note with his name printed on it above a telephone number. In Taiwanese she asked the clerk what it meant and was told that two men had twice been there inquiring about him. "I will take care of it," she said with a smile and extended her open hand to receive the note, which the clerk gave to her. The telephone number on the note looked familiar: Was this not the former military-police headquarters number? She would definitely call it later.

On the way to his second-floor room with Suzi Wu walking casually beside him, Charlie had no problem formulating three good reasons for initiating an in-depth relationship with this fascinating woman. (He consciously stopped at three.) Would she be receptive? Yes, provided he didn't rush her. He quickly conjectured likely reasons for her reciprocating. This whole situation could be a minefield! *Or worse*. He checked his watch. With some luck he'd be back with Marie in about thirty-six hours. Surely he'd be wise to forego attempting something he'd regret if he accomplished it.

Charlie entered the hotel room, dropped his bag, and casually assayed the space. "I guess it looks okay," he said to Hsiu-fen tentatively standing inside the doorway. "Let's go downstairs and get something to drink. I want to learn more about your life."

With no further ado Charlie and the lady stepped back into the corridor and went to the bar and cafe on the main floor. When Charlie returned to his room over an hour later, he was still charmed, and very much alone.

After a fitful sleep, in the early morning Charlie made his way along the corridor toward a stairway to the main floor. For maybe the hundredth time he allowed himself to muse about Hsiu-fen Wu's face and voice and mannerisms; images of her legs and physique he steadfastly refused to recollect. He was vaguely surprised to see two well-dressed Chinese men approach him from the opposite direction, and even more surprised to hear an accented voice from one of them say: "Dr. Grumbles?"

Charlie barely got off a "yes" and glance at one severe-looking face when he saw a brilliant spark in inky blackness. He heard a distinct Kr-aack! Then he felt a fist drive into his stomach. The realization came through layers of thick obscurity: he was getting hit, and again and again. He didn't even know he'd pitched face down onto the carpet.

At first Charlie was hardly aware of his hands being cuffed behind him. Abruptly he was pulled to his feet; by then he was aware only of pain as he tried to fall back down. But they forced him to stay on his feet and move with them along the corridor, then down the flight of stairs and out a door. Almost miraculously they jammed him into a car without pause. In a moment they drove away with him. No words were uttered, even by Charlie who emitted noises of pain and shock.

Only as Charlie felt the car surging forward (and stopping and surging again) did rage start to set in, although he was helpless to act on it. Eventually, in the bowels of Taipei, the car stopped, the door swung open, and Charlie was pulled (and pushed) into a vaguely familiar, dark old building, plainly a police center. The rage was mitigated when Charlie realized that he was the focal point of a well-attended, and very intense, interrogation that could only have been a gigantic mistake.

To Charlie this entire incident was more a mystery than anything else. His interrogators knew almost everything about all his activities of the day before, but they ardently wanted to know a great deal more, and try as he might, Charlie could give them not a whit of satisfaction.

Mainly they wanted to know to whom he had given the missile-guidance control units. What missile controls, he would ask. They'd tell him what he soon had to postulate, that he had brought missile-guidance controls into Taiwan, and they'd ask again, who got the so-called medical equipment? He always told them the recipient was Mr. Cheng, no one else. Initially they laughed; subsequently that same answer made them turn ugly, then outright vicious.

For whom was he a go-between? They much wanted to know that, too. Charlie could only answer, the U.S. government, of course. He readily predicted their response. (They had four or five other questions which they trucked out sporadically to throw him off balance or to cross-reference his answers.) Charlie had used his own passport and a tourist visa to enter Taiwan. This morning he realized that he was one tourist regarded as an enemy of the state, and he didn't know why. All he knew was that his interrogators were becoming increasingly angry with him, and they were outrageously arrogant idiots who deserved frustration and anger.

By eight that same morning Hsiu-fen Wu was busy getting ready to go to her job. She had contrived various pretexts to contact Charlie about meeting for breakfast or lunch or—at first she fantasized, then determined as a valid possibility—going on a picnic for two that very afternoon. But first to the telephone: she called the number on the note she'd taken from the hotel desk the night before. It was the Internal Security Service. To her chagrin she'd gotten no answer by calling Charlie's room at the Roma Hotel, so she called the Security Service number again (learning that the number got her the counterintelligence branch) and tried to cozen, then bully, information from everyone there. She even talked to that old fascist, former General Lau. Nobody divulged anything concrete about an American in custody. (So—something is happening there.) Suspecting foul play by somebody in the shadows, Hsiu-fen promptly advised her boss that something was amiss regarding a valuable ally to his private Cause, which—evidently—was again not as secret as he expected it was.

General Chang, of course, heeded carefully Hsiu-fen Wu's warning that he and his movement risked exposure as well as losing an ally. (How does that American know what he knows? What does he want? Chang plumbed his intuition and found a cipher.) To understand the situation as best he could, Chang summoned Colonel Tian for information and advice about Charlie and his role, and all indicators registered positive. Chang knew he had better pull some strings at once.

Charlie badly needed to be somewhere else, and then on his way home. If only he knew what these assholes wanted of him! After the first several minutes of interrogation he came to a realization that what he and Marie had often feared was now in progress: he was being set up to take the blame for something that had gone wrong. Of course he couldn't tell those androids what they were programmed to hear. He wasn't supposed to be able to do that. This compounded his rage, which he never quite revealed because as he told them over and over exactly what he knew, the arm twisting became literal, then intensified, and Charlie's outrage turned into fear.

Debbie was meanwhile having a change of heart. She, too, had been called by General Chang (a noteworthy event at the consulate). He requested her help in arranging the release of an American citizen wrongfully detained by the state Internal Security Service. (Chang never mentioned how he'd learned of that "very grave mistake.") Obliquely he told Debbie that Charlie was valuable to the Taiping cause and to rescue him was necessary. Debbie recognized a marching order when she heard one, and knowing The General needed her was like waking from an exhilarating dream and finding it real.

Charlie barely glanced at the five or six bored, angry faces and winced inwardly as he answered once again their main question the only way he could.

"Tsai-jing Cheng," he said flatly. "You know the answer."

None of the belligerent heads in the immediate vicinity even bothered to nod at Xinxin Zhang, a rat-like-looking man whose sole function in these proceedings was to cause Charlie acute pain. Which he promptly did with a calm, feral smile.

"You evil prick!" Charlie said to Zhang, who then proceeded to dislocate a few of Charlie's fingers.

Again Charlie was seized by abject numbing fear as his mind groped for a way out of this and could only hit against blank walls.

Colonel Tian was consciously applying some lore he had learned from his mentor and guide in all things worldly, General Chang. First the precept: Never rush important matters. Thus Tian allowed things to develop while he arranged to implement Chang's tactic number one: Always conceal your role in events by working through others. Thus Colonel Tian's closest associates, a senior agent in Counterintelligence and army Captain Chao, were taking appropriate actions. The American DIA agent whom General Chang often consulted (the woman with the fine physique) would facilitate matters.

Naked except for a sock on one foot, Charlie hung by his left wrist handcuffed to a pipe running below the ceiling of a basement utility room. His right forearm was broken; he felt sure that he'd lost forever the function of one kidney. If Xinxin Zhang didn't quit his work soon, none of the injuries will matter, Charlie thought when he'd drifted back into consciousness for maybe the fifth time. Either they'd stop trying to force something out of him or he'd die. Very soon. As a signature of their professionalism Charlie's inquisitors tried to avoid leaving obvious marks of physical abuse. The broken forearm was an accident, a testament to Xinxin's enthusiasm; it could be readily fixed and explained. Other than the broken arm and some cigarette burns in private places, plus a bruise on the side of his face from the hotel attack, Charlie's injuries were internal.

Almost involuntarily, while he'd been incurring many of those injuries, Charlie had contrived a strategy that he utterly yearned to implement. It caused him to return to consciousness as fully as he could, over and over. In retrospect beginning the next day, Charlie intuited that his "plan" probably sustained him in his ordeal; he had refused to die or even despair because he wanted so much to do it. It was astonishingly simple: slip his hand and wrist free of the shackle (or else pull down the pipe), place both feet on the floor, and with his one hand tear out Xinxin Zhang's fucking lungs. At the time, it seemed to Charlie that he was just on the verge of pulling this off.

Abruptly Charlie perceived a changing of the guard around him. Xinxin Zhang was evidently being relieved and replaced.

As Zhang washed his hands and put on his suitcoat and tie he and his replacement talked in rapid-fire Minnan. As prelude, the new man approached Charlie and perfunctorily punched him in the ribs. But the fist had been flattened; it stopped flush on bone and barely hurt. Zhang and his translator were on their way out.

"I am Captain Chao of Defense Forces," the new man said to Charlie. "We start at top. Where are missile-guidance controls you brought here? Who has them?"

Captain Chao spoke English well and needed no translator. Still, another person had entered the room; Charlie was aware of that before he responded: "Cheng . . . Mr. Cheng has them. Here, in Taipei."

The effort of saying even that caused Charlie to slip into a daze, partly because he anticipated a fist in the solar plexus or kidneys or lower abdomen. Contracting his muscles (and nerve) would have caused the blow to hurt worse.

Shockingly, it didn't come. Nor did Captain Chao speak. But Charlie did hear a woman's voice say something in what he took to be Mandarin. A pause. Her voice flared out again, but in English: "Chao, we must get him out now."

Charlie was aware of a chair being slid next to him and of someone standing on it. Somebody took hold of Charlie's stretched-up arm as the handcuff was unlocked.

The woman's voice, now markedly familiar, recurred right behind Charlie: "He looks good, eh!" Then she whispered urgently: "We need this man; he is one of us."

Chao voiced vocables indicating affirmation.

Charlie realized both his feet were on the floor but someone was keeping him standing.

Chao said, "I have requested authority to release him." The woman said, "You can say that Colonel Tian requests it. Also I have requested it for my government."

As he tried to stand erect Charlie was seized by unspeakable back pain that even blotted the throbbing in his head. He yelled sharply and sagged to the floor. Someone accidentally gripped his broken arm. But before all the space behind his eyes went black, Charlie was cognizant of having seen a clear phantasm (if not the reality) of Debbie Kassenbaum's face and form, which he later recalled easily.

Probably only a short time elapsed between Charlie's shout of agony and his awareness of lying covered with sheets on a stretcher borne into fresh outside air. He was quite comfortable now, and he was happy to find himself slid into a vehicle, likely an ambulance, for a fairly brief ride which he actually enjoyed. (Thinking the word "morphine" suddenly made him smile.) After they slid him out Charlie found himself being carried into a familiar entrance . . . into the Roma Hotel. (*Well where else are they gonna take me*?) Once he was back in his room he was surprised further by attention from two doctors and a stay-over nurse who had a radiant smile. "Hey, this is all right!" he said to her, and she beamed upon him and tittered.

Soon came the visitors. Debbie Kassenbaum showed up to explain to Charlie that he'd been arrested erroneously; they must have mistaken him for someone else. She was quite sure that was what had happened, she said, and Charlie nodded affirmatively, managed a little grin, and could say nothing in response. But he was sure that was not what had happened. Better not to roil the waters, though, he decided. Don't shake up Debbie, the person who'd helped save his bacon when he was hanging from that ceiling pipe. Try to get on a plane as soon as possible.

Somewhat to Charlie's distress, Debbie informed him that she had already telephoned Marie who would likely arrive in Taiwan late the next day. Marie's presence was bound to be very beneficial, Debbie averred with a broad smile. "I bet she can clarify something for me," Debbie added levelly.

Charlie had no inkling of what she meant, but if he had pressed her to explain her last remark, she would have allowed that she wondered whether Charlie—and Marie—had a "singular relationship" with General Chang K'ung. If they were his "allies under the skin," she needed to know so she could assist Chang effectively.

"Take care," Debbie said, and she was gone.

After a late lunch of broth and steamed rice, just before Charlie dropped into sleep Hsiu-fen Wu arrived. In his drowsy state Charlie found himself barely able to respond to her, let alone comprehend all that she said to him in her charmingly accented, often humorous way of speaking.

Mainly she was solicitous of Charlie's well-being. Was he comfortable? Did he need or want anything? ("Anything! I will get it, only for you.") She, too, mentioned "mistaken arrest," although how she had learned of it Charlie never knew. Charlie did register her real concern about him: it leapt out of her lovely black eyes and it palpably touched him through her voice tones. ("By God, we are on the same wave length," Charlie distinctly told himself.) Still, he was glad she didn't stay long.

Hsiu-fen Wu also left Charlie with a cryptic statement. She glanced about the room, put her arms across his shoulders, and said very softly: "Taiwan thanks you for courage. Please know this." To which Charlie could only crack a smile. He gave her a little wave as she walked away, trailing an invisible connection between them.

With sedatives after bland meals, it seemed to Charlie that only a few hours had passed before Marie walked through the door. Charlie was drifting in a theta-wave pattern, reluctant to go to sleep again because his dreams were usually so chaotic and supra-amazing. When he opened his eyes and beheld Marie's face coming close to him, reality had never looked so good.

"Hello, tiger," she said.

Charlie murmured something unintelligible. Then he said, "Me Charlie; you, Marie."

Marie had nothing profound to say, nor would she leave Charlie alone for more than a few minutes at a time. As soon as he was lucid Charlie could see the anguish staining his wife's soul. "It was all a huge mistake," he told her regarding his recent travail, to which she replied that Debbie had also said that. "You know I believe I made over $3,000 yesterday," Charlie tried to say insouciantly regarding the terms of his errand to Taipei, to which Marie rejoined, "You really are underpaid."

Only the next day when he and Marie were at the airport waiting to board their flight did Charlie feel at liberty to comment that he didn't understand what had happened to him. Nor did he know what had actually caused his life to be saved. Marie registered that, and when they were airborne they discussed it at some length, which was helpful preparation for Charlie who would have a lot to explain at his imminent debriefings.

"Debbie Kassenbaum says Taiwanese counterintelligence might have been suspecting you of helping some cult or some kind of subversive conspiracy," Marie said.

"I don't see why. All I did was follow orders; including hers," Charlie replied.

"Something covert must be going on."

"You mean weird. I never did anything that was…untoward, or even unexpected. You talked to Debbie Kassenbaum?"

"Oh, yeah. She showed up at the hotel twice after I got there. Plus she called me up. You were probably sleeping or in the bathroom every time. She brought us that box of chocolates you pigged out on."

"Ah," said Charlie. "Hey, I'm injured; remember. My body needs calories. [Beat.] Who brought that neat bunch of flowers you wound up giving to the nurse?"

"Oh, they were left by that lovely Mandarin woman we met before, the one who works for a crackerjack general. Suzi Wu. She came by yesterday when you were asleep. She seems to regard you as some kind of hero."

"I don't see why. I only did what I was instructed to do, including by Debbie. I tell you, this whole thing is one big horrific puzzle; more so by the moment. Uh, Suzi Wu is not Mandarin. She's a native Taiwanese. Comes from a very prominent family."

Marie found those last facts interesting. ("Does she actually use Taiwanese?" "Is her family mercantile or agricultural, or what?") But that was in passing. Of more immediate concern was Debbie Kassenbaum's connections.

"We better not trust that chick anymore," Marie declared.

"How's that?" The word "chick" had alerted Charlie to something being amiss.

Marie said that she intuited from remarks Debbie had dropped that the darling Ms.Kassenbaum might be somehow connected to a group or organization entirely outside the pale of her official capacity at the U.S. mission. Something potent, and maybe sinister, was gestating under cover in Taiwan. "We *do not* want to get too close to whatever it is," Marie concluded. "Definitely not."

"I've gotten more than close to something sinister goin' on," Charlie said as he tried to make a fist with his right hand, which he couldn't because of the cast from his elbow to palm. "Tell me more about Debbie," Charlie added. "What did she say?"

"She asked me a couple of weird questions about you and me somehow helping 'the cause,'" Marie said. "That's what got me suspicious. I mean, what 'cause'? How did we help it? She seems to want something from us, too, but she seemed to be . . . I don't know . . . acting on someone else's behalf. So who is that?"

Charlie told Marie about the woman's voice he'd heard when he was hanging from a ceiling pipe in the cellar at the former military-police headquarters in Taipei. (Of course he spoke in generalities or outright lied to omit details Marie didn't need to know.) The voice caused him a distinct mental picture of Debbie Kassenbaum, he related. Maybe he had actually seen her there. What the woman's voice said was most enigmatic: something about himself being "one of us."

"That computes, all right," Marie said. "I bet she's into something that's . . . well, that's not supposed to be going down." Marie pondered briefly then declared: "But we can't prove a damned thing about any kind of sedition, and we don't want any more risks. We are hereby disengaging ourselves."

Charlie, of course, concurred. "Somehow I get the impression sweet Debbie likes you," he added, "if you know what I mean."

"Yeah, well, that might be going on, too."

*

As though to substantiate Marie, at that very moment back in Taipei Debbie was taking sick leave from her job although she wasn't sick yet, at least not physically.

"I did it again," she chastised herself. "I let that fine hunk of a woman slip away from me—and with her man mostly intact yet!" She loosened a groan of anger mingled with frustration. Compounding her frustration was her failure to learn why Marie and Charlie seemed willing to help General Chang's Cause. All Debbie had managed to do in Marie's presence was make herself look "flaky," as some people would say. And let herself get really frustrated.

"God damn!" she said to the universe.

In the Wilshire Boulevard Federal Building in West Los Angeles a half-dozen very-senior intelligence officers struggled to understand how Charlie had managed to turn over M-11 guidance-control units to somebody totally unknown.

"I gave the stuff to Mr. Cheng, Tsai-jing Cheng," Charlie told them over and over.

Right.

"Mr. Cheng never received them," they told Charlie over and over, along with the fact that the loss was costly and potentially perilous. (Only then did Charlie learn conclusively that he'd been involved in a ballistic-missile technology transfer, and only months later did he read that selling the M-11 was outlawed by international accords.) Debbie Kassenbaum had more than covered her own involvement in this travesty. Not a scintilla of a hint existed that she had set up Charlie to take the blame for a mission totally miscarried, let alone that she'd caused it to miscarry. And the real Tsai-jing Cheng never learned what had transpired in his name during his absence from Taiwan.

"Better heal up that broken wing," an operations officer told Charlie, who was asked some routine questions and dismissed. In the process they paid him 6,600 dollars cash as promised.

"I've earned this," was Charlie's only audible comment on the matter.

"I'm sure he's earned every cent, but somehow he screwed up big-time," one of the debriefers remarked as soon as Charlie closed the door when he left.

"It might not have been his fault," another commented.

A consensus arose: the debacle might not have been Charlie's fault.

"We're still gonna need him," somebody asserted.

"We certainly need his wife and her language skills," someone else said.

Later, via FAX, a consensus recommended to Ray Rugowski in Houston that Charlie and Marie get an easy mission after Charlie's arm healed. Despite repeated requests for Marie's services from a DIA-operations station chief in Costa Rica, no errands would be available for Charlie or Marie until three months later, which was fine with them.

*

At Los Angeles International Airport on their way home after the Taiwan fiasco, amid throngs of people striding in the opposite direction a person fetched Charlie's then Marie's eye: a strongly rounded male figure in black, wearing sunglasses. Charlie pointed at him, Marie nodded: *Of course!* There's that same missionary priest again. At the moment he appeared lost in abstraction as he trundled off.

"Boy, it really is a small world, huh?" Marie said.

Chapter 9

Could it be that he—so often the observer—was himself under scrutiny on the airport-terminal concourse here in familiar Los Angeles? Father Bobby Jay Nobles distinctly felt being watched by someone he knew. But that hardly mattered. No, he told himself, as with everything else he could think of, in actuality it didn't matter at all.

Only some basic pleasures had motivated Father Jay to live and work from day to day for the last thirty-five years, and now they were wearing thin. I just need to recharge again, he told himself several times recently. That's why he'd returned stateside, he reminded himself: to rest.

His overriding problem, he was sure, was being too acutely aware of illusions that pervaded, really, all human experience. Everything he did, he was convinced, was either illusory or illusion-based. That conviction of awareness progressively eroded his effectiveness in the roles he filled. Unless he took a vacation soon, he'd be liable to overlook (even cause) dangers to people who depended on him. I might be a burnt-out case, but I've always worked around that, he sometimes coached himself.

After he would brief his Department of Defense employers on several matters, Father Jay would advise them of his intention to take a hiatus. (This was a need that recurred every few years or so.) They might even suggest he do something specific that would be recreational for him. Except for eating, sailing, rowing, and getting massaged regularly by naked Asiatic girls, nothing really appealed to Father Jay anymore as something he wanted to do. And except for second-hand knowledge he'd gained about a clandestine movement in Taiwan to establish a totally new political and ideological power on the world stage, he could think of nothing that stirred his imagination.

Father Jay acknowledged that he owed his fascination with that movement to the female covert operative in Taipei, the American with the Jewish name and eyes of a zealot. ("Yes!" Ms. Kassenbaum had said. "A country, an actual country, based on a synergy of Chinese values—some of which came from India back about the time of the Pharaohs—and, yes, some Western values chosen very carefully. It's not only possible, I'd say it's, well, *imminent*.") Father Jay had perceived the cynosure of Debbie's zeal to be General Chang K'ung, whom Father Jay himself admired. Before long he had apprehended that Chang commanded a small but formidable cadre of devotees.

And on the day he met and talked with General Chang's civilian adjunct, the humorously self-deprecating lady with the astonishing legs and heart-breakingly lovely face, he knew he regarded himself as a potential acolyte of whatever might be developing under Chang's aegis. If you can capture somebody's imagination or stroke his gonads just so, you can have his soul, Father Jay noted to himself on occasion. Thus he was amenable to doing whatever might be asked of him by anyone connected to Chang.

But first Father Jay would go to Baltimore to meet with his superiors in the Missionary Oblates, after which he planned to visit Rosslyn, Virginia, where a certain U.S. intelligence-using agency occupied office space. After that his *tabula* looked *rasa*, and he hoped to keep it that way because an easy agendum in itself could be energizing.

July 15, 1991
Mount Lavinia, Sri Lanka

"Y' know, I bet a person can really get off living in a place like this," Charlie remarked as he and Marie traversed the grounds of the beautiful hotel named for the mountain looming (it seemed) all around them. Where they walked, colors were primary but soft: mainly green and blue, with sprays of black and blocks of white (the latter two from tree wood and the stucco hotel walls). The land emanated something Edenistic.

"It is delightful once you get away from people pissing in the streets and the river," Marie said. "We'd better stick to the script."

They didn't know why this place had been selected as a "site," and they would never have violated the dicta of good form by asking. Two years before, they had been flown from Costa Rica to Rome to attend a conference of neurologists (incredibly) and to perform a similar job. This site was "a piece of cake," as Marie put it, because the Mount Lavinia Hotel was isolated and not crowded; moreover this lazy part of the afternoon allowed them to work almost unimpeded.

In less than two hours, acting without haste, Charlie and Marie had surreptitiously placed small (but not state-of-the-art) electronic transmitters inside table lamps, drape rods, and lavatories in three designated suites and a conference room. The final, least-tricky aspect of their job was to cement a pair of cellulose "growths" to nearby trees, each wood lump containing a relay transmitter. This they had to do without attracting notice. About twenty minutes of strolling the hotel grounds, interspersed with a little tree climbing and tomfoolery by Charlie (abetted by Marie), resulted in the job being completed. They had only to return indoors and initiate testing the equipment.

"Well, that was easy enough," Charlie said with a half-smile when they'd finished.

Marie cut a throaty laugh. They themselves occupied a suite they'd equipped.

"The world is a dangerous place," Marie said as they returned to their room to refresh. "We'd better make sure those little things are turned on; you know, in case we need to be overheard."

Charlie had already busied himself opening a complimentary bottle of champagne. His "Heeh-heeh-heeh-heeh-heeh-heeh-*heeh*" was audible at several yards. He proceeded to pop the cork near a certain table lamp, then poured the wine into champagne flutes held right up next to the same lamp. He and Marie stood under one drape rod and drank with gusto and appropriate vocables. Eventually they went into the bathroom and—Z-i-i-*i-i-i-pp*!—each opened a zipper. Just for effect they did that again close to that same table lamp and drape rod. (*A-a-a-h-h-h*!) In short order, they killed their bottle of bubbly with plenty of noises in the process.

"Oh, that was so good."

"What you mean, 'was,' white man?"

Fff-*boof*!! Marie had seized and opened a new bottle.

"It's all right; we're on vacation now."

Several miles up in the sky a satellite received and relayed distinct little sounds of fizzing liquid.

"Here's lookin' at you, dear."

"*Ahhh*!"

"A-h-h-h-h . . . ."

Standing next to that particular table lamp and under a certain drape rod, they drank deliberately for a while, overtly relishing every sip.

"Oh-oh," Charlie said. "I don't think we can turn those little things off."

"Hee-hee-hee! There's no way we can turn 'em off!"

"Hee-hee-hee-hee-hee!"

A bit later, beyond a continent and ocean, Marie was heard to remark, "You know, dear, I believe the path of *real love* is paved with all kinds of good yucks. Pretty much like now." And Charlie responded that he was utterly grateful to be alive to hear those yucks.

And later yet, vocal sounds of intolerable ecstasy were broadcast through a "bugged" table lamp, and to someone listening via satellite several thousand miles away, those sounds might have been deemed mere distortions. The level of intensity was simply too shocking.

Otherwise the Sri Lanka errand was remarkable because during an evening outing alone using the hotel Jeep, Charlie walked a little way off the road near the base of Mount Lavinia to scrutinize a growth of straight-up trees, and from dense underbrush about ten yards away he distinctly heard a very, very deep snarl followed by an impossibly long and sibilant inhalation (after which he couldn't recall getting back into the Jeep and putting it in gear); also because when Marie and Charlie toured Arthur C. Clarke University in Colombo they attended a lecture by a famous Indian-British novelist whom Marie deemed as "the real thing" and who quietly declared that he would continue writing about humanity as truthfully as he could until someone carried out the death sentence delivered against him by certain Muslim clerics.

One oddly remarkable development occurred as Charlie and Marie were being scanned with metal detectors outside the university auditorium before the novelist's talk: They spotted the back of someone so familiar that they froze in surprise. A moment later Father Jay tore a look behind himself, met their eyes, and smiled. To their additional surprise, he reversed his direction and with alacrity strode to join them.

After they'd exchanged handshakes, exclamations, et al, Father Jay declared, "I've been looking for you, believe it or not, although I'd never expected to meet you here."

Marie simply stared at him.

"You've been looking for *us*, sir?" Charlie said.

"Oh, yes. You see, I'm on vacation now, so I'm a little bit out of the loop. In fact I'm on my way to India. Just to have a little look-see." His shoulders raised, eyes widened humorously. "I've never been there, would you believe!"

I wonder what shade of green that is, Marie thought, transfixed by those eyes.

At this same moment Charlie thought—with an inward shudder—that he'd been checked out by eyes of maybe that same color at Mount Lavinia last evening.

Father Jay dropped a few dry remarks about building Christian missions amidst the very cradles of ancient religions and cultures, and "perhaps colonizing those wastelands in case they've got something we can use." Then he went on to relate how a few days prior to his holiday he'd made routine telephone calls to his order's missions in the Far East, and that's when he learned: "A very special person back in Taiwan had been trying to contact me, so she could find out how she might get a hold of you all."

Marie and Charlie presumed that person to be Debbie Kassenbaum, but she could probably contact them at will. "I'm speaking," Father Jay explained, "of that utterly charming Taiwanese lady who works for General Chang K'ung."

Beat. "What do you reckon she wants?" Charlie said.

"Search me," said Father Jay, who had his suspicions in this matter, thanks to Ms. Kassenbaum, but chose to keep them buried. "Let me give you her telephone numbers. You can call her up whenever you choose."

Thus he did, and thus Charlie and Marie found themselves with direct access (office and home phone numbers) to the day-to-day assistant to the person conceivably capable of repelling military invasion by Communist Chinese masses.

"We're honored, I guess," Marie said while Charlie (nodding concurrence) slid the folded slip of paper into his wallet.

"I think I would be," Father Jay said.

Charlie and Marie were lecture-bound.

"Have a jolly good time in In-jya," Marie said.

"Sir, I'm confident we'll be seein' you," Charlie said.

"But of course," said Father Jay, giving each a token hug.

Hours later, in a taxi going to the airport, Marie remarked that Father Jay emanated something she didn't dislike, but she distrusted it. "I couldn't help intuiting that here's a person who's missing something, something central. And he knows it."

"*Hmmpnh*. For what it's worth, at least a couple times I've gotten the impression he's . . . kind of like an onion," Charlie said.

Marie appreciated the comparison. "That's a notion upon which a person can meditate fruitfully," she said.

*

On the flight to Heathrow Airport en route home Marie raised the subject: Would they call the Taiwan telephone numbers Father Jay had provided? Charlie said he didn't know why not, but he felt chary about doing it. Marie said she felt likewise.

"I don't know whether to trust that lady or not," Marie said regarding Hsiu-fen Wu. "At least you do."

"Yeah, I guess she's trustworthy," Charlie said. "But, then, I'm not a woman."

That gave Marie pause, but she forged on: "Something's going on over there. Whatever it is, we don't want to know about it. I mean, why? We won't let ourselves get involved in Chinese affairs. Right?"

"Yeah, right. But there's some reason for those phone numbers coming our way."

And so they would telephone Ms. Wu and find out why she wanted to contact them. Both knew they had to do it.

*　　　　　　　*　　　　　　　*

Of course, the human mind needs to be stopped sometimes, but without going unconscious. Charlie was fairly adept at doing this because he had had plenty of practice in meditating. Marie had gotten less practice but she had developed her own ways of accomplishing more or less the same thing; she could suspend her mind and still be aware of only herself in the moment.

A major reason for doing this is to allow recent stimuli that a person experiences to be internalized and not simply erased by successive layers of living. Then peak experiences are less apt to be wasted. A main reason for humans to exist is to have peak experiences, which can be useful in looking beyond so-called reality.

Thus by this stage in their Lives both Charlie and Marie had learned to make sure that important things were kept simple as bedrock. For example: Living is best at its most intense, and it begs to be shared. Mutuality is prerequisite to Living well. By the way, I myself have seen scant evidence of this to the contrary.

I bring all this up to be helpful and to let you know that I have not forgotten you.

*   *   *

July 19, 1991
St. Petersburg, Russia
In their cluttered bedroom of the flat they had been so fortunate to lease upon their latest homecoming to dear St. Petersburg, Tatyana Platonov had locked the door, drawn the shades, and laid open a crate of books before she felt ready. Quickly she removed her shapeless dress. Feeling as she looked—oddly bulky—she pulled back the bedclothes and stood on the bed, just in case. What Americans call "super-cautious": I call this paranoia with method, she thought. If she dropped something now she'd be more apt to spot it on the bed; if necessary she could hide things under the blanket and shawl.

Tatyana could restrain herself no longer. She pulled off her underwear and let it drop next to her feet atop the bed, then she sat down and extricated five linen packets which had been padding her underclothes to make her bulge beyond belief in every direction. She didn't have to count the contents of those packets—that she had done several times in a hotel room in Singapore—but she did want to feel some of the contents. Which she did with great deliberation, her fingertips rubbing the edges and ends of no fewer than a dozen hundred-dollar bills, American money. She had brought home two hundred of those bills as a down payment.

"A-h-h-h-ha-ha! *Weeekh!*" Just like a silly bourgeois girl, she thought dreamily. But surely, she owed herself a great deal of self-indulgence. Over the past three months, while almost recklessly exploiting Andrei's position and access to facilities, she and three associates had managed to expropriate over twenty kilos, just under fifty pounds, of actual plutonium 239 from the former Soviet arsenal in Kazakhstan. Doing that had seemed to entail almost no problems, although they were under pressure to remove the material as quickly as they could before two well-known gangs of thugs took it. She had only to pay off her accomplices with the good-faith money she'd been paid in Singapore.

Her problems began after she had secured the plutonium in Andrei's laboratory. First came Andrei's and her relocation to St. Petersburg after almost ten years of fruitful exile in Kazakhstan. (*St. Petersburg in the spring! This must come from living right.*) Bringing the dangerous contraband home to St. Petersburg and then, with great anxiety, shipping it piecemeal to Singapore had indeed caused problems.

Did she expose herself and others to potentially lethal doses of radioactivity? Not if she took certain precautions and used cases lined with lead, Andrei had told her. (How does one acquire small lead-lined cases? How thick must the lining be? Where does one find equipment for safely transferring fissionable material from one container to another? Even Andrei had been unsure about these things.) Might the mobsters have learned that weapons-grade plutonium was in Tatyana's and Andrei's possession, or might the KGB, which still existed and had a proper role to play in this affair, suddenly come after them? Maybe. And then perhaps the biggest question: how safe was the address provided to Tatyana to which she had shipped six densely-heavy parcels? Tatyana had also to face the impossible matter of raising travel funds so she could go to Singapore, and then she'd had to leave Andrei for four days.

But now she felt comfortable in trusting the two Chinese purchasers whom she had gone to meet in Singapore. Arranging the meeting—a clandestine affair in a German-owned hotel—had been her idea and required force of personality and charm to effectuate. By the time they shook hands and parted, all three principals appeared to be satisfied with their relationship. Except for one thing, and so far as Tatyana knew it lay solely with her: the impassive and chilling intensity of that aristocratic megalomaniac whom she took to be from Taiwan caused her frissons of fear even now. True, he had shown her unfailing politeness and he had charmed her by being dashing and disarming at the same time. That was only his facade. Months later an image would occur to her: to be regarded at close range by that man was almost like being fixed on by . . . by a cobra.

*

While Tatyana hid her hard currency in a crate of books, on the third floor of a venerable Baroque stone edifice just beyond the neighborhood in which the Platonovs lived, Andrei Platonov was busy fulfilling his responsibilities as a member of the physics faculty at the University of St. Petersburg. This involved doing some teaching, yes—occasionally even on a high level—but mostly it required astute paper massaging. Foremost, Andrei had to justify both his proposed research projects (all related to cold fusion) and his faculty position, which carried a stipend perhaps sufficient to sustain a medium-sized dog. (At least his and Tatyana's tax liability was minimal, provided no governmental agency learned of their part-time employments.)

Taking a break to stroll about the old corridors on the third floor (perhaps to munch peanuts and raisins he'd acquired through bartering), Andrei wondered whether Tatyana had returned yet from her recent junket to—of all places—Singapore. Why Singapore, of course he had asked her, especially in light of the difficulties she had surmounted to finance the trip. In effect she'd requested he not ask her again. As soon as she could she would surely tell him everything, and that referred to not only her trip but other things in which she was involved, such as—most likely—disposing of the weapons-grade plutonium which Andrei himself had assisted her in "acquiring" in Kazakhstan.

Yes, he had rendered her nominal assistance, which turned out to be crucial. No, except for Sergei, his oldest and most constant friend, he had never learned the names of her accomplices in diverting nearly two dozen kilos of plutonium 239 from that Soviet arsenal to Andrei's laboratory facility. Surely Andrei knew some of Tatyana's designs: "Build for me a prototype of a small nuclear bomb," she had requested of him as they walked that snowy street in Alma-Ata. "Presume that you would have the necessary materials." And so he had done that, except for devising the detonator for which he had several options depending on how the bomb was to be used. Andrei often reflected he was fortunate this affair caused him paroxysms of anxiety only sometimes.

Eventually, after they'd returned to beautiful St. Petersburg, Andrei went to visit a former colleague who had given up science to work as a building-maintenance "engineer" in a modern industrial plant. (He needed to make more money.) That was when Andrei was struck with an idea for a much different design for small nuclear bombs, and thus how to best detonate them.

"What is that?" Andrei had asked his friend as they surveyed equipment necessary to keep the plant functional.

"Oh, that's a heating boiler," his friend replied. "We have a series of them."

"I know that," Andrei said. "What is this?" And he put his hand upon a bulbous cast-aluminum fixture that joined three feeder pipes going to the boiler about four feet off the floor. Gracefully rounded and painted black, the fixture might be regarded as a basic specimen of "mechanical art" (terms Andrei's friend liked to use); Andrei estimated its size to be about twenty-five percent wider across than an American football. Attached to it was a square plastic control case with an electrical conduit going into it. If the control case were empty, it might conceal a telephone pager, what Americans called a "beeper."

"Oh. That is a water regulator," his friend replied. "But the correct nomenclature, I think, is 'low-water cut-off valve.' Strictly a mechanical device; nothing profound."

"Ah," uttered Andrei, "I like it!"

Heh-heh-heh, Andrei thought as he finished strolling the musty corridors outside his office. By using just the shell of that industrial-sized water regulator, and the control case attached to it, he could devise a nuclear charge so cleverly functional that Tatyana would not only be proud of her scientist-turned-practical-mechanic, she could—if she were so inclined—demand the highest price for one if it incorporated plutonium 239. Andrei thus had to resolve a deep and treacherous dilemma, which now impelled him to retreat to seclusion.

*

Motionless at his desk, Andrei found himself doing something that would have been anomalous to his character even when he had been defeated by the full weight of the People's Soviet, plus ill health, desertion by friends and colleagues, estrangement from his children, and physical deprivation: He did a fatalistic little shrug. For the time being, he resolved, he would simply be the polestar of his wife's affections; everything else had to be relatively insignificant. To keep his status in Tatyana's eyes and heart he would do . . . anything. *Truly, anything.*

Abstractedly, Andrei scrawled notes legible only to himself: "Beryllium—only for triggering mechanism / no." "Cesium-137 = radioactive catalyst—Yes. Try it." (My problem is the reaction, he thought. Light will do the job if it is lasered; note that photochemical reaction requires light to be absorbed. Therefore a photocatalyst will be required.) Some of this was outside his bailiwick. He was a theoretical physicist—ah, yes—and a philosopher and fighter and lover (even despite what often felt like a dentist's drill going through his hip, among other afflictions). He was not an accomplished chemist. Nor a tinkerer. But he had made a prototype that would have worked, and now he'd improve upon it by using the shell of a boiler water valve as the casing, his own modification of a Japanese-made laser for the trigger, and (heh-heh-heh) a telephone pager to activate the laser.

Andrei wrote "magnesium?" on his notepad and promptly marked it out. (That was stupid.) Then he inscribed "ZIRCONIUM" in upper-case Roman letters. He would need some of that element to alloy the plutonium, especially high-grade plutonium.

I must find out: how much alloy will be required for two kilos of 239? In his mind's ear Andrei could hear himself singing out: "Oh, Ta-*tyahh*-na! Would you get a few grams of zirconium for me, please. We need it quickly!" And of course she would respond with, "Yes, yes; consider it done!"

(That coming evening, at home, this scenario actually happened. A week later Andrei had his zirconium which, Tatyana alleged, two unnamed contacts had "extracted" from the Institute of Physics and Power Engineering located about one hundred kilometers outside Moscow. "Were mobsters involved?" Andrei asked, and Tatyana averred they were unnecessary, for "things can simply disappear from anywhere" consequent to the power of money. Real money.)

Under "ZIRCONIUM" Andrei made another note: "Carbon-12. Pure—unnecessary?" he wrote in reference to an artificial diamond used as a kind of superconductor to transfer heat (or other types of charges). He truly hoped it would be unnecessary because it would be next to impossible to get, even for Tatyana and all her connections. But, will not a conduit in some form be necessary to maintain the reaction effectively? He would have to investigate that. Likely he would find other problems to solve and eliminate, any of which could catalyze new ones. Throughout his career Andrei maintained that his projects should be elegantly simple, devoid of excess technology.

Given that postulate, he had inferred that a charge constituted of a little less than two kilos of top-grade plutonium might be perfect for this project. It could vaporize perhaps a square mile of a city or military installation without causing Apocalypse. (*Heaven help me.*) Of course this caused him to address imponderable logistical questions, specifically how to ensure that the proper elements such as cesium-137, in the proper amounts, would be integrated in each of the final products.

In his mind's ear Andrei could hear himself singing out again: "Oh, Ta-*tyahh*-na! Can I go to wherever you shipped that plutonium so I can put your finished products together?" This would surely give her pause, for lack of money, let alone in amounts required to pay for long trips, was a true affliction they suffered every day.

Andrei felt his soul shrivel as he reflected that another pandemic affliction, one mostly peculiar to the twentieth century, was terrorism, which he defined as flagrant, intentional wrong-doing. And now Tatyana and he seemed bent on advancing it! *Even stupid, irrational young men know when they perpetrate evil, and here I am striving to provide them with means!* Thus he harbored a gossamer hope: somehow, he and Tatyana might yet avert fulfilling this project.

*

Two days after returning from Sri Lanka, following three instances of "telephone tag," Charlie made contact with Hsiu-fen Wu. The excitement he felt from this contact reached an intolerable pitch when she declared that she was asking a large favor of him.

Ms. Wu's younger brother and his "associate" (she used that term) were en route to Houston; probably they had already left Los Angeles by car. Both were graduate students, she said. They were intending to stop in Austin and they needed to make contact with people living and studying there. She had taken the liberty of advising them to contact Doctor Grumbles when they arrived. Would Charlie help them accomplish what they needed to do? Of course Charlie said he would, relieved by how easy this appeared—and disappointed by the mundaneness of it in ways he didn't want to admit. Late the next afternoon Marie telephoned Charlie at his clinic. "They're here," she said. She had already invited them to dinner and they had accepted her offer of basic accommodations for the night. Charlie would have to food-shop on his way home. "They like seafood and California wines," Marie advised him.

Thus Charlie came home to find two distinctly foreign young men in his house. He needed no time determining which one was Ricky Wu: the vaguely familiar-looking, cherubic fellow with the ready smile and bright black eyes and protruding middle (a physique very much unlike his sister's). Here was a man who enjoyed Life, Marie had decided. His associate, John Chen, looked ascetic and tough; he smiled rarely and appeared to be constantly holding himself in check. Charlie and Marie presumed that this was a man who considered himself on a mission.

The information these graduate students sought was of unexpected sorts. How long would it take to travel by car to and between certain U.S. cities (such as Dallas to St. Louis or Los Angeles to Seattle)? Some estimates were impossible for Marie and Charlie to make; plus neither could reckon how much time would be spent driving to the center of various cities. ("You don't just cruise into Manhattan or Boston," Marie said.) A big question: How would a person go about identifying photos of Chinese students enrolled at the University of Texas? Who would know how to match names with faces? Some questions were more prosaic: How can one avoid hassles in cashing checks? For Charlie and Marie the evening seemed long.

At 7:30 the next morning, after he'd made a brief telephone call (conducted entirely in Minnan), John Chen abruptly left with someone who showed up to get him. He barely said goodbye. Ricky Wu, all smiles and pleasantness, drove off for Houston immediately after breakfast. *Strange*, Marie thought.

While Marie was taking Julia to day care, Charlie got a telephone call . . . from Hsiu-fen Wu. He wasn't entirely surprised to hear her voice because he remembered informing her of his home telephone number two days before. She wanted to know what had transpired during her brother's visit and she wanted to express her gratitude to Charlie (and of course his wife) for assisting Ricky and "Lieutenant Chen." The first part of her call was business-like; the second part was friendly, engaging conversation.

When Marie returned a few minutes later, Charlie told her of the telephone call. A glance told him that her mind was busy synthesizing imponderables. After a moment, despite their running late in getting ready for work, Marie abruptly marshaled Charlie outside for a brief walk (just in case the walls or ceiling had ears). Between them they formed two conclusions before they returned:

"I think we've been assisting, in various little ways, some kind of underground opposition to the Kuomintang—well, now it's called the Taiwan 'Nationalist Government,'" Marie said. "A number of indicators are pointing that way."

Charlie's contribution to this was, "Let's hope that 'underground'—or whatever it might be—doesn't have ties with the Mainland. We don't need that kind of problem."

The other conclusion was less nebulous: "Do you feel kind of vulnerable now?" Marie asked. Charlie's contribution was that maybe they were lucky to be ignorant of whatever it was that had touched them. Marie had the final word on this subject: "I bet it's something we'd be afraid of, if we knew what it is."

****

From his balcony that gave onto a magical view of San Jose about three miles to the south, Sam Wallaby gazed at various shades of green blessing him from many levels all the way across his field of vision. He saw more than green: Bromeliads and three distinctly different kinds of white flowers splashed themselves on the welter of greens in unexpected places. As expected, something zestful charged the air. Sam loved being here, and in his heart he knew—actually knew—that Marie Overstreet would love it also. That realization alone had been sufficient cause to maintain his residence in Costa Rica even when he'd been rotated to other duty stations.

As DIA Station Chief Sam expected another full year in Costa Rica before he'd rotate out again. If he could stay longer he would. At first opportunity he'd contact Ms. Kassenbaum in Taiwan to learn how she had managed to retain her post for at least a few years. Right now, he'd just let himself ponder what he lacked, which was not much.

Twice married and divorced with no regrets about either, he had twice experienced fatherhood and done a good job of it. To him, "Success" in working for the Agency could be gauged by whether he'd made a beneficial difference in the lives of people his work affected; also by how much pleasure he derived, day to day, from his life as a covert-operations officer usually stationed abroad. Thus far in his twenty-four-year career, the final analysis for both those criteria was decidedly positive and plenty, but weighted a bit toward the enjoyment factor. Knowledge and understanding of human concerns Sam valued highly, and he strove to command his share. Evidence that he had done that, he thought, was the fact that he was usually happy.

But an internalized image of Marie Overstreet rose into his conscious and came into focus. Sam let it dominate his thoughts for several moments as he gazed at his vista. No doubt her husband's an okay guy but— But what? Yes! She needs a man who's adventuresome and unpredictable like me. She needs specifically me because I'll get her off like she's a machine gun.

Sam held onto the latter notion for several seconds. *Focus. Focus*: What would it take to make that possible? Maybe just one day. H-m-m. Use a little imagination. After a while Sam determined that if Marie would spend one day with only him, she would understand why he knew so many things about her, and one of the main things was that she needed to know a great deal about *him*. Once that happened, doors would fly open.

First things first, Sam told himself. One day seemed a modest objective. Surely he could arrange for that. He stepped into the second-floor living room of his "villa" and mixed a rum drink using grenadine and papaya juice so it would hold sunset colors. As he did that he mentally reviewed Agency "action items" in Central America designated for the next fiscal quarter, and almost unvolitionally he took up his telephone and called the homes of two officers who spent their work days in Langley and Rosslyn, Virginia. Sam had operational information to convey and, in return for it, a request.

When he concluded his second telephone call, Sam almost whooped with jubilation. *Oh-ho yes, my day is coming*. He would likely get the mission assistance he desired: Charlie and Marie would be asked to run a routine errand from San Jose to Bolivia and Peru and back. The job called for two people to do it even though it was easy and probably devoid of danger. And if Charlie were specifically designated to complete part of the mission in Houston—and connections between Agency contacts in Lima were to be out of synchronicity just a little bit, and thus (alas) delayed—Charlie might spend an evening and night alone in Lima and return directly to Houston, with nobody to blame for the gaffe except some DoD clerk for entering a wrong digit on a data sheet that was already electronically corrected.

Wide-eyed, Sam reviewed his scenario and found it seamless. He almost sang out, *I'm gonna have my day, yes*, I will! In that event, all kinds of preparations had to be made, almost all of them at his home. He tried to throttle down his imagination from overdrive. His heart was racing. Although he wanted to quash it, Sam cut a laugh that sounded demonic.

*

What Sam had projected for Marie and Charlie happened readily. After they met him for instructions and materials in San Jose, and then joined an American economy-tour which took them to the dazzling highland city of Sucre, Bolivia, where they made a "product exchange," the tour took them to Lima, Peru.

There a contact failed to materialize; Charlie had to sign off the tour and stay the night in Lima to complete assigned procedures the next day. Marie and her fellow tourists circled back to Costa Rica. She and Charlie expected to meet in Houston in about thirty-six hours. In San Jose she met Sam Wallaby outside the U.S. Consulate and told him what had happened.

"Oh," he said, and gestured toward a taxi instead of escorting her inside.

Marie regarded Sam quizzically.

"You are hereby debriefed," he told her.

Marie was charmed. "Where are we going?" she asked.

"Well, for openers I thought we'd go to your hotel room. It's a nice one, in Charlie's name. You can check in."

Marie was not about to demur. In the taxi en route to Hotel La Reyna she remarked about her last "errand" being part of a recent phenomenon: in the Sucre marketplace and at the Lima Sheraton neither she nor Charlie had ever gotten the sense they were under surveillance. She figured this was because the "Cold War" had ended.

"The times—they are a-changing," Marie commented.

Sam pondered that. He responded, "It's sure time for some changes."

Marie made telephone contact with Charlie shortly after she checked into the room in the small hotel Sam had found for her (and ostensibly Charlie). As she and Charlie outlined pending logistics, she noticed a floral bouquet and magnum of champagne set on an end table. And suddenly one thing else: *musicians* were playing local ballads just outside her door.

Abruptly the door came partly open and Sam stood at the doorway, backed by a string quartet augmented by a trumpet. "Look what I found!" Sam said, grinning. Then: "Oh! Sorry. I didn't realize you were on the phone."

But the music continued. Delighted, Marie told Charlie what was happening. In a few moments the band found their groove; telephone conversation was cut short.

"I thought, surely you jest," Marie said as she gazed at city outskirts through the windows of Sam's Land Rover.

"Oh, I never kid about dinner," Sam responded, peering over his steering wheel. "You need good food. Dinner at my house will be good and good for you. You'll be back at the hotel in two hours, three hours tops. Too bad your husband—uh, Charlie—can't be here."

Marie felt a heady sense of well-being after sharing the magnum of champagne with Sam in a party atmosphere with musical accompaniment and other hotel guests joining them at Sam's behest. Now they were headed to Sam's "casita" for a grilled swordfish dinner "by starlight," as Sam put it. "The key element in living well," he declared to her, "is not having a good housekeeper but a very good housekeeper."

"I wouldn't know," said Marie.

Sam resumed casually: "Being a good cook yourself makes for better dinners, especially when you have guests, so I always do the *piece de resistance*. Well, at least I put on the finishing touches."

During the rest of their twenty-five-minute drive they talked of many things and time flew for both. Mostly they talked about the key elements in Marie's Life, with Sam gently prompting her to open up about her aspirations and most heartfelt interests. The man really wanted to know, Marie determined, and Sam would have said she was right.

"What interests me most—intrigues me, actually—is the ultimate vision you might have for yourself and your time here on Earth," Sam averred. "Can you say what it is?"

"Making a difference," Marie responded instantly. "Not having lived in vain."

They talked about the fine points of how that aspiration might have animated Marie's Life. After several minutes Sam said, "And here I was afraid you might be a frustrated blues singer or choreographer."

"Those would be real turn-ons, of course. Like practicing karate in a group. Uh, believe it or not, I own some really crafty handguns."

Sam laughed lightly. "I suppose I should have guessed," he said.

For Marie, conversation with Sam Wallaby was good and satisfying, although the dinner she ate took preeminence. Sam proved himself to be a man who clearly knew how to cook, cognizant of how to use butter and wine and simple flavorings to achieve just the right effect. "Oh, God!" she said ecstatically, and that was all she could say for a while because swordfish had never tasted that good to any human being. The fixings—all simple and wholesome—were likewise "just right."

"I'm deeply honored to benefit from all the art and craft you've expended here, Marie said, meaning every word of it. She saluted Sam and his jolly housekeeper with her flagon of white Beaujolais.

"My pleasure," Sam said, meaning it as well, "and I think I can speak for dear Consuela."

Consuela, Sam's housekeeper at work nearby, smiled beatifically upon Marie.

"Well, time to get going," Sam declared. "I said I'd get you back in about two hours. Let's see what the morrow brings."

"No rush. Let's walk around outside your 'casita' for a while," Marie said.

"Actually it's part of a condominium," Sam informed her. "It's a complex of houses scattered over a couple acres."

They proceeded to tour the grounds, with Marie occasionally taking hold of Sam's arm as they strolled about dark gardens and lawns, inhaling fragrances of Central America at night, avoiding walking under monkey-laden tree boughs. ("Those howlers are nasty critters," Sam advised Marie, "but, well, it's their land we're on.") Eventually, for Sam, way too soon, Sam drove Marie back to Hotel La Reyna, the interim again proving pleasant and interesting to both. When they arrived at the hotel Sam saw Marie into the main entrance and kissed her hand impulsively before they parted. He didn't want to appear gauche to Marie but he felt she'd be charmed if he overstepped the line just a bit, and he was right.

July 31, 1991
About four kilometers north of Puerto Quepos, Costa Rica

"The country here is fantastic even if you hated the ocean," Sam declared to Marie over his coffee cup. "I hope you come back here someday just to see it. I'm talking soon. Very, very soon. I'd love to show you all kinds of neat places."

While he and Marie ate breakfast alfresco Sam drew a crude map on a sheet of notebook paper on which he denoted his favorite Costa Rica attractions. Marie felt engaged by his genuine enthusiasm for the countryside. Consuela had turned out the variegated breakfast and taken it by taxi from Sam's townhouse to his seaside cabaña where he and Marie sat at a patio table and wolfed it down.

"Is this good, or what?" Sam said ingenuously, seemingly referring to the food, but intending his remark to cover everything they were experiencing thus far today.

Sam had brought Marie to this resort "just for the experience," and plainly he was enjoying it as much as he hoped she was. The morning was yet cool, the sky powder-blue; birds and flowers were going crazy. Fishing off the coast was exceptionally good this morning. "The fish are jumping into boats for the hell of it," Sam declared.

"I'm having a great time," Marie said. "You didn't have to do this."

Sam asked Marie what she had planned for this morning and she said that she would like to see some of this favorite spots nearby and then take an ocean swim.

"And maybe do some shopping?"

"And maybe do some shopping."

So they visited special sights and shops and swam hard in the ocean and afterwards ate seafood at a beachside restaurant that could serve no more than three tables of diners at a time. And of course they talked a great deal, mostly about matters central to both. Not surprising to both, their interests were basically similar.

After lunch, as they took a final stroll on the beach before going back, Marie again told Sam that she was having a fine time. Then she added, "It's hard for me to imagine somebody with free will choosing to leave here."

Sam chose to let those notions gestate. Eventually he responded, "I'm planning on taking early retirement . . . here."

"Really? When?"

"Oh, pretty soon. Maybe next year."

Marie simply focused her sight on the line formed by water rolling rhythmically onto wet sand. Sam glanced at her face to see this. *Ah-hah!* He smiled inwardly. *The seed is planted. Cultivate cultivate.* Sam's craggy features brightened and turned boyish, a mannerism which (he'd perceived) caused Marie to feel comfortable. Although Sam knew he was in decent physical condition, he suddenly resolved to get into the best physical shape of his life beginning that very day.

When they arrived back at his cabaña Sam mentioned that the stretch of beach there was good, but only a few kilometers north it was prettier and even more congenial "to human aspirations." He'd bought this place to be his hideaway close to the ocean.

"I didn't know foreign nationals could buy real estate here," Marie said.

"I've been lucky; I won't bore you with details. I have clear title to this piece of heaven. I paid off my townhouse, but the title is in joint tenancy."

"A former wife?"

"Current business partners."

Offhandedly Sam mentioned having "a couple-few business interests" in country, but that was a subject unworthy of discussion. His professed main concern: returning Marie to her hotel room so that she could take her time getting ready to go back home. And that was what they focused on doing over the next two-plus hours. In the process Sam caught himself thinking that if he could not turn this vibrant woman into his lover someday, at least he would have made a good friend, although he really had *enough* friends.

By late afternoon, while he drove Marie from her hotel to the airport, Sam declared, "Just remember you've got a home here whenever you want it." He felt gratified that Marie fell silent, for he knew she was trying to envision the prospect of Costa Rica as her home.

At the terminal entrance Sam entrusted his beautiful silver-gray Saab to a valet so he could escort Marie inside.

"You don't have to do this," Marie said.

"Ah, but I want to! After we check you in let's try the pizza they sell here."

The man had definite charms.

A short time later they availed themselves shamelessly of various local refreshments including an odd cheesy pizza made and sold by an enterprising young man whose mother happened to be Consuela, Sam's housekeeper. Marie felt disarmed by the connections, and by the warmth with which people invariably regarded Sam. She noted the warmth was reciprocal.

Her mouth full of pizza, Marie remarked, "I wish Charlie'd been able to see the things I saw today." She said this apparently apropos of nothing.

"Yes, I wish he had," Sam distinctly heard himself say.

At that moment Sam admitted to himself that he felt some qualms about his role in engineering Charlie's absence. They were not deep qualms, but they disturbed him. Marie noticed the shadow over his mien. There was a brief, enigmatic silence.

"A penny for your thoughts," Marie said.

"Oh! Sorry." Sam graced her with his easy smile.

That was when Marie realized they were about to become part of a threesome: piercing green eyes beamed on them from a beefy face set atop a burly body clad in black, with a Roman collar peculiar to Catholic priests. Sam turned to behold Father Jay Nobles approaching.

"Ah, padre!" Sam said.

A lifelong agnostic more than slightly hostile toward all religions, Sam had been recently feeling his viewpoint softening. He had to regard Father Nobles amicably if only because the priest had been useful, sometimes critically useful, to not only the CIA and DIA but to various other U.S. intelligence services for at least twenty years. He seemed to do this selflessly; any remuneration he was due went directly to his oblate order.

Felicitations were exchanged; someone ventured, "It really is a small world"; and perfunctory questions were posed. Father Jay revealed simply that he was en route to Colombia; he'd stopped over in San Jose specifically to elicit help from Sam Wallaby on fairly crucial business.

So much for any final magical moments Sam might have envisioned between himself and Marie. He perceived Father Jay's eyes glimmer preternaturally when they focused on Marie. In short order the trio broke up: Marie headed for the gate, Sam and Father Jay headed for the U.S. Consulate. Before they departed the concourse Marie thanked Sam warmly one more time for his attentions. She extended her hand, which he took deliberately and kissed.

"I loved every moment," he said evenly. "I'll be seeing you, I hope soon."

None of the three doubted his statements. As he strode off, Sam found himself already trying to feature how he would accomplish statement number two. One thing was for sure: *all's fair in love and war*, he heard his mind declaim to the universe.

Chapter 10

July 4, 1992
St. Petersburg, Russia

By now, the major problem confronting the Platonovs was acquiring the lasers necessary to cause neutrons to penetrate plutonium and trigger a chain-reaction explosion. Moreover, those lasers had to be small enough for each to fit inside the shell of a water regulator for industrial boilers, on top the plutonium payload that would be encased by lead. Complicating things further, Andrei insisted on Japanese-made lasers.

Risking their freedom and Andrei's reputation, Andrei and Tatyana actually pilfered two model lasers, one from an industry exposition held in Gorky, some distance away, the other from a display at a technical institute in Petersburg, because they had to test at least two models and compare how they functioned before committing to a purchase. They finally lighted on the Sanyo model, for it was smaller and less costly.

Soon afterwards they found that purchasing ten Sanyo lasers would have been prohibitively expensive. But did they have to be purchased? Couldn't Andrei build his own? Actually, the year before, he had devised a workable gas laser based on a pair of Japanese models. His version would have been unusable for Tatyana's purpose, though, because it was too boxy.

Their main laser requirement was that it emit a beam of a wavelength that carried sufficient velocity to point of impact. Then of course it had to be reliable. Andrei simply didn't have available the basic materials to make ten of them. And since he was neither an engineer nor craftsman, he didn't have the skill to design and then fabricate a laser that would be compact enough to fit inside the space allowed. Despite being mathematically gifted, Andrei was so overwhelmed by the high number of rubles required to buy ten usable lasers that he resorted to a calculator to arrive at a valid figure.

"Beyond 100 million I lose track!" he said to his wife without exaggerating.

"Well, then, we shall have to steal them," Tatyana said. "That entails two problems: acquiring the correct model—a model which conforms to your prescriptions—and acquiring the currency required to . . . uh, 'acquire' the devices . . . uh, required."

Silently, they chewed on that for a while. Literally. At the time they were trying to eat whatever cut of meat Andrei had brought home and Tatyana had endeavored to cook. Presumably it was pork.

"What do you suggest?" Andrei finally said. "Can you suggest something?"

"I will work on it," Tatyana said, and within a week she was off to Singapore, a development Andrei hated. But her "meeting"—and the additional startup money it was to generate—would produce only half the solution to the problem at hand. The other half entailed finding and hiring the right person or persons to steal ten lasers more compact than a particular Sanyo model. Moreover the devices had to be brought to St. Petersburg for Andrei to test before sending (or taking) them to Singapore for integration in the final products. Tatyana would deal with those problems when she returned.

One consequence of Tatyana's clandestine enterprise had been the possibility that she (along with Sergei and unnamed accomplices) would acquire a reserve of high-yield plutonium solely to sell. Indeed, the opportunity for "diverting" more plutonium presented itself in Ukraine. Andrei was outraged by the very notion and categorically refused to help her accomplish that. ("A teacup of three-kiloton 239 could vaporize the entire heart of Kiev. It could incinerate all that we love in St. Petersburg and damage a good bit more," Andrei had told her. He added, "I would sooner fuck a live bear's ass than allow any more of that stuff to come into my laboratory.") Precluding the possibility of making a great deal of money was an ironic way for Andrei to exercise his renewed vitality, which Tatyana had caused him to recover.

On the day after Tatyana's departure for Singapore Andrei tried to imagine his wife meeting with strange men—true foreigners by his and her standards (indeed, foreigners to each other from what he'd inferred)—men with "deep pockets" as Americans liked to call them. By now, Andrei felt little concern about the possibility that his entire future lay bound up in the outcome of their meeting. Much more important to him was the total effect of this affair on the quality of Tatyana's Life and future. Perhaps for the hundredth time this year alone Andrei declared to the entire universe his deepest wish: Whatever she does, may her fortune be strong.

****

GUILTY PLEASURES

Her house emanated stillness from end to end. Bare varnished wood floors and cabinets had become dark gold in late afternoon sunlight. Charlie and the girls would be gone for at least an hour; they had taken along Cuddles and Ripper, the family dogs. Peace utterly reigned inside and out, broken only by a wren's "chibbee-chibbee-chibbee-chibbee!" somewhere out in the pecan trees. To enhance this atmosphere Marie had turned off all the air conditioners, leaving on ceiling fans to stir the air quietly.

"*Ah-h-h*," Marie said. This she repeated—much louder—after she'd poured out and sipped off a couple ounces of Rothschild brandy as she sauntered about her indoor demesne, her sole purpose being to appreciate it.

No place in the world can be as dear as your own special place, Marie thought with unqualified certainty and pleasure. To her, this whole house was her special place. It was "special" because people whom she loved actually lived here, and they loved her.

She was also living The American Dream, Marie told herself as she admired the walls and windows on all sides of her, then the expanse of ceiling; outside these walls lay their little allotment of rich earth covered with lawn and festooned with trees and shrubs and flowers. All this was hers (except for the shrinking mortgage on it). She strode to her dresser in her and Charlie's bedroom, and from under a layer of sundries in the top drawer she withdrew two bulging velvet bags. These she carried to the shadowy living room where she sat in her favorite chair.

From the blue velvet bag Marie extracted her currently favorite object: a dark-gray instrument of beautifully crafted metal with a made-to-order grip of inset polished oak, the Czech-made 380-automatic pistol called a "9 Browning," equipped with double-action cock and lock. *Oh God! Look at this*. Her breaths stopped coming as Marie held and beheld the weapon; for a while she simply didn't need to breathe. All she needed was to feel the gun on different parts of her hands, also on the tops of her thighs and rubbed against her face up to a temple.

Oh, yes.

Only some time later did Marie get around to opening the green velvet bag and perfunctorily hefting the nine-millimeter Astra Lama that she used to favor. (It still felt very good.) If you search out the best weapons, she'd often maintained, it's not necessary to get a Beretta, which she no longer owned.

****

As always, Mo Tzu felt despair mingled with dread upon his return to Beijing. Once again—my home, he told himself ruefully. All my Secretariat privileges. Everything emanates from one fact: my heart harbors mostly cowardice.

251

Lately, though, his cowardice had been gaining him unimaginable compensations. His current "adventure" (so secret that only two people knew about it, and they were foreigners) allowed him to speculate on a wondrous issue: whether he was really a kind of buccaneer, a nuclear-age freebooter. Someday, he fantasized, he might even copy those swaggering fascists in Taiwan who looked so good wearing small dark glasses.

Then there were his tangible rewards: passbooks for various bank accounts in his name that he kept in a safety-deposit box in the British bank in Singapore (thanks to Chang's open-handed trust). Mo Tzu had ensured that only he, in his official capacity (as Lin Piao), could access certain financial accounts and records being held for the People's Republic in Singapore and Brunei. He was thus assured of being able to take at least one more trip out of country, on the People's behalf of course, which would allow him to physically get to his own accounts at least one more time.

Lin Piao's ability to travel abroad carried limitations. Over the last six years his trips to Kuala Lumpur, Brunei, and Singapore—all on Chang's behalf—had become increasingly difficult to justify despite his always including some official governmental business. Suspicions might have been aroused, especially considering that during some of those trips he'd made himself impossible to contact. And that last trip to Singapore to meet with the sweet Russian scientist—along with General Chang—had followed too quickly his previous trip there. Sooner or later a committee, no less, would inform Lin Piao that his international-travel days were no longer necessary although there might exist no hard evidence of his wrong-doing. He was, after all, merely an Assistant Minister of Foreign Trade.

For now, Mo Tzu decided, he would simply fixate on four figures he had noted on an index card. Each represented a sum in his personal accounts—"bottom-line" figures they were called—either in U.S. dollars or Japanese yen. (He wouldn't dare use dollar or yen signs, of course.) These were special sums: each was comprised of his share of the account as his payment for serving as General Chang's lackey. The real bottom line: Mo Tzu could claim ownership of $75,000 (plus accrued interest) once he completed his job as linchpin between Chang and the Russian. That was not exactly a fortune, he knew, but an American idiom sprang to mind as Mo Tzu settled into a government-owned limousine and stared at his figures and tried to imagine himself fingering (and fondling) 75,000 American dollars: *Not too shabby*. For the sake of his sanity he decided against imagining what he could buy with that money, especially, say, in Thailand or Bali.

However, if my secret bank accounts in Singapore (plus a small one in Brunei) were discovered prematurely by anyone in the Republic, I am a fish flopping in a hand net, Mo Tzu reminded himself. The longer it took for him to culminate his linchpin role, the greater his chances of being found out. Prudence and wiles could not protect him indefinitely. *Perhaps, therefore, I am less a coward than I think! Perhaps I am skipping directly toward a chasm.* Yes, he thought, that might be the reality. And perhaps he was gripped by a soft madness! The abyss he projected looked most exquisite, and the closer he drew the more gorgeous it appeared.

During the rest of this ride into the very petals of Chinese civilization one could fruitfully contemplate those bottom-line figures again, Mo Tzu determined. Within a moment he had slipped out his index card and begun doing just that. It occurred to him that he might be investing the concept of "purity" with new meaning.

August 26, 1992
Mogadishu, Somalia

What the hell am I doing here? Charlie asked himself once again as he tried to stick himself to his seat in the bucking supply truck while the driver, a U.N. worker from Ireland, valiantly strove to miss potholes and ruts and still maintain fifteen-mph progress. Both men had ceased cursing the road. Each concentrated on absorbing shocks to his rectum and kidneys, and each tried to avoid breathing in too much Somali dust.

Charlie decided that probably deep-seated curiosity had driven him here. As appalling as he found this place, he felt a current of vitality going through him. Overseas errands were becoming rare, and his being here somehow seemed right for him.

This errand involved acting like a CIA operative under relief-agency-personnel cover. The object was to imply—in key quarters—official U.S. interest in the Somali civil war. This much Charlie knew. While he'd be playing his role, he would covertly pass on and receive information, the nature of which he didn't need to know.

Charlie soon found that the biggest part of his job was simply enduring the ambience and nonexistent sanitation facilities. In the meantime he got a chance to see and feel some of the essence of Somalia, and he found it hardscrabble but not harsh, a place of muted colors which people might love. Those people were handsome and engaging provided they weren't starving. Their curse (besides starvation) was their being dominated by large gangs of ruthless young men who were fed (to a minimal degree) and led by a few rich middle-aged men called "war lords."

Hey! You dumb shits . . . . Charlie would sub-vocalize this numerous times over the next two days as he'd find himself in range of a truck or Jeep crowned by a mounted machine gun and bristling with manic young "technicals" fingering automatic rifles. *What the hell do they think they're doing?* —Do they even *think*?

Eventually he determined that gang bloodletting in Somalia—called "clan warfare" by Western media—was largely a chemical phenomenon. Male hormones affected by diet deficiencies interacted with an alkaloid stimulant derived from *khat*, an indigenous plant the leaves of which were chewed by almost all the men. Thus the men's brains spun into a violence mode devoid of fear; their reflexes were wired to kill (or be killed); their hearts raced. Even if they could think, it wouldn't do them much good without food and work, Charlie determined. He decided to get some *khat* leaves and fold them into his wallet before he went home. Marie would be pleased with that and displeased if he didn't.

In short order Charlie completed the tasks entailed by his errand. Then for a day he simply had to make his presence public, which posed no problem because two lieutenants of Mohammed Farrah Aidid, the dominant warlord in that area, kept an office in a house next to a compound sheltering three relief-agency outlets. Thank goodness for this, Charlie determined, because aid organizations in Somalia were beset by marauders, many of whom were gunmen overtly loyal to Aidid.

Charlie had barely arrived at the compound in central Mogadishu when he realized that four young soldiers shadowed him in a tiny, stripped-down truck. That made it easy for him to keep a high profile, which seemed anomalous here. Aside from dying, the only thing that was easy to do in Somalia was to state the U.N.'s mission objective, which was to prevent more starvation.

Midday of his second morning in Mogadishu, Charlie shifted his profile to a U.N. compound in south Mogadishu where emissaries were to oversee a cease-fire between Aidid and General Mohamed Ali Mahdi, officially the interim national president and actually the other dominant warlord in Somalia. While en route, Charlie's driver, Tim, inexplicably drove their truck into the side of a house. Charlie had no idea that Tim had been hit in the chest by either a stray or sniper's bullet.

Wordlessly, Tim turned off the ignition and simply stared at a bullet hole near the corner of the windshield. Charlie looked about for the four soldiers tailing him and didn't see them. For a long moment Charlie's world felt devoid of sound and movement except for his own head and eyes casting about for a clue as to what to do next. It came quickly and very plainly. All around the truck young men materialized shoulder to shoulder, and every one of them carried a rifle ready to be used. More were coming, moving warily.

"*Ah, shit, man,*" Tim said through clenched teeth.

A face outside had fetched Charlie's attention; in a moment he saw it again: peering at the truck windows, a broad, light-brown face, clearly older than all the others. Charlie registered the man's high forehead and thinning hair; his white shirt, pens sticking up from a pocket. The fellow appeared to be unarmed; gunmen made way for him to reach the truck.

"Come out, please. Quickly," the man said to Charlie through the open passenger-door window. The brusque manner and even tones demanded compliance.

*

Mohamed Ghali, Doctor Ghali, was his name. He introduced himself to Charlie over tea in the patio of his villa—actually a well-fortified compound—after he himself had efficiently dressed Tim's bullet wound. (The bullet had passed right through Tim's upper chest and back.) Charlie, Tim, Dr. Ghali, and the contingent of gunmen had come at amazing speed in old trucks a good fifteen kilometers to a pleasant rolling landscape overlooking the southwest edge of Mogadishu. This was his family's primary home, the doctor had told Charlie.

"Why did your people abduct us? We meant you no harm," Charlie said.

"You were in Aidid's territory. We are anxious to capture anything we can from the son of a bitch. Actually, we are desperate . . . both to weaken his forces and strengthen ours."

"I forgot the name of the guy who's opposing Aidid."

"That would be Mohamed Ali Mahdi. According to CNN and the BBC, he is losing his war against Aidid," said the doctor.

"What's Aidid's first name again? Seems like everyone's got the same name."

"Aidid is named Mohammed."

"Oh. Well, can't you join forces with General Mahdi? He's probably got a lot of resources."

"We oppose that son of a bitch, too. We oppose him actively. Our only real ally happens to be my cousin Ahmed; his family operates south of Mogadishu, on the coast."

256

"Isn't that Aidid's territory?"

"Most of it, yes. We were there to harass him; we gave a show of strength to deter Aidid's forces from launching an offensive against Ahmed's house, which Aidid probably considers a troublesome enclave. My cousin and my house would be instantly crushed if Aidid and Mahdi got together. All opposition would be crushed—summarily—if those two ever got together and stopped ruining the whole country."

Thus Charlie perceived part of Dr. Ghali's purpose: to somehow derail the process by which Somalia was being destroyed largely by the struggle between two power grabbers. But something more basic was at stake.

"My family—my 'clan' as you might call it—we're being starved to extinction by the damned generals. We need food, immediately. Just as important, we need help—armed help—so we can keep our share of food once we get it. Otherwise we're dead. Not just my clan, but all factions which have not aligned with the generals. That of course means most of the populace."

"So?"

"Your country is preparing to help us, as we've been told. But even before that, *you* must help us."

"How would I do that?"

"We'll discuss possible measures this evening."

"This evening?"

"You'll be my guest tonight. Taking you back now would entail far too many risks; trust me on this. [Beat.] Your wounded companion needs more time to stabilize. His system has been shocked and he's lost a lot of blood."

"I'll do the best I can for y' all when I get back."

Charlie was about to expand that statement when his host cut him short: "You'll do more than that. As I say, we're desperate. Our soldiers might take desperate measures to get something to eat. They might even start with an American officer's liver. Say, tonight. Unless they have good reason to hold back."

"*Huhnh*! Where'd you learn English so well? You threaten me in English better than I could threaten you."

"Oh, I learned so I could go to university in your country, which I did, by the way. Then I went to medical school. Tulane University."

Charlie loosened sounds of surprise mingled with amusement. "Hold on," he said. "You're tellin' me you hauled yourself all the way to New Orleans just to go to school?"

"Yup. I did my residency in Canton, Ohio."

For a moment Charlie gazed at infinity. Then he said: "Somehow things got balanced out. You seem so rational for someone who's put in eight years in Louisiana."

"Well you wouldn't know it," Dr. Ghali responded.

"Sir?"

"Anyone trying to fight off those mobs of idiots working for Aidid and Mahdi—with the few men and resources I have to fight with—can't be very reasonable."

After a meager rice-based dinner garnished with warmed C-rations and figs, Charlie got steeped in his host's vision: "Put the brakes on the warring generals" while the U.S. launches and lands its promised aid mission to Somalia. Maybe Charlie could help accomplish that first part.

"And how do I 'put the brakes on the generals'?"

"Well, you can sap their willingness to wage war. That would help immensely."

"I suppose you have a plan?"

"Yes, I do. Even more simple than my vision."

And Charlie's host showed him two squat little bottles of a colorless liquid called magnesium citrate, an over-the-counter laxative probably available all over the world.

"This stuff is utterly superfluous here in my country," said the doctor. "But you might carry one of these bottles in your bush jacket, just in case you need it. And then you might, shall we say, use it. Use it where it might do some good." Dr. Ghali paused for effect. "You have it within your means to attend a meeting tomorrow, I believe shortly after noon, at the U.N. headquarters. Aidid's and Mahdi's main officers are expected to attend. They're going to announce pledges to assist the relief effort."

Charlie said, "All right . . . ."

"Water, especially cool drinking water, is very rare, but they are sure to have some for the meeting. Please accept this gift. Here, take both these bottles. If you can possibly treat their drinking water at the meeting, please do. For the sake of humanity."

"Y-uhh . . . ." Charlie took a few moments to clarify and restate the projected scenario. Then he asked, "Um, how come you don't give me poison to do the job?"

"You wouldn't do it. I don't have anything lethal anyway. Not even rat poison."

"I suppose I can give it a try," Charlie said. "I can't make any promises, though."

"Fine."

"There's not much to lose by trying what you say."

"You're a good man, Charlie Brown."

Charlie and Dr. Ghali shook hands.

"I'd better call my wife," Charlie said.

"Please don't reverse the charges."

Charlie had little difficulty telephoning U.N. headquarters in Mogadishu and inducing them to inform the U.S. Embassy in Nairobi of his whereabouts. He would arrive at the main U.N. compound in the morning, he made known, and he'd call the Embassy himself, at which time he'd call home. Would someone at the Embassy please alert his wife of his intentions.

After a fairly pleasant night enlivened by an impromptu jam instigated by local drummers, musicians, and dancers, Charlie's intentions came to pass. He and his host—with the lovely but anorectic-looking women of the household (all with radiant smiles)—said their farewells, and Charlie and Tim were whisked back to Mogadishu in pre-dawn darkness. Shortly after sunrise Charlie arrived at U.N. headquarters and was allowed use of a satellite phone. Upon calling the embassy in Nairobi and getting forwarded to a number in Langley, Virginia, he used a four-part code that enabled him to place a call in the 512 area. —*Ah, the Age Of Electronics!*— Within a few minutes Charlie found himself talking to Marie and little Lisa, one of whom was on the bedroom extension phone. For the sake of protocol, he tried to make his call sound like official business.

"A-b-5-star," Marie concluded when she apprehended that Charlie planned, on his own initiative, to subvert the warlords' business. The signal she used called for "taking out" principal targets—any way possible. They had never used it before. Five years earlier they had contrived it whimsically, almost as a joke, and somehow they'd retained it.

"'Maximum prejudice' is not an option," Charlie remarked, "but I will have to extend the mission; I'll miss this morning's flight to Mombassa, Kenya. I don't know when there's gonna be another one out."

"Oh," Marie said. "Well, you're a chiropractor. Make some adjustments."

"Roger that."

"You might need a roll." [Their argot for "have good luck."]

"I have it now. Y' know, it's too bad they don't give Nobel Peace Prizes for this."

"Look in the mirror next year," said Marie. ["Do what must be done."]

Charlie dismissed protocol. "Hey, I love you all, and I miss you," he said.

Charlie's purported reason for extending his errand was illness caused by something he'd eaten or drunk while in Dr. Ghali's "custody." He *dare not* go airborne. Plus, he made clear, he still had to finish his errand. Since he carried the pass and I-D of a NSA officer, he could leverage his way into attending the generals' meeting. If he succeeded in pulling off what Dr. Ghali wanted him to do, the effort might be worthwhile. He knew he couldn't *not* try to do something to help change the situation he saw; moreover he feared—literally feared—having regrets about wasting an opportunity to accomplish something beneficial to people. Marie had the same fear; that's why they made occasional references to looking into a mirror

*

Utilizing his cover and the willingness of U.N. functionaries to be helpful, Charlie had no trouble attending the meeting between Generals Aidid's and Mahdi's top officers. Already drowsy from the astonishing heat, he arrived a little early at the meeting room in a one-story municipal office building. After establishing his place in the back of the room, he got up to look for water. Next to a wall, near the conference table, there it was: a cylindrical, earthen, blue-enameled cask, perhaps three feet tall, covered with a lid, standing on a table. Cups and glasses and fresh paper cups stood on a table next to it.

Charlie walked over to the table with the cups, helped himself to a paper one, and asked the U.N. trooper working at a nearby desk, "May I?" The soldier nodded silently.

Overtly Charlie lifted the lid to see whether the vessel held sufficient water for him to have some. In that same moment he replaced the cover. He also slipped a little bottle he'd been covertly holding back into his jacket pocket. It felt noticeably lighter now. He drew some water via the little spigot protruding from the bottom of the cask and pretended to sip from his cup as several people approached behind him.

Four officers representing each of the main warlords had come to meet under U.N. aegis. They spoke in dialects of Somali but often whole English sentences emerged in the interchanges. Evidently they agreed on the U.N. demarche: their soldiers would not interfere with U.S. aid efforts. Charlie felt gratified to see that without exception the principals availed themselves of the water cask while they talked. Ironically, they seemed to agree on one other matter: the name Ghali came up; an officer on one side said Americans would call him a "scum bag," and opposing officers concurred. Charlie then took his leave, for magnesium citrate works "authoritatively," Dr. Ghali had told him.

*   *   *

You might recall having read that when the U.S. airlift arrived in Somalia that summer, the operation went smoothly, even beautifully. A major reason for this was suspension of the civil war in that country. The two main warring factions appeared subdued, as though their leadership was . . . indisposed. That situation persisted for a few days. Even armed looting in major cities was remarkably light. Only after several weeks did physical-safety conditions change for U.S. military relief-providers, mostly because of actions instigated by General Aidid.

Another consequence of Charlie's adventure was that from then on he and Marie possessed a legal and renewable weapon, of sorts, which they implicitly hoped they would never have occasion to use. That very hope probably accounted for why they had previously neglected to seek out something analogous to magnesium citrate.

Speaking of which, when Charlie reported back to Nairobi, on the same day that the U.S. airlift reached Somalia, he used his story of being detained by Dr. Ghali (and delayed by consequent diarrhea) to get paid an additional $2,500, which was granted freely. One reason for the bonus was that during Charlie's extensive debriefing, an array of "instructors" was grateful for his insights and grasp of the situation in Somalia. He seemed to have knowledge of it from the inside.

*   *   *

Austin, Texas

Marie professed the firmer grasp on family finances. "Figure we're somewhere between two and three thousand dollars ahead for the month," she advised Charlie over a sit-down lunch, "and that's not counting what you brought home from that last errand."

"I really can't say what we should do with the surplus," Charlie remarked as he and Marie lingered over coffee.

Both glanced about to ensure they weren't being overheard.

"Looks to me like we've laundered to the max," Marie said.

"Laundered" referred to their hiding undeclared income from the Internal Revenue Service, sometimes a real challenge they had adopted as a matter of honor. ("We can waste it slowly or they'll waste it for us, in a flash. They've always got pensions or perks to beef up; or how 'bout tobacco subsidies; or maybe they can destabilize a government someplace.")

They "laundered" mainly by investing in two legal businesses, both of which were likely to turn only marginal profits but which built equity. Their associates who ran the businesses—a restaurant-grease recycling operation and a firm that imported produce from Mexico—were esteemed people who paid their workers for doing real jobs.

"We could always buy a new and larger house," Marie joked.

"Yeah? For what?" Charlie said in his role as a crank.

"Uh, for your information," Marie said, "lettuce 'n' leeks and grease are doing kind of well lately. In fact grease has been goin' gangbusters for the last few months."

"The superior person knows how to turn adversity to advantage," Charlie declared. He was considering broaching (as he had several times before) the issue of investing in a tree nursery, but he knew of none available for investment.

"Well, we could always resort to the old pillow-case routine," Marie said, alluding to a belief that narcotics dealers often stuffed their cash profits into pillow cases. Once she and Charlie had actually done that when they had a few-thousand-dollars surplus. Thus Marie was glad she'd declined an errand recently even though her blood had urged her to take it. She'd also declined to mention to Charlie that while he was in Somalia she'd gotten two inebriated-sounding phone calls from Costa Rica, one firmly requesting her assistance in some arcane matter (Sam had already secured travel authorization and funding for her, he said), the other urging her to simply visit there. She did feel obliged to tell Charlie about one other telephone call she'd taken two days before: Hsiu-fen Wu calling from Taipei.

"Really?" said Charlie. "What did she want?"

"Beats me," said Marie. "But she sounded pretty earnest about needing our help."

"What did you tell her?"

Marie and Charlie stepped outside the eatery into sticky heat turned disgusting by an "ozone" inversion.

"I told her, really, in so many words, that we don't want to get involved in Chinese affairs. As far as I'm concerned, she and her boss are Chinese. Or close enough."

For a moment Charlie was nonplussed. As they strolled to his Honda Civic he said, "I guess that's right on. What did she say?"

"She said the matter is a U.S. concern. In fact she's going to be in Los Angeles, at the Century Plaza . . . m-m-m, in exactly one week."

Charlie felt a sharp surge of energy behind his sternum. "Ah kin remembeh," he said using dialect, "when smowg lahk this was un-*heard* of in Aoustin, Texas." Likely Marie understood what he was saying.

September 5, 1992
Los Angeles, California

Feeling anxious and more than a little foolish, Charlie stared at something deep within himself while he sat in the lobby of the Century Plaza Hotel, waiting for a group of "Asian tourists" to return to their base from a shopping spree.

He almost hadn't come; on the previous evening, though, he and Marie heard a recorded telephone voice-message from

Hsiu-fen Wu in Los Angeles entreating them to come and meet with her. (She used Marie's name but once; otherwise the message seemed directed exclusively to Charlie.) So here he was, like a macho marionette, wondering what was important enough to prompt her to telephone twice to request this imposition, given that Beverly Hills is not contiguous with central Austin, Texas. Charlie had another reason for anxiety: Marie had not only declined to come with him, she disapproved of the trip for reasons beyond Charlie's having to fly in first-class sans government money.

All those concerns evaporated instantly when Charlie spotted Hsiu-fen Wu enter the lobby amidst a touring group and he caught her attention and gauged her response to his presence. Plainly wilted by tourism and Los Angeles ambience, she brightened perceptibly when she saw him. *Oh god she looks radiant.* Hsiu-fen and Charlie did not embrace as they met each other but merely shook hands, yet each could tell that the other was checking the impulse to do more.

At first they talked about immediate, mundane matters. Charlie was sure that something important was pending but he simply let Hsiu-fen unveil it in her good time. Perhaps he would like to see her room, she suggested; the tour group had lodgings in pairs, what is called "double occupancy" in U.S. tourism circles. (Charlie had to transliterate her accent to recognize the words "double occupancy.") Fine, he thought, he had come this far, so going to her room would be inconsequential. In the smooth, cool elevator she told him that General Chang had paid extra so that she could always have a private room, and Charlie told himself he should have expected that. "I would think you'd have your own room," was all he responded.

And privacy Ms. Wu required because she was in this country to initiate contacts and begin enlisting help, she told Charlie after she had washed her face. Charlie nodded and waited for her to tell him more.

"New Taiping Rebellion will force our Nationalist government to reform from inside," she declared. "General Chang says our government will *have* to change; Taiwan society will then be allowed to grow independently. I am here because Taiwan needs the New Taiping Rebellion. Eventually it will help free my country from control by foreigners. As you know, Chinese came to my country before I was born. We need our own government; we need independence."

Again Charlie nodded. "As all nations do," he said. Then he requested some explanation of those cryptic words "New Taiping Rebellion" and what they applied to. (She said a "plan of action" to build "a new country.") Casually he asked Ms. Wu some basic questions about the "plan," such as how many adherents it might have had and whether it was illegal in Taiwan and how it would be funded, and she answered them cursorily. (The cause had been in existence perhaps six years; a large handful of senior military officers and likely a couple Americans were involved in it, she said. She didn't know how it would be capitalized, and it was neither legal nor illegal.) Hsiu-fen indicated that for the "struggle" to succeed, help would be necessary in America. Enlisting it was why she was traveling the country; help did not have to come from Chinese living here.

"Gee, whiz," said Charlie, "your general is planning a coup—a military takeover—and you're looking for help in America. For what?"

"It is not a 'coup' we are setting into motion, as you would say. It will be much different from military seizing power; you will see. Others will be involved, not only military. The government in Taipei will be left alone, and we will choose our destiny."

Charlie tried to feature all that occurring. After a moment he said, "All right. Uh, how will General Chang, how will the New Taiping Rebellion, actually do these things? I mean, what do they plan to accomplish and how is it supposed to work?"

"General Chang will cause great respect for the leaders of the Rebellion. The Rebellion must be recognized by all countries—but especially by the United States, also by the Japanese—as a real government that all countries must keep safe and nourished. So the government and people of Taiwan will be protected as well."

Charlie pondered that for a while. "Ah. And then Taiwan will be left free, to govern itself?"

"Yes."

Beat. Beat. "How do you know that?"

"General Chang assures me. He never lies to me. Also his officers believe this."

"Okay, so how will your leaders—the leaders of your Rebellion, specifically how will General Chang—gain such 'great respect'? I mean, people respect him now. Why will big, powerful governments respect him more? What can he possibly offer them?"

Charlie perceived that Hsiu-fen had anticipated his question, for she answered without pause: "I cannot tell you that now. Not yet."

"You mean, you don't know the answer, or you will not say?"

"Both. Some of what I do know, I cannot tell you."

"Ah. But why do you want my help? What can I do for the 'Rebellion' waiting to rise up in your country?

"You can make our job easier for us. You can arrange for logistics to be done here in this country, in different places."

"Like what 'logistics'?" Charlie said.

"I cannot tell you that yet."

Charlie saw Suzie Wu glance into space beyond the walls and ceiling as she considered saying something additional, and she did: "There is possible danger, and you must avoid it. If you help us, you will avoid the danger, very easily. That is why I ask you, please join with us."

"*Hohkh*! I don't think so, Suzi. Some of the things you've told me just don't sound right. Thank you anyway."

Abruptly Hsiu-fen outright implored Charlie to join in her endeavor. She—and the cause she represented—needed his help; she especially wanted to make sure he stayed clear of the possible "danger" she'd mentioned. Her earnestness was overwhelming.

What Charlie didn't know, Hsiu-fen presumed, was that this woman realized more and more clearly as she spoke into Charlie's eyes or absorbed the tones of his voice or studied the top and side of his head (covered by longish, soft brown hair bearing incongruous white patches) that she could easily spend the rest of her life with this man, and her life would be a rich one. With Charlie as her helpmate, her entire being would accrue dignity. Surely, she concluded, she would be able to work on a Ph.D. in the U.S. and at the same time be satisfied in all the ways she had always fantasized.

Was she being naive? She didn't think so. Fantasy had modulated to a vision. The vision was valid, supported by certain undeniable indicators, such as her urge to gently rub her inner thighs together after Charlie spoke to her, or the adoring way Charlie sometimes gazed at her and would appear helpless for an instant.

Actually, Charlie had intuited most of this even before this afternoon. He thought that she probably realized he understood her attitudes. He could accurately project some of the visions she had for herself. Usually their brains really did operate on the same wave length.

Charlie also felt rocked by the scenario of this desirable woman entreating his help—she was actually reaching out to him for partnership—in some vague course of action that might be catastrophic.

"Forgive me," he said, "but I don't think I can help you, and I surely can't help the New Taiping Rebellion, at least until I know a lot more. A *lot* more."

When she remonstrated, he pressed her for specific information she could not—or would not—divulge. *Cul de sac.*

Finally Charlie said, "Have you eaten lately? Are you hungry?"

Hsiu-fen desired no food, so Charlie proposed they go to the hotel bar, per usual.

Would Charlie like to learn something about the tenets underlying the New Taiping Rebellion and, perhaps, what his initial role might be if he assisted the effort?

"I tell you, Suzie," Charlie said without thinking further, "I'm good for one drink. Then I'm gonna catch the 7:30 flight to Houston."

*

Their short time together in the hotel bar was relaxed and pleasant. Each knew where the other stood on the matter they had discussed upstairs. No more need be said.

"I imagine your life is getting pretty exciting now," Charlie declared at one point. "Let me advise you, please be careful. Some kinds of excitement are addictive. Really. They can destroy a person, in different ways."

A moment of reflection for Hsiu-fen Wu. She responded, "Except for now, my life is much like it was before." She took another moment. "Addiction to excitement: I cannot really understand. But I will take your advice." Her face expressed pure animation. "I will compute what you say!"

To Charlie this exotic companion of the moment appeared—and undeniably was—utterly captivating. He released one of his rich-timbered, easy-going half-laughs, his head bowing briefly as he coped with being overwhelmed

Hsiu-fen Wu took the opportunity to gaze once more at the white patches peppered on Charlie's hair. Then for an instant she tried to take in the Gestalt of him.

What occurred next Charlie had never fantasized would happen. For three or four seconds Hsiu-fen Wu imagined, with tactile intensity, that Charlie stood before her utterly aroused and wearing only bikini undershorts and a singlet; ritualistically she helped him remove those underclothes. Mainly she was helping him get unbearably aroused. His throat emitted uncontainable sounds that stimulated all her skin to tingle. In just a few moments more . . . .

Meanwhile Charlie took his final sip of tequila "X-E-X" ("extra-especially-expensive," he called it). For a moment he rubbed the shot glass meditatively. Suzie Wu twisted on her chair a little and that fetched his attention. She looked at him levelly and said, "Have you ever been lover with an Oriental woman?"

Charlie's impulse was to request the question be repeated. No, he was sure he'd heard correctly. "Yes, I have," he answered, nodding.

"Very interesting! May I ask, how many Oriental women have you been with?"

Charlie gave that a moment's thought. Several years before, on the freighter from Hong Kong, he had calculated the answer to that same question.

"Oh, I don't know for sure. Let's say two or three . . . dozen."

Suzie Wu laughed lightly and dropped the subject. She thought he was kidding. Meanwhile Charlie was sub-vocalizing, *lady, you are dangerous my goodness*!

Soon Charlie had to leave to catch a departure flight for home. He had made a return reservation for late the next day, and now he regretted having made this trip, so he decided to expedite his return. Still, he felt flattered by Hsiu-fen Wu's attentions and grateful for the scant knowledge she'd revealed to him.

"Thank you for your confidence in me," Charlie said preparatory to taking his leave. "I'm sorry that I can't be of assistance to you and your cause." He wanted to add that he wished her efforts well, but that would not have been true. Recalling the words "New Taiping Rebellion" or the name of General Chang caused him a nauseating chill.

"We need you, "Hsiu-fen responded. "We want to make sure you are safe from danger. I want to make sure you are safe."

Oh what the hell try again. "What kind of danger are you talking about?" Charlie asked, and he got the response he expected: She couldn't say.

"Have a good time here," Charlie told Hsiu-fen Wu just before they parted in the hotel lobby. "Remember two words: 'addiction' and 'excitement.' Be careful now!"

When she smiled and gave her little wave, Charlie knew he'd miss her company starting the moment he stepped outside.

****

"So basically, from what I can see, that lady's representing something dangerous — at least potentially dangerous — and we don't know what, but I can't really feature it being, you know, a terrorist group," Charlie said upon having told Marie all he could think to tell her about his experience in Los Angeles that day.

By the time he'd gotten home and they were able to leave the house for a stroll to talk privately (always assuming electronic listening devices in their house), the hour was late. Best to discuss things before going to bed, though; let the subconscious work on issues overnight. Best also to leave the dogs at home if the issues are important.

"Maybe it's that chick, and not some terrorist group, that's really dangerous, at least as for as I'm concerned," Marie said.

Charlie heard that and thought about it, but anything he'd respond would not be clearly honest so he let it drop. Marie's remark also struck him as irrelevant, which Charlie knew might have been wishful thinking on his part.

"What I'm thinkin'," said Charlie, "is that it's not a terrorist group or terrorist organization we're confronting. It's a terroristic enterprise someone's fixin' to pull off."

"Whatever the distinction, drastic things are quivering under cover," Marie said. She added: "Now *think*. Did any other clues come up when Suzie Wu told you things?"

Charlie scanned his memory banks. He thought he had told Marie about everything, including Suzie Wu begging him to help her and the "struggle," and why.

"Well, she did mention something about a couple Americans being involved," he offered. "Now that I think about it, maybe somehow she sees a *connection* between us and Americans in Taiwan helping General Chang. And that computes, because why else would she confide in me—or us—the way she has? Once she even called me a hero."

"Actually, we don't know *anybody* working there. Except for Suzie Wu."

"And we hardly know her; not much more than we know Debbie Kassenbaum."

"Debbie Kassenbaum! Of course! I bet she's working for Chang, on the side. Somehow I bet she's assisting him *and* his 'Rebellion.' But, if so—so what? What if she is? They haven't done anything wrong. Yet. We'd never be able to prove anything if they did. The whole thing is just too nebulous; all we can do is back off. We can't even wait to see what develops: we're supposed to stay clear of Chinese affairs. *Period*."

"It's not really a 'Chinese affair,'" Charlie said.

"It's close enough."

Soon Marie brought up that during the past week she'd gone onto the University of Texas Internet site to learn something about General Chang K'ung, "the darling Ms. Wu's omnipotent employer."

"All I could find out about him was two essential facts," Marie said. "Aside from some basic data, like when he was born and when he attended officers' training school here in this country—which he did for two years, believe it or not—hardly anything is known about him. That's fact one. Somehow he's always been under cover. The other major fact is that he's fairly rich. His folks—on both sides, actually—had a good-sized fortune; I guess it all went to him. After that, almost anything else is conjecture."

"Well," said Charlie, "we do know that if China invades Taiwan, he's responsible for defending a quadrant of the territory. From what I gather, he can probably do it."

"All right," Marie said, "he's got military 'power'—what is 'power' anyway? He's got high-level authority in the military, he's got 'clout,' and he can wield it with a strong probability of success, for himself and for whatever he's trying to do."

"Okay. And we know he's got a lot of money—he's got 'buying power,' so to speak. All in all, I'd say he's got a lot of freedom. More than most folks."

"What motivates such a man?" Marie said rhetorically.

"What does it matter?"

"We'd know whether to take him seriously if he tried to do something weird. We'd know whether he's dangerous or not."

"Well, it doesn't take much to gather he's got a huge ego and a lot of pride. Otherwise he wouldn't be where he is. Right? He's probably a high-stakes gambler, too; so he's probably addicted to big excitement; you know, adrenalin-rush kind of stuff."

"Maybe. Anyway, let's give him the benefit of a doubt: let's presume that what's motivating him underneath all that, and underlying his compulsion to patriotism—he's career-military, right?—is a search for, a drive toward, some kind of *meaning* in his life. 'Meaning' with a capital M. Doesn't everything kind of . . . come together when you do that?"

Beat. Charlie remarked, "He's dangerous, all right."

As they returned to their front yard Marie concluded this discussion by declaring, "From now on we're going to have to be smart. We don't just keep ourselves clear of Chang K'ung—and whatever's goin' on over there. We stay *way* clear of that whole scene."

September 7, 1992
Taipei, Taiwan

"Major Chen, you are thoroughly evil," intoned Chang K'ung in Mandarin upon hearing his subordinate's suggestion for mitigating urban sprawl. ("Radioactive Filipinos and Japs will be fewer but far better Filipinos and Japs.")

They laughed about that and strode along a running track in smog-laden morning sunshine. As a rule they used code in references to setting off nuclear explosions. This time the subject was patently facetious, although each felt a serious undertone there. In the future even jocose remarks about "nukeing" would be said in code.

During the past four years at least a dozen officers much senior to Chen had explicitly sworn secret fealty to General Chang's vision and leadership, although the young major was Chang's confidant and sometimes-comrade. (Chang surmised this was probably due to his own narcissism or else it stemmed from complementary brain waves.)

Consequently Chen was entrusted with quietly carrying out the most critical tasks in launching the Cobra Cause. Thus, when the day would dawn to press his cadre of officers into decisive action, Chang would present them with a virtual fait accompli. Their commitments would then be irrevocable, precluding any turning back (or worse). Sometimes his own astuteness, Chang had often thought, was definitely inspired by intelligence beyond his own, which meant that he was blessed with great responsibility.

"Listen, John," Chang said to Major Chen. "You must ensure that all comrades named by Wu Hsiu-fen are committed to following our orders very precisely. You will do that by contacting each commando and each volunteer personally. That is step one. In the process, using your own methods, you will augment the information Wu Hsiu-fen provides about each volunteer. Be rigorous, be thorough. Is each man or woman undoubtedly reliable? I must be informed of any weak spots in our network.

"Next, if necessary, you must apply pressure to any of our comrades who might contemplate relocating—for any reason—during the next year. We need to be able to count on them, where they are. Please begin preparing to leave. Your itinerary is in your mailbox. It is subject to modification by Miss Wu. The dates of your absence will be finalized in twenty-four hours from this moment. Have you any questions?"

"By when shall I have returned? Am I allowed to ask Ricky Wu for assistance?"

"If Master Wu is available to help you, all the better. I shall clear your absence with your colonel. Take two weeks and two days. The final two days should be spent in Hawaii."

"*Hai,*" said Chen. "Heh-heh-heh."

Where the track curved Chen saluted and strode back to barracks. He and his general had determined long before that national military business and the Cobra Cause could intermingle—until that day when affairs outside the Cause would be irrelevant.

General Chang soon left the track as well; he would work out thoroughly that evening. Now he had to arrange final bank-draft deposits totaling $460,000 (U.S. dollars) to Mo Tzu's accounts abroad; that drain on his fortune was mostly destined for the soft hands of the Russian lady scientist, provided she delivered the detonators and they actually worked. *What good are fortunes if not for venture?*

Chang also faced the matters of where to safely store the warheads and how to ship them (also safely) to the U.S. for distribution. Security had to be seamless. Aside from ensuring operational efficiency, he had to maintain deep protection for himself. A minor misstep could lead to destruction of his revolution and preclude a high quality of life for untold millions. *Let me show all the world what we Chinese and Han can really do when our true potential is released and carefully cultivated.*

Chang was sure this would be the outcome once he fulfilled his vision of a Chinese state that would be truly Chinese throughout its fiber. Singapore provided a good basic model for what he envisaged, but it was simply not *pure.* The so-called Republic Of China was definitely not a worthy model; the government in Taipei would mainly be useful as a trading partner for Chang's new state. In Chang's view, a nation dedicated to promoting and nurturing unfettered Chinese abilities and capacities would be more affluent (per capita) and exciting than any country extant. Its culture would be inestimably higher than that of other countries because it would be *real.* Its influence would forever benefit the world. Its founder's destiny would thus, finally, be fulfilled.

And what of the founding genius's future role in this grand vision: essentially Chang saw himself wielding authority as an omnipotent senior statesman, what English speakers call "the king behind the throne." Even in the foreseeable future, "former-General" Chang K'ung would occasionally be the featured guest on television shows aired in, say, Europe or America. He would tell the world things people needed to know. Most importantly, he would divulge—with breathtaking grace—the keystone of his vision: "Real Chinese people, myself included, at last are enabled to live according to our inherited code, the code which our culture has evolved over millennia, and which we now implement as dynamic and expansive." If someone were to ask him if that wasn't perhaps a shallow mode of life, much like espousing capitalism as the be-all and end-all of human existence, he would have a ready answer: "Actually our code is comprehensive. It embraces whatever our positions might be within the whole cosmos even though the cosmos is beyond human understanding. —But I am not paid to be profound!"

Chapter 11

September 12-13, 1992
Kerrville, Texas area

"Oh, Ma-*rie* . . .

Oh, Ma-*rie*.

Oh, Ma-*rie*, la *bour*-geoi-*sie*!" Charlie sang as he and his beloved tooled over hills and through dales, penetrating Bandera County in their brand-new black Nissan Altima.

"Hold on there, ducks. I'm not the one who bought this car, brand-new yet. And black, just perfect for Texas heat."

"No, but you condoned my doin' it. Who insisted on this C-D player?"

Marie didn't respond. She focused on enjoying the ride, which at this moment happened to include inserting a ZZ Top compact disc into the player and snapping the air conditioner back on (the latter more a necessity than luxury a week after Labor Day).

As they neared their rural retreat (called "the ranch," their thirty-acre hideaway with a view), Charlie's assertion about Marie being "bourgeois" became increasingly immaterial. Their daughters were back in town having begun a new school year, and Marie and Charlie—utterly grateful to Jed and Benjamin for putting up the girls—were headed for a few days of relaxation. Maybe during the Christmas break they would bring the girls here with them.

All serious matters for discussion had been resolved before they'd left Austin. ("Did you bring the diaphragm?" "Did you put out the pooch food?" "How come you haven't been dealing much with vocational training as part of standard curricula?" "Don't undermine me when I'm trying to teach the girls how to develop a stronger sense of responsibility." Et cetera, et cetera.)

On top of all that, Charlie's mother, Marguerite, was waiting for them at "the ranch" with her husband of barely one year (Charlie's "step-daddy"), Bertram. They kept the place up by staying there five or six days of each month; if Charlie and Marie arrived when they were in residence, after a good visit they usually went back home to Austin. Charlie, Marie, and Marguerite believed that a place such as "the ranch" should be maintained by living in it. And Charlie and Marie much preferred to arrive there when someone had it "limbered up."

When they arrived at the ranch, which had most recently been a produce farm certified by the state as "organic," the pretty creek they drove alongside for about a hundred yards on their way to the house had never looked so green and full.

"We must have gotten some rain last week," Marie said.

"Oh, *God*," Charlie said.

When they parked and emerged from their car, Marguerite's voice proclaimed out the back doorway: "Hey, you're home! 'Bout time you got here!"

"Home"—a blocky, white wooden ranch house built over forty years before—emanated aromas of boiled beans, fried onions and okra and tomatoes, and freshly-baked bread. (Actually Marguerite had been experimenting with baking squash-and-apple muffins, and she'd added a batch of biscuits to ensure they'd have good bread.) Loud strains of "In the Mood"—Glenn Miller!—looped out from the front room.

"Bertram's practicing in the living room," Marguerite said. "Practicing" was understood to refer to dancing.

Indeed he was. A little hard of hearing, Bertram had switched to high-volume Tito Puentes and a new set of moves on the bare hardwood floor. He wore kung-fu slippers that made little clicking and sliding noises on the wood and allowed him maximum mobility. His lean face emanated utter contentment. ("Sometimes he's pure Zen," Charlie liked to say.) Marie often referred to Bertram as "the Fred Astaire of Central

Texas," but for more reasons than the obvious: to all who knew him, everything the man undertook he did smoothly.

They all enjoyed a good visit over the next two-plus hours, replete with various forms of sense gratification and silliness. At one point Marie even extricated her pump shotgun from behind loose wall planks back of the refrigerator, inserted some shells, and she and Bertram blasted away through open windows at cowbirds and grackles. Bertram enjoyed himself hugely, as he did in almost everything, a trait Charlie admired.

True to form, when the flow of activity made the back door of the house grow larger and compelling, Bertram declared something to Marguerite. They rose decisively.

"It's time we got back," Marguerite announced.

"Yup, it's about that time," said Bertram. "Hey, Maggie's got something for our man here." His white head nodded to Charlie.

"Ah, yes; that I have," Charlie's mother said. She fetched her oversized handbag from which she extracted a rumpled sheet of paper that she handed to Charlie. On it was hand printed a poem titled "A Rose from Charlie and Marie." When Charlie announced it was a poem with that title, Marie materialized next to his left arm. They read it aloud:

A Rose from Charlie and Marie

Almost from nothing
nothing but soil   some seed
ah, the seed   that was one thing
sunshine   water
some luck fending off
aphids   budworms   fuchsia mites
mildew of course   rust
deadly black spot

Dennis Frank Maček

Then comes synergy
exactly like love

Almost at presto!   consequent miracles
bush
blossoms
unspeakable beauty

The face of a rose
watches stars grow cold

Hollis Grumbles, Sr. 1/91

A few seconds passed.
"Well!" said Charlie.
Marie stood featuring the images.
Bertram sat wordlessly punctuating images in his mind with gentle nods. Marguerite resumed floating about gathering her things preparatory to leaving. She spoke to Charlie: "I found that last week in your father's things; I was pretty sure you'd want to have it. You and Marie. [Beat.] I know he worked on it for a long time."
Bertram looked up at Charlie's eyes. "What do you think all those images refer to in the poem?" Bertram said.
"I can't say I know," Charlie responded.
Marie's real self was still elsewhere.
"I think I do," Bertram said with a smile, then a gaze at things far away. He rose from his chair to join his wife. "Whatever you two've been doing, keep doin' it," Bertram added. And like a shadow he glided away.

*

"I tell you, before lunch there's nothing better than cold pizza—I mean room-temperature pizza—with a cold beer," Marie said happily as she and Charlie trudged hand-in-hand over arid terrain under azure sky. Here on their "ranch" in the Texas Hill Country, mornings usually felt fresh and bracing; with appetites sharpened, feelings of well-being took a person off the ground.

Where Charlie and Marie walked, the land was reverting to scrubland. Mockingbirds hunted, a hawk swooped. To the two city folk, Life showed itself as it really could be: a thrilling sequence of delights, dangers, and barely concealed mysteries. They forded the creek near their house and began making their way up a gentle gradient.

"I prefer hot biscuits and coffee as soon as I get up," Charlie said. "Cold rice and hot tea are good, but you need some fish or soup to go with it. The best thing is to have some brandy, preferably cognac, to spruce up your breakfast."

Indeed biscuits, coffee and brandy had been his breakfast that morning.

"Brandy, is . . . good," Marie said.

Now they strode in dry, clear air up the gradually ascending side of a geographic bowl. Soon they would be able to look across the hilly basin of their land or—turning north—gaze over a neighboring spread. Properties out here were separated by wire fences. A magazine laying cover down under a bush caught Charlie's and Marie's eye. (*What the hell is that doing here?*) Neither said anything; Charlie chose to stride out of his way to pick it up and look at the cover, which he did.

"It's a *Time* magazine," he announced. "This week's!"

He took it to Marie and they looked it over with keen interest. It bore no mailing label; it must have been purchased and brought to this area. But this spot was a few hundred yards from the rural highway; the magazine had been transported deep into their property through brush brakes and juniper stands. By wind, perhaps?

A few pages of the *Time* magazine had been folded in. Gazing at a full-page advertisement for scotch whiskey on the inside of the back cover, Charlie spotted what he thought was a word, inconspicuously inscribed in black ink on the white part of the ad: a trio of ideographs, perhaps a name, perhaps a reminder for someone to do something. There it definitely was, jarringly foreign.

"It looks Chinese," Charlie remarked as he showed the characters to Marie and underlined them with his index finger.

"Could be Japanese Kanji," Marie said as she scrutinized the ink markings. She experimented by uttering a few phonemes. "But why would a Japanese speaker be out here? [Beat.] What would bring a *Chinese speaker* out here?"

Marie and Charlie each cast a vaguely distressed look into the other's eyes. Without a word they briefly assessed the value of the site on which they stood and found it to be a likely spot, given the elevation and the inconspicuous little juniper thicket growing right there, from which to observe their house and not be seen from below.

They proceeded to examine the turf for any more indications of trespass. They found what might have been a footprint (maybe a men's size nine), and something else: behind the same bush, two inch-deep, perfectly round holes about ten inches apart in the ground that had recently been soft from rain. Each hole was the diameter of a quarter.

"They sure look artificially made," Charlie said.

"Yeah. Looks like somebody poked something into the ground here."

No clue appeared as to what had caused the holes.

"Well, maybe there's a perfectly natural explanation for how these holes got here," Charlie commented as he and Marie abandoned their search for more anomalous things.

"Maybe. And maybe this magazine just got blown here."

Eventually they backtracked to the creek and followed it to where it passed under the highway through a conduit. Charlie still clutched the magazine, intending to read a few sections over more coffee and brandy.

"Do you know," said Charlie, "next month begins a new tree-planting season."

Marie was about to say that of course she did (after so many years of knowing Charlie) when she spotted what struck her as a crumpled part of a photo wedged in flotsam and rocks along the creek bank. On a whim she picked it up, tugged it open, and stared. It was indeed half of a photo; the unposed subject was a man in a far shot.

"Who does this look like to you?" Marie said to Charlie as she showed him what she'd found.

They stared at the picture in disbelief because it was clearly of Charlie.

After a few moments Charlie said, "Gee-zus, what the hell's goin' on?"

"When do you suppose that was taken?" Marie asked.

Neither could say when or where the photograph was taken. They determined that it was at least three years old and likely set in a warm clime.

Marie allowed Charlie to utter what they now considered almost obvious: "I think . . . somebody's been tryin' to maybe . . . find us," he said. "They—or whoever—wanted to catch us out of town. Out here."

Neither considered speculating on a reason for that. Nor would they try guessing who would surveil them and whether the watcher or watchers had given up because they saw Marguerite and Bertram occupying the ranch house.

"This is too weird," Charlie said. He was about to add, "Eh, screw it," but Marie found her voice.

"This fact is impossible, it's intolerable!" she said. "I won't put up with it."

"I know. I just want whoever's been shadowing us to show his face," Charlie said as they began making their way back to their house, about three hundred yards away.

Marie said nothing.

"Let's just wait for him to come out," Charlie added as though they had an option. "There's probably no more than one or two of 'em. I mean, I'm sure there's not a big gang of

Droghistas lurking around lookin' for us. I mean, for what? We'll deal with 'im when he shows himself."

Still Marie said nothing; her mind had drifted to Provence as though she had never left France. After a long moment Charlie also began seeing—and feeling—images of forest and countryside along the San River. When they were back in their farm house they decided to report their being under surveillance to their primary instructor the next time they were called to do an errand. Four weeks passed before they could do that, and Jerry Callan, Rick Denton's replacement, appeared genuinely mystified by what they recounted, as did two other instructors. That was when Charlie and Marie realized what they'd intuited all along: the mystery of who was behind surveilling their country house would probably always remain a disturbing fact, not amenable to solution.

October 11, 1992
Bander Seri Begawan, Brunei Sultanate

"You might think this to be a great deal of money, yes, but for government projects the amount is trifling, even in the former Soviet Union," Mo Tzu declaimed affably. With a wry little smile he added, "Too bad this money is not mine!" He conveyed these attitudes through a translator to a prim, attractive young woman who had been tapping his data into a Dell computer that initiated the arrangement he desired.

Purportedly on behalf of the People's Republic, 280,000 American dollars would be transferred from Mo Tzu's account at this bank to the Central Bank of Byelorussia in Minsk. Those funds would be credited to an account held by the Director of Environmental Testing in the National Scientific Research Facility, which happened to be in St. Petersburg, Russia. Doctor-Professor Platonov would arrange for final disbursements to the Facility in Russia whenever Mo Tzu conveyed the code numbers to her, contingent upon approval of certain "projects."

To protect this "project funding," Mo Tzu had arranged for a Major J. Chen (who had a Kuala Lumpur, Malaysia, address) to receive the code as well, in case necessity dictated that the funds were to be returned. Mo Tzu was sure that he had left electronic footprints in this affair, but they would be visible only to parties who knew to look for them. With some luck his activities would never attract attention or warrant suspicion.

The slender, brown woman at the computer smiled at him reservedly and asked if that would be all (through the male translator). Mo Tzu replied in the affirmative and strongly considered adding, "Except I would like to meet you later for dinner. And later yet we could drive to a mountain top to view the moon, which I believe will be perfectly round and full tonight. Then perhaps you would like to see my hotel suite, which incorporates all manner of luxury."

Mostly the language barrier between them deterred Mo Tzu from saying this. Part of his frustration at the moment was the context of Brunei. There were so many places he would rather visit, where orthodoxy did not prevail and daily life integrated a raunchy underside replete with overtly available women. (*Ah, yes.*) The day was coming—making it happen was why he was here!—when he would spend open-ended blocks of time in Bali and Thailand, among other select places that required his investigating.

Outside the bank, as he looked for a taxi, Mo Tzu casually asked his translator: "Where does one find available women—any kind of available women—here in this city?"

Exactly as Mo Tzu expected, the translator regarded his query as a request for directions to Jupiter, then declared total ignorance of the commodity sought.

Mo Tzu had often—and rightly, he was sure—regarded himself as a gray man, always in gray clothes and stolid as a Russian. But his true colors lay under his grayness; he envisioned that one day his status would change; he would be in a position to exhibit his real self and let his personality simply blossom. All that would begin happening on the day he'd get paid in full for his services by that enigmatic fascist in Taiwan.

For openers he would prove that bourgeois Austrian Jew, Sigmund Freud, to have been right on target but pitifully underinformed. By the time he sampled enough female parts—along with all their personalities—to sate his curiosity and appetite, he would be a legend throughout Thailand and likely some other places.

After that, once he had clout, which comes of wealth from invested capital, he would sound the call for revitalization of his own government and start clearing out the stinking Party leeches (the Soviets had tried to dignify their function by calling them apparatchiki) starting at the top of the heap in Beijing. Anyone trying to do that would need military help, of course, and he could honestly say he knew the names of at least twenty senior-level army and air-force officers who shared his main contention, that the Party was dragging their Republic to oblivion and perverting the state's sole function, which was to foster—really, to cultivate—the lives of the people. Even Zhou Enlai and Zhao Tzu-yang, he believed, had somewhere along the way lost sight of their mission.

Therefore, Mo Tzu reaffirmed, he would continue to do General Chang's bidding by going to St. Petersburg in Russia where he would verify the progress purported in building Chang's damnable nuclear devices. Maybe on this trip he would meet a nice, bosomy Russian lady who would do anything for some real silk or batik.

November 26 (Thanksgiving Day), 1992
Seattle, Washington

"Sometimes real rewards come from doing small things," Hsiu-fen Wu said in Minnan to the male graduate student who had come fourteen hundred miles to receive an object from her that stood about twenty inches high and measured perhaps a foot across.

Surprised by the weight of it, the "student" hefted the package she had given to him in the crook of his arm. A medium-sized man with well-developed shoulders and chest, he regarded Hsiu-fen thoughtfully and responded, "Often great rewards appear small." This was coded dialogue as worked out by Major Chen and Ricky Wu, Hsiu-fen's younger brother, both of whom had "instructed" ten graduate students prior to each one coming briefly to Seattle for a meeting such as this one.

Try as she might, Hsiu-fen could not quite manage a smile. This business was serious, after all. As he took his leave the sturdy young man bowed to her slightly and she reciprocated. Whimsically she confirmed her perception that his face was prematurely lined and the deeper parts of his eyes were focused on something ineffable.

She checked off the "graduate student's" code name and the place (Urbana-Champaign) to which he would return—directly—with his mysterious package. Then she tore up the list and burned the pieces. Over the last several months all ten "students," actually they were elite commandos, had been dispatched to work on advanced degrees in or near various U.S. population centers. Soon all ten places would harbor one of the heavy little packages, and the commandos knew what to do with them. Hsiu-fen didn't know what was actually inside the packages nor did she want to know. She was under strict orders not to attempt opening one. In fact her first priority in this assignment was to ensure they remained closed. One relevant fact she did know about the contents: physical exposure to them was extremely dangerous. For Hsiu-fen, that was enough.

Ostensibly each package contained a molded cast-aluminum water regulator for industrial-sized boilers, exactly like the two unwrapped samples she had displayed to shippers, truck drivers, and clerks. Those were basically plumbing parts, painted black, with electric-wire conduits and a plastic control box attached to each; they weren't much of a problem to carry around. The packages, though, were anomalously heavy, exactly as though the contents were encased in lead, and they were extremely securely boxed.

Hsiu-fen's responsibility for the packages had begun in Hong Kong where she met two of John Chen's lieutenants and a soft-spoken Russian woman who introduced herself as "Tatyana." They were in the process of securing and wrapping the ten items. When that job was done, Hsiu-fen received final instructions and then contacted a shipper of Chinese-made industrial parts to send the items to Canada.

That initial Hong Kong business required the better part of two days. On the first day she met Tatyana—who charmed her at once by trying to talk to her in a language Hsiu-fen took to be Cantonese. (Of that tongue Hsiu-fen understood very little, even when it was spoken well.) She and Tatyana tried using French, then resorted to a few key words in English and a lot of mime and smiles. As things unfolded, Hsiu-fen caught a glimpse of a seemingly elderly man in the back part of Tatyana's hotel suite. Unobtrusively he took in developments for several minutes, then disappeared.

The next morning, when all four people involved met at a dockside storage building to transfer the ten packages to Hsiu-fen Wu's care, a fifth person was there, hanging back and looking on, the same "elderly gentleman" from the day before. Eventually he came forward, quietly said something in Russian to Tatyana, and in English spoke directly to Hsiu-fen: "If one box becomes open, please, you must get away far. At once! Understand?"

By then Hsiu-fen had already postulated that necessity, but she hadn't been keenly aware of it being urgent. Now she was. She nodded and looked into the Russian's kindly face and smiled almost despite herself. Astonished, she saw that behind his thin white beard he was not really old; perhaps his health had been undermined so that he appeared older. Plainly he still had vigor which invested him with a kind of thrust, and something else. Hsiu-fen had to respond to the quality he projected—and with her eyes momentarily locked on his, she did.

"Yes, I understand. Thank you."

They nodded to each other; impulsively each extended a hand to the other. Tatyana looked on with a little smile.

This must be the scientist, Hsiu-fen said to herself. At some point she had gathered that a "scientist" was at base responsible for whatever she was charged with delivering to the United States. The very hand she grasped had likely made— at least physically assembled—those dangerous items. With no real evidence, Hsiu-fen knew he was Tatyana's husband. Otherwise—and she was quite sure about this as well—if he and she were to meet someplace absolutely private, and if she then removed her clothes (as he would likely insist), she would see her own dark nipples lighten to pink as he whitewashed her insides.

*

General Chang had arranged to facilitate Hsiu-fen Wu's sending those ten packages to Canada, where they were securely stored in Vancouver until she smuggled them into Seattle, one at a time, using a variety of means to preclude detection of the lot. The section of warehouse in Seattle she was using as a distribution outlet had been leased exclusively for her by the current Republic Of China trade mission to Canada.

Hsiu-fen sighed deeply and gazed out the office window at darkness gathering over the Sound. Large boats and perhaps some ships were slipping toward the wharfs, many with lights already on. Somewhere in the bay a klaxon sounded; from a northerly tangent a bell seemed to answer it. Yes, off the land there was also much to do.

She hated having to leave. She loved this city, she loved this country. She even enjoyed spending time at this warehouse with its functional little office. She could see herself using the space to conduct aerobics and t'ai chi classes. And the lease was good for over five more months! A pleasurable connection rose in her ken: Wouldn't Charlie enjoy life here, with her to help him enjoy it? *Don't American men like to eat dim sum?*

Perhaps for the dozenth time, Hsiu-fen resisted the urge to telephone Charlie Grumbles. Instead she consciously resolved to focus on "covering tracks" (as Charlie might say it), for General Chang wanted her to erase all connections between herself and the items she had smuggled into the U.S. even though—if necessity dictated—she was protected by her diplomatic passport. She knew she had to return at once to

Vancouver and then proceed to Tokyo, Japan, to interface with some of Chang's contacts there.

December 3, 1992
New Territories, Hong Kong Colony

To Debbie Kassenbaum, this would be the most interesting—and unique—"vacation" of her life. Already she and her "family friend," a wiry, intense-looking Chinese man of indeterminate age purportedly named "Wu Ch'i," had eaten a gourmet lunch at a French restaurant and rented a Jaguar which he drove with great precision.

After leaving the Kowloon limits they traveled almost wordlessly for about twenty kilometers. Earlier "Wu Ch'I" had shown his personality to be delightfully expansive; now he seemed to sink within himself, not ignoring Debbie but no longer quite with her. She ascertained that he'd been functioning on a high brain-chemical-induced plateau; evidently the chemical balance had simply changed. Even the man's famous intensity appeared diluted. To Debbie's surprise, that hint of vulnerability enhanced his attractiveness.

The countryside left and right seemed virtually deserted. Sometimes they caught sight of a broad green river beyond roadside foliage and sparsely wooded hills. About one hundred yards from the south side of the highway appeared a compound of four brick buildings set up by the colonial government for some indeterminate function clearly deemed redundant. The light-beige buildings, three of them two stories high, were enclosed by a chain-link fence with a double gate giving onto the paved driveway. For whatever the place had been used, it looked forlorn now.

Debbie broke the silence and pointed when she spotted it. "Hey, General, I'll bet you a silk pajama—that's where we're going." General Chang snorted a laugh. He nodded affirmatively and a few moments later turned the black Jaguar onto the driveway.

Even before Chang braked at the chain-link fence he and Debbie saw four men inside the enclosure, all dressed in Western civilian suits, striding to meet them. Soon Debbie recognized the men as commandos selected by Chang to be part of his personal Delta Force (which he liked to refer to in English as "my Palace Guard"). Two of them briskly opened the gates and Chang bypassed the buildings to park in back.

During all this Debbie felt a definite sense of destiny arcing to fruition. *Things are coming to pass*! Anticipation began to make her thrum. Chang grinned like a small boy as he brought the car to a stop. "Well, Silk-Pajama Lady," he said, "is this a neat place to meet friends, or what?"

Behind the quiet buildings Chang and Debbie were joined by two of the commandos and, to Debbie's mind, a total stranger who was markedly foreign: surely Chinese but a different kind of Chinese, the product of a different diet and *Zeitgeist* and customs than the Chinese people whom she had known. He even wore a gray Mao-Zedong-style suit. Maybe incongruously, he had an easy, wry smile which made him appear to Debbie as being perpetually amused. This gray man is different, she decided.

"Mo Tzu!" Chang said as soon as he spotted the stranger.

General Chang and Mo Tzu greeted each other heartily. Despite their mutual dependence, they had met face-to-face only five times before.

A real study in distinctions, Debbie thought. Abruptly she realized that the contents of the brown paper bags Mo Tzu carried so casually were actually central to why they were there. Presently the Mainlander—by now she felt sure that's what he was—opened the larger of the two bags and pulled out an object fashioned of heavy black metal. He glanced about for the best place to put it, then he simply placed the black device with attachments sticking out of it on the asphalt underfoot. From his small bag he removed a plastic box with a lid which he pulled off to reveal . . . a duck egg.

Mo Tzu squatted before the black cast-metal ball—which looked a little rounder and shorter than an American football—and by taking out six small bolts (using only his fingertips) he removed a flange connection which had been attached to the bottom of it. An elbow joint was welded onto the flange. A braided strand of insulated wire ran through the elbow and flange and was still attached to something inside the ball.

By removing the flange Mo Tzu had exposed the hollow interior of the ball, into which he very carefully inserted the duck egg. Then he closed it up again and finger-tightened the bolts. Entering the elbow joint was about two inches of electrical conduit which came from the bottom of a gray aluminum box about the size of a box for a deck of cards. That compact gray box attached to the elbow joint by a bit of conduit became the cynosure of attention as Mo Tzu removed the cover on it. Securely packed inside, instead of electrical switches for the "water regulator," was a common telephone pager. Mo Tzu pointed out a double wire running from the bottom of the pager case into the conduit, and thus into the black metal ball. As nearly as Debbie could apprehend from the soldiers who did the translating, Mo Tzu announced, with a flat smile, what this really was: "Laser control," he said.

Chang nodded. Mo Tzu proceeded to demonstrate. A pause. Some exposition was required, punctuated by patting two spots on the black metal casing: "Inside here," said Mo Tzu, "explosive material loaded by scientist. Soviet weapons-grade, prepared for detonator. —But not in this one! Inside *other ones* sent to U.S.— In here, we put small laser! This is X-ray laser, very unusual, very intense." Again the bald smile. "Laser is attached from here . . . to pager!"

Debbie felt charmed by noting that a short pipe stuck out from each side of the metal ball though which water would be pumped if this regulator were attached to a boiler; these pipes were dummies, taped over and blocked off with three inches of lead. Mo Tzu paused again for Debbie's and Chang's and the soldiers' undivided attention. With a gesture akin to a flourish, he produced from inside his jacket a flat, collapsible cellular telephone that he opened. "I call; I page," he said (through translators), as he punched in numbers and listened. Then he quickly put back his phone and lifted the black water regulator, this time holding it out so Chang could hear the pager activate, which he and Debbie heard. Nothing else happened.

"*H-m-m-m*," Mo Tzu allowed, to which Chang was mute. Then Mo Tzu said something like, "Ah, but of course!" and proceeded to explain that the detonator could not possibly have worked because the laser beam was set to home in on X-Y-Z quantity and quality of radioactive material. It was perfected to operate only when put to final use. Unless . . . and at this point Mo Tzu displayed two tiny metal clips joined by a half inch of insulated wire . . . a sensor bypass were to be installed on the laser trigger mechanism. For that Mo Tzu requested assistance from one of the soldiers and from Debbie, for he was "not a mechanic," he said emphatically.

Together, on the hood of Chang's rented Jaguar, they reopened the black water-regulator casing, removed the duck egg, and partially exposed the laser device which Mo Tzu pried open with a small screwdriver he happened to have at the ready. Mo Tzu then spent about a minute—with helping hands holding things in place—attaching the sensor bypass to barely visible terminals inside the laser gun, which he re-closed and pushed back into the cast-metal casing. The duck egg also went back inside, and within a minute Mo Tzu was ready to try activating the detonator again. First he removed the apparatus from the hood of that "very elegant" car and put it back on the asphalt.

*

During this hiatus Chang K'ung looked on impassively. He could see where Mo Tzu's scenario was going, and he approved. In the meantime he was trying to capture implications of something Mo Tzu had said near the outset of this demonstration—the reference to . . . ah, "explosive material" (loaded by the Russian scientist) in devices exactly like this one sent to the United States. And something more: Chang and Mo Tzu were dealing with bombs designed to be *used*. Actually using them was integral to the strategy that would implement his vision. The realization this would be imminent caused him a psychic jolt. *I do what I must. Too bad for some. Life is short, maybe recurrent.*

Then where would he cause the devices to be set off? Where did he want them to explode? The issue was imponderable. The encased plutonium was already in or near ten U.S. population centers. But exploding all ten bombs would be immoderate, undisciplined, unwise, and therefore counterproductive. He had to determine how many to use and which ones. Resolving this was too much to deal with now. Postponing the decision would make it a delicious necessity. This whole thing mystifies me!

Mo Tzu was handing him a cellular phone, the antenna extended. Would Chang accept the honor of consummating this demonstration? Of course he would.

In Cantonese Mo Tzu uttered numbers and showed corresponding numbers of fingers. A soldier translated perfunctorily. Chang tapped the given numbers on the instrument. A female voice came on the phone saying in three languages, "Page accepted," and a moment later the pager in the small control box attached to the round metal casing hummed audibly. In that same instant—click, *bzzz!* The buzzing sound lasted a full second. (Mo Tzu later averred it was set for the maximum duration, 1.2 seconds.) Something seemed to have occurred inside the black steel ball. Mo Tzu unscrewed the flat bottom connection and removed it, as everyone present noticed an acrid, slightly appetizing smell accompanied by a stream of gray smoke. Except for two wet spots inside the casing and particles of scorched shell, the duck egg was obliterated.

"Ah-ha! It certainly works," Mo Tzu announced.

The implication of this was clear although Mo Tzu explained it briefly. If that egg had been weapons-grade fissionable material, properly primed—as was the case with all ten "water regulators" sent to the United States—the resultant chain-reaction explosion would have obliterated the whole complex where they stood and everything immediately near it. Mo Tzu added that ten X-ray lasers identical to the one inside the casing were packaged and stored in a vault back in Hong Kong. Chang had only to claim possession and send them to his associates in the U.S. to finalize arming the bombs there.

As he talked Mo Tzu couldn't help smiling broadly, manically. And Chang stood gazing at the mock bomb, deserted by his self-possession, a grin splitting his face.

Debbie broke their apparent spell: "What about pagers in those bombs we've got Stateside?" she asked Mo Tzu. "What if they don't fit or what if they don't work? Little details like that can make a big difference."

A soldier dutifully translated both ways.

Mo Tzu replied, "Oh, pagers are installed already in units sent to United States. Russians did everything. These lasers are easy to put in. General Chang—uh, 'Wu C'hi,'—can send lasers to U.S. by mail, no problem!"

Chang still grinned unvolitionally. It occurred to Debbie that possession of lethal power, especially a power that is ineluctable, pleases certain people immeasurably. — Vicariously, she might be one of them!— For a moment she tried to imagine a resultant explosion of the chain reaction that would have occurred if the duck egg had been plutonium. She really couldn't imagine it. The power of that blast would have been unspeakable, beyond comprehension, wiping out everything and everyone in the immediate vicinity. With a start, Debbie realized that for the past few moments her grin complemented Chang's.

As he drove Debbie and himself back to Kowloon, Chang chided himself for acceding to Mo Tzu's request for an extra thirty thousand U.S. dollars to meet incidental expenses and (they understood this without stating it) to pay him a bonus.

"Dramatics we saw today cost me a lot of money," Chang told Debbie.

"Was it for some kind of reward?" she asked. "How much?"

"He asked for thirty thousand, American. Also he wanted cash. Today. I'm glad I had only twelve thousand with me."

"Wow. Did you really give him that much cash?"

"Yes, I did, even though I have already paid him enough."

"I was wondering what that was all about. I saw you giving him money."

"At the same time, he was looking hard at you. First it was up and down, then he went from down to up. I think I know what he will do with some of that money—as soon as he returns to Hong Kong." Chang squeezed out a laugh of appreciation, then capped it: "Mo Tzu, you old rooster!"

Debbie said, "Good thing you can afford large gifts."

"I am not made of money. Those were American dollars! Not Taiwan."

Debbie let that stand while Chang found himself pondering: How many bombs? In which cities? Behind his eyes—a phantasmagoria of people, buildings, American landmarks he had visited, even loved—blown to bits, actually vaporized. *Resultant devastation—unspeakable, utter.* He turned to Debbie as he drove.

"How can I choose?" Chang said.

At this moment Debbie was on a different plane, her receptors opaque.

I immerse myself in evil, Chang reflected. Categorical evil beyond all doubt. *I do what I must.*

And two moments later Chang told himself—therefore I will do it well without reservation without fear. In English he told himself, if you're going to do something, do it right or don't do it at all.

That clarified one thing for Chang: his basis for action. He would choose his detonation site or sites by determining which would yield the highest severity of damage, much like selecting a military target. The realization caused him a frisson, for the choice would be his alone to make.

Debbie had returned from her reverie. Toward the end of it she found herself surmising how much Mo Tzu had been paid for doing General Chang's bidding. She guessed about $90,000 (American), which was close to accurate. She turned to regard her driver and saw that his attention appeared to be riveted on the road ahead. She thus envisioned the outline of their joint future: Together in this car, he and she had melded with a momentum and they were going to take it all the way to their destination, whatever that might be, and augment it with their joint will and combined strength. At her deepest level Debbie knew this was exactly what she existed *for*.

As the narrow highway sliced through a village about five kilometers from Kowloon and vehicular traffic had grown intense on this late afternoon, Chang had to focus on pedestrians and bicycles and (especially) trucks, which he did with real irritation, expressed often. This was fine with Debbie because Chang's contumely interrupted a change occurring inside herself that she had experienced before and didn't welcome, even though it would cause her a secret, mild pleasure. She decided to distract herself and Chang by enveloping them in small-talk touching on important subjects that were rarely, if ever, appropriate conversational matter.

"You're awfully rich, aren't you?" Debbie said.

"You could say I am wealthy," Chang responded.

"No, you told me you were filthy."

"Ha-ha!" (Chang was familiar with the Western expression.)

"I know generals get paid pretty well, but I've gathered most of your money comes from someplace else, like a family fortune or something."

"Correct. My salary is okay; I never spend money frivolously—except today. Most of what I own has come to me only because I have no brothers or sisters. My family was very fortunate, mostly in China."

"Ah," Debbie responded. Other issues in her brain begged illumination. "If China invades Taiwan, can you stop them?" she asked.

That captured Chang's attention. After a couple moments he said, "Yes, no. They can overwhelm us. They can eat us, but to swallow us could turn out to be fatal. We are not Tibet. In my sector of Taiwan, perhaps they would not be able to overwhelm us. I intend—I expect—we would kill them if they came, no matter how many would come to attack us. We would continue to kill them until they stopped coming. We have the technology, you know, as they like to say in the U.S."

"Wow." Debbie let all this register as they approached the Kowloon limits. After several moments she remarked, "So you've got a lot of authority and you command incredible military power; you say you can fend off the Chinese army, maybe. Plus you've got all that money et cetera that you've hardly used until recently, like today." Debbie paused to consider how to frame her questions. "What's actually your agenda?—Or is it 'agendum'?—I know you're planning something, shall we say, extraordinary; we wouldn't be here otherwise. Those lasers we're going to send off—are they part of your 'New Taiping Revolution'—or 'Rebellion' or whatever you call it?"

Chang felt slightly taken aback by the questions. "I thought you knew," he said.

"Only what I've learned through osmosis."

Chang gathered she meant she didn't know much. He responded with a grunt.

Traffic and people were stacking in every direction. The afternoon was draining away. There was still much Chang meant to do this day, including irksome chores such as driving downtown to claim his lasers. He couldn't delegate; his only source of assistance sat beside him in this Jaguar and she worked for a different government.

Chang knew almost with certainty that Ms. Kassenbaum— this young American intelligence operative—more than admired him. He had taken her into his confidence largely because, at base, she boosted his ego. And he and she did share a rapport. Now he raised another certainty which he'd previously disregarded: for him to fully exploit her idolization and their unspoken bond would be an impossibility. This woman, he had come to understand, hated being physically close to men. "Preference" was not an issue here; she was designed for the close company of fellow females.

Why am I thinking such things? *Of what possible relevance is this?* Chang asked himself in English and Minnan. He could see the answer in his mind's eye without having to turn toward his passenger. It concerned the way she was built, especially from the waist down. Beyond that, he felt stirred by the soft, blatant I-need-to-be-totally-satisfied-right-now attitude beaming out of her so naturally.

Without forethought Chang K'ung heard himself carefully deliver one, then four more carefully worded sentences revealing that he sought huge sums of money to realize his vision of a wealthy, totally autonomous Chinese country. It might be comprised of ten or, at probable maximum, twenty million souls. Singapore struck him as a template to use in designing it. Ideology would be irrelevant so long as the basis for its laws were core "Chinese values." He would be the CEO to ensure that those values would be permanent institutions; that might vindicate all his years of dedication to the now-forgotten Nationalist cause. Like Japan today or Britain of yesterday, his new country's global importance would grow incommensurately once he released the latent powers of its people, initially all of whom would be screened and selected carefully for citizenship.

"Wow" was Debbie's only response for a long minute.

"I know I am not realistic, but I can almost taste it!" Chang remarked.

"I really suspected you had something like that in mind," Debbie averred. "Let's say I smelled it cooking." (A wry, tight smile.) "So those lasers are going to be part of the preliminary stage, huh?"

"Correct. [Beat.] Once I begin the process—ka-*bom!*—developments will roll out quickly. I expect to see my vision completed long before I am old. [Beat.] At least before I am very old!"

"You know, you might be crazy," Debbie said.

"Maybe."

After about three minutes of silence, Debbie said, "Are you going to actually use the detonators? I mean, you know, *explode* some bombs?"

"Oh, yes. Empty threats are just . . . empty threats. The Revolution requires effective action or it will not get off the ground. No partial success can be acceptable."

"Wow. You're actually gonna explode bombs on U.S. soil?"

"Yes. I think pretty soon."

Debbie decided not to ask whether people would be killed or whether Chang intended to cause significant damage. His words "effective action" obviated that. "Well," she said, "what if they—the U.S. military—decide to nuke you right back?"

"They will have to destroy perhaps a quarter of Taiwan to do that, along with about half the population. Not a likelihood. That is key to my strategy. I call it my 'tactic a la Saddam.' You know Saddam Hussein might be crazy, but he's alive and well. Plus I intend to, oh, let us say, *oblige* the United States— eventually other countries as well—to sign nonaggression pacts."

"Your situation's a lot different from Saddam Hussein's. You won't have the Arab League or Russian diplomats trying to protect your rear end."

"I know. So be it. If I get killed, so be it. My own little life is meaningless, really, even though I am talented."

Chang gazed out with his inner eye for a moment before he said: "I can safely count on over a dozen high-level army and navy officers committed to my cause. We call it the 'Cobra Cause.' Those men are committed; they all have subordinates and they are committed. All of them have friends and family; I am sure we can enlist them. Most, maybe all, of the officer corps will join us—gladly."

"Do your officers know you're planning to set off nukes in America?"

"My cadre knows. My very closest comrades—they all know."

"Man, that's nuclear terrorism . . . ."

A few moments passed in silence. Chang said, "Miss Kassenbaum, your assistance has been invaluable, to me and the Cause. Will you join us? We would be honored if you were among us. I would be honored." He turned to look at her eyes. "Will you join us?"

Without hesitation Debbie said, "Of course." Beat. "I've considered myself on board even though you never asked me."

Chang pondered briefly and said, "When we get off the ferry I think we should conclude our business for today. We need to celebrate some things. Today has been a good day, at least for me! I owe you a grand dinner for all your trouble; it's the least I can do. [Beat.] Of course we have to stay at the hotel. We can try out their toney—is that the term?—restaurant."

"Sounds awfully good."

This is getting unreal, Debbie thought. She felt as though she had sat on a sponge saturated with warm, soapy water. Something was happening inside her that definitely needed resolution. As soon as possible.

When Chang and Debbie had arrived in Hong Kong early that day, they had checked into a new German-owned hotel with a name that resonated the nickname of a former British princess of whom many were fond. Even by Hong Kong standards lodgings here were very expensive, and Chang had a reason for choosing it: any guests or staff who recognized "Wu Ch'i" for who he really was could likely be counted on for discretion. Nobody, especially the local press, needed to know that the enigmatic ROC general had dropped into town *sans* bodyguards and accompanied by a nubile, white American woman.

In fact, though, four of Chang's commandos also had rooms at the "Lady D" (as it was nicknamed). They and Debbie got along famously. If Debbie were in actuality a misandriast, as she perceived herself to be, she was not entirely designed as one. "Men do have their uses," she would sometimes remark without elaborating.

When they'd returned to the "Lady D," while they waited for the lobby elevator doors to open, Debbie cut a sideways look at her escort to ascertain what she really wanted to do. Of course Chang appeared to her as he always had: inside those trousers and within that suit coat and shirt quivered lean, hard limbs and the torso of a cobra. Midway down the front hung a very short hose (ready to lengthen and harden and throb) and a small sack (ready to bulge and rise), and protruding behind the middle were small, tight mounds with an opening between them which begged (in Debbie's view) for vigorous violation.

Ah, yes. Debbie briefly reviewed all that, and went a little further: At the top of what she saw next to her there radiated a consciousness amenable to ecstasy triggered by deep, deep pleasure. Then there was the rich textured voice (bathed in testosterone and molasses) primed to vent that ecstasy. *Oh, damn.*

And here stood a man who could—and soon would—shape a moderate-sized country and probably shake the entire world. He really did have that ability. And more: within this man's grasp, depending entirely on what he willed, lay the fates of literally millions of people. He alone would decide where in the U.S. people would face nuclear disasters, and by what standards Chinese were to be incorporated in the new country he would generate. This was collateral to his military mandate to annihilate enemies presuming to invade Taiwan. "Annihilate": a fine word. *A key word.* Chang actually possessed the ability, the power (to use the term aptly), to annihilate. He could annihilate many, many vitally living humans, and he had taken the prerogative to do exactly that.

A moment later Debbie and that same man stepped onto the elevator and stood close enough together to cause their shoulders to touch briefly. In a few minutes, she thought, he and she would be disrobing and relieving themselves (et cetera) in rooms separated only by a wall.

Oh wow it's time to lube something up, Debbie remarked silently. She instantly envisaged something that needed no lubing: her own lower lips glistening under cotton now slippery wet. Absurd, she thought. *But there's the reality.*

Just before their elevator bumped to a stop at the top floor Debbie abruptly turned to regard General Chang again and, not surprisingly to either, their eyes met. Chang had been scrutinizing her; this each acknowledged. (Actually Chang had just mused on how much this woman physically resembled Hsiu-fen Wu, although Debbie's curves were better developed.) When they paused at the door to Debbie's room Chang said, "Your room or mine? —As they say in America." He was speaking apropos of the dinner they would share that evening away from public view. They briefly discussed the logistics.

Abruptly Debbie said, "Come in." She unlocked and opened the door. They stepped into her room; she closed the door decisively.

"I'm not really hungry yet," Debbie declared. "Right now all I need is maybe a snack; a little fuel. If I eat a whole meal I'll get bloated, slowed down."

"All right then," Chang said. "We will have more time to bathe and rest. Dinner will come later." His mild perplexion caused by Debbie's behavior in the last few moments had already ebbed. He spoke his next words to her back as she strode across the room: "A good, long shower and a nap, also a drink or two, might be just the thing."

Chang watched Debbie bend from the waist to open a small leather case placed on a chair. She wore an expensive black dress and shoes with inch-high heels. The effect was understated stylishness, just right for Hong Kong. The hem of the dress rose as she bent, which presented to Chang's gaze the backs of well-toned legs. Many times before he had marveled at the radical roundness of her rear, obscured today by her full-skirted dress; for a moment he was favored with an intriguing hint of what she had there. The urge to examine it closely (very closely) became overwhelming. Chang found himself considering taking on the challenge to physically exploit this woman's devotion, hopeless as victory might be.

Debbie had removed something from the small leather case. She had straightened her back and was looking over her shoulder and speaking.

"You can have a drink here," she said. "I'd better have one, too."

"Fine. I will relax before my shower-bath."

Chang felt his perplexion beginning to return. Debbie turned to walk back to him. In both hands she lightly held a bizarre object; she spoke into Chang's eyes.

"You can take your shower here," she said.

That captured Chang's total attention.

"In fact I'll take one myself," Debbie added.

A dissonant moment of silence passed between them. Debbie had crossed the floor to stand before Chang K'ung. She held the outre object in front of her as though it might be an offering. Chang regarded her quizzically; Debbie felt compelled to explain.

"I need to learn something," she said earnestly. "I want to get into—I'm trying to discover—certain realities."

"The realities—do they concern me?" Chang asked.

"Oh, they do. I want to get to the bottom of something, so to speak."

"Will it give you real pleasure?"

"I don't know. I think so."

Debbie extended her arms to proffer the object laying across her upturned hands.

"Do you know what this is?" Debbie asked.

Chang looked hard at the thing. He answered "yes," but tentatively.

"The English word is 'dildo,'" Debbie said. With her right hand she gripped the base of it and made a little thrust. "You know what it's used for?"

"I can imagine."

"Of course. Please, come make yourself comfortable, General. I want to show you something else."

Debbie motioned to a chair and kicked off her shoes. As Chang seated himself Debbie raised her dress and in a few quick movements removed her panty hose which she threw aside. Then she casually removed her cotton panties which she handed to Chang and which he accepted with equanimity.

"They're a little wet and sticky," Debbie said. "I'm going to use these." And from a suitcase open near the bed she extracted not one but two panties, both dark (one mauve, one cobalt blue) and glossy. "These aren't real silk," she said, "they can really stretch."

Chang felt an internal alarm start to go off but he was truly intrigued, especially as Debbie enlisted his help in removing her black dress. Clearly he was actually going to get the chance to examine her wondrous nates.

"First we need a shower," Debbie declared, "and something to drink."

After their joint shower and a couple glasses each of mediocre dry champagne along with some sushi, Chang found out in short order why Debbie had displayed the dildo; also that she hadn't produced two panties inadvertently. The dildo, she off-handedly made clear, was for her—to put to use. And one of the panties was to be worn by . . . Chang, who was in no way charmed by her desires.

"Please," Debbie said. "You know I'm revulsed by men, but I want to know you. I mean really know you. This is the only way I can do it. I need to do it!"

Chang was budged but unmoved. Still, he couldn't help being transfixed by the nakedness squatting before him. (He sat on the edge of the bed wearing—at Debbie's urging—only his military identification tag.) "I want to get to the bottom of something," Debbie declared as before. "I can't really say what it is. Let's say I need to probe some mysteries, I guess you would call them. It's an obsession of mine."

"How do you hope to do that?" Chang asked.

"I'll show you!" Debbie said, and seemingly from nowhere she produced a huge tube of a Taiwan-manufactured petroleum jelly that Chang recognized instantly.

Chang didn't have to look at what Debbie grabbed with her other hand. He knew it was the phallus, and it caused him a shudder. That shudder—a sure sign of latent fear—he hated above all things. Then he had to consciously quash that fear as he noticed Debbie pulling a broad, simple black strap out of her leather case, then a thick white silken string bearing a series of small knots.

"I can promise you this much, General," Debbie said earnestly. "You won't need to fuck again for at least a week."

She and Chang each gulped at their champagne.

"Hee-hee-hee-hee! You'll never go back to regular women," Debbie declared.

"Heeh-heeh-heekh," from Chang.

Debbie stood up and put the strap around her waist and buckled it snug before she induced Chang to help her step into the mauve panties—and accept the dark blue ones she proffered insistently. Chang thought it strange that Debbie placed the belt buckle on her left side, under her bottom rib. Then he spotted the leather flag-staff holder, very much like those used to bear flags in parades, attached to the belt and laying over her pubic mound. He surely would have said something if Debbie hadn't turned on the radio loud.

*

About a half hour later Chang acknowledged to himself that Debbie had been right about one thing: he couldn't now imagine wanting or needing sex again, ever. His psyche and seminal vesicles spent, he gazed at Debbie lying near him and tried to smile at her, but with no success. He decided to indulge himself by visually taking in her fine breasts and abdomen, all lean and hard-looking and symmetrical. He admired her accessory: a delicate gold chain from which a bezel holding a solid gold coin hung between her breasts.

A narrow space of bed lay between them precisely where they had been so intensely together a short while before.

Debbie opened her eyes and caught his gaze and smiled at him dreamily. She, at least, could smile, Chang thought.

"I found out what I wanted to know, I think," Debbie said.

"Good. And what is that?"

"You're . . . you're just a man! Like any other, probably. You're . . . a man."

"Really?"

"Yuhh . . . I was ready to spend this evening and all night trying to get into, you might say 'lay bare,' what's going on. I mean, inside you. I wanted to know, I needed to know, what you really are."

Chang could say nothing.

"What makes you so . . . potent," Debbie added.

"And?" Chang said.

"Well, you're . . . a man."

Debbie regarded Chang levelly and (to his mind) smiled endearingly. Then she said, "But oh, my, a super-messy one!"

They eyed the area of bed—and the darker spot in the middle of it—which lay between them.

Chang almost smiled. "I didn't think I had all that in me," he said. [A Minnan interjection.] "I have never had such experiences in my life. I thought I would die!"

Chang glanced about for the white silk string with the row of knots.

"You're quite a woman," he added. "Where did you learn all those tricks?"

"Oh, in the Orient."

They laughed about that.

Their relaxation together prompted Debbie to grasp at metaphysical connections. She realized that Chang lived by something special which she had begun to comprehend only that day: a vision, some might call it a "dream." Whatever it actually was, it animated him, it caused him to thrust at heights reasonably off limits. This man was consequently very dangerous. Definitely—one to be feared, but not by her. Debbie allowed herself a delicious frisson different from the ones she had felt several minutes earlier. Inexplicably she asked, "How'd you get that scar on the back of your left hand?"

"I put it there. As a reminder."

"Ah. Does it work all right?"

"Sometimes maybe too well. For example, I should have told you things about our Cobra Cause long before today. My regrets that I did not."

"Ah, well, I'm behind you one hundred percent now. You know I'm part of your team until I die. I promise you, I'll do everything you ever expect me to do."

"Thank you. I am grateful for your commitment. Already you have assisted our cause, such as today."

Feeling thrilled and gratified, Debbie knew her life was changing irrevocably. She decided that she had better take care of business stateside, get her house in order, while there was time. She asked Chang for permission to do that. From now on, she apprised him, she would report to him first in all matters of importance.

Chang was not surprised by that but he did feel flattered. He also felt a surge of satisfaction: this evening he'd examined carefully the bare backside of this well-kept woman, and he'd found it to be better—far better—than he had fantasized.

Debbie watched Chang gingerly rub his own backside, grimacing as he did that. "I guess people get kinda used to that after a while," she offered. She turned on her side to regard perhaps the most dangerous man in the world, lying naked only a body's-width away from her on rumpled bedclothes.

"I wonder what would've happened if that Chinaman— you know, this afternoon, out in that place by the river—what if he'd slipped real plutonium into that steel casing instead of a duck's egg . . . . Would there be anything left of us? I mean, would they find even a trace of our bodies, or that we'd even been there?"

"We would have been vaporized," Chang said. "Assuming the plutonium to be the right grade, and primed properly."

"How do you know you can assume that's what you'll be using? I mean, how do you know that's what you've got?"

"I deal only with people who possess integrity."

"Wow" was all Debbie could say for a few moments. In the silence that followed she finally said, "We should celebrate!"

Debbie sprang off the side of the bed to stand next to it and stretch luxuriously. "I can honestly say today's been the high point of my life," she announced.

Chapter 12

December 6, 1992
Austin, Texas

Similar to a pair of spoons, atop their bed Charlie and Marie lay on their side to make as much contact between themselves as they could. For the sake of variety they had lit candles inside small, intricate lanterns from Pier One to cast intriguing light patterns on the walls and ceiling. The room was redolent of a toasty fragrance hinting of fruit unknown.

"Remember in Xian when the room was lighted sort of like this?" Charlie said.

"That's what prompted me to get those little candle holders," Marie said.

They stayed as they were, happy for everything. Almost.

"I've gotta get up by six tomorrow," Marie said. "I'd better get to sleep."

Charlie released Marie so she could get up and pad her way to the bathroom, returning shortly to don her nightgown and get under bedcovers. Charlie used the bathroom, then pulled on boxer shorts and a T-shirt. Marie's and Charlie's bodies displayed their proclivities combined with their genes: Marie with her wide shoulders and large breasts and butt still displayed easy athleticism; Charlie looked agile and moved vigorously, his rounded chest and concave belly a little inconsonant with the tubular fat deposits around his hips. Marie likewise bore patches of fat, the product (as in Charlie's case) of genetic programming and probably too much beer and ethnic cuisines.

As they moved about preparing for bed Charlie declared, "This working for a living is the pits! And we're some of the lucky ones: we don't have to go to regular jobs."

"We're actually kind of like 'yuppies,'" Marie said. "Yuppies *manqué*."

"Oh, really? I thought we were 'grumpies,'" Charlie responded. "You know what a 'grumpy' is, don't you?"

"Um, no . . . . I've forgotten."

"A 'grown-up, mature person.'"

Easy laughter.

"Anyway, we're just lucky," Charlie said. He arose and moved to extinguish the candles, then thought otherwise. "But even *we* can't escape the grind. It's the daily push-push-push that makes people get old; that includes us. I'm gonna drink part of a beer."

Charlie left the room to get a longneck bottle of brown ale. When he returned Marie's eyes were closed but he knew that she was awake. He sat on the edge of the bed again and swallowed beer. "How 'bout some for you?" he asked. As he'd expected (he hadn't brought a glass), Marie declined.

"Well," Charlie said, "we'll be takin' a break around Christmas. Head out to 'the ranch' and recharge a little. This time the girls'll come with us."

For several seconds neither said anything. Mention of "the ranch" recalled for them buried images of finding that discarded photo of Charlie amid the weeds there during the weekend after Labor Day. Charlie drank quietly. Abruptly, Marie brought up the name Ricky Wu. Surely he would enjoy seeing "the ranch," she remarked, adding that he seemed to be a decent, likeable chap, to which Charlie concurred. Marie had made a connection: "the ranch" and Ricky, Hsiu-fen Wu's graduate-student brother. The next connection followed inevitably.

"His sister Suzie is quite some lady," Marie said.

"Oh, yeah; she sure is."

"She's drop-dead lovely; surely you've noticed. Y' know I got the distinct impression—maybe it's an intuition—that she's attracted to you.

Is it that obvious? Charlie wondered. He uttered the first notion to cross his mind: "We have a kind of rapport; I've got this musk."

"I'm serious."

"I'm kinda serious."

Time oozed, barely.

"A rapport—that's about as far as it goes," Charlie declared, gazing at the ceiling. "During the course of a year, any year, I see literally hundreds of good-looking women. Austin, as we know, is packed with 'em, girls and women both. Maybe one out of ten or twenty I might have some kind of . . . I don't know, brain-wave connection with. —Or maybe it's pure physical chemistry, some kind of interaction that happens.— In one year that's quite a few connections. The end result's always the same, though."

"Yeah, I know," Marie responded. "The same applies to me, except to a much lesser degree. Seems like most of the men I run into are plain jerks."

"I'm sure some of the ladies are, too."

"Yeah, well, I'm sure Suzie Wu's not one of 'em."

Charlie let that pass. He was thinking of something else: "I really can't imagine getting . . . you know, actually close to anyone who's not Marie," Charlie declared. "If she's not Marie, I'm not interested. I mean, not really; even though I might look twice once in a while."

"When's the last time you looked twice?"

"Um, I don't know. Today I suppose. I can't say."

Charlie knew that was only partially true but he didn't want to recall evaporated details. Meanwhile Marie was deciding to pursue a point.

Casually, Marie asked: "Don't you ever at least *consider* trying to hump one of those 'connections' you sometimes make? I mean, look at Suzie Wu."

"Nope. If she's not Marie, I'm really not interested. Just 'getting off" I don't need. It's got to be . . . you know, natural."

To Charlie, the gratifying act had to feel right by his experiencing Marie's features and characteristics; otherwise it would not, in fact, be "natural." Marie understood his parlance perfectly.

Marie and Charlie lay silent, holding each other's hand. Expecting to hear familiar sleep-breathing, Charlie was surprised to be listening to Marie speak to him in a matter-of-fact tone with an unrushed, even cadence.

"If I ever catch that Taiwanese chick trying to crowd me out—I mean try to take my place in any way—I'll kill her," Marie said. "I don't care if she's helped us before, or how nice a guy her brother is, or how important her job is for General what's-his-face. If she ever tries to scuttle me, I'll snap her neck."

"All right," Charlie responded, at a loss to say more.

"First I would get her; you second," she added.

That was all. Still holding hands, each mused for a moment on how readily "pillow talk" ranges beyond romance and whimsy.

****

December 8, 1992 (Saturday)
Los Angeles County Airport

Feeling dysrhythmic and cramped internally, Debbie Kassenbaum took plenty of time to claim her luggage, check in at Southwest Airlines for the first leg of her flight to agency headquarters in Rosslyn, Virginia, and—most importantly—stabilize her gastrointestinal processes before proceeding into nebulous territory. After two Alka-Seltzer ingestions, she felt ready to take the first step of her primary mission.

In the office provided her by the INS she called a number in Austin, Texas, and Marie answered. A moment later Charlie picked up an extension and joined in. Post the usual preliminaries, Debbie declared, "I really need to see you in Dallas tomorrow, just for a short while."

"I'm afraid that won't be feasible," Marie said with finality.

"What's goin' on?" Charlie said.

"Look," said Debbie, "it really is important I see you. That's why I'm staying over in Dallas instead of going on. I'll go right to your house and stay till I find you if I have to. Help me out, would you! I'm trying to help *you* out."

She would not disclose anything more except that she was expected to appear at agency headquarters on Monday to discuss recent developments in the Pacific Rim Basin.

"Do you need to see both of us tomorrow?" Marie asked.

"It would be to your advantage if you both came. Trust me on this."

Marie went silent as she reviewed her plans for the next day. Although she herself had been dismayed all her adult life by the practices and very purposes of organized religions, she wanted her daughters to be habituated to weekly church attendance (most recently at the downtown Episcopal church), and that required her first-hand leadership. She had plenty else on this Sunday's agenda.

"Did you say 'recent developments' overseas?" Charlie asked.

Debbie's response implied that events were pending in which they, Charlie and Marie, could be involved. Charlie thought she might be referring to imminent errands.

"Where can you be reached in Dallas?" Charlie asked.

Perhaps ten minutes later Marie and Charlie ambled hand-in-hand down the middle of their quiet street, disdaining use of the sidewalk as was their habit unless their daughters accompanied them. Marie held Clarissa the schnauzer on a leash.

"I tell you, that bitch is into something deep," Marie said referring to Debbie. "We've seen signs of it before, as you might recall. We don't want to get ourselves sticky with it—whatever it is she's into—if only because it's probably, you know, Chinese."

Declining to raise the distinction between "Chinese" and Taiwanese, Charlie concurred. He and Marie remarked on Debbie's longevity in her post in Taipei; maybe she was kept on by some chicane connections. Charlie could still recall a woman's voice in English coming through orange fog as he drifted into consciousness while he hung by one arm in a cellar in Taipei.

"Aside from the possibility of our getting a little vacation," Charlie said referring to undertaking an errand overseas, "we've gotta see what the hell she wants. I don't want some shit coming down on us—while people are taking our picture behind our backs—because I didn't check something out. If maybe an errand comes up because of this, well, we don't have to take it, y' know. Regardless, we'd better see what's goin' on."

"This is sort of like a home-repair project," said Marie. "Probably neither of us can do a good-enough job without the other."

December 9, 1992 (Sunday)
Dallas, Texas

"This is really an imposition," Marie muttered perhaps for the twentieth time. "It had better be worth something."

She and Charlie had made their way to the fourth floor of the Dallas-Fort Worth Marriott and were striding along the final stretch of hallway to Debbie Kassenbaum's room. They were dressed for chilly weather; Charlie carried a gift bottle of wine.

"Debbie's still pretty young," Charlie commented; "she's been living abroad for a long time. I'm dubious about this being actually important. But maybe the upshot will be they're gonna need us to do something in French Tahiti or, how 'bout near Bangkok."

A minute later they reached Debbie's door and knocked. When the door swung open Debbie stood before them looking a bit peaked. "So nice of you to come," she said. "How are you?"

"Oh, I've had better days in the jungles," Charlie said.

"He's had better days in the jungles," Marie said.

They stepped into Debbie's room and at her behest made themselves comfortable in heavy chairs around a thick-topped table. Debbie barely looked at the bottle Charlie handed to her. She wore a melon-orange Mandarin pants suit and sipped from a mug. "Tea?" she asked, and they accepted. Debbie fixed two mugs of tea while she told them of her current trip to Rosslyn, Virginia. (The visit was elective, but soon it would have been mandatory.) She averred being plagued by a gnawing headache, and that prompted Charlie to give her a neck adjustment which rendered partial relief.

Then sweetness and light were suspended. In a straightforward manner Debbie informed Charlie and Marie that "the tricks" which she knew they had "pulled" in Taiwan three years before were known about by others; she didn't say who the parties were and what was actually known. She eschewed expressing judgment on Charlie's and Marie's alleged actions. She added (while resolutely withholding Father Nobles' name) that they were "suspected of" perpetrating similar "tricks" in the Philippines nearly eight years ago.

Debbie would brook no demurs from Marie or Charlie. What was known was known; period. Whether their "tricks" would be considered treasonous might be moot, but in their case allegations of treason would require very little proof. That vague point was left to hang in the air ominously.

Still, despite her shock and dismay at what Debbie knew, Marie felt sure that Debbie was bluffing. Revelations of treasonous behavior would have brought swift retribution, at least during the Cold War. Probably only Debbie knew of Marie's and Charlie's "tricks," and she didn't know much, and most probably she wanted something from them. This Marie posited decisively. Charlie, meanwhile, was simply incredulous about everything Debbie had said, except for her disclosing knowledge that he and Marie had done something irregular three years before.

"Tell us more," Marie responded to Debbie's assertions.

"You tell me," Debbie said. "I mean, I'm going to face people who know things. They're gonna want explanations. I'm just trying to help out."

"Help out whom?" Marie said.

"Well," replied Debbie, "you for openers. I've also got a job to do. People in my agency are gonna want to know why you helped insurgent elements abroad. —Yeah, yeah, aside from what Charlie said in debriefing that time in Los Angeles, word is, they want the *whole* story.— Other agencies happen to be involved, you know. For instance the FBI, CIA. They're gonna want to know what was really going on. It's got all kinds of domestic ramifications."

At this point Charlie, who had been standing and casually stretching, bent awkwardly to put his mug on the table. He fidgeted with things on the table top before he sat down again. Clearly he was preoccupied by what Debbie said. Still, Marie was sure he had winked at her.

Debbie had switched to drinking orange juice. She took a swallow from her tall glass, which by now was only half full, and replaced it on a silver tray on the table, then sat back and waited.

Eh what the hell, Marie coached herself. She looked into Debbie's eyes and spoke with deliberation.

"We can't tell you much—you know, about ourselves and what we did—because there's simply not that much to tell. Believe me. However . . . we do know some things that—" And here Marie broke off for a second. "We do know some things," she resumed, "that your associates in Taiwan will consider critical. Yeah, it's critical stuff."

That sent the discourse caroming in a direction no one could ascertain. Marie waited noncommittally while Debbie and Charlie scrambled to grasp the import of what she had served.

After a long moment Debbie said, "My associates in Taiwan?"

She grimaced broadly and hunched forward in her chair.

"Right," said Marie. "Prominent people out there with whom you're connected. Not necessarily on your job."

Beat. Debbie attempted to say something. Instead she cut a sharp groan, stood up looking stricken, and bolted for the bathroom where she slammed the door shut.

Wide-eyed, Marie turned to Charlie. He smiled in response and very deliberately produced from his sport coat pocket a small bottle of clear liquid which he displayed to her then replaced. She knew the liquid was magnesium citrate because he had told her what it was when he'd filled the little bottle over their bathroom sink at home. "This is strictly for pranks," he'd said matter-of-factly. Now he had just pulled a magnesium-citrate "prank."

Marie and Charlie sat at the table and drank their tea. Charlie spotted a box of cookies on a counter top and helped himself, offering one to Marie (accepted). They could now speak privately provided they spoke in low tones.

Marie declared, "That little bitch is trying to get something from us."

"I noticed you're tryin' to give her something," Charlie replied, "and I don't know what it is."

"I don't either," Marie said. "Remember, we've been intuiting she's got big-time connections overseas. We've been presuming that for a long time, for good reason. Now we find out she's got some kind of goods on us. —It's actually kinda shocking— We'd better draw her out. Find out what she knows, what she wants."

Charlie pondered then said, "Fine. Let's keep her off balance. We'll find out what she's got in mind, and I want to know who else knows what she claims to know."

Sounds of commode flushing emanated from the bathroom. Water running. Soon the door opened and Debbie rejoined them, her complexion wan but her insides unburdened. "Sorry," she said and returned to her chair.

"What really do you have in mind to do?" Debbie said to Marie.

Impasse. After glancing at both women Charlie simply waited.

Marie decided to shoot from the hip: "Look, if you want to help us, all you have to do is not volunteer anything. If somebody pointedly asks you something about Charlie or me—whatever the question—well, just answer what you can prove. Period; that's all. That'll help us; and we can just keep quiet about things that . . . are best kept secret."

Marie paused for effect and resumed: "Now if you want to help certain parties . . . say, in Taiwan—or maybe someplace else—we might have very useful information, call it critical information, for that person. —Uh, for the parties involved I mean."

Now Debbie had something to ponder, and she took her time doing just that, meanwhile resisting the temptation to partake of more tea. She felt dehydrated. She also needed psychic support: seeing herself returning to agency headquarters for debriefings and then to her own stateside residence in Falls Church, Virginia, made her quiver inside. (Would she have the fortitude to face all the finality she intended to precipitate?) The anxiety clashed with another kind of quivering: anticipation about getting directly involved in Chang's cause and the array of consequential events that would shake the world and— sooner or later—affect this captivating woman seated at the table with her.

Charlie caught the women's attention by overtly looking about the room. They followed his eyes for a moment.

"We don't know if anything's being recorded here," Charlie said levelly. "We do know that if there's some kind of insurgency or rebellion or whatever goin' on, let's just say in Taiwan—well, the word we've heard is some Americans are in on it. 'Intrinsically prejudiced,' goes the jargon. Or maybe it's just one American; it's hard to say."

Then Charlie very explicitly raised both his hands to a level with his nose and laid one index finger over the tip of the other to form a capital T. He looked Debbie in the eyes and held the T for a moment, even pushing it a few inches toward her nose for effect. A nod from her confirmed she grasped his reference: T'aip'ing. Prefaced by a hint of smile Debbie spoke levelly to Charlie and Marie.

"Not to worry. I'm not recording anything. —I'll use the word."

She uttered the word "*T'aip'ing*" and left it to hang in the air.

"Unfortunately we know about things that are critical," Marie declared.

Beat. Debbie decided to posit Marie's averments as true. "Can you give me some kind of idea of what it is that you have?" she asked Marie.

"Well, let's say that the party for whom you're concerned is . . . involved in activities that are not exactly secret," Marie responded. Pause. "There have been leaks. People who shouldn't know certain things, know things."

"Is it dangerous? I mean, are the leaks critical?"

"Probably they are."

"What's your source?"

"I can't tell you. I'd love to, but right now I wouldn't dare. It's not one source."

Charlie simply stood near the table and nodded abstractedly, affirming in effect whatever Marie asserted. He tried to look earnest but he maintained a little smile because he was simply amused. He wondered where this interchange was going; he wondered what Marie was going to say next. *How did she come up with this stuff?*

Debbie decided to drop all pretext, and for that she was rewarded.

"Do you believe in General Chang?" she asked, her eyes boring into Marie's then Charlie's eyes.

"General Chang is a great man," Marie responded. "We know that to be true."

Charlie still nodded, but emphatically.

"I'll be in touch," Debbie said.

"Just keep everything cool when they ask you things at headquarters," Marie said. "Don't volunteer stuff. If they ask, only tell 'em what you know is absolutely verifiable."

"I'll do the best I can," Debbie replied.

And that was that. Only when they were back in the busy airport terminal did Marie and Charlie broach discussing their recent event with Debbie.

"We still don't know what that chick is up to," Charlie remarked after ensuring minimal privacy.

"We do know she's working for Chang K'ung," Marie said.

"How do you know she's actually 'working for' him?"

"Well, she's getting something from him. She's in his service."

"Maybe she's doin' it for love," Charlie jibed.

Marie cogitated before she spoke: "What's the *It* that she's doing? That's what I want to know."

Later, when they were airborne toward home, Charlie picked up the topic again. "We'd be wise to just stay away from that woman," he said abruptly, staring at whiteness outside the window.

Marie concurred. "Too bad we know something about what she's mixed up in."

"She says she'll be in touch," Charlie said. "She's probably gonna want to know stuff, like what kind of assistance we can give General Chang or whomever. Ostensibly we've got 'critical information' Chang needs. So what do we tell her?"

Marie answered without hesitation: "We do everything we can to keep her away."

"Unh. Well, what if we have to produce something?"

"We don't 'have to' produce squat. All we have to do is keep her away; the possibilities are infinite. But the object is to stay clear of whatever's going on."

"All right by me," Charlie said.

"We'll handle it," Marie said. "One way or another."

****

Consonant with Charlie's experiences since puberty with developments deemed inevitable, after he and Marie met with Debbie Kassenbaum, nothing relevant happened. Time passed, and Debbie did not get in touch.

Imminent Christmas and New Year's became history. More time passed. Marie found comfort in feeling forgotten by people outside her and Charlie's teeming Life. The prospect of performing "errands" had dried up. Evidently the same could be said for the menace presented by Debbie and her connections (either domestic or overseas). Neither Charlie nor Marie knew how the vagaries of bureaucratic existence and skiing injuries suspended their affairs.

Conversely, by being principally involved in those same vagaries, Debbie Kassenbaum found herself shocked numb for a while. After tedious debriefings in Rosslyn, Virginia, she learned that she had been reassigned; all her tactics for averting that no longer applied to her job. Her next assignment: Brazil. (Braa-ziill?!) She had a choice, of sorts, but if she were to maintain a position that provided real assistance to General Chang, simply resigning her job and returning to Taiwan as a private individual would have been counterproductive. Moreover she felt a lingering loyalty to the agency that had nurtured her for so long. Her next destination, then, would have to be in Brazil.

Then, when Debbie had tried to contact Chang, she found him incommunicado. Only by returning to Taipei to tie loose ends in her elapsing assignment—and then using a few days of vacation leave—was she able to learn that he had broken a tibia while skiing and was demoralized by his incapacity. When they met and talked in his mansion, Chang confided that he faced a struggle to regain his confidence. The broken leg bone precluded his practicing Tae kwon-do and doing most kinds of training; he was not even able to do T'ai chi properly. Once he recovered, he'd have to get back into shape; that would be almost like starting over. For a while even some kung fu practitioners would be able to best him in a full-contact match.

That was for openers. Diminished confidence undermined Chang's ability to cope with larger problems: the General Staff had lately been reorganized and Chang found himself manning a new assignment. New technology besieged him; he had to integrate and utilize (effectively, perfectly) weapons systems barely imaginable only five years before. He had to scramble just to maintain his status in the army. Something as minor as getting Major Chen reassigned to Chang's new staff entailed a struggle.

Debbie took all this in and told General Chang what she thought: the best way for him and her to cope with their recent setbacks was simply to overcome them--aggressively. She handed over a sheet of paper. When he was ready again to implement his vision, he could reach her in Brazil at the designated addresses and phone numbers. She too would be ready.

During this visit Debbie and Chang began to share a very meager dinner he had prepared for himself, but with a look of disdain she decisively put down her chopsticks.

"Look," Debbie said, "if you want bones to mend you're going to need a lot more calcium; you need more protein. You're not in some concentration camp."

With no more ado, Debbie telephoned a high-toned restaurant she used to patronize and insisted that Chang order delivery of a multi-course dinner. Then she left him with the admonition to get back into shape and contact her soon. As she walked away Chang leveled his gaze at her back and, starting with her long black hair (tied close to her head), intently took in every inch of her down to her ankles. In that five-second interval Chang knew, absolutely knew, that within a year he would contact her and she would rejoin him, perhaps at this very same place, and together they would take all the final steps to transcendent personal fruition.

GUILTY PLEASURES II

Normally Charlie wouldn't have indulged himself thusly, but on a spring evening following a stout session pumping iron (et cetera, et cetera) at the Hyde Park Gym, his whole being reached for refreshment. Plus Marie had gone to a faculty meeting and the girls were quiet in their rooms. Besides, he needed recharging before he undertook the monthly chore of tending to family finances. As for those finances: he'd best delve into something else first. He owed himself a treat.

First (always)—security before pleasure. Charlie ensured that drapes were drawn and house doors were locked. He also checked on the girls again; one was reading (very good), one was already asleep (very, very good). —Heh-heh-heh.— Casually Charlie opened a huge dictionary on a stand in his and Marie's study and turned to the O's. There he found ten one-hundred-dollar bills bound loosely by a strip of postal tape. Good, good. He found (and riffled) another stack of ten bills in the W's. All right . . . . Opening another dictionary and eventually a Bible he fingered three more clutches of hundred-dollar bills, all the while humming a happy improvised tune. From under a potted cactus Charlie extracted, counted, and replaced 670 dollars more.

These batches of money were his and Marie's "ill-gotten gains," acquired during the last few months through unrecorded cash transactions stemming from their various activities. (They sometimes called it "walking-around money.") Charlie's partnerships had yielded further undocumented cash rewards, all reinvested. Heh-heh-heh-heh-heh.

The first objective, of course, was to beat the IRS. "Make it and keep it" was Charlie's motto. The point of that was to put it to good use; otherwise there was no sense in acquiring it. Using money effectively (and anonymously) presented a welter of problems, serious problems, which Marie usually resolved as a matter of personal honor.

Leaving only parlor and kitchen lights on, Charlie lay atop the covers of his and Marie's king-sized bed clad only in boxer shorts. Of course, he thought, some of his obsessions were irrational, absurd. Fine. The satisfactions he and Marie derived from putting money into a private school for maladjusted kids or the Austin Battered Women's Center or the Nature Conservancy justified the feel-good experience as an end unto itself. In perfect concinnity Charlie contemplated this notion as his muscles and mind slid into deep, deeper softness.

In St. Petersburg in the Russian Republic, Tatyana Platonov regarded her own satisfaction as a secondary thing, even a bagatelle, in relation to accomplishing her reason for existing (aside from the lives she had given to her two children, of course): Her Andrushka—simultaneously reading and planning lectures in the living room with his cassette player insinuating Mozart to his brain via headphones—embodied her Life, and he badly needed corrective heart and lower back surgery before he could Live fully.

What Andrei did not know—although Tatyana had left explicit directions for him to learn otherwise if something catastrophic were to befall her—was that, by Russian standards, the two of them were actually quite wealthy. In various places—her sister's safety-deposit box in Petersburg and in two banks abroad—Tatyana had hidden nearly 100,000 dollars in American currency. (Twenty thousand of it she could put her fingers on within a half hour.) Despite the language barrier between them, the dour Chinese gentleman had helped her deposit cash in German and Swiss banks. The agreement they had worked out in Singapore was that he would deposit the balance owed to her upon his receiving final authorization to do so from the intense-looking man often addressed by the English word "General." Final payments would total another 100,000 dollars in hard currency.

As Tatyana rammed lunch remains into their battered little refrigerator, she reflected that her dreams for the past several years were about to come true except for one damnable thing: on the preceding day Andrei had received at the Institute a cryptic telegram from "Mo Tzu," the dour-looking gentleman, declaring that Tatyana do nothing until (ostensibly) further notice. Period.

Thus Tatyana's plans—and Life—and aspirations—were in abeyance. Evidently something had gone awry. All she knew was that she had performed in full her part of the agreement. She had done so beautifully. Neither Chinese gentleman could harbor any complaints or qualify his satisfaction with her work or her products.

Well before 1992 had ended, Tatyana had managed the actual manufacture of Andrei's detonators. She had sent them piecemeal to Mo Tzu's "environmental testing firms" set up in the Philippines and Brunei. She'd received signed receipts accounting for all ten devices. She had since finessed all manner of financial arrangements to pay for her final "research trip" to Singapore. All she lacked was the final signal, and she felt utterly unprepared to wait longer.

*   *   *

Let me explain something that you have probably intuited about the motivations of Tatyana and Andrei and Charlie and Marie that I know to be true. This is basic to understanding each of the couples as a unified entity, into which they had evolved quite naturally.

But first a preface: after Marie and Charlie returned from Xian, China, they had a discussion with Hollis Senior, who remarked that he wished he had focused his Life on accomplishing things that were more . . . "universal." He cited "enriching Lives and fixing Lives" as feats that "partake of universality." These he could attribute to Marie. More abstract achievements, such as causing people to know joy or enlightenment (sometimes difficult to tell apart), he called "divine." He put it neatly when he said, "Once you do something that's divine, or when you experience something divine, the event can never be nullified."

For Charlie and Marie that perfectly expressed their psychic mainspring, which was to try to do things that augment reality in a way that transcends time and the material world, much as love does. Thus they intended their Life to be meaningful. In their own ways, Tatyana and, especially, Andrei strove to do likewise.

Of course accomplishing that necessitates making all sorts of decisions involving imponderables. Unified couples who Live vitally have to make devilishly tricky decisions all the time. So Charlie and Marie and Tatyana and, I would say, Andrei evolved a principle that enabled them to act fruitfully and they abided by it: If you can project that you will regret not having done something, for heaven's sake do it.

Allow me to endorse this for you.

*   *   *

April 13, 1995
Austin, Texas

On a whim, Marie answered her telephone this mid-morning instead of using her answering machine to screen the call. Her reward was to hear the melodious voice of a young woman stretching to reach her from days almost forgotten.

"This is Debbie Kassenbaum. Remember me?"

"Of course!" Marie replied. "What are you doing? Where are you?"

"Well, I'm in transit," Debbie said. "I thought I'd check with you so I could plan ahead a little bit."

"I don't know if I can help you much anymore," Marie said.

"Well, maybe you can. Is it possible to talk to both you and your husband?"

"Charlie's at work of course. We'll both be here, say, six hours from now."

"Fine. I'll try calling you then."

With a reciprocal "fine" from Marie, the call ended. Marie tried to shunt it from her mind for the rest of the day and she mostly succeeded.

When Charlie came dragging home from planting trees in a county park (discrepant to Marie's earlier declaration of his whereabouts), he seemed barely concerned when Marie told him of Debbie's making contact. Except for one thing: Marie and Charlie had set a dinner date for that evening with Jed and her husband Benjamin, Marie's and Charlie's closest friends. (Friendship with Jed stemmed from nearly the origin of Marie's identity as "Marie." It extended, seamlessly, to Benjamin Ethan Berman, "Mr. *Uber-Mensch*," whom they liked to call "Benny"—a name he barely tolerated.) The occasion was designed to fortify both couples for the rest of the work week. Anticipating Debbie's telephone call partly subverted the evening because Charlie and Marie wondered whether something big was in the offing that might involve them.

Of course she didn't call. They had no idea of how to reach her or they would have tried. At first the dinner date turned out well anyway, and the two couples enjoyed Latin-American-style food at an haute-cuisine restaurant near the huge university. Later they opted for "sin" by smoking overpriced cigars on the restaurant veranda.

Ever since they had become a foursome, the couples disagreed with each other (sometimes trenchantly) on most issues. Only one thing did they agree on categorically: the main benefit from being united with another person—the *raison d' etre* for personal partnerships and marriage—was enjoying the pleasure of the other's company. They endorsed the corollary that a person does a better job of living (and enjoys Life more) when he or she is in partnership with someone important; the mutual effect is synergistic.

During get-togethers, Charlie's—and usually Marie's—designated role was to be a civilized crank. Benny and Jed had the temperament of devil's advocates, so that was their role vis-à-vis Charlie and Marie. The couples' arrangement always worked well, as it did on this evening—until after they'd begun relaxing outdoors with their cigars.

Benny—supported by Jed—had been waxing ecstatic about the benefits and pleasures of being "on the Web," as he and Jed utilized the Internet daily. They (and Marie) waited for Charlie to say something like, "For what?" probably adding: "I don't do nearly enough reading and working out as it is." But tonight Charlie had fallen reticent. Marie offered remarks about all the newspapers, magazines, journals, and books she'd been unable to read of late, then she too slipped into a study.

"So, what's new with y' all?" asked Jed, ending a long blank space.

From Marie and Charlie: nothing.

Benny's incongruously *goyish* blue eyes turned earnest as he spoke to Charlie and Marie in turn: "Hey, what's really goin' on lately? Are you thinking of, maybe, doing some more work for the federal government? Nahh! Why do that, right?"

Charlie and Marie regarded Benny and Jed as though the gathering had just convened on Saturn.

Jed and Benny knew very little about Charlie's and Marie's errand-running activities; over the years they'd learned only some basic facts, which they really weren't supposed to know at all. What little they'd been told had been divulged under strictest confidentiality, for Charlie and Marie regarded their vows of secrecy as ever binding.

At last Charlie spoke in measured tones, choosing his words carefully as Marie gazed at his face to monitor his words and thoughts: "It's possible that some real horrors we've gotten wind of might be fixin' to happen. I don't know where, but I expect here, somewhere in this country. —It could be . . . lethal."

"Are you talking about . . . maybe some kind of terrorism?" Benny asked. "Like, nuclear terrorism?"

"I can't say."

"We don't know yet," Marie interposed.

"Are you trying to find out?" Jed asked.

Marie and Charlie allowed as that was a good question. Maybe they *could* learn what might happen.

"What are you going to do if you find out that it will happen?" Benny asked. "Can you report it somewhere? You know, where reporting will do some good."

"We honestly don't know," Marie replied, and Charlie nodded concurrence.

"Sheesh!" Jed said.

"Well, you can't just let it happen," said Benny

"Can they really stop it from happening?" Jed mused aloud.

A gap of silence until Charlie said, "Y' know, it seems a little unlikely that we could stop it. We're talkin' credibility here. I mean, who's gonna take us seriously?"

Jed asked, "Well, don't spies know who to report to, you know, directly, so you can get direct action? I mean, don't you have access to channels that put you in touch with people who handle that sort of thing? Seems to me you would."

Marie said, "We're not spies, dear."

"Hah-hah!" Benny blurted with a wry smile. "Once a spy, always a spy."

Marie gave a snort, Charlie shook his head. A moment or two passed.

"Look," Benny declared. "You can always do something. Hey, read my lips: There's *always something* you can do."

Jed spoke levelly into Marie's eyes. "Does it look like it's gonna be catastrophic?"

"We don't actually know enough to conjecture properly," Charlie interposed.

"You should find out," said Benny.

"Well," Jed declared, "looks like you'd better do something. You can count on us for whatever *we* can do."

*

May 5, 1995

"Would you believe, I'm still around," Debbie Kassenbaum had told Marie over the phone on the preceding evening, then she happily related that she'd been "tying loose ends" and was in Houston on her way "overseas."

Marie had declared straightaway, "Even if I were at liberty to divulge anything you might have found useful, which I'm really not, it's probably long outmoded."

Debbie had conceded the validity of Marie's assertions but she wanted to ensure that "certain weak links" be exposed. "It'll be my last bit of 'damage control,'" she said. Her method would be simple: enjoy a face-to-face lunch with both Marie and Charlie on her way through Austin en route to California.

"I'd like to see your part of the country before I go back," she said.

Meeting in Charlie's and Marie's home had been precluded by the concern about possible "bugs." Thus Debbie, Marie, and Charlie met for lunch at a gourmet Mexican-cuisine restaurant called Eva's in downtown Austin. A good lunch was needed by all. Before they went in Charlie said to Debbie, "Listen, you're welcome to come stay at our house for as long as you'd like. You can rest up, wash up, whatever. There isn't much else we can offer you, though."

Debbie registered that, but the business at hand took precedence. Fifteen minutes later, her tastebuds having done acrobatics from an array of *salsas* and the *chilequelis* for appetizers, Debbie dug into her chicken-mole enchiladas and almost instantaneously all her body cells stretched high and cheered.

Still, Debbie Kassenbaum was nothing if not dedicated to her commitments. Even as she extracted her second forkful she said, "Look, if there's anything we need to know, *anything*, even if it's passé, I'd better dig it up so we can look at it. We—I won't mention names—can't just let something go if it might have been important. You know?"

Silence from Marie and Charlie. Debbie resumed chewing and swallowing. After a while she spoke again: "I thought some information you had was so important—so critical—you implied you could only deliver it personally. In fact, you did mention security leaks." Beat. "I've been instructed to find out what they were. Or what they are." The question of who "instructed" her was left unspoken.

"Anything we know—whatever we knew—is obsolete," Marie said. "And, yuhh, if it were current we'd only disclose it personally."

"Well," Debbie said, after downing a mouthful of food, "you can tell me, or you can tell . . . someone else. I think you know who that is. —Seems a lot easier to tell me."

Charlie declared, "What we had isn't current, so we're reluctant to bring it up."

Debbie directed her major concern to Marie: "How do you know it's obsolete?"

"I can be pretty sure about most of it," Marie answered.

"But not all of it," Debbie said.

"I suppose that's right; maybe not all of it," Marie responded and looked to Charlie who glanced her way and nodded.

Neither Marie nor Charlie was happy with this game. On that Sunday afternoon in Dallas almost two and a half years before, they had simply bluffed Debbie, with whom they would have preferred not to deal at all. Except for the menacing but sketchy information Charlie had allowed himself to learn from Hsiu-fen Wu, they actually knew nothing of importance about the New Taiping "revolution." And they surely had no critical or useful information to provide Chang K'ung and his associates, other than "the darling Ms. Wu" (to use Marie's words) having breached her general's secrecy in her effort to recruit Charlie's help.

Marie and Charlie decided this game with Debbie had been sustained too long; moreover it carried the potential for being the opposite of harmless. They separately determined to stop it before it went further.

For a little while Debbie focused on finishing the mole enchiladas in front of her and clearing the reddish-brown sauce from her plate with a corn tortilla. Then she looked up at the two chewing faces at the table with her and declared: "Listen, we're not talking about some little game or something that some Chink fascists are playing on the other side of the ocean." Resolution had hardened her voice.

"This is the first time I've heard the word 'fascist' in a long time," Marie said.

"First time I've heard 'Chink' in a while," Charlie said.

Charlie and Marie spoke the next sentence almost in unison: "We're out of the loop."

"That's your choice," Debbie responded. "But remember this: there will be repercussions, sooner or later. I presume sooner than later."

Charlie surveyed the remains of his meal. He scooped green sauce and melted white cheese onto a corn chip; he picked at his salad. Marie leaned back in her chair and sipped red wine thoughtfully. After a while she spoke to Debbie.

"I hate to ask dumb-ass questions," said Marie, "but what kind of 'repercussions' are you talking about? Cite for us one 'repercussion.'"

Charlie muttered something in concurrence.

"Look," Debbie said, "I can't tell you a whole lot. But, well, let's say stuff will happen. Gross stuff; gruesome occurrences. People—all kinds of people, many people—are gonna want to know why, and how. You don't want them coming after you. And they might. [Beat.] Uh, that's not quite all." Debbie chose her next words carefully: "This much I can tell you: some places in this country will be physically dangerous places to be in."

"So, how do we avoid those places?" Marie asked.

"Not a problem," Debbie replied. "If you're on our side. If you're with us."

Charlie snorted. "I don't think so," he said, recalling his conversation with Hsiu-fen Wu in Los Angeles back in September of 1992.

"I tell you," Debbie said, speaking impulsively to both pairs of eyes focusing on her from across the table, "if you're considered to be against us—against our Cause—that could be a really dangerous, uh, situation in days to come."

Charlie and Marie registered this threat noncommittally.

"I would think you'd want to avoid that hanging over you," Debbie added.

Charlie snorted. "I can't say I give a rat's ass," he responded.

"Well, what is it that you propose?" Marie asked in her most reasonable tones. "You know our position."

With a glance at his wife, Charlie, the mellow man of reason, sat back to listen.

"Look, what is today?" Debbie asked.

"Thursday," Charlie said.

"Hmmm. Okay. Five days from tomorrow afternoon, in Singapore, you'll get your chance. If you really had something important for our Cause—I can tell you, it's a cause that's going to affect the whole world—you'll get your chance to present it, no problems. Exactly as you wished before, you'll be able to deliver it in person.

"If your information is obsolete or non-critical, well, so be it. But only one person is in a position to make that determination, and if you can't tell me, you can tell it to him yourself, personally. That is, if you really have intelligence, and if you really care about the Revolution. I think we can call it a revolution, given that it's going to really impact on the world."

"For a long moment Debbie confronted silence. For the sake of thoroughness she decided to play her bottom card by adding, "Your own safety might be at stake, you know. I'd say it probably will be."

"We'll give it some thought," Marie said.

Charlie said, "We'll think about it." His mind arced into the next week and surveyed the contents of the days. "We really don't have time right now for any trips."

Debbie tersely clarified particulars: On the eleventh of May, that coming Wednesday in the U.S., she herself would introduce Charlie and Marie to "a giant" (whose name she still avoided uttering) if they were to meet her in Singapore. The meeting and introduction would take place ("believe it or not," she said) at the Raffles Hotel, probably in late afternoon. No rooms would be available at the Raffles on that day or the next; Charlie and Marie would be able to get a good room at the Far Western Hotel less than a few blocks away.

"Trust me on all this," Debbie declared as her lunch partners listened impassively. She wondered whether she was persuading them to her will and decided that probably she was. Then Debbie brightened as she commented that Charlie and Marie would actually be able to meet "a giant among men" and they might aid his Cause.

"We'll give it some thought," Marie said again. Charlie nodded. Both wondered why the event was going to take place in Singapore, but neither bothered to ask. Everyone noticed that nobody had used the word "Taiping" during this lunch.

Marie broke a brief silence by asking Debbie, "Aren't you supposed to be on assignment somewhere? Like, overseas."

"Well let's say I'm on extended leave from the Agency," Debbie responded, smiling. "I decided I'd like to take a vacation and drive to LA. See parts of the country I've always missed."

Understood by all three principals were the words, "while I have the chance," implications of which Charlie and Marie found disturbing.

They parted amicably enough. Debbie declined Charlie's reiterated offer to refresh at his and Marie's home. No further mention was made of meeting soon in Singapore. After a little smile and wave, Debbie simply went on her way to Los Angeles and points far beyond. Holding hands till the last moment, Marie and Charlie parted for their work.

At home with their daughters that evening, after watching CBS Evening News, as Charlie trimmed and seasoned red snapper fillets in preparation for cooking, he asked Marie if there was something significant about the Raffles Hotel in Singapore. She replied that it was an historical gathering spot in the days when Singapore was a British colony and "Brit-lit types" liked to visit the place, the name Somerset Maugham springing to her mind. Maybe that's where the "Singapore sling" cocktail was invented, she added.

All that meant little to Charlie. As he finished preparing the fish while Marie chopped salad ingredients, he ventilated what they'd both been pondering: "I wonder what all she knows about us. I bet she doesn't really know much." The reference was to Debbie Kassenbaum, a subject they had carefully avoided raising until now.

"Oh, she certainly knows a lot about one subject in particular," Marie said.

"Well, yeah, of course."

That was all they meant to say now because of their precaution from years past: walls might have strange bugs. But after a moment Charlie declared, "Well, there's one almost sure-fire way to find out the things we need to know. Until we do it, we're just stumblin' around in the dark, or worse. Marie guessed correctly what he meant: learn certain realities from Hsiu-fen Wu.

"But when?" she asked. "Five days, remember?"

"Tomorrow. Maybe tonight. I'd better get on the phone if I'm gonna do it."

Charlie could only conjecture that Hsiu-fen was in Taiwan and would be amenable to seeing him. If that were so, he would visit her immediately. Telephoning her would have to be done from his clinic; if the phone there was bugged, so be it. And if Charlie were to travel to Taiwan immediately, he would have to secure airline-ticket reservations and make arrangements to be absent from his clinic for about a week. That notion pulled him up short.

What might happen in that week? Would they—Charlie and Marie—be able to accomplish, successfully, whatever they might have to do? Mainly, would they both return safely from doing it? Separately, privately, Marie and Charlie answered the latter two questions: Of course. And that was the way it would have to be.

Also of course Charlie could not reach Hsiu-fen Wu directly. Finally, late that night, she did answer at one of the two telephone numbers Charlie had been using twice every hour. When Charlie heard her voice, and especially when he felt the warmth in her response to his making contact, his anxiety receded to the ether. Everything became brightly easy.

Yes, Suzi Wu would be available for him to visit her as soon as he could get there. *Great.* He would leave as soon as he could get on airline flights; he'd call her "the moment" he arrived in Taipei. Thus Charlie realized that he was committed to a course of action undreamt of a day earlier.

Getting airline reservations, notifying his clinic partner of his imminent absence and plausibly justifying that, and waking Marie to tell her of his plans without sounding excited (and inexplicably pleased) were suddenly easy to do. Finally setting aside his hot telephone, Charlie sat quietly at his desk and found himself envisioning pending scenarios, the most prominent involving him—and expectedly Marie—going to Singapore in a few days.

To do what in Singapore? Charlie allowed himself to make projections, and what he saw—the direction, the ultimate actions—he and Marie might have to take, left him shaken, nauseous. The exciting anticipation he'd felt in generating his own mission, beginning with a spontaneous trip specifically to visit an intriguing, receptive woman, had given way to dread. *Boy I sure hope this is gonna finish up being just a middle-age illusion.*

*

Shortly past midnight, as Charlie prepared to leave his clinic (conceivably for the very last time, he reflected), he impulsively picked up the phone again. His mother and Jed and Benjamin he'd intended to call later, when they were awake. But maybe Benjamin knew about something that Charlie should look into very seriously. It could make a huge difference. The superior man who Lives in the moment, also prepares for the moments he can see coming. Years and years before, Charlie had spent numerous minutes on several occasions framing this set of ideas in English.

Charlie was lucky: Benny and Jed evidently were still awake. He briefly told them that he—and possibly next week Marie as well—had to go overseas to "look into that matter" they'd discussed at the restaurant in April.

"Benny, remember when you did your EMS training," Charlie said, "you told us about that expert poisoner you knew. I think you said you'd met him when you were between medical school and pharmacy school."

"How did you know I went to medical school?"

"Jed told me."

"Oh. Yeah, I knew some poisoners. There were actually three of 'em, all related; they're all brothers or cousins." Benny added that "the poison brothers" owed him favors for his helping them avert two murder charges. Charlie asked Benny to arrange for him to meet them.

"Sure. When do you want to meet?"

"Tonight."

Benny said the only problem was they lived in Lockhart, a farming-ranching town exactly thirty miles from downtown Austin; plus it was late. Charlie wanted to meet them anyway, if only because he would benefit from a drive in the country and feeling space. Thus it was arranged, and Charlie embarked on a three-hour fool's errand.

He actually met with "the poison brothers," three congenial young men with strange obsessions, but all he accomplished was learning that ricin, a protein derived from castor beans (thus undetectable after ingestion), was precisely—and only— what he needed. Utterly lethal and quick-acting stuff, he could carry it as pocket dust or shoe powder through international customs, no problem. Transmitting it required a solvent, and Charlie's hosts could provide one, free of charge. And of course the man who processed castor beans (and wouldn't overcharge for a handful of powder) was nowhere to be found that night, and Charlie returned home empty-handed, his future—and likely Marie's future—appearing too clouded to envision.

At about seven o'clock that same morning, Charlie sat at the kitchen table rousing himself with coffee and relating his recent experiences to Marie, who was busy getting Lisa and Julia ready for school while she coped internally with pending events. Marie might soon be under the same duress as Charlie but hers would be amplified: If she were to join Charlie overseas during the next week, someone else would have to take care of the girls; meanwhile her own projects (and deadlines) would have to be suspended. Worse, she wouldn't dare presume that she and Charlie were going to return home safely and directly. She knew that Charlie harbored the same lack of presumption.

"Whatever happened to prudence," Marie said when Charlie finished recounting his late-night experiences. "Don't

Buddhists believe in prudence anymore?" Then she half-whispered to Charlie, "That ricin you wanted, were you planning on giving it to—"

Walls could maybe hear things. Marie slanted her eyes with her index-finger tips, then formed a circle with her right-hand index-finger and thumb tips and placed the circle on each of her shoulders: impressions of epaulets, a Chinese general. Charlie nodded yes. For a moment Marie looked stunned.

Then Charlie declared, "It's possible, we might have to, um, handle things in a very . . . uh, direct sort of way."

Before Marie took Julia and Lisa to their respective schools, Charlie gave each girl a strong, protracted hug. They knew he would be leaving on a trip that morning; ostensibly he'd be gone most of the following week. Charlie's reasons for holding them tightly stemmed from his much different prospects, which Marie understood too well.

When Marie returned from taking the girls to school, Charlie was mostly packed to leave. He showed Marie that he was taking his own passport—with visas to Taiwan and Singapore—and his most recent Special-Status passport that had been issued by the U.S. State and Defense Departments; it was a document he was supposed to have returned after their last errand abroad. (He and Marie each kept one despite strictures against retaining such documents.) The Special-Status passport did not bear Charlie's real names. "I'm hopin' not to use this thing," Charlie said.

Charlie also hoped to not make use of two little bottles of magnesium citrate he'd packed in his toilet kit (the fact of which he overlooked mentioning to Marie). But mainly he didn't want to use the arrangement for contacting Marie that he and she devised when they briefly strolled the street in front of their house: If Charlie were to find himself facing a job too large—and too critical—to undertake alone, he would telephone Marie on two successive midnights, Texas time. He was bound to succeed in making contact at least once. The sole fact of his placing the calls would be their signal: she was to meet him at the Far Western Hotel in Singapore by the morning of the eleventh.

The exception would be if he explicitly wanted to preclude that from happening. "In that event," Marie declared, "just to be sure, at *some point* to say 'C-X-1, blue." That would be the signal they most wanted to use ("Cancel priority one; all is cool"). To both it would become like a mantra.

"Let's hope this is just a false alarm," Marie said before they went back inside. "And if it's not, well, maybe the two of us might decide we can't save the world. We're not exactly equipped, you know, to take on a well-founded conspiracy. Our firepower is really limited!"

"Yeah, well, I'm surely hopeful," Charlie said. "It all seems so *unlikely.*"

When they stepped back inside their house Charlie was delighted—and subsequently unspeakably relieved—by what developed next. First Marie asked him how his packing for the trip was going, and Charlie replied that it was almost finished. Marie looked at a clock; so did Charlie. The hour was barely past 9:00 a.m.

"What time does your flight leave?" Marie asked, although Charlie had told her.

"*H-m-m*, 11:20," Charlie said.

"Good. There's time. You finish packing. I'm gonna take a quick shower," Marie declared. "You need to be good and relaxed for the trip."

Chapter 13

At about the time Charlie's Southwest Airlines 737 was touching down at Los Angeles International Airport, Chang K'ung finished a solitary workout in the officers' "health club" and hurried to his car still wearing gym togs. He had at least a dozen major things to finalize in the next four days, the first being to implement his own vision of how to most advantageously deploy Taiwan's recent acquisition of American F-16 fighter-bombers. His vision of where to place those and all other jets under his command was governed by very special considerations, what he called his "hidden agenda," which people assumed he meant ironically.

"Home," he said quietly to his Japanese driver. During the drive he would re-study the proposal he intended to present to the National Defense Council in the morning.

In fact Chang *constantly* advanced a hidden agenda known only to members of his top-secret cadre. For instance, the American jets would be used to defend, if need be, a nation which did not yet exist. How Chang and his officers deployed those jets might very well deter attack upon that country by, most likely of all, the Republic Of China, which would actually host the new country. (Chang would name it after he received consensual advisement from his cadre.) If that wasn't a "hidden agenda," Chang had often mused, no such phenomenon existed.

Even for Chang, too many preparations required his complete attention. Near the end of the next week, solely at his discretion, Chang would calmly speak into a telephone and issue the orders, probably two orders to be executed simultaneously (although he contemplated a third as well) that would make the civilized world recoil (to put it mildly). He would also utilize coded Email to alert his operatives in the U.S. that action was imminent. And once his orders were carried out, he and his cadre would do things seen only in fantasy novels and movies.

After the physical damage of small nuclear explosions—mere tokens but causing real devastation—huge governments and military establishments and economies would have to react to what he had triggered and, most importantly, do what he demanded. Entire populations would quail. Chang and his organization had better be ready to keep themselves impregnable while they seized the most powerful governmental throat on Earth and maintained their momentum until all their demands were abundantly met. The trick would be to keep the bastards cowering, Chang had postulated; this was a major tenet he had preached to his lieutenants. Thus, to maintain pressure he wouldn't hesitate to nuke again, maybe hitting Washington, D.C.

Was all necessary communication equipment in place? Yes.

Was their "fortress" ready? Well, mostly.

Would everyone have his orders precisely clear, definite? Incredibly to Chang, he was still working on that. He reminded himself that some orders he could not possibly issue until the last possible moments. His mind vectored tangentially . . . .

Pittsburgh I never liked Pittsburgh. Maybe, Chang thought, Pittsburgh would be the locus of his third explosion. Los Angeles was a given (as they say in the U. S.); Detroit—no problem with that. Chicago had been a strong possibility, but Chang had always liked Chicago; no telling where his commando would set off the explosion there and what it would ruin. Initially hitting Washington, D.C. struck him as similar to using a trite metaphor or cliché in a poem; it would lack freshness, individuality. Chang regarded Pittsburgh balefully since the city had been greatly improved in recent decades and its citizenry had turned snobbish about it.

Which targets he selected would make little difference, Chang was sure, so long as the damage, although limited in scope, would be total destruction. If he could have been more certain of the placement of his people in Japan, he would have surely opted for an initial target there as well. (Kyoto would not be harmed, but Chang had different plans for various Japanese cities.) That was one reason he would meet with the Russian scientist's wife in Singapore: to arrange to secure additional detonators and a backup explosive or two.

Thank goodness we're going to Singapore. There he and the key members of his "revolution" would meet to clarify expectations; at the same time they could relax and reinforce each other's resolve, away from their usual stresses and demands. Once they returned to Taiwan they would feel refreshed and motivated. The time in Singapore would also allow Chang himself to focus better on meeting all the prerequisites to the fateful steps he planned to take.

Maybe I really am what they call an "evil genius," Chang told himself in Minnan and English, unable to resist a wry smile. In Singapore, everything would get sorted out.

May 7, 1995
Taipei, Taiwan

Feeling more than slightly dysrhythmic, by the time Charlie passed through Republic Of China customs at Chiang Kai-shek International, Saturday evening had deepened into night. Flight delays compounded by fierce squalls between Hawaii and Wake Island had cost him over four hours. (Taipei time was past 10:00 p.m.) Ostensibly his visit was occasioned by chiropractic science and business, a cause worthy of advancement, although he knew only one doctor of chiropractic in Taipei. Several times during this trip he had imagined himself being met inside the airport by "the darling Suzi Wu," but he knew that vision to be purely a fantasy.

Almost exactly as Charlie had fantasized, as he walked to the luggage carousel Hsiu-fen Wu materialized next to his right shoulder and strolled with him wordlessly. For a moment

Charlie felt too flushed with pleasure and surprise to say anything.

"Suzi! Am I glad to see you!" Charlie said at last.

He turned to make eye contact and saw that Hsiu-fen looked tired. Later he would learn that she was sleep-deprived from tracking his flights.

After several more steps together she said in a thin voice, "Too bad you come so late, Chahrdree. We missed having good time at my cousin's wedding."

Charlie felt rocked. He hadn't been called "Charlie" in a cadence such as he'd just heard—and with that peculiar Asian-female resonance—for at least fifteen years. His only response was to curse sincerely the airlines and weather.

Once outside the airport terminal Hsiu-fen and Charlie set about implementing their agenda. Hsiu-fen knew in her heart that she had a program she wanted to see effected, but she resolved not to acknowledge it. (This foreign man emanating his lightness and richness, after all, was connected to a formidable wife.) Conversely, apart from his being dazzled by everything about this richly textured Woman (spelled with a capital "W"), Charlie had come here specifically to realize goals.

"I've got to find a hotel room," he declared as they strode into a VIP parking area and he felt a gnawing lack of vigor from the knees down.

"I have hotel reservations for you; no problem," Hsiu-fen told him.

Soon Charlie found himself being led to a red BMW which he thought he had seen before despite the pristine appearance of it. "Ah, I see you've still got the Beamer," he said. "It's actually comforting to see a fine car like this survive the traffic in Taipei."

"Oh, Taipei traffic's not so bad," Hsiu-fen said as she unlocked her car by remote control. "This is same kind of car, but newer model."

"Really? How much newer?"

"Third time new," she said, showing three fingers.

Charlie was impressed.

Soon they shot into teeming Taipei for a night-time tour to refresh Charlie's perspective on the place and to allow space for conversation. Since Hsiu-fen had already reserved a hotel room for him, Charlie felt free to pursue a primary item on his agendum: whether Hsiu-fen and Debbie Kassenbaum worked closely together in their connection to Chang K'ung. "I know that you're General Chang's right hand," Charlie commented as he and Hsiu-fen talked of many things. "Ms. Kassenbaum — Debbie — is she the general's left hand, or what? You know she works for a U.S. spy agency."

By this time, about ten minutes into their drive toward the center of Taipei, Hsiu-fen appeared more animated. She smiled in the dark as she contemplated Charlie's question; then she laughed lightly.

"Nobody can say, not even General Chang," Hsiu-fen responded. "All I know — Chang trusts her; also he needs her. For what, I don't know. I know she likes certain kinds of women. [Beat.] Not my kind!"

Good, Charlie thought. The right hand doesn't quite know what the left hand is doing. As Charlie dismissed the issue of Debbie's sexual design, Hsiu-fen said, "I thought you and Miss Kassenbaum work for the same intelligence agency."

"Oh, maybe sometimes," Charlie responded. "Other times I work for . . . other agencies. They're all part of the same thing. It's called Department of Defense."

With that Charlie hoped to imply what he wanted Hsiu-fen to posit as given: that he, Charlie, was privy to deep knowledge about Chang's secret modus operandi, even Chang's intentions. Substantiation: he knew that Chang would be in Singapore on Wednesday and the occasion was important. He even knew the name of the hotel Chang would stay at (having guessed correctly that Hsiu-fen had made his reservations there). Charlie's problem lay in expressing hints of his knowledge gradually, plausibly, while displaying corroboration before Hsiu-fen would give it. Thus he said rather abruptly, "You'll be going to Singapore with Chang on Wednesday, won't you?"

That must have caused Hsiu-fen a little jolt, because how did he know that?

As soon as he could, Charlie mentioned the Raffles Hotel by asking how long in advance Hsiu-fen had booked reservations there. To his credit, Charlie thought, he had displayed knowledge of secrets with the mien of someone alluding to mere common knowledge. The implication was clear: he knew a lot.

Hsiu-fen responded freely to Charlie's queries. Meanwhile she pointed out occasional landmarks en route to a traffic artery on the north perimeter of the city. Charlie felt distracted as they passed by the Sheraton Taipei without even slowing down.

"Are we going to the Hyatt Hotel, or what?" Charlie asked.

"We are going to Hotel Roma," Hsiu-fen replied.

"The *Roma*?!"

Charlie had nightmarish memories of his last stay at the Roma, when he'd nearly been killed by plainclothes police abducting him from there and where Marie had suffered pain when she saw him there afterwards. Hsiu-fen's perceptions were entirely different. Her memories of being at the Roma with Charlie (especially of assisting him after the police took him back) often caused her soft pleasure.

"I thought you prefer the Roma," Hsiu-fen remarked.

Charlie explained his attitude. Hsiu-fen explained hers. Each was careful to keep Marie's name from the equation. In a little while they arrived at the Roma and Hsiu-fen helped Charlie check in and saw him to his first-floor suite. (It would do just fine.)

"I need some cold Japanese beer," Charlie declared. "The humidity's killing me! Would you care to join me for a drink in the bar room? I distinctly remember there bein' a funky ol' bar in this place."

Hsiu-fen said, "Sure. [Beat.] If you are buying!"

In what seemed like no more than three to five minutes to both, Charlie and Hsiu-fen were on their second round in the Hotel Roma bar room, Sapporo beer for him, Suntory with water on the side for her, and they had barely begun to touch on all the topics that came up, even though their dialogue leapt and bounded ceaselessly.

One mundane subject: How long would Charlie be in Taipei? Maybe three nights. He had business in Taipei; his next stop might be Singapore. (That caused Hsiu-fen's eyes to flicker.)

Amidst many light moments, a much more important subject: Likely intentions underlying the actions of Hsiu-fen's employer. This Charlie barely touched upon. The name Chang K'ung came up but once between them. Still, Charlie did send home the notion that a major reason for his coming to Taiwan was to "discuss" this matter with Ms. Wu. Fact-finding was not part of Charlie's purported scenario; he was there to "discuss." But that should be done after, say, lunch the next day, which Hsiu-fen said would be fine.

They contemplated a third round of Sapporo and Suntory but disdained that as redundant. The hour was past midnight; they were sated and tired. With little ado they rose and left, casually walking close to each other. (Charlie almost offered Hsiu-fen his arm, but in a moment of lucidity decided not to.) Their route to the hotel lobby passed the corridor down which they could see the door to Charlie's suite. Hsiu-fen said something about going there and using his bathroom. While they strode wordlessly down the last thirty or so yards to his door they drew closer together.

Once inside the suite Charlie said, "Ladies first" and gestured toward the bathroom. Hsiu-fen disappeared but left the door ever so slightly ajar. Charlie noticed that and stayed in the small front room. After a minute or so he idly turned on the television set to watch nubile Chinese post-adolescents singing popular American songs in English, a phenomenon he mildly enjoyed.

When Charlie completed his turn in the distinctly Western-style bathroom, he returned to the front room to find the post-adolescents still mouthing words on TV but the audio was off. Hsiu-fen sat sleepily on the sofa, barely watching the screen images. Charlie sat next to her and realized he felt woozy.

"Tired, huh?" Charlie said.

The response in a small voice sounded like "*hai*."

Charlie leaned back, at a loss as to what to do next. He thought he would close his eyes for just a minute. Before he did that he uttered, "Hey, it's Sunday morning. *Good*." He heard the same response in the same little voice.

Charlie and Hsiu-fen each recalled waking during some segment of the morning and making expedient arrangements for more comfort. When they woke up after daylight, Hsiu-fen had been lying across the bed, partly covered by the spread, with her shoes, dress, and jewelry off; Charlie had risen from the sofa (feeling surprisingly well rested), similarly unburdened. Only the bathroom light was still on.

As Charlie padded into the small bedroom he gestured to the semi-open door to the bathroom and told Hsiu-fen, "Last one in—is a turkey!" He gave her a token chance to get there first, then he bolted for the doorway and won uncontested. From then on, for both parties getting ready for the day was a fairly pleasant matter of making do, facilitated by the hotel furnishing two toothbrushes and a pot of hot tea.

Hsiu-fen took time out to make two expedient telephone calls; she told Charlie that one was to her "condo," the other to her brother. Charlie was sure that she had used a different language for each, a perception later borne out. Barely an hour after arising they left the hotel and took a taxi about two miles to a restaurant Hsiu-fen recommended for a breakfast of porridge and some kind of stew over rice with fruit and pastry, all of which sat well with tea.

"I must get New Taiwan dollars so I can repay you for this meal," Charlie said while he and Hsiu-fen relaxed before dessert.

"They will accept U.S. dollars here. Gladly. [Beat.] You said you want to talk to me about some things. Better if we go somewhere else."

"Right. Do you have some place in mind?"

"I can think of many places," Hsiu-fen said with a smile which momentarily paralyzed Charlie with unexpected pleasure.

Hsiu-fen's plan was, "as they like to say in U.S. media, 'revolutionary'": take the day off, entirely. She could—and did—propose all kinds of pleasant things to do. Charlie, meanwhile, had to remind himself that his role mandated he not ask obvious questions because impliedly he knew all about Chang's machinations. Eventually he'd probably tip his hand, but the longer he put that off the more credible he would appear. He glanced at Hsiu-fen and could see she was intent on enjoying herself as she drove them to a shop she wanted to visit.

Soon Charlie accompanied her into a boutique to help her select an outfit for the day: deep-yellow not-too-tight shorts, polo shirt (with broad black bands across it), and woven-grass sandals (Italian-made). Charlie appreciated the way she combined decisiveness and astuteness. She even picked out a pair of wicked sunglasses in less than thirty seconds.

As this morning surged along Charlie was dazzled by Hsiu-fen looking more radiant every time he took her in. *The only reason you're not hooked up with someone permanently is nobody's a good-enough match—God what a prize are you to spend sixty years with.* This skein of notions, Charlie reckoned, must have run through his mind about five times an hour most of the day. And all the while he had to consciously refuse— adamantly preclude—imagining what this Woman looked like and how she felt to the touch and smelled under her polo shirt and shorts. Nor would he dare project how she might use her legs and various other God-given equipment in certain intense situations.

After having refreshed and changed clothes back in Charlie's room at the Roma, Charlie and Hsiu-fen took a drive to the southwest edge of Taipei, and Hsiu-fen announced that she had a new idea. But first they must stop at a particular shop that catered to upscale Western tastes. There they bought two magnums of champagne, a large insulated-plastic hamper, and plenty of "blue ice" for transporting the magnums and medley of comestibles they picked up to sustain themselves over a long afternoon. "Champagne is a wonderful idea!" Hsiu-fen exulted. "As they say, now we can live dangerously."

Departing from the highway they headed east and south on progressively narrower roads into a dramatic valley and then around a cluster of large verdant hills. Hsiu-fen turned her BMW onto a gravel lane paralleling a gentle, green gorge; with effort she managed to stay on the track, even when it almost disappeared, then passed under a highway. About thirty driving seconds beyond the highway overpass their trail ended at a brake of desiccated brush. Hsiu-fen skirted the thicket, slipped past a sand hill, and came to a stop as . . . she and Charlie were momentarily blinded by sunlight reflected off blue ocean. Only a narrow beach of beige sand separated them from water.

"Wow!" Charlie said. "Where did all that water come from?"

"How about this?" Hsiu-fen said, herself delighted by the sights. "Now you see why they called this '*Ilha Formosa*.'"

She was referring to Portuguese sailors naming this land "Beautiful Island," a point Charlie now appreciated.

The beach stretched way off to the north and south. A few fishermen's boats were out on the surf; a handful of ships were visible plying the horizon of blue meeting blue. Nearby to the south Charlie and Hsiu-fen could see part of a village. Although not a fisherman, Charlie found himself wishing that he was out on the surf in those boats, doing exactly what the fisher folk were doing.

"A good day for fishing," Hsiu-fen remarked. "Week after next I will fish here."

"It sure pays to get out of the big city when you're in Taiwan," Charlie declared.

Without another word between them, Charlie and Hsiu-fen left her car to cross the beach to touch ocean barm, providing them an opportunity not to be wasted. At water's edge they removed their footwear and waded into cool green, going out as far as they could and stopping to let the surf caress their legs up over their knees. For a while their minds simply wafted over the water.

After they'd turned to plod back to dry sand (both smiling serenely), Charlie asked Hsiu-fen whether she came to this beach often. She explained that the highway nearby was the route she drove to her family's home, but she came down this way too infrequently because of her commitments in Taipei.

"My mother, my sister, my father, many relatives—live in T'ai-tung; maybe two hundred kilometers south from here. That is south of your Tropic of Cancer, you know. We have beautiful home with mountains next to ocean. Also we have home in Hsi-lo; one of my brothers lives there, farther south in farming country you would like. Maybe next time you come here—maybe next week if you stay—we'll make special trip so you can meet some of my family."

"Wow. That would be nice."

Both had spoken bemusedly but sincerely.

Curiosity prompted Charlie to ask, "Your family—is everybody Taiwanese? I mean, full-blood Taiwanese, your mother and your father."

"Not quite, but close. We have a little, only a little, Mandarin Chinese on both sides. We suspect a little Portuguese, also a little Japanese, maybe sneaked in."

With a smile she made a charming little gesture using her fingers on one hand to convey smallness. Her suave attractiveness was not lost on Charlie.

"It's too bad China regards Taiwan as a breakaway province," said Charlie.

He and Hsiu-fen completed returning to her car and opened the doors. They sat together wiping sand from their feet and replacing footwear.

Hsiu-fen said, "No, China doesn't think what you said. Only Chinese leadership says we are part of China. —If you call that 'leadership.'— Chinese people don't care abut Taiwan, except maybe to come here to live." She gazed at the sky for a moment, then declared: "Absurd to say this is China. Taiwan is Taiwan, maybe to you 'Formosa'; we are not Chinese. We don't like Chinese!"

They drove the coastal highway south past a few villages and parked again where a path took them to a shaded ledge overlooking another beach. Hsiu-fen spread a quilted cover on the shale and made a command decision: Now was the time "for some danger."

Thus Charlie opened a magnum of champagne which they sipped from clear plastic flutes as they stared over ocean. Soon they began nibbling their picnic snacks (except for a brie which Charlie ate with gusto). Everywhere he looked, Charlie thought, colors were pure and dazzling. But he had to approach something quite abstract, beyond the physical present.

"General Chang K'ung—the man who is your employer, your actual leader—he sure looks Chinese to me," Charlie remarked after some moments of preoccupation.

"General Chang is part of occupying force. The army he belongs to occupies our country," Hsiu-fen responded. "He is different kind of 'Chinese,' you know. Mandarin class; has different culture, even different genes. Also—"

After a long moment watching Hsiu-fen gaze at ocean Charlie said, "Also what?"

"I think," said Hsiu-fen, "he loves Taiwan."

Charlie realized that he'd just been provided a handy window. *Steady* . . . . Don't press it, he thought. "More champagne?" he asked, to which the reply was affirmative.

In small helpings they finished the whole magnum (an off-brand that Charlie forgot the name of a minute after he'd hidden the empty bottle in the "Beamer" trunk). The wine was a great idea, the origin of which neither could recall: it facilitated all kinds of talk and meanwhile they laughed a lot.

One subject recurred a few times and caused Hsiu-fen to glow perceptibly when it did: "I really like it here, Suzie," Charlie would declare. "I'm sure I would love your country if I got to know it better."

And "Suzi" would respond with vague, gentle urgings to experience Taiwan further, to which Charlie responded with vague, tentative promises. Eventually Charlie capped the subject by saying, "I think a man could be very happy here." He purposely left off the clause, "once he's figured out how to pay the bills." In that moment he glanced at Hsiu-fen to see her grinning overtly and he realized that his remark would make very good sense indeed if Hsiu-fen were an integral part of the equation. *Damn it's not just the "bubbly" thinking.*

Charlie stole a moment to restore his focus.

They drove for about an hour down the East Coast Highway and made good time until they reached a town called Taroko, near a huge, beautiful gorge. They went to a secluded inn that Hsiu-fen seemed to know well, and after a light lunch they drove inland on the East-West Cross-Island Highway.

Charlie was in a constant state of awe as they slipped through one gorgeous valley after another. "Wow-ee" was the word he used most.

"I thought you would like this," Hsiu-fen said.

"Does General Chang ever come through here?"

"Yes, very often. I think he builds a house—or something, I don't know what— somewhere here. That's one reason I think he loves Taiwan."

Eventually they were able to turn north. Hsiu-fen concentrated on following the narrow highway cutting between mountain ranges while Charlie scrutinized a map to ascertain possible landmarks. He determined they were about six kilometers from Chosho, a mountain-river town located at a highway junction.

Wild landscapes afforded Charlie space for work. He leaned back in his seat and looked ahead as he spoke, choosing his words carefully, his tone matter-of-fact: "I hope you know that certain people in the United States—very knowledgeable people who work for the Defense Department—consider General Chang to be . . . well, let's say . . . highly dangerous. The expression is 'loose cannon.' They say he's like a loose cannon sliding all over a ship, smashing things and people. (Gesticulations.) You understand?"

Hsiu-fen nodded.

Hoping that he sounded plausible, his tongue and brain perhaps too limber from the wine, Charlie continued, "Word gets around. Japanese and Philippine governments have been advised. Also European governments. For sure, Australia and Indonesia. They're all watching Chang closely. Plans—U.S. military plans—have been made. At least that's what they tell me. You should know this."

Charlie decided to stop there. Wait for the effect to show itself, he thought.

Hsiu-fen said, "Okay. So?" She looked straight ahead, impassively.

Now Charlie had to choose his words especially carefully. He felt sure that Hsiu-fen would spot any lapses in his explanation; if she didn't quite believe him, she wouldn't help him as much as he needed. Moreover the champagne he'd drunk taxed his powers.

"Some people are worried about actions the U.S. military is preparing to take right now," Charlie said. "They're worried that Chang is gonna do something outrageous, and then Taiwan will be mostly destroyed." (A sweeping, emphatic gesture.)

Hsiu-fen's attention was now in thrall.

"You've got twenty-one million people here; this island is so beautiful," Charlie mused.

"Why do you say Taiwan faces destruction?" Hsiu-fen asked. "From what?"

"Well, from nuclear retaliation," Charlie said.

"But why?"

"You tell me." And Charlie felt almost inspired. He added, "If you help me, I'll tell Chang what I know about this. He needs to be warned. You need to be warned. We're talkin' about a very dangerous situation, Suzi."

In the next minute or so Hsiu-fen simply repeated the essence of what she had told Charlie nearly three years before when she was with the tourist group in Los Angeles. The champagne began diluting Hsiu-fen's constraint, though, for she concluded by divulging that Chang and "fifteen or twenty" of his officers in "the movement" would be meeting that week in Singapore to make final preparations before they took "first action." (That terminology was Chang's.) She also referred to a "Mainlander" being in attendance to help procure some things from the Russian scientists, who might also be there.

"You mean at the Raffles Hotel," Charlie said knowingly.

Hsiu-fen nodded and said, "Chang says we must begin now to prepare for the future. He said the way to do that is to plan how we will maintain, uh . . . you know, *momentum* . . . after the movement begins."

"Ah. *What kind* of 'first action' are they gettin' all ready for?" Charlie asked. "I mean, what exactly are they going to do?"

"Would you believe, I don't know."

"What do you think they're fixin' to do?"

"I am not involved in that part of General Chang's revolution. Purposely—I'm sure—he refuses to tell me a lot of things. Even when I ask. So I try not to ask. I refuse to . . . speculate what Chang plans to do."

She doesn't know. She knows.

"When will they take 'first action'?" Charlie snapped.

"Oh, I think in about a week."

"A *week*?"

"About one week. Maybe from Wednesday or Friday. I really can't say."

"*Wow* . . . ."

They were almost in Cho-sho which Charlie presumed to be a mountain-resort town but which was actually a nexus for processing coal and cement. Infrastructure was built for industry.

Abruptly Charlie asked, "What is the aim of that 'first action,' do you think? The first goal, the first objective, of the New Taiping Rebellion—what do they actually want?"

"As I told you, they want to cause great fear. Chang says in order to succeed, the Revolution must first of all make other governments tremble."

"Ahh. I suppose Chang and his bunch want to do that so they can demand all kinds of things—and get 'em. Like tons of money, and protection. We know Chang's rich, but he can't fund starting up a whole new country. [Beat.] How did he pay the Russian scientists?"

"He used his own wealth."

"I would think it's kind of dangerous for him to deal with Russians on a private basis. Chang seems too smart to expose himself like that."

"The Mainlander helps him."

"Ahh. Well here is one thing you've probably guessed: your New Taiping Movement, I presume that's what you'd call it, is planning to use Russian nuclear weapons. How they're gonna be used, only God and Chang know."

"Chahrdree, it's not my business what General Chang decides to use."

"Well, if he uses nukes they're gonna be used against the United States. That's what people in our Defense Department think, and for good reason. You want to know what's gonna happen if he does use nukes against the United States—Ka-*blaam!*—Massive retaliation. Right here, in your Island Formosa. That is your business, Suzi."

This time Hsiu-fen was the one to say "wow" after which she drove wordlessly.

The outskirts of the town rising on both sides and ahead of them incorporated small open spaces akin to vacant lots. Charlie requested Hsiu-fen to stop, and she responded by pulling over next to a plot sprouting cabbages and tomato plants. Charlie had reached a decision that brooked no distraction. What is it?" Hsiu-fen asked, turning off the ignition.

"This might sound a little weird, but I've got good reasons for this," Charlie said.

For a moment Charlie hesitated without intending dramatic impact. His own trepidation (fed by a scenario he hated to imagine) made him pause, along with his awareness of one thing else that would short-circuit any man's mental processes: this Woman (with a capital "W") was unmercifully lovely and dear to behold.

"Yes?" she said.

"I must meet with General Chang—privately. It's very important, to him and to you; it'll only take a few minutes. First I must ensure that nobody else is present when we talk. That is crucial."

"Oh, Chahrdree, that is simply not possible. Goodness. He's so busy even I cannot talk to him in private. We're preparing to leave the country for his conference."

"You're referring to going to Singapore, I take it."

"Yes, for four days. Now General Chang is ... preoccupied."

Charlie pressed his cause unsuccessfully. Hsiu-fen prepared to restart her car. Ever more distinctly they heard the untoward blare of pop-rock music, which caused Charlie to finally glance at the car CD player.

"Oh-oh!" Hsiu-fen said and hurriedly put the car in "Drive."

Too late. From around a corner, filling the narrow street and coming toward them inexorably: a procession of vehicles led by a flower-festooned black sedan displaying (flush against the windshield) a large, framed portrait photo of an elderly Chinese man. Three or four sedans behind what Charlie realized was a hearse rolled the source of the "music": two black minivans equipped with electronic speakers. Each van bore an elaborate platform on the roof, and a bonus that interrupted Charlie's breathing: on each platform three slender young women clad in bikinis danced sinuously and sang off-key to the music, their black hair flipping and swinging, their faces and teeth and torsos glistening in the afternoon sun.

"I'll be damned," Charlie said as the hearse and minivans passed by. He stared at the line of black cars still to follow, all of them garlanded with flowers, some carrying that same portrait photo. He knew this was a funeral procession, but the female dancers left him disoriented.

"This is a funeral; isn't it?" Charlie said.

"Yes, it is," Hsiu-fen replied. "It should brighten that old man's journey."

Hsiu-fen twisted in her seat and inexplicably (to Charlie) rendered a token *namaste* toward the procession. Charlie did a little bow. They waited as about two dozen vehicles succeeded the minivans, followed by a twelve-member band playing a dirge.

"Gee whiz," said Charlie.

Hsiu-fen was following the procession in her rear-view mirror. "He must be important businessman or landowner," she commented. "Maybe some gangster boss." She paused to look harder into the mirror, then added, "I see them going into a field; there is what you call a cemetery."

Without a word they went to join the funeral, which was about to be conducted by a Buddhist priest. In the cemetery the band had stopped playing; several dozen people were gathering around the hearse and two minivans now parked close to a concrete dome high enough for a short man to stand inside. The rock-music tempo picked up and the volume rose noticeably.

Almost as Charlie would have fantasized (and to a degree actually did), the female dancers (all of them pretty) responded to the music accordingly. And then some: the song ended; before the next number started all the bikinis came off and went flying. People shouted and clapped. For several minutes the scene was breathtaking.

Charlie uttered the obvious into Hsiu-fen's ear: "I bet that old dude is goin' to heaven with a big smile!"

Hsiu-fen nodded. "As big as a lake," she said.

Charlie realized that everything about Hsiu-fen pleased him. When the music stopped, as the burial service got underway she and he drew closer together and listened respectfully to the priest's and monks' chants.

My goodness, Charlie said to himself to help calm his soul. He allowed his mind to dwell on a thought he'd captured in recent minutes. With her clothes off, the accomplished, lovely Woman gently brushing against his right arm would easily rival—probably surpass—the professional beauties they'd seen undulating on the platforms. *She'd show 'em a thing or two.*

Charlie gazed at the side of Hsiu-fen's head, took in part of her face and neck, and entertained a thought on which he'd refused to focus till this moment: Given half the opportunity—which he himself would not consciously arrange—he could pull off Hsiu-fen's shorts (and whatever she had under them) with his teeth, and lick her until she screamed. —*Wooh!* Yes he could, and maybe would if he were drunk enough.

Ah, but she wasn't Marie. In Charlie's psyche, a transparent wall forever separated him and Hsiu-fen Wu. There was no getting around it. Real intimacy, with someone other than Marie—to Charlie that simply was not a desirable outcome. It didn't even seem possible. *Sorry!* he told himself, or might yet say to Hsiu-fen.

All day (and the last night) Charlie and Hsiu-fen had been careful to avoid referring to his wife or mentioning Marie's name. That might have to be reversed soon, Charlie thought as he and Hsiu-fen backed out of the crowd at the burial ground and returned to her car. So far today, Charlie determined, he hadn't accomplished his purpose. He had merely become convinced that he was privy to imminent nuclear terrorism and potential disasters. If he had to cozen this Woman to get his way, and harmlessly use Marie to do it, he decided, he would. Covertly, partly to test his resolve, Charlie managed an appraising glance at Hsiu-fen, first at her head and face, then he tried to take in all of her. *God she's dear though.*

"Let's go somewhere and drink our bubbly. I'm gettin' thirsty," Charlie said.

That they did, this time in a sandstone-floored coniferous glade with a creek spilling down a tiny waterfall and running through it. The place was on an estate to which Hsiu-fen was welcome, she explained modestly, because of her family connections and her position on General Chang's staff. Charlie said he felt remarkably at home there.

"We have to go back to Taipei soon," Hsiu-fen said as she sipped her champagne and gazed at surrounding green poking into azure. She gave a soft, protracted sigh.

"I guess so," Charlie responded. Abruptly he said, "Suzi, what do you hope to be doin' in one year from today?"

Charlie saw an endearing smile as Hsiu-fen thought briefly. She answered, "I would like to begin study for—what is it called?—Ph.D.—at a good American university."

Hsiu-fen explained that she had interests in at least three fields in the humanities plus a few areas of history (one of which was modern European history). If she were free to pursue her heart's desire, she didn't know how she could choose.

For a moment Charlie tried projecting himself into Hsiu-fen's shoes. He proceeded to speak carefully: "The University of Texas in Austin, Texas, where I live, would be perfect for someone just like you." He explained that the university was huge; it offered almost anything Hsiu-fen could imagine studying. Plus the town would suit her well. He let her think about that for a while; she asked and he answered questions about the university and city.

Charlie had to make a decision, and did. After a little gap of silence he said, "Get a U.S. student visa; also get transcripts of the work you did here, at the university in Taipei." He knew that she had a master's degree in something technical. "Then come to my home, immediately. You can see what the university is like first-hand. If you want, you can walk there and apply, no problem. If that is what you want to do."

Hsiu-fen had difficulty comprehending what Charlie was really proposing. At first she thought he was being facetious. But, no, he said he was serious. He almost demanded that she act promptly.

"What would your wife say if I arrived at your home with my suitcases?" Hsiu-fen asked with a lopsided grin.

"Oh, not much. She won't be there. I mean, she has her own life; we're not . . . *together* anymore. She's movin' to Washington, D.C. Looks like it's gonna be for good, permanently."

"Oh. How is that so?"

"She wants, you know, a high-level career. She can work in the National Security Agency. They want her. That's fine; she should go. I have my own life. You'll see!"

Charlie said all that as though he were commenting on the weather. Hsiu-fen looked—and felt—dazed. Preoccupied, she began picking up the wine flutes and basket.

Charlie capped the topic: "We can get you enrolled and all set up and everything —before this fall semester."

For Hsiu-fen that scenario transcended fantasy. She got paid well from her job on General Chang's staff, so she did have savings. She could also sell her car and live comfortably on the proceeds for maybe two years. As for Charlie . . . the dear man and all he could offer might actually be hers exclusively if she chose.

Charlie quietly walked alongside her as they returned, one more time, to her car. He, too, felt dazed; even numbed. But he was able to focus on one principle: he had to compartmentalize all thoughts of the consequences of whatever he'd set in motion.

"This is crazy!" Hsiu-fen declared when they were seated inside her car again. "I have a job to do. General Chang depends on me. My family depends on me to be successful."

"I'm sure you've done a good job for everyone," Charlie said. "As far as I can see, you've been very successful. Probably Chang still needs you, but not for long. If he does something crazy, he'll be dead. Maybe Taiwan will die also."

Hsiu-fen flashed a distressed look.

Ah, Charlie thought; what he had said felt solidly right, her expression confirmed that. He just hoped the champagne wasn't thinking for him. (Thank goodness for the brie and bread and ham.) At least the alcohol blunted doubts: *Chang's got nukes all right.*

As Hsiu-fen found their way back to the main road Charlie waited prudently, then followed up: "I don't want to see your country destroyed; I don't want to see it damaged. Help me talk to Chang—in private. I know certain things. Maybe I can stop him."

"That's impossible; I told you. We're going to Singapore."

"Well, I can meet him in Singapore, then."

Brief hesitation. "We'll see," she said.

"It's important that I warn him," Charlie said. "We don't want him to use what he's been getting from the Russians. [Beat.] After we calm Chang down, you and I, after we persuade him not to be crazy, maybe you'll want to try living for yourself. Now wouldn't that be good!"

For a few moments Hsiu-fen said nothing, although Charlie felt a great deal going on behind her dark glasses. Finally she turned to him.

"What do you mean, I will live for myself?"

"You might want to come join me. Life is good where I live. I can help you follow your dream."

By the time Hsiu-fen returned Charlie to the Hotel Roma daylight had turned brassy and shadows were lengthening. The long day and champagne had taken a toll on both. Charlie knew that Hsiu-fen must also have felt belabored by the notions he had raised for her that day. During their final hour on the road they had spoken only cursorily about Charlie meeting privately with Chang in Singapore and Hsiu-fen going to study in Austin, Texas—as Charlie's guest—and thus serving her country "from a distance." Marie's status with Charlie (indeed, her very existence) had not been raised again, nor had the notion of Taiwan being set upon by U.S. military power consequent to Chang's "first action."

Now parked outside the Roma, Hsiu-fen implied that her night was designated for meeting family and personal commitments. She explained moreover that she would be preoccupied by her job as of the next morning because she would go abroad with Chang on Wednesday. "Only a person who is wise and fortunate has no boss," she remarked with a trace of smile.

Then Charlie thought she leaned toward him, perhaps to be kissed, and he took her right wrist and hand in both his hands and gave it a warm squeeze before gently releasing it. If he kissed her even on the cheek, he feared, he might be lost.

"This weekend has been wonderful," Charlie said. "I wish I could thank you enough."

"Try *shiay-shiay*."

"*Shiay-shiay*!"

"As you once said—the pleasure is mine."

"Will I see you in Singapore?" Charlie said into the open car after he'd alighted.

"If you wish."

Charlie closed the door and waved; Hsiu-fen smiled at him, her radiance unmistakable, and gave a little wave back.

Unfortunately, yes I wish, Charlie thought. He stood stationary and waved once more as he watched her car move away, then glide up the street and disappear.

As Charlie dropped into a fitful, dysrhythmic slumber in his suite at the Roma, Tatyana Platonov arose from a phantasmagorical one. She could still hear Andrushka's soothing tones as he spoke to her in dreams. But other dreams left imprints of Asian male faces—Chinese men's faces— menacing and demanding but promising coveted rewards. The more prominent of those faces, the intense and handsome one, smiled at her charmingly as he spoke with flair through interpreters, while he strained to hold back a promise of pending catastrophe.

As Tatyana had expected, Andrei was already gone, in search of whatever medical care he could find today for his congested heart and arthritic lumbar vertebrae, infirmities he insisted he could overcome with a few advantages from capable surgery. Although she was barely awake, Tatyana immediately set about exploiting her privacy by finishing preparations for her final "research trip" abroad. She profoundly hoped it would be her final trip. For sure, it would be the last one she'd take without Andrei.

All was not in readiness because of a complication: According to the gray-looking Chinese man named Mo Tzu, the other Chinese man, the driven-looking one (did he not sometimes reveal the look of a fanatic?) was insisting on obtaining an additional kilo of weapons-grade plutonium plus the bomb prototype Andrei had devised. Tatyana had been informed that her final payment would be fifty thousand American dollars larger but contingent upon her providing what "the General" wanted, regardless of their established agreement.

Thus Tatyana's preparations had had to include inducing her friend Sergei to "redirect" six more of the biscuit-sized tablets of uranium which she had to pack and send to a warehouse address in Singapore. Then she'd had to persuade Andrei to hand over the cumbersome prototype he'd built—not an easy task—and she had to pack it among her belongings for the trip.

Whatever I must do, Tatyana told herself, I simply will do it. She knew that so far she'd been lucky: she had succeeded. If she kept on succeeding, one day Andrei would reap the benefits of her rigors. He needn't realize all she'd undertaken and risked; he needed only to benefit. Then one day he might begin to apprehend the caliber, the incredible quality, of her love for him.

*   *   *

You might remember when Charlie and Wu Hsiu-fen decided to purchase two magnums of expensive champagne for the afternoon picnic, and then wondered how in the world they had decided to do that: did you intuit perhaps a familiar third party at work in that goings-on? Yes, I do "get around," as people like to say, so I have been exposed to some basic realities. Probably I have good reason to mount a pulpit sometimes.

364

Rarely will you hear judgements from me about human ethics for one very good reason which I raise below. Still, I have to be appalled when elite members of the human race become fools. This happens every damned time someone makes a thrust at overcoming what he or she perceives as a meaningless (or potentially meaningless) existence by doing something that is clearly wrong.

People—maybe all people—sometimes forget they have the ability to intentionally *not* perpetrate wrong-doing. Often they say that God tells them to harm or kill other humans (in the myriad of ways your race has invented). And that is not only being intentionally stupid, it is arrogance, tantamount to wild chimpanzees expecting you to climb their trees to illuminate micro-processing for them, which you would surely decline to do even if they begged you from a temple.

Now granted, ethical issues and principles often become obscured, involuted, maybe inverted. Regardless, I would bet that not harming other humans, at least not intentionally, requires very little mental brilliance.

*   *   *

May 9 (Monday morning), 1995
Austin, Texas

All day Sunday she had functioned in a state of dread; by evening she'd fixated on the predicate that he wouldn't call her. When the telephone rang at a minute past midnight, Marie actually felt relieved that the call had come.

Charlie sounded as he always did: mildly amused by most things, matter-of-factly or wry about concerns at hand. What he said, though, was definitely serious. "Looks like it's a code red, sweetie." His tone changed to earnest as he outlined the scenario of himself and Marie meeting at the Far Western Hotel in Singapore on Wednesday.

"You're absolutely sure this is going to be necessary?" Marie said when they'd concluded reviewing logistics.

"I'm afraid it's no false alarm like we hoped," Charlie responded.

"Shit," was all Marie could say for a long moment. Then she said, "All right. Do you know what, more or less, we're gonna have to do?" (She was recalling Charlie's relating his attempts to buy ricin.)

"I think so," Charlie said.

"Are we really up to it?"

"We'd better be!"

That was exactly the answer Marie feared—and needed— as the basis for action. "I'll call the hotel as soon as I clear customs," she said. "Then I'll just taxi on over."

Everything was straight. Charlie capped their plan by uttering the long-unused code words "black before white, ducky," which signified, "bring both passports; but use the other [DOD-supplied] one."

That was it. Their joint destiny was drawn as far as they dared to envisage.

"Lest we forget first priorities," Marie said, "I love you, sweetie."

"I love you," Charlie said. "More than I could ever say."

*

From a medium-close metaphysical distance Marie observed herself as in a mainstream movie of the 1990's: formidable woman on the telephone dutifully averring her vulnerability.

"I'm scared," she told Jed, whom she'd roused from bed by phoning her right after Charlie rang off.

"Can you tell me why?" Jed asked, her wits startled to wakefulness.

"You know what we talked about at the restaurant that time? We—Charlie and I—might have to take matters into our own hands. Uh, so to speak. Regardless of . . . uhm, possible consequences."

"Hooh! I don't like the sound of that," Jed declared.

"Well, it can't be too big a thing, really. Charlie and I can only do what's, you know, possible, feasible. There's only two of us; we're not exactly suicidal."

"That's a relief. What can we do to help?"

As expected by all concerned, Jed and Benjamin would provide plenty of help in caring for Julia and Lisa and the dogs and the house during Marie's and Charlie's absence. Jed understood that was for openers. She and her husband—and all their mutual friends with Charlie and Marie—were to pull for, give psychic support to, if feasible pray for, Charlie's and Marie's safe return from "Charlie's working vacation" abroad.

"Let's hope it's not gonna be too-tall of an order," Jed remarked, featuring her dearest friend going off to a foreign land to fight secret evil, exactly as would be expected of an empowered woman of the 1990's. In fact, that was how *Marie* regarded her own intention of going to Singapore, but with an added dimension of real anger.

****

Waiting outside the terminal for his Transaereos Aguila flight from Bogotá to Singapore, Father Nobles remarked that he was about to embark on yet another mission for Our Lord's Mother despite his growing aversion to long-distance travel.

The man to whom Father Nobles spoke was a well-dressed Hispanic U.S. citizen who would return to his office in central Bogotá within the hour. He had just given a packet to Nobles along with verbal instructions regarding Nobles' role in an investigation into the fates of three U.S. intelligence operatives recently abducted from Indonesia.

"Good thing for us you're going to Singapore," the man said. "We need your nose."

"No problem for me," said the priest. Overtly he glanced about to see if anyone could overhear him. (Negative.) "I wonder," he added, "might those 'disappearances' be connected somehow to a covert dissident movement some people have mentioned might be brewing in Taiwan."

"I'm not aware of any dissident movement in Taiwan, let alone one that's, y' know, dangerous," the man said.

"Ah. Well, I'd presumed I was hearing just speculation." *Good. His bunch doesn't know anything. We hope.*

The man—Jim Montes, probably CIA, maybe NSA— produced and casually displayed a white envelope to which he spoke in reference: "Everyone tells me you don't accept money. It's here, though, if you want it."

"Thanks. It still goes right to my Order. I just have to cover travel and incidental stuff; that's already taken care of this trip."

"All right," Montes said. "Good luck on your various missions, Father."

When they parted Nobles thought wryly, I'm a goddamned double agent! He knew he had come to regard his protecting the New Taiping Rebellion as a sacred mandate. Over the past three or four years in various ways he had intimated salutary comments about General Chang to U.S. intelligence organs. (His aim—which originated with Debbie Kassenbaum's suggestion—was to deflect possible suspicions about Taiping activity.) Had he been privy to anybody harboring even vague suspicions about Chang or his officers, he surely would have advised Ms. Kassenbaum of same.

Nobles liked dealing with the lissome, reserved Taiwanese woman Chang employed as his primary aide, but Debbie Kassenbaum was the one person with whom Nobles actually shared a rapport. What they had in common was their attraction to particular abstractions.

Nobles had determined that General Chang was the quintessential gambler. Evidently, Chang was standing himself up to risk everything (including his own life and liberty) in a quest for something other than glory or money. (He had more than he wanted of both.) To Nobles' mind, Chang might have been egoistic, but that alone could not have been sufficient motivation for Chang's willingness to risk all. Thanks to Debbie's need for a confidant (who would understand her and could respond in subtle English), Nobles had come to know a great deal, though not everything, about Chang's design for a "revolution," including it being founded on some kind of ideals.

Debbie knew something about those ideals because she was close to Chang, at least sometimes. Neither she nor the priest, though, cared much about "Chinese values" (which Debbie had heard Chang evoke occasionally). But they did envision that Chang's intentions might cause some effect in the overall scheme of reality. For sure, on a mythical level Chang was trying to accomplish precisely that. By staying connected with Chang, their lives might be part of something consequential, which was more than they could have said for themselves before all this. And much more elemental: they found Chang's modus operandi to be breathtaking, "like meeting a tiger in the park," as Nobles expressed it.

****

Truth be known, Charlie thought when he'd settled into his seat aboard a Singapore Air flight bound for Singapore, he actually disliked traveling. There were so many other things he preferred to be doing, especially now. For a long moment his mind drifted over Rocky Mountain foothills in Colorado—sites of seedling-tree farms, then over Central Texas and home. — *No sense in thinking about that now.* — The jets outside had been fired up; flight attendants had completed preparations. Right on schedule, the big airliner taxied away to go airborne.

Would he ever see Taiwan again? Of course he would! Provided that some day he'd so desire. Thank goodness he'd be seeing Marie before long. Too bad they'd have to meet in circumstances both hostile and vague. "Shit!" Charlie said to nobody. The man next to him heard but ignored him.

369

Once they would meet with General Chang—a prospect Charlie now regarded as a probability—they might learn that he actually meant well. He might, in reality, be a benign pillar of rectitude who intended no harm to other human beings. Or— he might be so well protected that they would be powerless to stop him from doing anything he wanted to do.

Yeah yeah yeah.

Charlie and his fellow passengers were well aloft, the island of Taiwan beneath and out of sight behind them. *Thank you Father Of All for my constitution and talents, physical and mental*, Charlie thought-said to the entire cosmos from which his being emanated. He could see himself—comfortingly— seated in shade near the forest edge (smells of nearby cooking gracing the Earth), learning to convey his prayer properly. Now he added, *Grant me—i beg you—additional courage if i need it. And strength of will if i need it.* That was possibly good, Charlie thought. Then he added, *Grant me great cunning; i beg you.*

Oh, God! Marie said to herself as she felt the pang drill right through her again. —*Shi-i-it!*— She tried to push her back into the airliner seat while she watched a mental replay of herself telling Lisa and Julia: "So long, not 'goodbye,' sweeties. All right?" They—her darling little girls—couldn't know that "goodbye" might be a distinct reality—applied to both their parents—when Marie and Charlie would pursue and meet some kind of fate far away.

Although she could relax on the Singapore Air flight out of San Francisco, Marie still felt her psyche and vitality stretched thin by the logistics this trip entailed. She was going to Singapore because she had to meet Charlie. She thought. "Am I crazy, or what?" Marie said aloud, and people next to her heard it.

Lord, Marie prayed, *grant me strength, and wisdom! Wisdom to discern what I have to do. Grant me—and my husband—wisdom and strength.*

After she had drunk a vodka gimlet Marie thought that if she and Charlie had to carry out something especially drastic during their sojourn in Singapore (she refused to feature any possibilities), they would require a great deal of cleverness. Thus she prayed also for extra degrees of cleverness.

Chapter 14

May 11, 1995 (Wednesday morning)
Singapore

"I'm glad it's not the thirteenth," Marie remarked, "although I'm not superstitious."

"Listen, by the time it's the thirteenth here, we'll already be back where it's the twelfth," Charlie said, referring to recrossing the International Date Line.

"D' y' think so?"

"Yes I do."

Charlie checked his watch. He sat in an armchair and watched Marie unpack luggage in the Far Western Hotel room Charlie had secured for Mr. and Mrs. Charles Weingarten of Philadelphia, PA, USA. (One might claim to be an ophthalmologist, the other a high-school teacher and coach.) Each had professed fondness for Singapore: its orderliness, its pleasantness.

"I suspect the theatre and music scenes here are a little thin, though," Charlie had commented.

"Well, I've never heard of this place being exactly a hotbed of political activism, either," Marie had said.

"Nary a brew pub in sight," said Charlie.

Yet nearly everyone they'd had occasion to deal with in this Chinese city-state exhibited a kind of savvy about everything that came up. One exception—for both—was (incongruously) a Malaysian cab driver who seemed to be outright prescient. ("I mean, how in the hell would he know all that?" Marie said, astonished by the driver having called her "Marie—uh, Mary" and then his mentioning "Charlie" when she referred to her husband. "I know!" said Charlie, who'd been equally astonished by his contact the previous day with that same cabbie.) These things they had talked about shortly after Marie's arrival. Again Charlie checked his watch. Singapore time was almost noon.

"D' y' really think she'll call?" Marie said, referring to Debbie Kassenbaum, whom Charlie had taken some pains to contact. No such name was registered at the Raffles Hotel. Still Charlie felt confident that Debbie would respond to his messages. Marie then asked Charlie what he thought their agendum was to be.

"We want to meet—and talk to—General Chang. But strictly in private."

"Ah. Regardless of what you've heard and gathered about Chang and his droogs—and their intentions—we really don't know enough," Marie declared. "I mean, if Chang were to walk in here right this minute, we wouldn't even recognize him. That's how much we know."

"That's partly true."

"So?"

"So we find out more. Right from the source."

"And then?"

"We'll see. I mean, we're not gonna just go crazy and break necks, then ask the world to understand. You know I've been rehabilitated since my days in the jungle."

Marie had yet other serious concerns, such as what Charlie had learned from his recent stay in Taiwan. In a few short sentences he told her. They still had no concrete proof of General Chang's intentions, but any reasonable suspicions they harbored were sufficiently confirmed.

Resignedly Marie said, "Someone's gonna have to do something, and looks like we're It."

The telephone rang and Charlie took up the receiver, intoned "hello" and listened.

"*Ah*. It's for you," Charlie said to Marie and handed over the phone.

Within a moment Marie said into the phone, "Why, hello, sweetheart." And a moment after that she said, "We'd like to see you, too."

A few minutes later, upon ringing off, she told Charlie, "Looks like we've got a lunch date at the Raffles, with darlin' Debbie. Maybe some kind of meeting afterwards."

Lunch at the Raffles turned out to be a lavish buffet with tables alfresco being highly popular. Neither Charlie nor Marie ate heartily; mostly they sat outside—where they could be seen—and waited. Soon Debbie joined them, and discounting a foolish-looking grin which disappeared after their initial exchanges, she radiated sheer exuberance. Seated and talking animatedly at Marie's and Charlie's table, she sampled a tempura dish as though food was redundant. Marie thought she looked thinner.

"You're looking fine," Debbie said to Marie at least twice in the first ten minutes, each time ignoring Charlie's eyes.

Eventually Marie asked Debbie when they could meet General Chang.

"Oh, this afternoon, I suppose," Debbie replied. "Is that good?"

She was informed, in measured tones, that the meeting would have to be strictly private. She demurred: the general was busy; was that demand really necessary? Quietly, matter-of-factly, Marie and Charlie held fast. They could not tell Chang anything substantive, they said, if they couldn't tell him privately. That was reality.

"I'll see what I can do," Debbie responded. "I can't make any promises, though."

"Is General Chang around here someplace?" Charlie asked Debbie as he glanced about at fellow diners.

"Oh, yuhh," Debbie said. "Back in there."

They pressed her to identify a table amid a clutch of small tables close to the back dining-room wall. It was occupied by an imperious-looking Chinese man, elegantly dressed. He was enjoying a macho moment with the gathering of middle-aged men much like himself seated at nearby tables. He appeared not to notice Debbie and the two Americans glancing his way, but knowing Chang as she did, Debbie felt sure that he perceived everything relevant to himself.

Silently Charlie said, *Ah, the enemy.*

So that's the enemy, Marie thought and found herself fascinated.

Five Chinese women sat sprinkled among Chang's retinue, all of them in low profile and attentive. Charlie felt a pleasurable jolt at seeing one of them. Hsiu-fen Wu didn't look his way, but Charlie felt certain that she had seen him. As he gazed at her sitting at a table with two of Chang's officers, Marie's voice recaptured him.

"Do I see what I think I see?" Marie said, and Charlie followed her eye to spot a familiar burly figure in a black suit and Roman collar on his way out of the dining room. At first Charlie's mind wouldn't yield the priest's name, but Charlie knew that if he could look into the man's face he'd be startled by the bright greenness of the eyes beaming back.

"What next?" Charlie said.

Debbie asked, "You know him?"

"Sure do," Marie said. *This'll enhance our credibility.*

Debbie said, "I'll go see what I can do," and she arose, did a little bow, and ambled away to rejoin General Chang's party. Charlie and Marie simply sat at their table and waited. As they did, they heard live American dance music starting up across the hallway from the dining room. Marie poured out fresh cups of tea and Charlie began picking at his brandied mango. Both realized that Hsiu-fen Wu was standing alone about ten yards from them. Marie recognized Hsiu-fen almost immediately and felt disordered.

Suzi Wu belonged to the "enemy"; that was why she was here in Singapore. She was also partly responsible for Marie and Charlie having come here, perhaps on a fool's mission. Conceivably, Suzi Wu might have lured them here so they could be neutralized if Chang or his claque deemed them dangerous. Or conceivably she was angling for something altogether extraneous: a weird kind of chemical reaction seemed to occur between Charlie and Hsiu-fen when they made eye contact a moment later. Might that have stemmed from a shared intimacy? The question lingered but evanescently.

Charlie beckoned Hsiu-fen to his and Marie's table and she complied. He rose and introduced her to Marie.

"We've already met. Six or eight years ago," Marie said.

"Ah, right." Showing a large smile, Charlie took a moment to overcome disorientation. Hsiu-fen's responses were terse, detached.

Would she care to sit down? No, she should return to the dining room.

"I have done what you wanted, Chahrdree," Hsiu-fen said. "General Chang says he will meet with you. Tomorrow morning at ten o' clock. He says he wants to meet you at the Far Western Hotel; a good place would be in the garden they have there."

She turned to leave, and would have if Charlie hadn't said, "Why on Earth does he want to meet at the Far Western Hotel?" Neither Charlie nor Marie, both startled by this news, could determine if that would be a good thing or not.

Hsiu-fen turned back to the table. "Chang thinks a change of scenery would be good. At Far Western they have better breakfast menu; American-style food."

Ah. *So far, so good.* Would their meeting be strictly private? That she didn't know, but she doubted it. Well, would she try to arrange that? Yes, she would try her best. "Please do," Charlie said, and two earnest faces averred how important that was.

Abruptly Hsiu-fen turned and left. During a few moments of silence afterwards, Marie pondered the importance of meeting Chang privately. She was sure that Charlie, now gazing inwardly, was projecting the particulars of that happening.

"Uh, what if we can't convince Chang that he'd be stupid to try using nukes on the United States?" Marie said. "I'm sure he could make a case for the Dark Side."

Charlie glanced about in a few directions and then responded, "Well . . . . I guess we'll just have to kill him. I mean, what else can we do?"

Marie said nothing. There was simply too much to say.

*

About ten minutes later, in a reception room converted ad hoc to a ballroom and bar room, Charlie and Marie waltzed to the live music they had heard starting up. They didn't recognize the tune at all, but they had decided they might as well relax; try to clear their minds of baneful clutter, foster accurate perspectives.

After a wordless interlude between them, Marie took the lead. "How are we supposed to, you know, do what you said?" she asked. "I presume you weren't speaking figuratively." The reference: killing Chang. Charlie could only shrug noncommittally. Marie continued, "They've got laws against that, you know. I've heard they're pretty stringent here."

Charlie said, "I know."

Wordless again, they waltzed to music Marie called "brain candy" amidst four or five other couples, mostly Americans. Finally Charlie remarked, "We probably have to do it, though."

Marie said, "I know it."

They glanced toward the bar set along the wall. Heavy drapes blocked out early-afternoon sunshine; parts of the room reposed in shadow. Marie and Charlie spotted Father Nobles perched on a high stool, sipping a gimlet and gazing their way. He didn't appear to be looking at them, at least now.

"Wouldn't y' know we'd see him here," Marie muttered.

Charlie said, "Good thing this ain't a fox trot with me chewin' gum; I've got enough to think about."

"Well, here's something else for you," Marie said, looking over Charlie's shoulder toward another shadowed wall where a number of white-topped tables were about to be occupied. "I believe we're soon to be studied by our allies from the Republic Of China."

With a "Really?" Charlie turned Marie so he could see what she meant. Indeed. Drinks and small plates in hand, a number of well-dressed Chinese men, with perhaps four Chinese women among them, were settling among the tables for a postprandial respite. Charlie noticed Debbie walking away from a table and thought he saw Chang seated there. Although he didn't actually get a view of Hsiu-fen, he felt her presence causing him a sweet, painful thrum.

After a turn and a deep breath Charlie said, "I wonder if Chang knows who we are."

"I'll bet he sure does," Marie said.

At that moment Chang was allowing himself total bemusement as he gazed at the American couple dancing languorously near the middle of the reception room. Did they know he was present? They knew. Were they talking about him as they danced? Probably. He didn't care who they were; they didn't look familiar. What do they know? How did they know it? —He surmised they had to be intelligence operatives, but that accounted for really nothing.— And, yes: What do they want? They seemed to have clout: twice today Chang had been pressed to meet them. Wu Hsiu-fen had proposed that quite firmly; Ms. Kassenbaum had seemed anxious for that to occur. Moreover in both instances Chang had been urged to meet the couple privately. He finally agreed to that, with misgiving. *What could be so damned important?*

At lunch Chang had asked Ms. Kassenbaum questions about that American couple (still dancing out there) and he'd learned precious little that was important. One fact stood out: inexplicably the man, Charlie, had tried to help the T'aip'ing Cause back in the spring of 1991, at great personal risk. Chang indeed recalled the time Debbie urged him to cause an American to be released from interrogation before he died. That event simply did not compute. Chang then asked Ms. Wu the same questions about the couple and her answers corroborated Debbie's.

All right . . . . Chang requested Debbie to inform the pair that he would meet with them in strict privacy, same appointed time and place. On a whim he now asked Ms. Wu if that couple were really husband and wife, or was their relationship less personal, or perhaps more personal.

"They are married to each other," Hsiu-fen said simply.

"Ah, but one should never claim certainty in matters taking place far away from home," Chang declared with a wink. "They might really be lovers."

"No. They are married to each other."

To Hsiu-fen's mind, Charlie and Marie did appear to be firmly together. After a quick review of what she had seen of them that afternoon, no indication emerged to the contrary. But would they be together, intimately, during the night ahead? *Probably they would*. Hsiu-fen felt turmoil churning at her core, a very sad commentary.

Meanwhile Chang watched the couple, "Charlie" and "Marie" as they were called, saunter off the dance floor hand-in-hand, to be met by Debbie Kassenbaum with his message. Yes, he would meet with them privately (although openly); he wouldn't dare not to. Destiny had only begun its smile upon him. A tiny flaw in this stage of development of his Cause would likely be magnified to the hundredth power later. If that couple—Charlie and Marie—could help him avert a catastrophe, he would elicit, gladly, everything they had to tell him.

Chang decided to interrupt Ms. Wu's apparent reverie: Did she know the ancient Han maxim regarding how a strong man must tread across Victory's threshold? She said no, she didn't, so Chang edified her: "Very lightly," he said.

*

When Debbie had met them on the edge of the dance floor and told them, "Well, you got your wish. General Chang says he'll be glad to meet you in strict privacy tomorrow morning," Marie felt their fate was sealed. Evidently so did Charlie. The silence between them was almost palpable while they departed the Raffles and walked back to their hotel.

"*Brent*. You know, I bet he's a great kid!" Charlie said as they strode the busy sidewalks. That was virtually the only thing either said during their quarter-mile walk.

In their room at the Far Western, after a nap and glasses of room-service coffee, they abandoned safe-dialogue rules.

"What exactly do you have in mind for Chang?" Marie said.

They hadn't looked for bugs or even turned on the television.

"I mean, if we've gotta kill him," Marie continued, "how on Earth are we supposed to do that? You can't just say, 'excuse me,' and grab him by his damned neck."

"Let's hope this place isn't bugged!"

"I don't care if it is," Marie said, glancing about the room. Actually she did, but the prospect seemed remote, redundant. "We need a real precise plan," she declared.

"Well, first we reason with him. We tell him basic 'facts,' such as the NSA and DIA knowing about his Taipings and their plans, even their MO. —We don't know how they know; we're just lowly field operatives. Right?— We mention names. Colin Whiteburn's a good one, if he hasn't retired. Debbie Kassenbaum knows who he is. Since we admire Chang and all that he's tryin' to do, we're here to warn him. We ask him, please, not to do anything reckless. Given that won't work, we'd better have made friends with some of the staff in this hotel here. We're gonna need their help if we expect to do what we've got to do— *and* get outta here okay."

****

Before going to dinner in the hotel dining room that evening Charlie made sure to take along his pocket screwdriver and a pair of channel locks he had borrowed from hotel maintenance. He had already set out his little bottles of magnesium citrate, and he and Marie had painstakingly rehearsed how they would pour out the contents surreptitiously.

Some things are simple and straightforward, Charlie maintained. "If we can just put this stuff into someone's tea, it will work. He's gonna be indisposed for a while. He won't be able to defend himself worth a damn. If we take the trouble to arrange things right, unless there's a typhoon or somethin', we'll be clear of this country before anybody suspects us of anything. Now, other things can be tricky, but we'll be goin' with the flow."

Marie shuddered internally. She could visualize some of those "other things."

"D' y' think we'll make it back to Texas?" she said.

"Yes, I do."

*

In line with their need to get out of Singapore immediately and smoothly, they settled on booking a JAL flight to Tokyo scheduled for departure at 11:50 the next morning. The hotel staff helped out as well: Yes, their check-out would be automatic as of 11:00 that morning. A taxi would be waiting with a driver known to be quick. And one thing more that was arranged (for a fifty-dollar price): the sliding doors giving onto the patio-garden from the lobby would be inexplicably locked for at least five minutes *after* Charlie and Marie had come in from the patio at about 11:00.

Before dinner, Charlie and Marie casually exited the lobby through sliding glass doors to step onto the patio where the next day's breakfast would be served alfresco. "Ah. This is how we draw the drapes across the door," Charlie said, tugging a vertical white cord on their way out.

They found the patio a pleasant place for dining with several tables occupied. Beyond the swimming-pool area the courtyard was gracefully unstructured. Tables stood beside trees or bushes, some stood in the open; a portable bar set under a canopy was being stocked for evening use. An unpretentious white-bricked outbuilding standing between the pool and lobby entrance provided lavatories for patrons outdoors.

"We should eat out here," Marie said. "I want to be totally familiar with the whole fabric of this place."

381

"Fine. We can sharpen our focus."

They strolled to the white outbuilding, barely twenty yards from the door, and from there surveyed the setting. For a few minutes they pointed out tables each thought would serve them best when they would meet Chang for breakfast.

"The main thing is that he won't opt to go to the lobby when he needs a toilet," Charlie said. "We're lucky they've got restrooms out here. Damned lucky."

"Yeah, I'm sure," Marie said. Then: "Hey—what if it rains tomorrow?"

"We find some way to cope."

"What you mean, *we*?"

They were momentarily interrupted by a demure-looking, buxom Caucasian woman passing near. She might have been sixty years old, clearly worn down, not well kept, but emanating cultivated intelligence—and some indefinable quality both formidable and definite. Marie perceived all this about her, and for an instant their eyes met. Pale blue eyes beamed a smile at Marie; the rest of the lined face radiated good humor and will. To Marie's mind even that woman's blocky powder-blue dress looked right on her.

"*Bonsoir, madame!*" Marie almost sang, her smile going broad.

The older woman responded appropriately adding in French that the evening surely had possibilities. She reciprocated Charlie's respectful nod and moved on.

"Well, she's not French," Marie commented to Charlie.

Soon a waiter led them to a table in the open with small garden statuary and shrubbery near it. Very pleasant, quite private; it had struck them as one of the most feasible spots to meet Chang the next day.

"No doubt it would help to get here early, before Chang and his droogs show up," Marie said, her point being that they should ensure meeting at one of the four tables they had determined would serve to their advantage.

Something else, though, was playing on Marie's mind, something decidedly major, and she was loath to capture and raise it. After a waiter took their order, as they settled back in their chairs and sipped a sweet, cold Indian rice drink, Marie glanced about to ensure privacy, then expressed the issue: "I suppose we're gonna do in Debbie Kassenbaum, too; huh?"

"I don't see how we can just, you know, let her go."

"I don't either. I was just wonderin' if you did."

"No . . . . We'd be in permanent danger if we did. Not from her. From her mouth. God knows who'd listen to her, but anybody at all is bad news for us".

"I know. We have to kill her for us."

"Do or die; it's a good-enough reason."

Both noticed a familiar burly figure wearing a black suit and Roman collar pass through part of the courtyard to enter the hotel lobby. Whether he had seen them was moot. They might have waved to him had they not been so intent on discussing their plan for Chang K'ung's and Debbie Kassenbaum's future.

"We could just blow this whole thing off," Marie speculated. "We could go home—tonight—and wait for whatever is going to happen—to just happen. Then if we have to, we plead ignorance; just so long as we keep ourselves clear of it."

"Yeah, we could do that."

That was no good. Nor would it work to concentrate on killing Chang K'ung while leaving Debbie free to tell tales. During the next hour-and-a-half they focused themselves on the job they had come to do while they ate a light American-style meal and discussed—often quite specifically—the logistics involved. Here were the tables; there were the bathrooms. Cause the targets to go into those bathrooms. Ensure they would not come out alive.

"That's why I brought this screwdriver and channel locks," Charlie said and he patted his suit coat pockets. "That flat stone over there'll help." He got up and picked a stone out of a shrubbery bed and casually placed it under his chair. After he and Marie finalized a few more logistics, they paid their waiter and went to respective restrooms.

*

Marie had been waiting outside the white outbuilding for a good five minutes before Charlie came out to rejoin her. She noticed he looked exercised.

"That was kind of a tough job," he remarked to Marie's inquisitive look.

"You mean you did it now?"

From Charlie: affirmative. Marie glanced at his right hand to see it holding, against his trouser leg, the flat stone he had showed her earlier.

Their referent was Charlie's stratagem of rendering the locks inoperable on the restroom-stall doors. He and Marie had planned to do that later this evening when chances of being seen would be minimized. Impulsively Charlie had already done the job in the men's restroom, although he took little pride in it.

"I only had two stalls to do, but—hookh!—I sure mauled 'em," he said.

Accomplishing that same job in the women's restroom, where Marie had found three stalls to alter, would best be done as they'd planned, at about 9:00 p.m. when most dinner patrons had left. Thus they had only two other chores to do at the moment.

"Maybe we can find some good, firm cushions in the club room they've got here," Marie suggested, and they decided to go there next. They wanted to use cushions more substantial and firm than those they'd found in their hotel room, and not as large and intractable as those in the lobby.

"If we're smart, we'll put the cushions back when we're through with 'em," Marie said, and she felt an internal quake that actually made her grimace.

"We need to stop at the main bar and see if they'll sell us a magnum of champagne," Charlie said. "I don't want us depending on room service tonight. Not tonight."

"That's right," Marie said, and she and Charlie paused to register what each saw.

His back against the portable bar in the patio, gazing their way but focused on the ambience overall, Father Nobles ("call me Father Jay") sat dreamily cradling a highball.

"Well, I'll be damned," Marie said.

Beat. "What the hell, life is short," Charlie said. "Let's go visit with him." In an awed tone he added, "I wonder if what they say about him is really true."

"What's that?"

"He's over five thousand years old."

Nobles made eye contact with Charlie and Marie as they overtly headed his way; he gave them a little wave. Ten seconds later they were shaking hands and exchanging greetings and truisms about how small the world had become ("and it keeps getting smaller," Nobles said).

"Last I heard, you were spotted in Alaska, like this morning," Marie said.

"Well, that's true," Nobles said.

"Aren't you supposed to be in Patagonia or Peru or maybe Portugal?" Charlie said.

"Yes, I'm there," Nobles responded.

"Ha-ha-ha!"

With a level look into the great green eyes Charlie asked, "In all earnest, what brings you to Singapore, Father Jay?"

"I imagine I'm here for pretty much the same reason that you are," Nobles replied. "Beyond that—and my work for the Lord of course—I can say no more."

Tacitly they abandoned that subject. A brief conversation ensued, animated by mutual feelings of congeniality. They parted with assertions of surety they would all meet again soon.

For Marie and Charlie there was champagne to buy; they had to make a telephone call to Jed, which they made sounding as light-hearted as they could manage. Then there were two cushions to expropriate from lounges in the hotel, and three locks to disable on women's toilet stalls back in the patio. And there was the night ahead.

"Listen," Charlie said when they were back in their room and he was opening the champagne bottle, "tomorrow morning we focus—one step at a time. Boom-boom-boom. It's done. Then we get out smoothly, without rushing: one, two, three. We stay inside the current we've set in motion, and we keep directin' where it's goin' to go."

Marie was undressing near a vanity table. She responded, "Fine. That's good. We stay in the groove until everything's done. Okay. Now, we've got airline reservations. I want us to hold this image in our minds: we're getting on that plane; we're airborne; we're looking down at this very place. Okay?"

Charlie was all for that. Soon he added: "Okay, now we've got to rest up so we'll be sharp tomorrow, so first we've got to relax."

Marie was all for that. Both left unspoken the notion that even with their focus and imaging, they had no certainty they would ever be able to relax again.

When Charlie gazed at Marie, what he did know, beyond a doubt, was that all he beheld — every inch of that person — was ineffably dear. He lived for her presence. And Marie, taking in Charlie, knew (without question) that he and all that emanated from him was way, way, way beyond any value known to humankind. Would she give everything in her power to secure his well being? Yes, presuming Lisa and Julia wouldn't be harmed if she did. And would he do the same for her? Of course.

"I love you, you know," Marie said, her eyes dancing and delving deep into Charlie's.

The texture of her voice, the feel of it, as she said that became part of Charlie from that moment on. He knew this was happening as it occurred. And all the times afterwards when he recalled that moment he remembered he had known it was eternal.

*

Spent and satiated, Charlie and Marie lay gazing at the ceiling and holding hands. Final tracks on a Mozart compact disc played softly in the half-light of their hotel room. Thoughts about the next day had been consciously banished.

Marie annulled that arrangement. "Let's hope that everything we've tried to do in Life actually amounts to something," she said after several moments of silence between them. "Just in case we don't do anything more."

"What's gonna stop us, except for maybe a plane or car crash or something?" Charlie responded. "My only real sweat is Chang's bodyguards. If they get in the way, well, I guess we just back off. All right? If we—if I—can just stay clear of 'em, it's only a matter of us gettin' out of here before they know anything. We've got it all worked out. Right?"

"Yeah, well, we just have to stop two people from doing or saying anything, ever again," Marie said.

"Sure looks that way, from what I've heard."

Still holding hands, they stared wordlessly at the ceiling.

"We can always back out of this right up to the last moment," Charlie said.

"Yes, we can. D' you want to?"

"Sure. But I won't. Do you?"

"We'd have to, y' know, live with ourselves."

"I think that's what I fear most. Aside from you gettin' hurt, I mean. And the girls gettin' hurt. It's the possible regrets I can't stand to even think about."

Marie nodded. "Well," she said brightly, "let's see what the future brings."

"Yeah. Let's see how much good we can do."

Marie let go of Charlie's hand and got off the bed to fetch her cognac flask. She found it without aid of additional light and poured two generous shots. One she handed to Charlie.

"Here's lookin' at you dear," they said in unison as each raised a glittering little amber-filled glass to the other.

May 12, 1995
Far Western Hotel, Singapore

They had slept later than planned, and getting themselves ready for breakfast and departure took longer to accomplish than they'd expected. Still, by 9:30 a.m. Charlie and Marie burst from the hotel lobby into the patio, expecting to head for and occupy the most desirable table at which to meet with General Chang. The plan was that each would then go to a lavatory in the small outbuilding to stow the two white plastic bags each now carried.

Barely three paces down the flag-stoned walkway they heard "Marie!" called in a woman's voice, and they found themselves exquisitely irritated to see Debbie Kassenbaum standing in wait. Everything she wore was black (short-sleeved blouse, tight slacks, sandals); her face wore a smile both disarming and smug.

"He's over there," Debbie said and gestured toward a table perhaps twenty yards to the right of the small white building. The setting emanated pleasantness: table shaded by a tree bough and close to a flower bed. It was also centrally located in relation to everything, including four other tables each occupied by a solitary watchful man.

Charlie and Marie discerned a semi-familiar figure seated where Debbie had gestured. An Asian man, perhaps middle-aged, handsome and lean and looking a bit foppish in his white linen suit and wide-collared blue shirt festooned with a broad gold-and-white silk tie. They had seen him only once before, at a distance. Still they recognized, waiting specifically for them: Chang K'ung, General of the Republic Of China. At the moment he sat conferring with two well-dressed Chinese men of about his age.

Charlie said to Debbie, "I thought we'd be meeting him in private."

Debbie replied that the conference in progress would adjourn presently. A private meeting was next.

Marie asked Debbie if she would join them to provide introductions and "lubricate the tracks a little," to which Debbie was readily amenable.

"We'll just freshen up a little and get rid of this trash we've accumulated," Marie said pleasantly. "See you at General Chang's table—in five minutes, okay?"

Debbie nodded. Marie and Charlie strolled off to the outbuilding where they would separate and go to restrooms. En route Charlie glanced at Chang's table and remarked to Marie, "That fellow's got good taste. Look at the suit he's wearin'."

In fact Charlie owned a suit remarkably similar to Chang's, and he had almost opted to bring it for this occasion. Instead he wore a glossy blue-gray business suit that looked a bit rumpled even though it wasn't. It accommodated Charlie's standard blue T-shirt and thick-soled shoes and his need for roomy pockets.

"Looks like those pants are painted on her ass," Marie muttered in reference to Debbie's tight black slacks. "I hope she can get 'em off all right."

*

Chang K'ung sat at the breakfast table and sipped orange juice with Ms. Kassenbaum after saluting his departing associates whom he would rejoin at the Raffles. No monsoon rains in sight, only a few tourists in the patio; soon he would be eating American-style food replete with rashers of crisp bacon and cups of drip-brewed coffee. Ah, yes, a fine day to be alive.

Chang listened for birds singing and glanced about at stunted trees. For some reason this courtyard appeared devoid of birds, which he thought was just as well. Bodyguards were in place; he had looked around and made eye contact with two of them. He saw Marie first, then Charlie, materialize from the restrooms and begin making their way toward him. Each smiled at him with a nod as they came over.

"It's still a little early," Marie said to Chang. "Is it okay if we join you?"

"Please do," Chang replied, and he rose quickly and did a little bow.

Handshakes. Introductions by Debbie. Everyone got seated and a waiter was summoned. Breakfast menus were required; in the meantime tea and biscuits for everyone, also orange slices with powdered sugar. The waiter disappeared.

"Breakfast is on us," Charlie said.

"We'll see," Chang said.

For a few moments no one said a thing more.

"I don't guess you really need me anymore," Debbie said abruptly. "General Chang lived stateside for four years; he knows English better than I do."

She rose to leave but Marie asked her to stay for tea, to which Debbie acceded with a smile.

Chang glanced into Charlie's blue eyes, then his gaze shifted to Marie's dark eyes, her facial lines, her scar. He had seen her walking strongly in the dark slacks she wore; now he wished she weren't wearing that neutral-colored sports jacket because it obscured her upper-body development which was probably wondrous to behold and fondle, he decided with a frisson.

"You wanted to talk to me about something?" Chang said directly into Marie's eyes. Marie found his accent engaging, and he spotted her flicker of a smile.

"We sure do," Marie responded.

Charlie took the wheel and decided to head right for the top.

"Word has it, sir, that you're fixin' to set off some nukes."

Chang had resolved that nothing they'd say would surprise him. He looked at Charlie then Marie levelly. "So?" he said with genuine off-handedness.

"So everybody should know they're wrong. Otherwise the situation is dangerous for you and your organization, for your Cause."

"We're here to warn you," Marie jumped in. "People in the wrong places are getting anxious. We know they've got itchy trigger fingers, and that's the real problem."

At that moment Charlie found himself glancing about for Hsiu-fen Wu. He saw no hint of her presence in the courtyard but he felt she was close. Now he regretted trying to cozen her on Sunday; what he'd done was tantamount to sacrilegious. Concurrently, Chang heard himself asking Marie and Charlie about their sources of information, and of course they responded exactly as he would have in their place: with a wry, smiling shrug.

Marie declared, "Let's just say that we're here as private persons."

Charlie took it: "We appreciate—we admire—your New T'aip'ing Cause."

Intolerably long silence.

Chang said, "Go on. Please."

"We're here to warn you," Marie repeated. "People might get killed."

With a nod toward Debbie Charlie said, "One of Ms. Kassenbaum's old superiors, Colin Whiteburn, says Taiwan will get hit. Bad. And I believe him."

"H-m-m-m-m," Chang intoned, and he allowed himself a few moments of contemplation while the waiter put down a sizeable pot of tea and placed cups and little dishes all round. A busboy brought menus and Chang snatched his up and perused it.

"Look at the number three," Chang announced in reference to breakfast options, and he told the busboy to call back the waiter. Before long all had ordered something, even the preoccupied Debbie.

"This is on me," said Chang. "I am overpaid."

"Well, okay. I am not," said Charlie, leaning back in his chair. He glanced at Marie, who seemed to be taking cues from Debbie by sitting forward intently.

Looking mostly toward Marie Chang said, "Your source of information is missing one important thing: people will die. My intent is to present something that is real; I have no desire merely to frighten your government or your population. When people see reality, comes real fear." A short glance toward Charlie. "As for Taiwan destruction, I doubt it will happen. Even so, we are protected by civilian population; maybe by other things. If there is reprisal we counter-punch. —Boom!"

"Hmmpnh!"—from Charlie. Marie looked at Chang askance.

In the next few moments all sipped their tea; Chang bit into a biscuit and chewed with obvious pleasure.

Marie turned to Chang. "What can you hope to gain from nuclear terrorism?"

"Oh, I hope to gain the usual," Chang responded. "Money, women, fame. I would like to be in movies."

"You could play yourself!" Charlie jibed.

Chang acceded that.

"This is sociopathic talk," Marie declared, to no apparent effect.

For a while everyone concentrated on tea and biscuits and orange slices. Soon the meal would arrive. Charlie stood up briefly to stretch his back, his hands pushed into his suit coat pockets. "The bed we had last night is pretty rough on a normal human person," he explained, and Marie was struck by the irony of Chang nodding his empathy.

When Charlie sat down again—a little awkwardly—he said to Marie, "Pass the tea, would you, dear."

Marie did more than that. She took the teapot and rose from her chair to stand over Charlie and pour tea into his cup. When she'd finished, Charlie reached up and touched her forearm affectionately, causing Chang and Debbie to avert their eyes.

Marie bore away the teapot, and ceremoniously—and a bit abruptly—stepped behind General Chang's chair. His cup was half full and he had ordered coffee to be served with his breakfast. Marie filled his cup anyway. He did a little bow and acknowledged her courtesy by taking a sip of the tea.

"This is good," he said and sipped again.

"How 'bout for you, Debbie?" Marie said.

Before Debbie could reply Marie had stepped behind her. Again Marie poured out as much as she could. "Since I'm up," she explained. Debbie responded with a "thanks" and perfunctory sips.

Marie sat down again. Charlie took a drink of tea and momentarily pressed a napkin to his mouth to block a little cough.

That was when Marie chose to ask, "What brings you to Singapore, General? I mean, is there some special occasion in progress here? It looks like you've got your organization, your whole team, assembled for action."

At first Chang's only response was a flinty look. Then he said, "This is not my whole team by any means."

"Ah," was all Marie could say, with a nod.

"You mean Mr. Whiteburn hasn't briefed you?" Debbie said.

Charlie felt alarms go off. He had met that DIA Assistant Director but once, and that was at least four years back.

"I will answer what you asked," Chang said. "We are here to put final touches on forming our new country. You can say we are fine-tuning our plan of action, making sure every man and woman knows exactly what to do. We will use—we will try to use?—structures already in place, if you want to know. So our job is complicated; without very careful planning we are lost before we begin. I want to *make sure* we hold back nothing. We bring everything forward to be examined, or resolved when necessary."

"General Chang never stints," Debbie remarked.

"Word is," Charlie asserted, "Stage one is set to happen pretty soon, huh?"

Despite his resolve Chang felt alarmed. This fellow, Charlie, might know far too much. That in itself wasn't alarming. Whatever agency he represented was supposed to know nothing about the New T'aip'ing Revolution. Nothing at all.

"Maybe. Maybe very soon," Chang responded.

Two waiters bearing trays approached their table; conversation was suspended. As soon as the waiters were gone, even while he dug into his scrambled eggs and bit off crumbly bacon, Chang asked Charlie and Marie whether they still worked for American intelligence.

"*Of course,*" Marie answered. Beat. She and Charlie said in unison: "Why do you ask?"

"Because you helped, or you tried to help, our T'aip'ing Cause. That is not, I think, standard operating procedure for a spy agency. I think you tried twice a few years ago. You even gave us the parts for a missile-guidance system if I am not mistaken. It's a very good one, by the way; very advanced. But we hope never to use it."

"Well, fine," Marie said. "As we have told you, we admire what you are doing. The trouble is, not everybody does. That's why we have come here—to warn you."

Despite their credibility, Chang did not know whether to believe that. His insides were starting to quake; perhaps it was the black coffee on top the tea he'd drunk. Fresh cantaloupe went well with eggs and crisp bacon and hotcakes, but he wasn't used to such fare. For some reason he glanced at Debbie. Her expression conveyed abstraction, also physical discomfort. She had hardly touched her scone and fruit.

His mouth still full, Chang said, "We never recruited you. Yet you tried to help us; now you try again. What do you gain from your attempts?"

Charlie deferred to Marie who declared: "It's really kind of abstract. We want to contribute to justice in the world; we try to make a difference. Plus we need challenges, stimulation. Ultimately, we desire some kind of *meaning* to our lives. You know?"

"Ah," said Chang, preoccupied now by many things. He felt he had more primary concerns than listening to fools (or heroes) utter abstractions in a language foreign to his, although he did follow the skein of Marie's ideation and he felt comfortable with it.

Debbie announced, "Time for me to say—excuse me!" She smiled all round as she rose from her seat, then walked in a diagonal line toward a table set near the courtyard wall. Plainly she was headed to join the familiar burly figure dressed in black who was seated there reveling in the morning.

Chang noted with some interest that Marie's eyes fixed on Debbie's movements. For an instant Chang thought Marie was preparing to bolt from their table, and he was right. That would have happened had Debbie left the courtyard.

When this interruption had passed, Marie turned to Chang. "Uhm, since you ask," she said, "one thing we have gained is being able to learn all kinds of things."

A moment elapsed before Chang asked, "What things are those?"

He can actually look reptilian, Marie thought as she responded, "Things about ourselves. Things about our own culture, about other cultures. Things about you, even."

"Ah."

Charlie was making a show of preoccupation with eating eggs and waffles, but he was listening intently. He looked up at Chang, and their eyes met.

"You should know, then, you owe me your life," Chang said to Charlie.

"Really?" Charlie was totally engaged. Marie's eyes beamed on Chang.

"Yes. Remember that time—I think in 1991—when police were killing you?" Chang said. "They had you in interrogation cell in army-police headquarters, back in Taipei. Is that right? Do you know why they stopped? Because my people got you out, under my orders."

"You know, I've often wondered about that," Charlie remarked. "I thank you for that. My wife and children thank you. Probably you did save my life."

"It was the least I could do."

For a few seconds Charlie allowed his mind to drift back to that time. Inadvertently he said: "Ironical, isn't it?"

Chang could not respond to the rhetorical question. Marie had also heard it, but she didn't think it was cryptic at all. She suppressed a frown turned upon Charlie.

Marie and Charlie watched Chang's eyes suddenly widen. His face began to contort below the cheekbones. Marie's and Charlie's hearts leapt. Anxiety was over. All-out action would be now.

But not quite.

Almost in horror, Chang beheld Mo Tzu and Tatyana Platonov approaching his table escorted by one of his officers and one of his personal soldiers, along with two young Asian men whom he recognized as translators. In fact he had arranged to meet Mo Tzu and Tatyana at this place shortly after 11:00. But the hour was barely 10:30; he hadn't finished breakfast. He had yet to conclude meeting these two Americans with whom he wanted to maintain a useful relationship. And—*oohkh!*—his gut was cramping sharply. He wondered if he could stand up and walk without bending forward. Soon he would have to excuse himself; that was for sure. Now was a dismal time to deal with the Red and the Russian.

Charlie and Marie perceived that new arrivals were about to obstruct their path of action. Almost ferociously Marie tore a look across the patio at Debbie. She was still seated at Father Jay's table. Marie's and Charlie's eyes met, and each conveyed to the other a simple resolution. They would hew to the path.

Between them Charlie and Marie had managed to covertly pour almost the entire contents of one of Charlie's little bottles of magnesium citrate into the teapot they shared with Chang and Debbie. Masterfully, Marie had accomplished this when she had stepped behind Chang and Debbie seated in their chairs, just before she poured their tea. The depleted little bottle she had simply palmed, eventually passing it to Charlie, who put it in his pocket.

Of course Tatyana and Marie and Charlie recognized each other from the evening before. Again Marie addressed Tatyana in French and got an apt response. So, Marie thought, she must be the Russian scientist who supplied Chang with nukes; probably she did that in order to survive the Stone Age looming in Russia. Charlie found himself shaking hands with Mo Tzu and guessing him to be the Mainlander to whom Hsiu-fen had referred on Sunday. (Hsiu-fen's voice melodiously recurred in his mind distinctly mentioning, in passing, Mo Tzu's real name.) Chang K'ung meanwhile was explaining to a translator that he was engaged in other matters until 11:00.

Marie glanced up to spot Debbie rise from the table near the courtyard wall. In the next instant she would surely bolt for the restrooms in the small building twenty yards beyond this table. Marie stood up and tried to appear preoccupied while she kept Debbie in sight. Debbie continued to talk to the priest even though she was pressing a forearm against her midsection and bending forward noticeably.

Charlie watched Marie rise and take two steps to stand over him; desultorily she glanced in Debbie's direction. Charlie apprehended the situation and offered Marie a smile and reached to touch her arm again. Marie glanced into Charlie's eyes and nodded.

"Time to rock 'n' roll, I think," Marie said quietly and began moving toward the restrooms just as Debbie broke from her conversation and scurried for the same destination.

Charlie looked evenly at Chang K'ung and distinctly heard his internal voice say *You're next you dick*. At the moment Chang was successfully dismissing his most recent visitors, his left-hand fingertips holding a rasher of dark bacon at the ready. But Chang's face showed acute physical discomfort.

Now alone with Chang at the table Charlie spoke off-handedly as he rose from his chair: "Mo Tzu—he's from the People's Republic. What's his job? He looks vaguely familiar."

Chang had bitten into his bacon. Charlie stretched and looked about. "Lin Piao," Chang said unexpectedly. "He is deputy minister of . . . something."

"Ah. Excuse me also," Charlie said. "I'll be right back." He began striding toward the small white building housing the restrooms.

****

Remembering the last time she had drunk tea in Marie's and Charlie's company, Debbie would have wondered—had she been able—whether a connection existed between her infirmity then and her distress now.

As she made her way into the lavatory the overriding concern of her existence was to relieve the intolerable pressure—with stabbing waves of more intense pressure—building inside her entire midsection all the way into her cervix. Her only other thought regarded how she could most quickly push down her tight pants. She lurched into a stall and managed, with sheer determination and good luck, to do that. She would have locked the stall door but she didn't have time. Besides, the lock was broken off. She noticed this fact as she realized that someone else in dark slacks had entered the restroom and stood still (for a moment) outside her stall.

By taking deliberate, measured steps, Charlie tried to appear not to be walking slowly on purpose. He gazed idly toward the patio wall in various directions; actually he was trying to note the positions of Chang's personal guards. He spotted three of them (and a possible fourth) sitting alone trying not to look watchful. A well-dressed Asian man whom Charlie vaguely recognized from the day before, probably one of the officers in Chang's cadre, sat talking intently with a female counterpart. Father Jay sat engaged by a plate of French toast and various side dishes. No other patrons remained in the patio; a few bored hotel staff moved about perfunctorily.

Charlie hoped—fervently—that the staff would do what he had paid them to do when the time came, which would be soon. He took a ragged breath as he visualized for an instant Marie doing what she had gone to do behind the white wall several feet away. *Whoah!* Exactly as Charlie had projected, Chang K'ung hurried past him, making for the men's lavatory. Charlie also hoped—profoundly—that Chang had motioned his bodyguards to stay back. They all appeared to be in place.

Unvolitionally Charlie quickened his pace but strove to appear nonchalant as he followed Chang into the restroom.

*

Debbie could not have cared less about anyone standing outside her toilet-stall door as she sat down desperately, very short of breath, and went light-headed from intestinal relief combined with oxygen deprivation. She groaned loudly as she felt discomfort and outright pain suddenly let up.

The stall door swung open. Debbie's eyes widened as she wordlessly watched Marie step directly toward her clutching a large brown cushion. Other than possibly a single spark bursting behind her eyes, that was the last thing Debbie saw on Earth as Marie pushed the cushion into her face and forced her head forward—and held the head almost entirely motionless.

Even at her most robust, Debbie's strength could not have overcome Marie's. Within a minute her head simply lolled into the cushion, all other physical movement having ceased. Marie let out a gasp but continued to press Debbie's head and the cushion together for at least another minute, her own breathing still rapid and shallow.

"Gee-zus!" Marie said as she finally let off pressure on the cushion. Something made her look behind herself, and she felt a shock exactly like being jabbed in the back by an electric cattle prod.

*

One moment earlier Chang K'ung had felt he'd never known such distress, and now sitting in the commode stall he couldn't know enough relief. He was sure the pressure dilating his intestines was released just barely in time to avert his gut exploding.

"*Ya-a-a-a!*" Chang bellowed even before he could take an overdue breath. As he gasped for air, the door two feet in front of him yawned open and he felt his breath catch.

Charlie strode into the stall gripping a large brown cushion with both hands. He paused imperceptibly, intending to smile or say he was sorry. Instead he let the cushion drop as though something extraneous had occurred to him.

Wordlessly Charlie bent forward and reached out to put the palms of his hands on each side of Chang's head, gently pressing Chang's temples. Chang decided not to attempt smiling and simply grimaced. He wondered, fleetingly, what the cushion was for. Looking inquisitively into Charlie's face, all he saw was stolidity. The man must be affected by the odor, he thought, as he raised both his hands to touch Charlie's wrists.

Looking intently into Chang's eyes, Charlie said, "You need this," and with no overt effort he gave Chang's head a sharp jerk to the right causing the cervical vertebrae to shift. Done correctly, the movement would have placed those bones in better alignment, but that was not the case here. Nor was that intended.

Chang cut a yell that might have carried outdoors. All he felt was pain and rage. As though to countervail the pain in one side of Chang's neck, Charlie immediately jerked Chang's head the other way, this time perceptibly making a hard move but not cracking any vertebrae.

The pain was too excruciating for Chang even to cry out. At first he saw only yellow and scarlet, then black. His eyes opened for an instant. He saw a square of brown material about to be pressed to his face, the last thing he would see on Earth as a living human being.

With his right hand Charlie had taken firm hold of the back of Chang's head. Charlie's left hand gripped the cushion; he set his feet firmly apart while his left arm and deltoid pushed hard. When Chang could finally will to resist, all his cells were oxygen deficient. The struggle lasted barely beyond a few seconds and never got very intense.

"Hoohkh!" Charlie said after about two minutes when he let off pressing the cushion into Chang's face. Then he had to drop the cushion again to grab hold of Chang's shoulders and reposition the body to keep it from pitching forward. Charlie tore a look over his right shoulder and glimpsed the side of a black suit pass the open stall doorway less than five feet behind him.

"Shi-it!" Charlie said as he snatched up the cushion, pivoted about, and vacated the stall to confront the interloper. During one instant, he did manage to hope (sharply) that Marie was having good luck

*

At the moment that was mostly so. Marie used a one-handed shove to push Debbie's body against the commode tank so it wouldn't slump forward and fall to the floor. Then she spun around and barged from the stall, gasping for air as she set about dealing with the woman who had looked through the partly open doorway to glimpse what engaged two women at one toilet.

If not for the feeling that a giant fist was squeezing the inside of her stomach and womb, Marie would have been surprised to see that the intruder was no stranger. Outside the stalls Tatyana Platonov inquisitively awaited Marie's approach. Marie came into the open and gave her a baleful look. Despite no real knowledge of the situation around her, Tatyana comprehended most of the reality underlying what she had just seen. Even the fact of Marie placing the cushion in a white, opaque plastic bag corroborated Tatyana's realizations.

Marie knew she had to make a big decision. Again she assessed the Russian woman: At least twenty years Marie's senior. Skin and teeth not well maintained but physically fit despite deprivations. Lucently intelligent. Probably she understood what was happening here, Marie determined, then asked herself: *Ah, but does she care*, does she have a *stake* in it?

"Smells pretty bad here, huh?" Marie said and perceived incomprehension. She repeated the idle question in French and got a nod.

For an instant Tatyana placed the fingertips of her right hand on her downed eyelids. Then she lifted her hand away and allowed her eyes to reopen.

"*Je n'ai rien vu!*" Tatyana declared. She hadn't seen anything, she said, and now she needed to hurry into one of two vacant stalls and lock the door, which had no lock.

Marie swung the door open and went in after her.

"*C'est a cause des nerfs*, huh?" Marie suggested, since overtaxed nervous systems sometimes cause people to see delusory images—or occurrences.

Emphatically, with an appalled shrug, Tatyana agreed. "*Je suis tres nerveux*," she conceded because she'd been under considerable stress lately (which really was true, especially now), and she repeated that she had seen nothing.

Marie nodded firmly once, her expression forceful, a bit severe. She leveled an index finger at Tatyana for a second. They were now accomplices, Marie conveyed as she stepped backward and vacated the booth.

Marie still clutched her bag with the cushion. A second identical bag and cushion, her backup to use if the other had been removed, she'd leaned against the wall under a sink basin. Before she retrieved the second bag and went outside— profoundly hoping to see Charlie intact and alone—she forced herself to check inside the remaining stall in case someone had gone in there. She also checked immediately outside the restroom door and saw no one near.

With a final admonition to Tatyana that she had seen nothing at all unusual—and waiting to hear it audibly confirmed—Marie placed the bags holding the cushions under her arm and strolled outside into smoggy sunlight.

*

Charlie and Father Jay Nobles had found themselves confronting each other in a situation neither could have foreseen. They didn't know what to say to each other. Nobles gave a slight nod of a greeting.

402

"Mornin', padre," Charlie said. "What brings you by?"

"Oh, the usual. You've been busy!" Nobles remarked and slipped into the vacant stall to find the door lock disabled.

Still clutching his cushion, Charlie barged in after him. For a moment he crowded the priest against the commode. He was thinking that if he did not kill Nobles right then, he and Nobles would have to appear in the open, outside, immediately. Killing Nobles could have subverted everything; it simply was not in the plan. Armed men were on the alert outside. Time had been passing; Charlie felt this fact acutely. He wrapped his right arm across Nobles' back and heaved, pulling him from the booth.

"Come on," Charlie said into Nobles' widening green eyes, "we go outside. *Now*."

That was what they had done, with Charlie pressing his right arm firmly across the priest's upper back and brooking no resistance. On their way out the restroom door Charlie paused only to pick up the white plastic bag he had dropped next to a sink; he slipped the cushion into it before exiting. Another white bag holding a backup cushion he simply left there.

*

Stepping outside the white-brick lavatory building, Marie was more than slightly surprised to see Charlie and Father Nobles standing together and chatting on the short walkway to the lobby entrance, in plain sight of everyone in the patio. Or they seemed to be chatting, as Charlie casually tucked a white bag identical to Marie's under his elbow.

No more than a minute earlier Charlie had finished telling Nobles that he, Nobles, had seen "nothing untoward or even unusual." Then: "If you even suggest to anyone that you did, sir, I'll kill you myself," Charlie had said matter-of-factly. "And if I can't, you bet your life we've got people who will." Bluffing the priest Charlie had done naturally; he never thought to use the title "Father." Nobles hadn't the will to assess and perhaps defy Charlie's threat, for he had become torpid with the realization that someone—and some thing—he considered inestimable no longer existed.

Charlie added, "One way or another, sir, *we-will-kill-you* if you talk. Is that clear?" And he had gently placed his arm over the top of Nobles' shoulders. "I'll do my best to break your neck. [Beat.] You know I can do it."

For a kinetic moment Charlie had gazed flatly into the great green eyes. Barely perceptibly he had caused his arm to rise across the back of the priest's neck—and turn rigid. By then Nobles had clarified internally some facts and issues: What was done, was done. Jeopardizing his own life by incriminating Charlie would serve no good purpose. Life was sweet! Why end it prematurely? Perhaps he could have resisted attack from Charlie, he thought, but who else might be primed to kill him for informing on Charlie? He gave a shrug. "I didn't see anything unusual in there," Nobles said to Charlie with sufficient conviction to sound credible.

As Marie approached them she saw Charlie motion toward her, causing Nobles to look her way. Loudly Charlie declared, "See! You're outnumbered already. She and I are with different agencies, by the way."

"How'd it go?" Marie asked Charlie quietly.

"Not too badly. Uh, there's been a hitch. Father Jay's forgotten about it, though."

"I hope so," Marie said, and she stepped around Nobles and moved close to his broad back, almost flush against him for a second. "All of us hope so."

Marie felt a tension between Charlie and Nobles not evident from a few feet away. Nobles nodded affirmatively. "I didn't see anything remarkable," he declared.

Marie glanced about in different directions looking for Chang's personal guards. She thought she saw only three of them seated at tables. Nobody besides herself and Charlie and Nobles and a waiter was standing or moving in the patio. "We'd better get going," she declared.

"We have to leave," Charlie said to Nobles. "We're expected elsewhere." Charlie also looked around for Chang's bodyguards but lost track of how many he spotted.

With little token waves, Charlie and Marie left Nobles standing on the walkway as they headed to the hotel lobby entrance. They observed the middle-aged Chinese man they'd seen earlier apparently en route to the men's restroom.

"Bye!" Marie called out to Nobles and heard a response much like an echo.

*

They briskly entered and closed the sliding glass doors, and, by arrangement, a clerk from the lobby materialized to lock the doors while Charlie said "Let me help," and he closed the drapes across the glass. He and Marie strode to the registration desk at the other end of the lobby. En route they paused to drop brown hotel cushions onto a divan; they wadded and discarded the white plastic bags in a trash receptacle.

"So far, so good," Marie uttered.

"We'll make it," Charlie said.

At the desk Charlie flashed their stamped-"paid" receipt, Marie waved farewell to staff members, and she and Charlie walked out the front doors, perhaps more quickly than they wanted to. Just outside the entrance a maroon Toyota taxicab engine started up when they appeared. They hurried to it, opened a back door, and clambered inside. Their flight bags were on the seat.

"Ah-ha!" Charlie said, and he and Marie marveled at how efficiently people respond when they get paid more than they expect.

"To the airport," Marie told the driver, a black-haired Asian man wearing a white baseball cap.

The response came with a slight British accent: "I know."

Marie and Charlie looked at each other for a second. Poking a fist clutching a hundred-dollar bill over the front seat, Charlie asked the driver whether he accepted American money. About five seconds later, after stopping at a traffic light, the driver turned around to reply and accept the money, and Charlie and Marie were taken aback to realize that he was the same—seemingly omniscient—driver who had delivered each of them to the Far Western Hotel on previous days.

"Hey, do you remember me?" Marie asked after a moment.

The driver glanced perfunctorily at his rear-view mirror. "Of course," he said. "I remember your husband, too. Three days ago."

Stunned silence in the back seat. They passed the Raffles Hotel and soon turned onto a boulevard.

Marie said, "We must arrive at the airport before 11:30."

"You have a Japan Air Lines flight before noon?"

Two edgy voices from the back seat: "Yes."

"We'll take the fast way," the driver said, and he caused the cab to dart into the inside lane, then he drove it onto the median strip, barely missing a palm tree. Marie literally screamed.

In the next instant the driver cut a sharp left, then another left, and they passed by the other side of the palm tree they'd nearly hit a moment before. Even Charlie couldn't say anything because he had Marie (and their two flight bags) jammed against him as two wheels of the cab rode on the median strip and the two wheels on Charlie's side rode on street. Thus they slipped past one car then another and another (with several centimeters to spare) until the driver cut in front of a truck to jam them into the inner lane.

At least two police sirens had started up somewhere in the immediate vicinity. Marie and Charlie heard the driver mutter something unholy. In spurts of speed he wheeled the cab around one corner, then another. They went up the street a few blocks until the driver pulled into an arterial street on which they traveled for a half kilometer to another artery, which led them to a palm-lined highway that he entered with ease.

"You will arrive at airport in eight minutes," the driver said. "Ten minutes tops."

"Gee-zus," Charlie said, "God must be with us."

"No problem," the driver said. Beat. "My name is Ray. I learned how to drive in Miami; you know, USA."

"Ah. That explains a lot." —From Charlie.

During the final minutes of their ride, Marie quietly conferred with Charlie about whether suffocation as cause of death can be revealed by an autopsy, and Charlie said that usually it was. As though he was privy to their concern, Ray spoke to them over his right shoulder: "You picked a good time to come here! Singapore has one coroner. She's in Hawaii until next week!" His voice sang with jubilation.

Charlie and Marie refused to consider what they believed they'd just heard. They merely glanced at each other and strove to restore their focus.

Not only did they arrive at the airport terminal on time, but Ray took them through a service door and down a hallway to the back of the Japan Air Line desk where their ticket purchases were expedited. After their flight tickets were validated at the gate Charlie and Marie still had to pass through customs, which they did readily by showing their U.S. DOD passports. Visas had not been required. True to Singaporean form all was accomplished in an orderly manner. Ray stayed close to them on the other side of the green cordon swag. Before proceeding they paused to shake hands with him.

After the goodbyes and best wishes Ray added, "All is well that ends well, as some people say. You must be proud!"

By now they were so inured to this man's prescience that they let themselves be arrested by his glittering black eyes and luminous smile and they simply didn't respond. Charlie intended to say "You're one helluva guy; you know that?" Instead he searched the beaming brown face because something else captured him.

"There's something . . . familiar about you," Charlie said to Ray. "Do I know you from someplace, from before?"

"Not in this Life, buddy."

Charlie half-way expected that answer. Marie felt this exchange to have been somehow normal. With smiles they turned and left as Ray tendered them a final wave.

*   *   *

I imagine you guessed who Ray the taxi driver actually was. Implementing roles like that can be expected of me. But let me explain that even though my function in Charlie's Life caused important effects, I had to do something singular during that climactic episode in the lavatory at the Far Western Hotel.

My job has rarely called for me to advise or motivate Charlie, but his and Marie's situation had become overly perilous that morning as they endeavored to terminate Chang's and Debbie's activities on Earth. I was sure that Chang would have struggled manfully to survive suffocation; first he had to be fully disabled. Time provided no margin: Chang's bodyguards were anxious and vigilant. Plus I knew that Marie needed my help, and I cannot do two things exactly simultaneously.

So I intervened. I reminded Charlie of Marie's counsel by long-distance telephone that time he was in Somalia: "Chiropractors make adjustments," I told him. "Now is the time to make one." That was when he decided to place his hands along the sides of Chang's head and alter his neck alignment. In that moment I also influenced the way Marie averted disaster by simply conveying to her conscious mind the essence of the word "rapport." It definitely helped her despite all the dissonance she was experiencing.

Then I had to promptly get back into my current role and ensure my cab ran well. Doing that was a challenge not nearly as demanding as filling the function of a lady corporate executive working for E-Systems in Dallas and manipulating federal covert operations, but fairly analogous to the job I did as a German merchant seaman advising Charlie about life while he taught me how to be a paramedic aboard ship. Boredom for me has usually been a luxury.

*   *   *

Only when she felt the airliner stop climbing and level out, herself and Charlie now clear of Singapore, did Marie feel free to comment on their recent events. "Looks like we've done our bit," she said. "I think we're gonna be okay."

"I refuse to worry about any fallout—unless this plane turns around and goes back," Charlie responded. "Thank *goodness*, we did what we did."

They fell silent for several minutes. Each was experiencing numbness gradually giving way to a thrilling realization: They had done something actually monumental! And they might not incur any adverse consequences. Finally they let themselves feel it: exhilaration, completely unreserved. Ray the cab driver had a good point.

Seemingly apropos of nothing, Charlie turned to Marie with an idiotic grin and said, "To quote Muhammad Ali or Mick Jagger or somebody, 'Truth is stranger than fiction.'" And she knew exactly what he meant.

At about this time Marie began to feel overtaken by something else rumbling from depths within her. She was almost astonished. As she fixed on a flight attendant's jovial, pale face she could think of only one word, a Japanese word: *bento*.

"*Bento no arimasuka?*" Marie said to the flight attendant, attempting to use elemental Japanese to get or buy a lunch.

Charlie recognized that word, and his eyes widened and he felt tense facial muscles loosen as he declared, "I can't remember the last time I had a real meal!"

They each ate a *bento*, a Japanese lunch, then each had another. Except for one beer which they split, they contented themselves with tea to wash down the food because they still had to maintain a modicum of mental sharpness. After they ate and availed themselves of the flight toilets and began to feel more relaxed, Marie heard herself reflect aloud: "He was an evil jerk," and Charlie knew the reference was to Chang K'ung.

After a moment Charlie remarked, "He really was bigger than life, though."

Marie responded, "So is Fidel Castro or Saddam Hussein. Look at that turkey who's running Zaire into the ground. John Wayne was 'bigger than life.' What of it?"

Charlie pondered briefly before he answered: "I think Chang had a grand vision. And probably he was the only person on Earth who could have brought it to fruition."

"He was actually fixin' to kill a lot of people just so he could have what he wanted," Marie said. "That's intentional wrong-doing; and he was aware of it."

Charlie was feeling unexplainably empty despite the *bentos*. He endorsed everything Marie had just declared but without enthusiasm.

Marie was about to say, "Look. Hitler was an idealist. So was General Tojo." Instead she said, "Well, I'm pretty sure about something else regarding Ho Chi Chang."

Charlie rose to the bait.

"I know why we've only seen pictures of him in high-necked uniforms," Marie said. "Even when he was on vacation, you might have noticed he kept his collar buttoned and wore a tie. Do you know why that was?"

Charlie bit.

"He was trying to hide the circumcision scar around his neck!"

Before they dozed off they inventoried five worst-case scenarios that could ensue from their joint accomplishment that day at the Far Western Hotel. The first would have been arrest in Japan with extradition back to Singapore, the last would have been assassination at home by Chang's vengeful lieutenants. Perhaps except for the first, the scenarios looked highly unlikely.

"I tell you," Charlie said again, "I refuse to worry about fallout."

"Right. Whatever comes down the pike, we'll deal with it."

"*Right.*" Charlie's mind was already at home with Marie and their daughters.

"You can say that ours is an allegorical tale," Marie commented, bemused and nettled by a desultory sense of something undesirable that she'd first noticed in the taxi after they had left the Far Western Hotel. Until now she couldn't identify it but now she could. She was feeling unexplainably dirty.

In Tokyo they never left Narita Airport, nor did anyone bother them during a two-hour-plus layover before they went on to San Francisco. Except at Customs, they were just anonymous Occidental *gijin* en route to wherever they belonged. They found that realization comforting, and it was enhanced by an irony: their presence was utterly insignificant despite their having committed crimes which likely precluded all sorts of adverse impacts on Japan in the future.

"As far as these people are concerned," Charlie observed, "we don't exist."

"Well, what do they know, anyway?"

Something about this situation, along with a casual observation Marie had offered about a family of Chinese Americans (also en route to San Francisco) waiting on a bench nearby, inspired Charlie with an idea. At first he dispelled it; then it seized him.

Did he have a telephone number for a certain office in Xian in Shaanxi Province in China? Yes, it was on a stained card stuck in a pocket of his dob case which served as his toilet kit. Did he have the yen to make a long-distance call? No, but he had a Sprint International Calling Card. No, he would be stupid to use that, but he could get yen fairly readily from an exchange desk upstairs. But how could he telephone anybody in China if he couldn't speak the language? The family on the bench across the aisle were probably native speakers, and they looked awfully bored. Whatever he envisioned was complicated; it would require probably most of an hour to accomplish. They still had almost two hours to kill.

Charlie bounded from his seat. Before long he and Marie (motivated by boredom) had approached the Chinese family, introduced themselves, and asked of them an interesting favor: Would one of them mind helping Charlie place a telephone call to Xian in China? It might be important to people living there. Family members briefly squabbled among themselves to determine who wouldn't help. After a while they left as one (taking along all their stuff) to assist in making the call. Six family members closed around Charlie and Marie at a public telephone in a corner of the passenger area, excitement rising like steam. Passersby had to try hard to ignore the event.

Charlie punched in numbers and deposited yen; he heard a recorded message and passed the phone to Samo, the father, who told him to add such and such numbers. The operator butted in to inform him that another thousand yen were required. Charlie tapped the numbers and Marie pushed in yen.

At last Charlie heard someone in a parallel universe speak on the other end. He passed the phone to Samo who said something into the mouthpiece, waited, and excitedly asked something of his son, Ralph. Ralph uttered a Cantonese word; his father repeated it into the phone. Beat. Beat. Samo listened intently, and his eyes grew large as saucers.

"Internal Security!" Samo announced, astonished.

Charlie took the phone from the man's hand and spoke into it precisely and emphatically.

"Zhang Yimou, please," he said. To make sure he was understood he repeated "Zhang Yimou" two times, very distinctly, and added Samo's single Cantonese word for "director of organization," also Ralph's Cantonese word for "please." Marie helped elicit the translations. After waiting for several seconds a gruff voice came into his ear and Charlie believed that he'd been spoken to by "Big Yim" Zhang, Director of Internal Security for the Shangri-la known as Xian and for all Shaanxi Province.

"I am Charlie, American agent," Charlie said into the phone. "My wife is here also. You remember us—The Garden hotel." (Damned if he could recall the dates!)

For thirty tedious seconds Charlie heard himself trying to explain in very rudimentary English that Minister "Lim Paw" was a traitor consorting with Taiwan generals in Singapore. Despite hearing no response from the other end, Charlie felt sure he was being listened to. He heard a melodic, semi-metallic dee-dee-dee-*ding*, and he thought the call was being recorded. Finally an operator, a woman speaking distinctly in Japanese, interrupted this exertion and Charlie simply hung up. "Good try!" he declared to the wide-eyed assemblage, and he and Marie walked away.

Charlie had no way of gauging the effect of his telephone call, or whether his message had even caused one. And Director Zhang no longer worked at that location. But Zhang's ambitious successor listened to Charlie's voice, which he dutifully recorded. The words would not be disregarded, and Charlie's intuition about political and bureaucratic power apparatuses, especially in a context where governmental machinery is repressive, would turn out to be valid: once insinuated, a little poison, no matter how insignificant or thin, gets utilized almost infinitely.

As they sauntered back to the bench to resume their wait, Marie asked Charlie, "What was the point of all that?"

"Public service," Charlie answered. "That washed-out-lookin' guy from the Mainland—he was consorting with a genuine terrorist. He knew what Chang was fixin' to do. Plus he's a traitor. I'm sure he's some kind of high government official, so he gets paid good money while he's, you know, consorting. I say screw 'im. It's the least we can do."

"That works for me," said Marie.

Chapter 15

Upon her return to St. Petersburg from Singapore, Tatyana projected a dialogue between herself and Andrei, who was busy teaching at the Institute when she arrived home. "Most fools can look heroic and splendid when dealing with misfortune," Andrei would conclude. "But turning thin fortune into huge personal gains—now that is the work of a superior soul."

What thin "fortune"? Andrei was due a vacation and stipend (sufficient to maintain a medium-sized dog) when the current academic term at the Institute ended. He would then be free to accept brief lectureships in Scandinavia or Yugoslavia, and Tatyana would be expected to accompany him. Now that they had some freedom, they could leave and simply never return if they chose to be expatriate paupers.

Their only resource was about sixty-four thousand American dollars Tatyana had cached in various places after paying Sergei and other associates for helping her to "acquire" and secure those nine kilos of plutonium that were to drastically alter her and Andrei's Life. Sixty-four thousand was scant reward for all her exertions and all those hazards she'd endured for so long. That was because her operational expenses had grown geometrically and she had been too generous in paying accomplices; moreover, Mo Tzu had deposited some of her payments in a Singapore bank which she now considered off limits to preclude a connection being discovered between herself and Chang.

Tatyana did feel fortunate to have inside her underwear a down payment of nine thousand U.S. dollars from Mo Tzu for yet additional plutonium, which would no longer be of use to him or his late employer, and which she was now disabused of having to produce. She thought it unnecessary to reimburse "Mr. Mo," nor did circumstances afford her the opportunity for that in the aftermath of those apparent assassinations at the Far Western.

Of course Tatyana considered herself especially fortunate for not having seen anything unusual that day in the hotel lavatory despite those delusions from her "bad case of nerves." She had not even been detained for questioning by Singapore police after those untoward events at the hotel, perhaps because their staff no longer included Russian speakers (a sad commentary). Oh, she was definitely grateful to be home!

At last Tatyana heard what she might respond to Andrei's declaration about a "superior soul" and their own thin fortune: "We will make do with the resources we have and 'go for it,' as they say in the West, while we are able." And that would be the final word, for Tatyana had resolved that she and Andrei would jeopardize no further their chances of revamping their Life.

****

Who would have dreamed our saga would end this way?
Lin Piao's shock from the news of Chang's death had almost undone him. Having been forced to instantly clear himself of any hint of implication in assassinating Chang had jolted Lin further. But worst of all, the probability that one day soon he would be undressing beautiful Thai and European girls—had vanished. All those possibilities of sweet adventure in years ahead—evaporated. And that blood-quickening ambition he had once harbored to someday be an effective revolutionist by wielding authority based on his wealth from investing the money Chang had paid him—hopelessly naive in the light of reality.

How depressing my situation yet I can sink deeper. Even if the New T'aip'ing Revolution were to live on somehow, "Mo Tzu"

415

now lay unceremoniously buried. Lin still had access to bank accounts totaling over one hundred thousand U.S. dollars in Brunei and Manila, but to utilize them now would have entailed defecting straightaway, a prospect for which he felt dismally unprepared. His final payment from Chang for his efforts and personal expenses, which he would have received at about noon on the fourteenth, could have made spontaneous defection feasible if he were to combine that money with the funds in his accounts. (He cursed himself for having used cash to pay the Russian lady for additional plutonium because it came from his personal funds. In her place, he would never have returned it.) Now, just to keep his position at home safe, Lin had to focus on eradicating every trace of association between himself and Chang K'ung.

Yet Lin Piao would learn that he was still on high ground compared to the spirals his career (and life) would take during the years ahead. Within a few months, he would diagnose his reputation as having been infected by a mysterious virus that he had no means to fight, and for him paranoia would turn out to be a most reasonable condition. After that dark day in Singapore, one glittering notion did illumine Lin's prospect of his future, and it alone sustained him in the midst of his deepening-gray world: Somehow he would take revenge, total and unqualified, on whoever was responsible for costing him so much.

Thus even before departing Singapore for Beijing on the day after Chang's death, Lin set in motion his effort to get that revenge by using the only means he could find. As the cynosure of Lin's new focus, Father Jay Nobles would at first find himself actually amused by the ironies in the situation.

*   *   *

Truly important things are hard to identify, and you might find comfort knowing that I myself can list no more than six

416

or eight "eternal verities" that are actually eternal, and half of those might ultimately fail the test of reality. Consider this: when Earth has been incinerated, will "truth" or "justice" even exist? Will "right" and "wrong" exist? Grave issues of national or historical import are worth addressing in this context.

How does one know what the truly important things are? Mainly by being receptive to discovering them. Usually they emerge in the form of others' faces or some kind of beauty. When Jed, Marie's old friend from the teaching profession, told Marie and Charlie they had been missed when they were gone to Singapore, and that the spring flowers in the fields and along the river were still there for them to see again, she crystallized and implied most verities that actually are eternal.

You might ask how a person would best Live with those things perceived as truly important. My only advice is this: Do not let yourself get bored once you connect with the good and true. Human beings seem pathologically susceptible to profound boredom. Most colossal mistakes in human history have been instigated by people simply being bored. Please consider yourself warned.

*   *   *

Even though he couldn't remember his exact choice of words, Charlie often recalled the sound of his own voice directed to that vulnerable (and, yes, dear) soul, telling her what he thought she wanted to hear. Her face juxtaposed on azure and framed by rugged foliage on both sides of her, she listened to his lies and likely believed them. (One reason for that was her big, true heart, a fact Charlie couldn't bear to contemplate.) He had needed Hsiu-fen's help, and on the mountains back in Taiwan he had used her desires and goodness to get it.

Sooner or later it's gonna come back at me, he told himself almost every time he evoked memories of his last stay in Taiwan. Probably Hsiu-fen was neither vengeful nor disposed to meanness, but she was formidable and her qualities had been abused. Still, Charlie was sure that even she could not release him from his karmic debt.

Actually, Charlie had considered telling Marie about what he had done to elicit information from Hsiu-fen before he'd gone on to Singapore. Travel-related exigencies on the final leg of their journey home took the upper hand. Later he was glad he hadn't divulged his lies because almost certainly Marie would have felt at least a trace of betrayal, a development Charlie would have found abhorrent. A smart man should learn some things from his previous failed marriage, he thought. Willingness to overlook his own contretemps was one of them.

Coincidentally, Marie had learned from her previous marriage not to probe matters in which she would find things she couldn't abide. In Singapore and upon returning home, she hewed to the wisdom of simply waiting for Charlie to disclose relevant information. If it would turn out to be unacceptable information (although it couldn't be *very* bad, she thought), she would know what to do.

*

"I think it's important we get rid of these passports," Marie had told Charlie while they were still airborne from Japan en route to San Francisco. "We're not even supposed to have 'em anymore; remember?"

Use of U.S. Department of Defense passports was generally not recorded in countries with which the U.S. had certain compacts, although some customs officials informally noted the bearers' names in case they needed assistance in country. That hadn't been the case this time out. Officially, Charlie and Marie had not left the United States in about a year, although they would have had trouble explaining why they had purchased international airline-flight tickets.

About forty-eight hours after returning home from Singapore, Charlie finally took the illicit passports behind their garage and doused them with gasoline and set them afire.

Reducing them to ash took three such treatments, after which Charlie dug up two patches in their backyard and tilled the ashes under. "*Sheesh*, that was like trying to kill a pair of those big brown mice," he told Marie afterwards.

A day later each got the telephone call they'd been expecting, requesting them to appear separately at the Federal Building downtown. Of course they complied, and each related earnestly that during their last meetings with Debbie Kassenbaum (in Dallas and in Austin) she hinted at having learned about some clandestine "activity" or "underground movement" that might destabilize countries in the Pacific Rim. She'd divulged no specifics, saying only that she had learned what she knew by accident, and that she intended to investigate it.

Was Debbie all right? The last time they'd seen her she looked hyperactive, tired. (They couldn't have known she was dead.) Maybe by now she was some kind of hero! Yes, they'd heard about General Chang's death on CNN; it meant very little to them. They'd been out of town at their "ranch" recently and hadn't been anywhere else. That was their story, and they steadfastly maintained it.

Conscience dictated that Marie and Charlie insinuate one exceptional element into their story even though it caused them to return to the Federal Building one afternoon to repeat everything to the FBI: Debbie Kassenbaum had casually, maybe inadvertently, mentioned to them on two occasions that she thought nuclear explosives had been smuggled into the U.S. and distributed to as many as a dozen population centers, all of them in proximity to a major university. In that context she had named General Chang as a possible source of the explosives, but she'd disclosed nothing else specific.

Were Charlie and Marie believed? They thought so. Not to have believed them would have been unreasonable. "We're tryin' to get away with all kinds of things," Charlie remarked to Marie after their initial interrogations at the Federal Building. "We're doin' fine, but we might need some luck if we're gonna succeed."

Marie understood the primary reference was to their killing Chang K'ung and Debbie Kassenbaum with impunity, but more things were subsumed, from their illegal use of special-issue passports to the modus operandi they employed on some of their "errands" that had caused them to learn of Chang's plot. Now they were trying to help eliminate Chang's nuclear devices: Could they do that without tripping on the curb?

"I hope so, because we've got a Life," Marie declared. "That's enough of this stuff." Charlie couldn't agree with her more emphatically. Often he could smell the odor thick about him while he did something anomalous and savage in a particular lavatory in Singapore. He felt sure Marie had the same lingering experience even though she mentioned it but once.

Only gradually did a major facet of reality overtake them, and it surprised them.

"Y' know, I believe we could stand a change, almost any kind of change, so long as it's not detrimental to us or the girls," Marie declared to Charlie about three weeks after their final interrogation by FBI agents downtown.

"Yeah, I know it," Charlie said. "If you ask me, we actually were 'excitement junkies' until we got weaned from it. You might say we fell off the wagon recently, and now we're payin' for it."

Marie understood that "falling off the wagon" referred to their exploit at the Far Western Hotel (which they'd coded as their "last great adventure"). A little later she let herself reprise and enjoy the psychic surge she'd experienced when she had answered, affirmatively, Jed's query about whether she and Charlie had succeeded in "saving the world." So Charlie was right.

****

During this same time, near the west edge of metropolitan Beijing in a far-flung "suburb" totally indistinguishable from dozens like it, mysterious goings-on had been in progress but were low-key enough to allay local curiosity. After a while the sporadic (usually semi-weekly) occurrences of a black government automobile stopping behind a shuttered, barred municipal storage building and disgorging two men who went inside for an hour began to appear normal.

"Why am I here?" Father Jay Nobles would say to the two men at some point during those occasions. Invariably the older, authoritative one (who might not have understood a word of English) would say something in Cantonese, and the other (who looked shriveled but somehow less gray compared to the first) would say in English that Nobles was there to divulge certain items of information.

At first Nobles was baffled. He had no idea of where he was or how he'd gotten there. The information demanded of him he couldn't comprehend enough to provide.

"Who are you, anyway?" Nobles would sometimes ask the older man.

"I am the ghost of Mo Tzu."

Nobles would dip into his historical knowledge. "Mo Tzu was a great general. I believe he is considered a bold, innovative leader," Nobles would say.

And the response would be some version of, "One day you will know."

After a few weeks of solitary confinement mitigated (alternately) by two silent jailers providing outdated *Time* magazines and occasional scraps of meat with his rations of rice and porridge—Nobles concluded that he'd been abducted from Singapore to China (conjecturing this happened after he'd been drugged, which was the case), and he recalled that in Singapore he had once seen "Mo Tzu," who now wanted him to reveal who had killed Chang K'ung and why.

All right, he decided, he would comply (with certain reservations) if he received assurances that he would be released when he did and that he wouldn't be named (to anyone) as the source of the information. When he advanced this bargain it was ignored, although Mo Tzu never struck him as murderous or even unkindly. Four more weeks later, after he'd lost about thirty pounds, failed at two escape attempts, and been bored beyond his threshold of tolerance, Nobles' intention to negotiate evaporated.

"Answer all my questions completely," Mo Tzu ordered one day. Almost mindlessly, Nobles did exactly that. His inner walls were atomized; he could withhold nothing. If he didn't know the answer to a Mo Tzu question, he made one up. His interrogators returned and repeated the questions on the next day, and the day after and the day after and the day after that.

Now sometimes Mo Tzu actually smiled at him. And Nobles was given little rewards, notably a toothbrush and salt, a chunk of smoked pork, several bottles of beer, a daily candy bar (imported), and finally a jar of whiskey. On the fifth consecutive day of questioning they catered to his oft-repeated wish: he was given a fairly recent, rumpled copy of the *Hong Kong Times*.

When Nobles got the newspaper, he promptly sat and read voraciously under an unshaded light bulb until he was interrupted in about twenty minutes by one of his jailers opening the door to his makeshift cell. Under Lin Piao's stern supervision, he was invited to leave the room and walk down a hallway, which he did with sheer delight. As he strode along enjoying the deliciousness of physical mobility, he was barely aware of being struck on the back of his head by something hard. He had no such awareness of his throat being slashed a minute later as he lay on a tarpaulin.

Despite his revulsion, Lin Piao closely monitored these actions which he himself had commissioned. The matter of disposing of Nobles' remains had been meticulously arranged. Only his tape-recorded voice would survive the day, and not for long.

"Wash that thing off at the drain," Lin told the two men who worked for him as jailers. "Put it in the truck after dark exactly as we planned."

I think I know all I need to know, Lin advised himself. I will use it most effectively regardless of risk no matter the cost.

Lin had resolved to use the facts he'd extracted from Nobles to get revenge as token compensation for the losses he'd incurred when Generals Chang K'ung and "Mo Tzu" died in Singapore. He alone had access to three of Chang's foreign bank accounts; in sum they held over a hundred thousand dollars, enough to enable him to live moderately well for at least two years without using his own funds if he defected. (He often wondered if he had the fortitude for that; usually he thought he did.) Almost as relevant, he knew how to make contact with men who would do anything for absurdly small payments, even in *yuan*. Proof was the ease with which he'd arranged Nobles' being abducted and smuggled into the country and then held prisoner.

But Lin could never have foreseen the degree to which his intentions would be blocked—time after time over the next few years—exactly as though he were cursed, a notion he came to posit as demonstrably true. Revenge thus became even more imperative. Some mornings he would recall convoluted, gratifying dreams in which he set the process in motion.

****

At first Hsiu-fen Wu had simply been in shock when she learned of General Chang's death. The bizarre circumstances surrounding it, including her own government's reluctance to acknowledge it, had extended the shock effect. Fully three days passed after she'd learned that Chang was dead before she psychically acceded that he was actually gone. That he'd been murdered (somehow) along with that woman who had become his sole confidant struck her as certain. The question of who had killed him was irrelevant to her, although of course she wondered whether Charlie and his wife had some connection to the event. (She'd never seriously suspected they had caused

423

it, for the idea was too inconsonant with her perceptions of them.) Mostly she wondered what happened to Charlie after his meeting with Chang K'ung. She didn't know for sure that they had met, but she presumed they had.

Soon after Hsiu-fen had returned to Taipei, even before she had finished setting Chang's military business in order for his successor (who was yet to be named), she tried telephoning Charlie's and Marie's home in Austin, Texas. Were they intact and safe? She needed to know that. All she learned was the sound of Marie's recorded voice stating what number she had reached and that she should leave a message, which she felt unable to do.

On her fourth attempt at making telephone contact, her nerves taut from the many changes in her life and its nebulous future, Hsiu-fen said simply to the recorder, "I hope you are well. Please call me in Taipei." She decided not to identify herself or leave her number. Charlie—if he was alive and well—would recognize her voice and know how to reach her. Lisa Grumbles, who heard that message and erased it, either took it to be a stranger's mistake or she simply forgot to tell her parents about someone requesting a call "in Taipei."

*

"Y' know, we could always go 'bourgie,'" Marie remarked to Charlie one night as they lay abed and had just finished reading.

Charlie understood her code word for activities they considered shamelessly bourgeois, such as purchasing unneeded vehicles and boats and furniture, or undertaking unnecessary home remodeling, or going on expensive vacations to places de rigueur. Systematically trying out local restaurants they already did, but only when that pleased them.

Charlie lowered his foresters' newsletter and briefly pondered Marie's proposition. "Yeah," he said, "I guess we could. But, we do *not need* a new house. We've got all we can handle just Living."

"That's fine. I think I'll try setting things up so we can, you know, distract ourselves for a change. That'll be good."

Thus Marie set about finding desirable ways for her and Charlie to pass gracefully through the glaring, withering summer. "We're sort of in prolapse," she would remark to Charlie or Jed to explain some of her uncharacteristic behavior eruptions, such as taking long shopping excursions. In that vein, under very little pressure, Charlie even took Marie and the girls on one of his trips to Colorado and then to Oregon. Since they went by auto, the endeavor drastically resembled a "family vacation," a phenomenon Charlie adamantly disdained. By August Marie found herself trolling for more work editing and consulting; she accepted a larger teaching commitment for the fall. Meanwhile Charlie at long last raised his fee to twenty-five dollars per adjustment.

Marie had maintained, and Charlie had acknowledged, that a phase of their Life had passed: they did no more "errands" nor would they accept any more; yet they had recently put their Lives on the line (along with their children's futures) to permanently block Chang K'ung from killing people. Since they had succeeded in everything and survived, their mission henceforth was clear: they had to fulfill the fact they were alive. Thus Marie determined they had to adjust to a phase of Life analogous to aging, and they would adapt to it, and use the adjustments to their advantage. When she articulated that last point to Charlie, his face beamed his pride in her attitude. "Fine by me," he said.

January 23, 1996
Hsinchu, Taiwan

Gazing out her office window from the city's newest high-rise, Hsiu-fen Wu decided to give in to the whim she had resisted dozens of times since early the preceding summer. She got up and left her office to look down the corridor to the reception area: all quiet, her associates gone, staffers on break. She decided to gamble: probably she could justify telephoning the United States at government expense, even though the number she would call was to a private residence. Hsiu-fen settled behind her desk, prudently took a deep breath, and tapped numbers on her agency telephone. Connections occurred, lines hummed; her hands trembled and she had to remind herself to breathe. Finally she gasped as she realized the last connection was occurring. Hsiu-fen sat motionless and listened to a telephone ringing many thousands of miles to the east and north, in a household in which, she presumed (correctly), the evening meal had long been completed.

After four rings someone picked up the speaker. From across the ocean Marie's composed, resonant voice said "Hello." Chagrinned, Hsiu-fen didn't know what to say. She sat frozen, trying to apprehend the situation to which she'd gained electronic entry.

Was that music in the background? Hsiu-fen thought so. The womanly voice came to her again, tinged with good humor probably founded on happiness: "Hel-lo! Anybody there?" Still Hsiu-fen sat as though frozen, and the disconnection occurred.

What if Charlie had answered? Would she have said anything intelligent? Hsiu-fen had to wonder this, although she felt sure that she would have said the right things and then asked the right things. Was Charlie happy? Was he married? What was he mostly doing with his life? (She knew that he was called "Doctor Grumbles," but she had no idea of what he was a doctor in.) Would they meet soon? She would have told him her own schedule was very flexible.

Clearly Charlie had lied; Marie was an integral part of his life. To think otherwise struck Hsiu-fen as absurdly naive. She recalled quick images of Charlie and Marie dancing and interacting with each other at the Raffles Hotel one oppressive afternoon. *I should have known that woman would answer the telephone.* (For a few moments Hsiu-fen speculated on Charlie's most likely reasons for lying to her. Given, he wanted to meet Chang K'ung in private. Were those his only reasons? Maybe. Did she attract him? Yes. Did she attract him strongly? Yes. This explained little or nothing.) *I must be missing something.*

Hsiu-fen was long reconciled to Charlie having been right about Chang's vision and probable tactics being too dangerous for anyone's good. She was also sure now that Charlie had been right about something else: she could serve her family and country more effectively if she first cultivated her own good. That was why Hsiu-fen had exploited, almost recklessly, her late employer's clout and reputation and the myriads of favors owed to him (also to her) by people in very high places. With ease she had "networked" her way (to use an Americanism she'd adopted) into the diplomatic corps for a few unsatisfying months, then transferred laterally to a deputy directorship of intelligence operations for South America, a job she found to be anything but boring.

Oh, yes. Hsiu-fen felt positive about one thing in her future, and almost sure about something else: She would have the Life to which she aspired and to which she was entitled. Soon she would be in a position to go afield and seize it any way she deemed best. (In the process she would remove herself from the advances of that aggressive Major Chen.) And Charlie, with his blue eyes and boyishness and American home, would be a definite part of her intended Life.

****

"Sometimes I think I'm gettin' old," Charlie remarked to Marie a few nights after the second consecutive Christmas when they had received warmly worded greeting cards from Taiwan and Costa Rica. One, addressed to "Charlie Grumbles and family" was signed "Suzi Wu," the other, addressed to "Marie Overstreet and family," was signed "Sam."

"You're probably no older than the last time you thought that," Marie said as she got into bed. She wore a short, low-cut nightie and—she expected Charlie would notice—nothing else.

Despite only dim lamplight in their bedroom, Charlie noticed. He had come out of the shower feeling worn out by his day at the clinic and a hard weightlifting workout at the gym, for which he'd been ill-conditioned by over a week lay-off caused by holiday obligations. (Already he anticipated the next day being a short one.) But his condition began to change once he got close to Marie.

"I hope everything's still workin'," Charlie said as he burrowed under bed covers to get closer to her.

Charlie had refrained from putting on the boxer shorts he customarily wore to bed, and this Marie noticed well. Just outside their bedroom a compact-disk player emanated Miles Davis creations, utterly cool.

"I'd say it's startin' to work just fine," Marie said after they'd made all kinds of mutual physical adjustments accompanied by much tittering.

"Uh-huh!" Charlie said, giving in to projections of pleasures rather than fantasies.

"Uh-*huh!*" Marie said, doing likewise and rising from under Charlie to emerge on top disabused of nightwear. In a little while their special scent and noises made Charlie prudently tear a look past Marie to see if the door was closed, which it was. *Ah yes.* Then came total abandon, doubly. When Charlie could open his eyes to behold her, Marie had never looked so amazingly good to him, and to Marie Charlie had never been so unspeakably dear. Even after the ecstasy, everything was almost unbearable.

Eventually Charlie spread covers over Marie and they lay quiet for several minutes. They held hands, their faces open to the ceiling.

Charlie spoke haltingly: "It's really hard to, uh, you know . . . believe . . . At least, for me it's hard to believe. Someday . . .y' know . . . we won't be doin' this."

"How's that?" Marie demanded.

"Well, we won't be here, on Earth."

"Hey, that's a great topic to bring up."

"It just seems so . . . incredible."

"I know."

Gap of silence.

Marie said, "Maybe we can leave together, somehow."

"It'll be a bitch if we don't."

Another gap.

Marie said, "We will always be *we*. I just can't believe otherwise."

Charlie gave a deep little laugh. "I think by now you're stuck with me."

At the moment they harbored more or less the same notion: some things can never end. To believe otherwise would be like saying that the *source* of their abilities to love or create or understand . . . can die. For Marie as well as Charlie, that did not seem possible.

****

If Gansu Province was not the end of the Earth (as they say in the West), it lay athwart the frozen footpath leading to it. Lin Piao, formerly the honored "Mo Tzu" in General Chang's envisioned New China (and always aware of the elevated status which had almost been his), squinted through cutting wind and dry snowflakes to assay his new demesne. He had never known such desolation. With nowhere else to go, he stepped back into the stalled train. If the tracks ahead were clear, it would take him—and his wife and two grown sons—on the final leg of a journey to veritable exile in the provincial so-called capitol (the name of which he could barely pronounce). Only one positive thing could come of this: his situation would likely get no worse.

Somehow, somewhere, Lin's career had been nudged into a helix by some process inexplicable. Was a widespread conspiracy at work to undo him? Maybe so, but Lin could identify no part of it. Was he the loser in some secret vendetta? Perhaps, and it was elaborately, brilliantly hidden. He was aware only of some vague innuendos against him, all intimating that he'd been somehow disloyal to the Republic and therefore—most importantly of all—to the Party apparatus. Yet no one, anywhere, had ever alleged anything specific about him. He had long stopped wondering what happened.

Aside from what Westerners called "horniness" (never something to titter about) Lin's most primary problem was straightforward and (formerly) anomalous: he could not arrange to leave the country even for a day. Fate seemed to have locked him in. No matter how he contrived things in the various jobs to which he'd been posted in the last two years, he could not get out of China. Now he would be lucky just to get out of Gansu Province.

In Lin's envisioning, the hundred thousand dollars of General Chang's money languishing in secret bank accounts abroad that only he could access would someday, somehow, be used. *By him*. The conviction alone vested his life with a purpose. As he gazed out the train window at darkening frozen wasteland, he was pleased to know that the animus of his existence—having his revenge on that American couple whom he had learned so much about from that worthless priest—was actually causing him to feel warmth emanate from his core.

With a rare smile, while he reflexively ignored his hard-bitten wife, Lin addressed and instructed the two sullen young men in his company whom he called his sons: "You know, of course, that where we go many of the populace are Muslims."

Yes, they knew. And so?

"We will learn something valuable from them."

Did he feature learning anything in particular?

"Islam teaches—Islam imparts—patience," Lin intoned.

*

March 12, 1999
Austin, Texas

Looking ahead to the university being closed for spring break, Marie could see herself deserving a respite from intellectual overload and teaching responsibilities. Probably a short vacation—preferably in Costa Rica, if she could get a good deal at a resort she'd heard about—might be the perfect means to recharge her faculties. She decided to broach that prospect to Jed, who might have been likewise needful. First she broached it to Charlie, despite already knowing his response:

"I was thinkin' of takin' Lisa on a forester's expedition up north," Charlie said, referring to gathering seedlings in Colorado. After brief discussion he added, "Looks like we'll be takin' separate vacations; that's about as bourgeois as you can get."

"Well, I can't say that's a good idea," Marie said. "It's more than a few levels below the trips we used to take—remember, back in a different life?"

Charlie loosened a vocable, nodded, and indulged in a short reflection.

Even if an "errand" were offered to them, they would decline it now. Their reflexes for operating out of country, like their appetite for same, were probably blunted. They had too much at stake to take any unnecessary risks. "That sure *was* a different Life," Charlie commented.

*

March 31, 1999
San Jose, Costa Rica

By 11:00 a.m. Hsiu-fen Wu had been able to extricate herself from the Taiwan diplomatic-mission office near downtown and had gone to meet her favorite lunch date, this time at the Costa Rica tourist-visa office. Why Sam wanted to meet her there, she couldn't have guessed. Maybe he was trying to make their lunch together appear work-related.

"Hey, Suzie, you're early!" Sam Wallaby called to her as soon as she stepped inside the visa office.

Job-related or not, they embraced heartily before Hsiu-fen displayed her diplomatic identification card and seal at the entry desk.

"You look great," Sam remarked as soon as he could.

"Hooh! I think I am pie-eyed. As you say."

"Well I hope it's from too much fun."

"I wish."

Hsiu-fen did look weary. Her duties as chief of intelligence-gathering for the region encompassing Mexico and Central and South America were onerous by any standards. The operation in which she worked Sam characterized as "cost-cut to the bone." To Hsiu-fen's mind this was the price she paid for freedom and upward mobility.

By achieving "clout" (Sam's term for success in her case), Hsiu-fen would gain freedom, which to her meant being enabled to use all her capabilities and be sufficiently rewarded for doing that. Resultant fulfillment and dignity would help restore honor to her family. Thus far she was successful, even beyond expectation. But as Hsiu-fen had become more aware of her biological clock winding down, she felt the time was overdue for her to focus on a different objective: fulfilling her own deepest yearnings. To accomplish that, she had even devised a timetable.

"Let's go in," Sam said to Hsiu-fen. "I'll show you something interesting."

They were admitted to the bureau, where Sam led Hsiu-fen to a desk in the middle of common-use office space on which stood a Dell computer and printer. The female clerk seated at the desk smiled up at Sam and pushed a sheaf of print-outs toward him. He and she interchanged pleasantly in Spanish and Sam took up the print-outs, scanned the top three pages, and removed one, which he handed to Hsiu-fen.

"Take a look at this," he said to her, and when she did he pointed to an entry under the heading "Turistas—USA."

Hsiu-fen saw the name Mary Overstreet, which meant nothing to her, but the point of origin, "Austin, Texas," waved a flag.

"Is Charlie coming here?" she asked Sam.

"I don't see his name anywhere," Sam replied. "Looks like his wife's coming, though." And very vaguely, Hsiu-fen felt the timetable for her future begin to telescope.

During lunch at a working-class restaurant both favored, the two still-unlikely associates became confidants, a development toward which they had been segueing for the past six months.

"I know you're interested in Charlie Grumbles' . . . uh, situation," Sam averred right after they'd placed their order. "You want to know about his life. I've gathered this from little things you've told me."

Hsiu-fen allowed Sam's insight as true. And she revealed she had had similar intuitions about Sam's interest in Charlie's wife, based mostly on the way he had referred to Marie during various occasions over the last several months.

"True enough," Sam responded. "So we—you and I—have a lot more in common than just our work." (An emphatic little gesture.) "Uh, your work and my job."

"We have a chemistry," Hsiu-fen ventured. "I believe in that. Don't you?"

"Yeah. Chemistry, and our brains working on the same wave length. Something like that."

They nodded in agreement. After only a few minutes of discussion over salad, even before their entrees arrived, Sam felt free to say, "You have serious plans for Charlie, don't you?"

Hsiu-fen said, "Maybe. I think you have plans for his wife, Marie."

"Let's say I would have, if I could. It's only desire."

Each fiddled with utensils for a moment or two.

"If you have desire, you have goals," Hsiu-fen declared.

"Ye-uh . . . that's true. I'm not what you'd call a homewrecker; I have no desire for that. But I *could* be, I suppose. I don't know . . . ."

They allowed that subject to slide away, but they had crystallized an understanding. And to Hsiu-fen, a psychic door she was vaguely aware of possessing suddenly opened a little, which caused her to feel a comforting strength.

Later, when they had finished their grilled fish and while they debated whether to order dessert, Sam remarked abruptly, "You know, you really are a lovely, vibrant woman. I'm sure Charlie's going to be one very lucky fellow."

Hsiu-fen accepted the compliments with easy grace. "Maybe we can help each other," she offered.

Sam affirmed that, then he said, "For openers, if Marie's going to be here alone, I'm gonna make every effort to spend time with her. If I find out something that might be useful to you, I'll tell you right away. Now that's for openers. Between now and the next time I see you, let's give the matter some thought."

Sam intuited that Hsiu-fen was already looking ahead to Marie's arrival in country for reasons only Hsiu-fen could explain. He didn't know that across the table from him at this very moment an eruption of violent images was flashing across Hsiu-fen's mind, and she sat horrified by what she saw.

Hsiu-fen had to make a rigorous effort to appear to be listening to Sam as he commented about the deteriorating political-military situation down in Colombia, a situation to which he was privy. Despite that government's strides toward effecting internal peace, Sam said, insurgencies were increasingly endangering American lives and U.S. interests in that country. Within the next week Sam might have to go there to do some work, he said, as probably his "last hurrah" before he retired from his Agency job.

Again Hsiu-fen envisioned violent images, now clearly involving—and physically consuming—the formidable Marie Overstreet. Most compelling, everything she saw was plausible. Could she *cause* the evil scenario she envisioned to actually happen? Yes, she could if she had the right kind of help which, probably, she could arrange to get. *God have I come to this?* Hsiu-fen wondered in either Minnan or Taiwanese, and her subconscious response affirmed that she had.

Sam had finished talking and Hsiu-fen bestowed upon him a bemused, feminine smile known to charm all men.

"Call me," she said.

Austin, Texas
About the same moment

"You really are the light of my Life," Charlie said to Marie. He had always considered it pure understatement when he said that to her. Marie knew it to be true, and she responded with a look of unfathomable endearment.

Charlie and Lisa were almost set to leave for northern New Mexico; Julia had left earlier to be with her friend's family. Marie was also getting ready to leave for her short vacation trip, which she would take alone since Jed had gone to Hawaii.

"We should be back mid-day Friday," Charlie said. "I want to talk to Lisa's teacher before school lets out. Plus I need to get by the clinic before the weekend."

"Boy, the weekend seems a long way off," said Marie. This was Tuesday. They were expecting a separation of five days.

"You can be sure I'll be plenty horny for you by then," Charlie said softly, trying to avert being overheard by their little girl.

Marie gave him another soft look. Charlie allowed himself to replay a series of images from the night before when, utterly spent and satiated, they lay naked and holding hands on their bedsheets. That was when Charlie said what Marie usually remarked on similar occasions: "*This* is what I was made for, you know."

And Marie had slowly turned her head to regard him and said, "We've been on a great ride together, haven't we?"

Her remark struck Charlie as unrelated to everything in the moment. He pondered it briefly and responded, "It's been a *beautiful* ride!"

Charlie suspected what turned out to be true: For the rest of his Life on Earth he would recall those words from Marie at least once a day, usually fondling each one in turn, with great pride and wonder. And for most of that week, Charlie regretted not having told Marie the same thing she had said to him as they prepared to travel separate ways that morning. Later, he felt grateful about his omission because sometimes it helped him grasp a tiny bit of detachment.

What she said just before their final so-long was, "Remember, I can't imagine living without you."

April 1, 1999
Aguas Zarcas, Costa Rica

She had barely checked in at the resort office, and as sticky and grimy as she felt from her trip, even in her hurry to reach her bungalow and use the *baña*, Marie wished Charlie were striding alongside her. The resort, called "El Tucano," was located in the back country—an area Marie and Charlie had only read about—and when Marie exploited the opportunity to gaze across a lovely green river at pristine jungle (flashing with incredibly colored birds), she missed Charlie all the more.

"Gee, whiz!" she announced to the world, and she decided to go back inside the bungalow only to pour herself a drink to help her enjoy the setting better.

To Marie's surprise the telephone was ringing as she stepped inside. Expecting the caller to be the resort owner, she was doubly surprised to answer the phone and hear a familiar male voice and it wasn't Charlie's.

"*Hello*, beautiful lady! Welcome back to La Costa Rica," Sam Wallaby's voice declared happily.

Almost instantly Marie felt at home. After she and Sam exchanged felicitations and gambits, she was surprised by his disclosing that he might not be able to see her before she went back.

"I'm supposed to be retiring, you know, but it looks like I'll have to go down to Colombia, in the state of Quindio, which is not too far from Panama, and rescue some Americans or something," he said. "By the time I get back you might have flown the coop on me."

"I really can't feature you retiring," Marie said. "I'll be here through Saturday."

"Well, it's possible I'll get back to San Jose in a day or two, and then get over and sweep you off your feet."

After they rang off Marie felt both relief and disappointment. She thought Sam could never sweep her off her feet, as he'd said only half facetiously, but it would have been fun to see him try.

"Wooh!" said Marie, and quickly replenished her brandy.

*

San Jose, Costa Rica (same day)

Sam had done what he'd said he would, and as shadows began to lengthen he sat at a sidewalk table with his favorite (and easily most attractive) foreign counterpart.

"Ye-uh, she's here all right, and she's alone," he told Hsiu-fen Wu. "I really don't know what's going on with her and Charlie, though. I couldn't see fit to ask her."

"Can't you go to find out?" Hsiu-fen asked.

"I'd sure like to. Believe me. Right now, though, it looks like I'll be going down south for a bit. You know, Colombia. It's something I've gotta do."

"Ah. Man of integrity," Hsiu-fen said lightly.

"Maybe sometimes."

"Will it be dangerous, what you must do?"

"I hope not."

"I hope not, too. Really." Hsiu-fen's own sincerity surprised her pleasurably.

Sam talked about when he would leave (probably the next day) and how Hsiu-fen could locate Marie in the back country (not easily). For several minutes they discussed the situation in Colombia. Both understood that sometimes Hsiu-fen could do her job simply by tapping into Sam's knowledge of a situation, based on reports he'd seen from a variety of first-hand sources.

Hsiu-fen found herself intrigued by everything Sam told her about the escalating level of violence in Colombia. Foreigners there could find themselves in life-threatening situations. A thought arose in Taiwanese: *Is this not a portent?*

They parted after a pleasant forty-five minutes together. Sam had to get home; Hsiu-fen had a "date." As Hsiu-fen watched Sam recede from her sight she found herself envisioning once again scenarios too dreadful to retain: Explosions. Skeins of invisible bullets pounding stucco, rending metal. Desperate men bearing automatic rifles and grenades charging in different directions; men in uniforms firing weapons from behind ruins. Idiots. Maniacs. And—*unavoidably*—Marie somehow afoot amid that viciousness, unable to step beyond it. Completely disappearing—Hsiu-fen shuddered psychically. Then she felt her forehead contracted, her jaw clenched; she consciously directed herself to relax. After a few moments the realization dawned: some things she had wildly fantasized were now resolved, for she would cancel her date that evening and go to Aguas Zarcas in the morning.

Hong Kong (about the same time)

Dismayed by his feeling like a foreigner in a city he used to call his second home, Lin Piao stoically tried to mask the emptiness this temporary assignment was causing him. On very short notice he had been tabbed to substitute, briefly, for a member of the Republic's trade mission to this former British possession. He was in no position to have declined. But despite his seniority in dealing with Hong Kong relations, his mission status was decidedly most junior.

Thus largely ignored, Lin had some freedom to follow his fancies, so he made a solitary visit to the old Queen Victoria Hotel. There in the wonderful bar room he was delighted by a waitperson actually remembering him from those times in his heady past when he had been an honored guest at the hotel. *Who else might remember me in my prime and glory? Perhaps a large number of people!*

As he sipped and savored a martini, his drink of choice when he traveled abroad, Lin allowed his memory to run out a series of estimable faces from his past. Most belonged to bankers and service-industry captains such as hoteliers and chefs (and perhaps a few high-priced prostitutes). But after Chang's and Madame Platonov's, the most significant faces belonged to a few senior ROC military officers whom he had hardly known but who used to regard him with deference. Likely, they were thriving in Taiwan as they had been when Chang K'ung was alive.

I would be surprised if any of them realizes the extent of his good fortune. As always occurred when Lin looked back, everything he associated with Taiwan arose in tandem with a desire, now an obsession, both hot and steely: Total Revenge. Any way he could get it. Not by his own hands—probably—but directed by him. Somehow.

Impulsively Lin extracted from his identification packet his old white-on-black photostated Ministry-Office-Building permit. Several numbers on the face of it, when combined correctly, and with the addition of two one's and a zero, actually comprised a telephone number. Knowing that telephone number was by far the biggest secret of Lin's life because when he had used it, say, from Brunei or Manila, only one person would answer (twenty-four hours per day unless he was in the shower): General Chang K'ung.

Could Lin recall that digit combination correctly? Easier than he could recall his wife's name! To check himself, he did it (with ease). Casually he looked around the sumptuous bar room: to everyone there, he hardly existed.

This might be the perfect time to try using it. But why? To see who, if anybody, answers. For what? In case .... *Revenge.* He didn't have to complete the thoughts. He simply removed himself to the right end of the bar where he remembered making telephone calls years before. There he ordered another martini, laid down a few hundred Hong Kong dollars, and requested to use the telephone. As developments unfolded for him this evening, Lin almost conceded to a sense that some things were actually preordained. After he'd tapped in Chang's secret telephone number, to his surprise—and acute anxiety—instead of a dead line he heard a series of short buzzes. For an instant the line fell silent, and a man's voice in a different world said in Minnan, "Colonel Chen here."

Lin remembered the name of Chen, General Chang's most trusted subordinate, a mid-level officer named "John" whom he'd met twice, only briefly, but whom he recognized as Chang's alter ego, a generation removed.

"I am Mo Tzu," Lin said in Cantonese with quiet emphasis, and despite the language differences between himself and John Chen, Lin imagined he heard the young officer snap to attention.

Lin knew that this was neither the time nor place for a private conversation between two people who did not use a common language, but he suddenly decided to at least try to establish contact with his past and with people who could wield freedom as a weapon. And to his immense pleasure his boldness found reward. As both men utilized their vague acquaintance with each other's language, Mandarin and Cantonese met electronically and melded in ways prescribed by blood. However haltingly, they managed to communicate with each other.

Lin (sporadically assayed by fellow bar patrons) brought the loud process to conclusion by announcing, "We will meet tomorrow at 5:00 p.m., at the ferry landing, Hong Kong side." He had a proposition to offer, and that would be a feasible time and place.

For his part, Chen declared, "Sir, I will be there." To decline would have been unthinkable.

Chapter 16

San Jose, Costa Rica
April 2, 1999

With glances at the sunrise beyond the balcony of her apartment on Calle Madero, Hsiu-fen Wu found herself acting entirely on her whims. (I may be half crazy, she thought, but my desires lie deep.) Exactly why she was going to Aguas Zarcas that morning she refused to define. After she'd left Sam Wallaby on the previous evening she had notified Lorenzo Garcia, a local driver contracted by the diplomatic mission, of her intention. He would pick her up at 08:00.

Do what I must do. There was no good reason to temporize. Marie had long had her day. Wu Hsiu-fen—specially gifted, indisputably hard working and sacrificing—was equally deserving of fulfillment (and happiness) as Marie. Who could deny that? A change—likely a drastic change—was required to remedy the disparity between them. And now Marie was alone outside her own realm, a development that had to be providential.

Hsiu-fen took up her telephone and called (not awakening) her friend and admirer, ex-General Zhou, one-time pillar of the New T'aip'ing Revolution, now posted to Bogotá as charge d' affaires for Taiwan's diplomatic missions in South America.

She could almost hear Zhou's face split into a smile when he realized who was talking to him. Of course he would help the luminous Miss Wu in any way she wanted. Nor could anything be too irregular for him to undertake on her behalf.

When Hsiu-fen asked whether Zhou could arrange for one or two Republic Of China citizens to be temporarily incarcerated (on any charges that might be feasible) in the Colombian state of Quindio, he laughed. Consider it done, he told her, whenever she wanted it. He asked if she was aware of dangerous "hostilities" in that area and was informed that she knew that guerrilla warfare seemed to be fairly intense around the city of Pereira. Could General Zhou arrange for the incarceration to be effected in that city? He gave it some thought: No problem with that. It could be arranged that very morning.

Briefly they discussed a few logistics such as how temporary the detention would be and who might be involved (employees of an oil-drilling-equipment company owned by ex-Colonel Tian, who used to be one of Chang's personal favorites). Then Hsiu-fen vented her main wish: to hire an assassin, a local sharpshooter, to kill someone whom she would take to Pereira.

That caused Zhou to pause, mainly because they had been talking on an unsecured line. But they were speaking in Minnan, and Hsiu-fen invoked General Chang's name.

"Tell me more," said Zhou.

"I will tell you, sir, that she is the American woman who—along with a consort—met with General Chang K'ung on the morning of his death. They met him at the American hotel."

Ah. Zhou remembered that woman quite well. He had seen her and a man, presumably also an American, meeting with General Chang (and his female companion) over breakfast at the Far Western Hotel. He himself had been there; afterwards he'd been detained for questioning in connection with Chang's death by Singaporean police.

Hsiu-fen allowed Zhou to draw his conclusions.

"So you want her killed?" he said.

"Yes. Please. I will pay whatever the assassin requires."

"Again, that should be no problem. But I will tender payment."

"I will reimburse you. I have plenty of money."

On that point Hsiu-fen stood firm. Without so stating she made clear that this undertaking was for her a matter of honor. Zhou was truly impressed by her fierce loyalty to the memory of their dead leader. They suspended finalizing key details regarding Marie's appearance in Colombia until Hsiu-fen would have met with her.

"I will need good luck in making things happen correctly," Hsiu-fen declared. "I must avoid precipitating anything . . . unseemly . . . here in Costa Rica."

"I understand, dear lady. I wish you all good fortune in your endeavor," said the honorable Zhou Qiang.

They would talk again that afternoon or evening when Hsiu-fen would call Zhou using a cell-phone number he provided.

After she'd hung up, while she readied herself for her drive into Costa Rica's back country, Hsiu-fen realized that the tumor of remorse inside her had shriveled to a mote. In its place she couldn't deny a burgeoning feeling of elation. And that was appalling! Thus she determined she could cancel the plot simply by not calling Zhou later that day, although she couldn't feature herself turning back now.

While Hsiu-fen waited the last ten minutes for Lorenzo to pick her up, she indulged herself in a faux French pastry she had bought after she'd met with Sam the past evening and cancelled her date. Gazing out from her balcony she took several moments to reflect on what she was ultimately striving to accomplish. *What do I think I will get from Charlie?* She decided to acknowledge it: What she wanted from Charlie, what she expected of him, was . . . everything. Nothing was to be withheld. For a true bond to thrive between him and her she had to be satisfied, she had to know, that he was hers in every way, exclusively. If she had to eliminate any obstacles to his commitment to her, well, she would erase them, whatever—or whoever—that might be. She couldn't see otherwise.

Shortly before twilight Marie leaned forward on the deck railing outside her *cabaña* to stare at the darkening forest on the other side of the river. Birds of various sizes sailed into it; bats of different sizes sallied out of it. Fireflies flickered on both banks of the quiet green water. From scattered points, monkeys called out as though conspiring something serious. Marie smiled in her awe as images and shades of color transmuted from moment to moment.

She sipped cognac from the small snifter she had been holding, then sighed. Imbibing it felt so good in such a setting, despite her tongue having been numbed by too much of the local *aguardiente* she had been offered throughout the day.

"Ah-h-h!" she vented happily to everything before her, and almost simultaneously a musical voice off to her right rose to the deck to meet hers: "Hed-droe!" it sang.

Marie glanced toward the source of it, then turned to regard a vaguely familiar face and form approaching the deck.

"Hello to you," said Marie, momentarily stunned by seeing this visitor from contexts totally foreign to this one.

"Your friend from Taiwan!" Hsiu-fen identified herself. "Also from Singapore."

For Marie, the "small world" of Father Nobles had suddenly become smaller. "Come on up," she said and resumed fixing on the forest across the river.

Hsiu-fen joined Marie at the railing and together they gazed at nature receding in the dusk. After a few moments Marie declared: "Charlie loves rivers and trees. He'd love it here."

"Ah," was all Hsiu-fen could respond.

Another moment passed before Marie asked, "Are you staying here, I mean, are you staying at this resort?"

"No. I came here to see you."

Marie regarded her visitor levelly. "Come inside," she said.

They went into the cabin and Marie turned on a lamp. "Don't mind the mess here, please," she said. "I'm on vacation."

She motioned to a settee; she and her guest got seated. After Marie's what-can-I-do-for-you, Hsiu-fen related her report about two Taiwan citizens being incarcerated (wrongly) in Pereira, Colombia; and her job—an urgent one in the circumstances—was to effect their release. For that she needed help, crucial help, from someone who could speak Spanish well and who was savvy in South American ways. Thus she had come to Marie after ten hours of riding on back-country roads to find this resort.

"How did you know where to find me?" Marie asked.

The answer she'd half expected: Sam Wallaby had told her.

Marie had other questions: Couldn't Sam do a better job of helping? Could Marie get Republic-Of-China diplomatic status to enter Colombia? (She had no visa to that country.) If she went to Colombia to help, when would they leave and return?

Hsiu-fen answered that Sam was too busy "trying to retire"; she hated to impose. Her other answers conveyed images of an easy trip. It would take most of the next day. Barring bad weather and earthquake, they would be back either that night or, perhaps, the following morning. Visa problems were already resolved.

"Isn't that kind of a dangerous place to be goin' to?" Marie asked.

Reports of danger there were exaggerated, she was told; still, the hostilities in that part of Colombia gave Hsiu-fen's objective more urgency.

Marie felt reluctant to go even though Hsiu-fen's mission might be important. However, it looked potentially interesting, if only because it would afford Marie the chance to learn more about the impressive Suzi Wu and what kind of work she was doing. But most intriguing: Marie might learn what Suzi had experienced during the last four years resulting from General Chang's untimely death. (Of course, Marie would allege knowing only what she had heard on television news.)

After thinking about all this while she poured shots of cognac for herself and Hsiu-fen, and while each enjoyed their initial sips, Marie again leveled her gaze at Hsiu-fen's earnest face and declared the inevitable:

"Well, I guess I could use a trip to Colombia."

"Oh, thank you! This is very great relief."

"No problem. I think. But it's gonna cost you a mighty big lunch."

"Sure!"

And with this, Hsiu-fen featured herself released onto the chute that would promptly deposit her—just like that fictional Victorian-era English girl—in a metaphysically distant place from which she could never return unchanged.

****

April 3, 1999
Pereira, Quindio state, Colombia

Strong. I do what I must do all the way, Hsiu-fen had told herself several times during the last twenty-four hours. But now, seated in the taxi, she added: *What have I leaped into?*

She stole a look at Marie and saw calmness. Simultaneously she was startled by a perception she had realized the day before at the resort: Marie looked older than she had expected. This caused Hsiu-fen comfort for reasons she knew to be irrational.

Suddenly Marie said, "Geez-us! Watch out!" This was directed at the back of the cab driver's head as Marie and Hsiu-fen found themselves hurled directly at a manned roadblock that the driver avoided smashing into only by wheeling the cab into a U, then abruptly turning into an alley. This was the second time the driver had done this.

Marie reached to touch him. "Take it easy. No hurry," she declared.

That seemed to work. The driver used a more leisurely speed to wend them through outlying barrios and skirt roadblocks, taking them ever closer to the central part of the city. Behind his sunglasses the driver appeared stoical, but Marie regarded him as a crazed *kamikaze*, consonant with everything else she'd experienced on this trip to the beautiful Andes.

For Marie and Hsiu-fen, the flight to Colombia had been maddeningly late; their landing had been rocky. As soon as they'd exited the airport they saw recurrent military activity. Their route into town showed signs of recent fighting. Marie regretted her decision to come here and heartily hoped they

446

would reach the municipal-government complex without incident. So far they'd been lucky, she thought.

With a jerk the cab sped up recklessly, and Marie and Hsiu-fen saw why: a gun battle between a squad of government soldiers and irregulars was in progress right next to an intersection through which they were passing. "*Mierda!*" the driver spat.

They didn't try to dissuade him from speeding clear. A few moments later the cab topped a small hill in a crowded working-class neighborhood; on the decline it turned onto a wider road vectoring to the right. To Marie the street looked deserted; she was pleased to see some open spaces in a few of the blocks they passed.

Exactly as though they had reached their destination, the cab slowed and stopped at the edge of the road fronting ramshackle two-story houses. The driver put the transmission in park and turned to Hsiu-fen. He spoke furtively, hurriedly; Hsiu-fen sat mystified until she asked Marie, who hadn't heard all the words, what the driver had said.

"I think he said this is Park Street," Marie replied.

"Oh." Again Hsiu-fen sat looking mystified, immobile.

Again the driver turned and spoke to her, this time urgently but with more clarity: "*Andele descolgars de carro conmigo.*"

And again Hsiu-fen asked Marie to translate.

"He wants you to get out of the car with him."

"Oh." —Said with a focus on something extraneous. — Are you sure?"

Marie admitted puzzlement. Then to her surprise Hsiu-fen swung open her door and slid out to the street to join the driver, who looked anxious even behind his dark glasses. Marie heard—or thought she heard in Spanish—"We leave the road," said with urgency. Utterly astonished, she watched Hsiu-fen and the cab driver bolt across pavement to the other side of the street where they disappeared from her view.

What the hell's going on?

As Marie reached for the door handle to leave the car, something tore through the edges of the cab roof, buzzing past her head very dangerously close. She knew that was a bullet but she couldn't frame the thought until splinters flew at her from both front-door windows taking another hit.

"Damn!"

Marie dropped down on the car seat and pushed open the door Hsiu-fen had exited, intending to make for the street. She wanted to get low outside the cab and keep it between herself and whoever was shooting. Of course she had no idea as to the source (or sources) of the gunfire, only that more rounds tore through the cab perceptibly close to her.

As Marie pushed herself off the car seat through the partially open doorway she felt something unthinkably quick and hard smash through her right ankle. It happened so completely that she felt both pain and numbness as she heaved herself away with both arms, knowing already that she was disabled.

"A-h-h-h-a-a-kh!" Marie hit the pavement next to the car and scrambled to keep herself shielded, aware of at least two more rounds violating metal and glass above her. *Meant for me. If this doesn't quit I'll be killed,* she thought, and pulled herself close to the front wheel of the car, hoping hard that the gas tank wouldn't explode, which did not happen although she distinctly smelled gasoline.

Gunfire at the riddled cab had ceased. Marie lay on the road with one hand pressing the cuff of her slack above her injured ankle to stanch blood flow. She had no idea of what to do next; all she could do was feel gratitude that Charlie wasn't there, for he surely would have tried to shield her and probably would have died.

Marie spotted soldiers moving toward her from down the street. Up the street, people scattered for cover, but several briskly came toward her. *Oh no!* The situation Marie saw was not a delusion, and she pushed herself under the edge of the taxi.

In the next moments rifles opened up from both directions. Marie could only lie flat and hope for good luck in the crossfire. She couldn't see other guerrillas attacking the government troops from three directions, trying to encircle the soldiers who retreated and disengaged.

The whole exchange took less than two minutes, although to Marie it felt like a long ten minutes. More time oozed by while nothing happened. Then Marie realized she was looking up from under the cab at grim young men and women with rifles looking down at her. All wore civilian clothes, frayed and dirty. Soon they were joined by several comrades. Marie thought they looked very young, resolute, and underfed. Every one of them acted skittishly, attuned to the likelihood of army reprisal.

At least four times Marie had to shout her name, nationality, and explain why she was in Colombia. Finally the guerrillas helped her get out from under the cab. She leaned on two of them while others applied a tourniquet to her leg above the ankle. They gave her analgesic tablets that she washed down (unvolitionally) with canteen water.

Concealed by foliage and trash across the street, Hsiu-fen observed Marie's situation and felt more grateful than frustrated. (*The woman is alive!*) Somehow this might work out for the better, she thought, while resolving not to be defeated. But now she had more immediate concerns: *If only I survive this! I will try hard to live a better life.*

She didn't know where the driver of the ill-fated cab was, although she expected he would come back for her (which he did some minutes later). At the time he was crouched in a cluttered alley talking on a cell phone to report his having completed his job. A minute later Hsiu-fen saw Marie being lifted onto the back of a stocky brown man as the guerrillas began melting from the site.

They moved quickly, first on foot then by vehicle, to the suburbs Marie had passed in the cab. Although she had slipped into shock Marie recognized certain landmarks such as a vast garbage dump. She also spotted obvious places where the guerrillas could have left her for rescue such as a church and market, but they never stopped at those places. What they wanted her for Marie couldn't conjecture; she only knew it was to her detriment.

After nearly an hour of traversing *barrios* and skirting military and police checkpoints, the guerrillas holding Marie joined a large group of their comrades on the southeast edge of Pereira. There they had a stronghold of a few square blocks of huts and row houses from which they forayed. Marie was taken up a short hill to a one-story stuccoed row house which served as their headquarters and overlooked the hardscrabble neighborhood. The leadership would determine what to do with her whenever they next got together. Marie meanwhile was left to drift in and out of consciousness and worry about contracting gangrene and how to get to and use *la letrina*.

Lord if I survive all this I'm gonna be more careful till I die. This she resolved, when she was lucid, many times over.

*

By late afternoon Sam Wallaby had arrived at the Pereira municipal-government buildings and been ushered to police headquarters where he promptly met with the mayor and a colonel of the army. He knew it was urgent because he'd been summoned by the U.S. Embassy in Bogotá, the regional Colombian army chief, and by Hsiu-fen Wu. They had contacted him easily and he'd arrived quickly because he worked from the Quindio Public Safety Directorate at the state capitol in the adjacent city of Armenia. By the time he met with Hsiu-fen he knew that Marie Overstreet was the American woman captured that day by leftist insurgents.

"So what in the hell was she doing here?" Sam demanded of Hsiu-fen, who told him that Marie was helping her secure the release of Taiwan citizens detained by local authorities. The effort was to have taken only one day.

When Sam asked her for details Hsiu-fen related: "Civilian fighters, you call them guerrillas, attacked a military patrol. We were coming here in taxi and got caught . . . right in between. I got away; driver got away; Marie is wounded, I think in right leg or foot. She could stand on one foot. I saw her do this, then they took her away. She went on piggy-back."

Sam said, "Thank God! It could have been a stupid, horrible waste. I would never have imagined . . . ." The scenario was too absurd to contemplate.

Sam caused Hsiu-fen and police to identify the ambush site on a wall map. Then he and various soldiers tried to determine which way the rebels had gone and where they might be. Meanwhile Hsiu-fen allegedly had her own work to do and she arranged for escort to the Quindio prison. She felt satisfied that no one would accuse her of complicity in Marie's travail, let alone substantiate any link between her and the initial shooting. She would simply wait for the outcome of it all, then try to turn it to her advantage.

After a half hour of conjecture with a number of policemen and soldiers, Sam determined the southeast corner of Pereira to be his focal point. "I need a Jeep and a driver," he said.

Sam felt he could have driven himself anywhere in the Americas in the all-terrain vehicle consigned to him; he requested a driver in case he'd be busy with matters other than transportation. To countervail needs for luck Sam knew he'd have to be resourceful.

When he set out to find Marie he carried only one twenty-dollar bill in *yanqui* money and about five thousand pesos in Colombian currency; not quite enough to kill him for (perhaps). But he carried an authentic promissory note drawn on the country's most prominent bank; it was already co-signed by the bank's director in Medellin. The amount was blank as was the principal signature.

Sam also took a holstered flashlight, a machete, an infantry shovel, and two canteens, one filled with fresh water, the other with rum. Plus he took a pint flask of brandy. His most important equipment was a first-aid kit for army field medics, supplemented with morphine-loaded hypodermic needles, Seconal pills, and a few paregorics, plus a half-dozen fair-quality cigars. He had managed to induce some soldiers to sell him their nutrition bars. The field kit and supplies went into a thick canvas satchel with an attached shoulder strap.

Sam could have packed a sidearm but disdained that. He had a stubby combat knife concealed under his belt buckle. He could shoot a jet of acid several yards from the eraser end of an orange wooden pencil displayed in his shirt pocket. That was all he would need, along with a transponder concealed inside a worn-looking cake of soap, which he carried in a pocket of his bush jacket.

With barely an hour to dusk, Hsiu-fen, standing outside police headquarters, watched Sam climb into an idling vehicle and get taken away. On the off-chance that he'd see her, she waved firmly and was surprised to see him wave back. She resolved to tell Sam, as soon as she could, that she had suspended her designs on Charlie because of her first priority: assisting citizens of her country. She had needed Marie's help to do her job well in Colombia, she would tell him. The Man of Integrity would understand this.

Sam and his driver, an army corporal wearing mufti named Fernando, passed through a half-dozen military and police checkpoints until the road stopped at a barricade of building rubble, rocks, and two burned-out cars. Even in the half-light, snipers could have hit them from various points beyond the barricade.

Sam didn't hesitate. Gripping his satchel, he bounded from the ATV and clambered over the barricade, expecting Fernando to be waiting for him under nearby trees. On the other side of the rubble he strode down the street until he met some people.

Police and army officers back at headquarters had primed him with two *noms de guerre*, and Sam inquired about them a few times to no avail. Then he asked only to be directed to "The People's Army," and people assisted. Twice he was asked what he wanted; he replied that his girlfriend was there and she was wounded in the leg. Plainly here was a man on urgent business.

In about a half hour, accompanied by seven or eight curious or concerned people, Sam topped the low hill capped by the stucco row house, at the first entrance to which he was detained by a clutch of heavily armed men. After he told them why he was there—and that he represented no government, which was true in effect—they led him inside to await summoning.

The room in which Sam waited for about ten minutes was furnished only with a chair, a stool, a bare table, and a stump of a candle for light. A curtain covered the doorway; just outside he could hear people moving about, weapons bumping or scraping cement walls, orders being declared, brief colloquies by youthful-sounding men and women. He was aware of references to the "older" *gringo* at hand. Sporadically he listened to a radio newscast emanating from nearby.

When Sam was led into a room with a door and electric lighting, he found himself scrutinized by three dark faces belonging to people seated at a simple table, two men and a woman, all thirty-something years old. A fourth person, a woman of like age, appeared to ignore him as she worked on electronic equipment along the far wall. Sam nodded curtly to each of the three faces and stood silent until asked his business.

He told them that his "close, dear friend" was the wounded *gringa* they were holding, that in no way did he represent any government, and he was there solely to aid his friend. They listened impassively. Then silence.

Sam dispelled the deadlock, first by drawing his wallet, then by removing the pesos and dollars he carried and spreading the money on the table, meanwhile demonstrating that he had no more.

"This is all the money I have. For your cause."

He displayed his sincerity by voicing a terse plea to be allowed to help Marie. The three faces searched each other, nods ensued, agreement emerged. A woman's voice told Sam, "Yes. Go ahead. Do what you must."

"Thank you," Sam averred and nodded to each in turn, then to the fourth person who had turned about to observe him.

Three voices enunciated an order, the door swung open, and two men beckoned Sam from the room. He followed them outside the house, passing among several armed people milling about; then he was led to the next entrance. When Sam saw the door opened for him, he fully expected, beyond any doubt, to enter a place at once forbidden, sacred, and somehow mortally dangerous. He felt positive that his life was about to change drastically. Lord help me, he prayed despite himself as he stepped in.

From outside and within, the house looked identical to the one Sam had just left. He passed a room with a curtain covering the doorway. But in the room with a door and electric lamp—instead of communication equipment along the far wall, a pallet lay over a layer of straw on the floor. Marie—motionless but emitting desultory vocables—lay uncovered atop the pallet. To Sam the room smelled bad but didn't reek, probably because the lone window held no glass and the shutter was ajar.

At first Sam was hard pressed to provide Marie much relief. She was sick from the water and drugs they had given to her. She was weak from loss of blood, dehydration, and inability to eat. Pain further sapped her capacity to cope with anything. She drifted into frequent bouts of oblivion. Still, Marie recognized Sam almost as soon as she got a good look at him.

"Thank goodness you're here," she said, and Sam felt a thrill beyond words.

He helped her get a bit less uncomfortable, then focused on assaying her damaged ankle. When he first saw it he uttered an expletive. On closer examination he determined it was manageable. Blood loss had been stanched; the main problem was painful sensitivity caused by the bone break. Sam had to perform serious first aid, which was not his forte. Then he had to induce Marie to drink the purified water in his canteen and to eat a nutrition bar. He fashioned a crutch for her from a rifle stock someone had given to him so she could pull herself up to move about.

Over two hours had elapsed. The morphine and liquid combined with nutrition definitely got Marie to feeling better.

"Think y' can get me outta here?" she asked when she sat up on her own power.

"Eventually. Yeah, I think so."

"Listen. Tell Charlie where I'm at, but tell 'im I'm gonna be okay. —Okay?"

"Yeah, sure."

Marie became insistent about her request. She wanted to preclude her daughters and Charlie getting excessively worried. Again Sam acceded. And he did resolve to comply, although contacting Charlie was not one of his priorities. Finally he kissed Marie warmly on the forehead, squeezed one of her wrists, and declared it was time to arrange for removing her.

*

"She needs medical attention immediately," Sam told two of the commanders, a man and the woman.

Already people were sleeping in the row house. Sam knew that unanimous consent among the commanders was prerequisite to moving Marie, and that would entail waking the other man and possibly the second woman he had seen earlier. All right, he said, that must be done. The man and woman to whom he spoke didn't concur, and the woman, heavy-eyed, abruptly broke off discussion and left the room.

That left but one *subcommandante* to dismiss Sam or to deal with him, and Sam decided to play his trump card. The man, called Luis, appeared to be the oldest member of the group; he probably had a family. If he did, he might be susceptible to money, Marxist or not.

"Have you family?" Sam asked absently as he felt in his jacket pockets for something elusive.

455

"My wife is dead."

"Your children, are they alive?"

Nod, affirmative.

Sam produced the bank draft. With a ballpoint pen he filled in two-hundred thousand pesos, signed it above the signature of the bank president, and left the signee line blank. Urban guerrillas knew how to cash such instruments with impunity.

"This will be good," Sam averred, looking Luis in the eyes. "For whatever purpose you see fit."

Luis glanced at the check but didn't touch it.

"The amount is inconsequential for a North American," Luis said. "She might be worth a million yankee dollars."

"Nah. She will die before you are able to make your demand known. And who will pay it? As her dearest friend, this is all I have to offer, Luis. I ask that you help me. Please."

Luis appeared irresolute. Sam waited and tried again.

"If you don't help us, she will die. I will die."

From the visible effect of his plea Sam ascertained that Luis was now on his side.

"I think I can carry her to a place where we will find transportation," Sam said.

"I will advise my comrades of this tomorrow," said Luis. "Maybe then you will take her away."

Sam tried again. Again he was told maybe tomorrow. *Shit*, he uttered silently as he saw the matter closed.

Luis wrote on a half sheet of unlined paper: "Please help Mr. Wallaby meet with me on 4 april, 1999

Subcommandante Luis"

His signed title and name dominated the bottom part of the paper.

As he handed the paper to Sam he said, "By eight o'clock would be good. Nine o'clock . . . maybe too late."

"Thank you" and "until tomorrow" was all Sam could say.

He gave Luis a cigar and departed the headquarters office and went back next door to see Marie. She lay looking comfortable, now covered by two shawls Sam had gotten earlier.

The light was still on; Sam saw her eyes open as he spoke to her evenly.

"They might let me move you tomorrow morning. Sub-commander Luis [he stressed the name] is aware that you need prompt medical attention. In the meantime, I've gotta go back and make sure we'll have transport. Is all this clear?"

"Yes," Marie answered. "Will you tell Charlie and the girls not to worry?"

"As soon as I can."

Sam left her with the Seconal, a hypo of morphine, another nutrition bar, the pint of brandy, two of the cigars, and both his canteens, along with instruction to use the rum primarily for wheedling favors from guerrillas guarding her.

He also left the foil-wrapped bar of soap he'd been carrying in his pocket, from which—he thought—he had removed the tiny transponder. If he had, he wondered later, what had he done with the little device? He thought he'd hidden the thing inside his first-aid kit. But from his last moments with Marie, all that he could recall vividly was indulging himself in kissing her forehead again, along with another squeeze of her wrists.

"Have a good night," Sam remembered telling Marie as he turned to leave her, and he heard a soft response that sounded like "Thank you."

*

When dawn had begun to open, Sam Wallaby sent Fernando out from the vehicle in which they'd spent the night (uncomfortably) to find something for them to eat, preferably with coffee. Fernando had had success; thus Sam was fortified to go back to guerrilla headquarters and—he profoundly hoped—return over the barricade bearing a disabled, much-beloved person.

At seven o'clock, after requesting Fernando to wait for him until at least evening (which both presumed and hoped wouldn't be necessary), Sam set out in high spirits to complete his mission. When he'd safely cleared the barricade, he decided

457

that he might try to contact Charlie during the coming night. But that was barely a concern.

This morning looked brilliant (though a bit misty); to Sam the effect was undeniably salutary. A few people were out and about; when he and they made eye contact they usually waved or nodded. Apparently word had spread about the lone, formidable-looking *yanqui* toting a medical kit, bound to rescue his lady love. (He never had to show his safe-conduct pass from Sub-commander Luis.) Sam thought the *barrios* he traversed, all cramped and crumbling, many bearing unmistakable signs of gunfights and fires, were about half inhabited. He saw no evidence of any kind of industry and had to wonder how residents there supported themselves, although he did see a few shops opening and clusters of vendor stalls coming to life.

As Sam strode along, internally projecting things he would have to do that day, twice he was pleasurably distracted by radio music—*salsa*—emanating from open windows. For him that made the high point of the morning. Without analyzing his lot, he realized he'd rather—much rather—be doing this than anything he had ever done.

By his own reckoning, Sam's route between the barricade and the hill capped by the stucco row house was about two kilometers long. He mentally noted difficult or dangerous spots along the way that he would have to bypass on the return trip, aware that he would gladly carry Marie inside a vein of quicksand or fresh lava at least that far.

Just after Sam had mused that his getting killed in crossfire or by a maniacal sniper was not his main concern because if that happened he wouldn't realize it, he rounded a corner and gazed up a block-long hill to spot the guerrilla headquarters. At that same moment, sputtering gently, a faded, nondescript little sedan likewise turned the corner and passed him. Sam glanced over his shoulder at it. The front-seat passenger, his window down, casually rendered a gesture of greeting. Luis, on his way to work.

"*Commandante!*" said Sam, a bit surprised. He strode up the street after the car, becoming more keenly aware of a jet-plane roar inside a bank of low clouds beyond the hilltop—and then seeing the jet plane, reflecting sunlight from wingtip to wingtip, in the second before it dropped into a shallow dive and almost instantly pulled back up.

It might have been an American- or a French-made fighter jet. Sam couldn't tell whether it ejected or simply released a payload before it swooped over.

Intolerably gross noise slammed into Sam's inner ears. He saw the row house and Luis's car completely obliterated by orange and yellow light in a long instant. Pieces flew skyward and everywhere.

As Sam stared, horrified, everything on the top of the hill less than a block away ceased to exist except as pieces of flying and raining-down rubble.

"Geezus!" Sam said. His whole being froze. Then he had to resist running uphill to the smoke-enshrouded spot, a purely futile act.

The urge to self-preservation made Sam bolt in horror toward safety on the other side of the barricade. That was a good thing, for the area lay in the grip of a closing pincer movement of Colombian army units bent on extirpating rebels. En route, as he clambered over rubble in haste to avoid crossfire that had already begun, Sam's shoulder bag slipped away and fell into an aperture at the base of a wall where he had to leave it. Just as Sam rejoined Fernando, government troops closed off the route he had used.

****

At first Sam could not entirely believe he had seen what he had seen. For three hours he waited with Fernando; there was no going in again. All he could do was return to police headquarters.

By the time Sam returned to the municipal-government buildings, seemingly everyone there with whom he associated knew what had happened. Army and police officers, a few city or state officials, at least four Americans connected to the consulate corps—all regarded him with relief. Some congratulated him on returning safely. Those who knew of his personal reason for undertaking the mission commiserated with him.

Soon after his arrival Sam watched television news footage of the surprise attack on rebel-held *barrios* and was positive that he got a good look at the hill where the row house had stood. Now, except for debris, the top appeared to be vacant, level. Later, from a radio broadcast he heard about the "discovery" and complete destruction of insurgents' headquarters within the city limits of Pereira. He knew that he would never learn with surety whether he had directly contributed to that occurring by having carried in the military-supplied transponder, which he had taken on the advice of police officers and the army colonel and which he thought might be useful in rescuing Marie. He knew he would never attempt to find that out.

As many times as Sam related his experience of that day, to U.S. State-Department and intelligence operatives, to Colombian officials, and to journalists, he still had to tell it all to Charlie and Hsiu-fen Wu, which he did, dutifully. Hsiu-fen he apprised later that day. Charlie he managed to contact the next evening. After both those episodes he dissolved into tears without realizing it until he saw them roll past his nose.

"I'm going back there tomorrow," Sam declared after he had told Hsiu-fen about what he had seen. "Maybe they'll let me go through. It's something I've gotta do, God damn it."

"I am sorry for this," Hsiu-fen responded evenly.

After a brooding moment Sam remarked, "You're the one who could benefit from this, you know."

"I know, but I am sorry," she said. "I wish . . . other things."

*

460

The next morning Sam did go back to the late site of the guerrilla headquarters—and Marie's last point of existence on Earth. He didn't expect to find anything recognizable amid the rubble, and except for the destroyed car in which he'd last seen Luis, he found nothing to examine or commit to memory. Marie had completely vanished. Not a trace of her existence had survived. To Sam's perplexion, a well-dressed Asiatic man accompanied by two army officers and a local resident also inspected the site. The Asian and the officers nodded affirmatively among themselves as they walked about and appeared to ignore Sam as though he were a journalist.

When Sam contacted Charlie by telephone he found himself narrating details to a person who was essentially in shock.

Charlie had already received the news from the State Department and then from different sources. Regardless, Sam concisely told Charlie whatever he could think to relate. Charlie responded with a dullness which belied the anguish and tumult he was undergoing. Even though they hung up perfunctorily, both men understood that Charlie was grateful—and he would always be grateful—for the details that only Sam could have provided about Marie's final day.

During that same evening Qiang Zhou managed to contact Hsiu-fen Wu, partly to congratulate himself on arranging what she had wanted, partly to emphasize his willingness and ability to do whatever else she wanted.

"Colonel Tian said he personally walked upon the site where that American woman was held prisoner by insurgents," Zhou told Hsiu-fen by telephone. "The Colombian air force—totally dedicated to quelling rebellion—could not be restrained. I am informed—unequivocally—that she no longer exists."

"That confirms what I hear," Hsiu-fen responded.

Setting the matter aside, Zhou added that perhaps he and lady Wu could meet in Bogotá that weekend.

Hsiu-fen expressed her gratitude for great favors well done. Unfortunately she was ill from her own recent experiences, she said. (This was partly true.) She had best go home as soon as she could travel.

Privately Hsiu-fen acknowledged that her mental processes astounded even herself. She would go home, indeed: she would travel to her future home as soon as feasible. Charlie might need her consolation. For sure, he needed her. And she was ready to fill every role open to her. Eventually, she expected, she would transcend, perhaps justify, her responsibility for committing outright evil.

*   *   *

*   *   *

We have learned that everyone—during those private, deepest moments that people cherish—feels a longing for something unknowable. When we're alive on Earth that "Something" can't be known because we had forgotten, so to speak, what it is. We can only feel a deep, deep longing that never goes away. I think you know what I mean, even though being conscious of that longing might occur only once in a while.

Now Charlie and I can explain what happens: while we're on Earth we feel a pull toward home. That's exactly what it is, a constant pull. And we are blocked. For a time we simply can't go home because we have to stay in our own Lives. But that pull is a major part of our going home. It's something we all need, and most people are glad to have it, despite the melancholia we feel when we savor it

*

I can verify what Marie has just told you from my own experience although we're talking about a sweet mystery of existence. We, Marie and I, would reveal it better for you if we could. We have yet to learn the reasons for it.

462

I will add something: Our deep, deep longing, as Marie calls it, opens the way for us. We, all of us, have to eventually go home. When we do, the longing makes our partings less difficult. Marie and I hope we can ease the way for you by what we have just said here.

*   *   *

FINALE

Some disclosures about Charlie and his existence without Marie might be helpful now, and I can provide them.

Beginning the moment he realized that Marie no longer existed on Earth, Charlie decided his Life was over. Before his shock had dissipated he actually went to Quindio State in Colombia and scrutinized the site where Marie had last breathed, then returned home and methodically began dismantling his existence.

He had found no trace of Marie's presence in Pereira, for which he felt relief because to him her departure seemed more dignified by completeness. He wished not to recall the name of the resort at which she had stayed in Costa Rica, and he successfully misplaced information about it, so he never went there to retrieve her belongings. That sad business fell to Sam Wallaby, who undertook it to his detriment.

I could not really blame Charlie for his overall decision, nor would Marie have, although I tried to persuade him otherwise. Life, with a capital L, if a person can *Live* it, is an outright gift, an exquisite gift of divinity; a person must never decline such a thing. Charlie knew this, but he must have determined that it no longer applied to him. Presumably he regained his mental clarity (which for several days had been frozen to opaqueness), yet he never changed his attitude or decision about his Life having ended. This was despite his bonds with his children and all his ties to human reality.

463

Benjamin, Jed's husband, heard that Charlie had stopped practicing chiropractic and was selling his clinic.

"What's going on?" he asked Charlie. "Are you gonna work for somebody, or what?"

"No," was all Charlie said about the matter.

Marguerite Grumbles, Charlie's mother, tried to allay his despair to no avail. He simply told her, "I don't want to be attached to life-support systems."

The focal point of Charlie's existence was tending to his daughters, who were adapting to their mother's passing with more facility than Charlie thought imaginable, even though he felt unconvinced that they fully understood she would never, ever return to them. Telling his nine- and ten-year-old daughters about death—specifically their own mother's death—was the hardest thing Charlie had ever faced up to and done. When he sat them down and revealed the facts to them—while trying, with fair success, not to appear devastated and to apparently be in control of immediate reality—they surprised him by their ability to comprehend what had happened in their Lives and what that was going to mean. He would never know the degrees to which they suffered in secret, partly to protect him from their distress.

Of course neither Lisa nor Julia could fully realize the meaning of their mother's death. For that Charlie required assistance and reinforcement from concerned people such as his own mother and Jed and—most unexpectedly—Janette, Marie's older sister, who came to Austin for a week from West Texas. (Charlie thanked heaven, literally, for them all.)

And in unexpected moments during the following few months the girls would derail Charlie's psyche by asking questions such as: "If I talk to Mama, will she hear me?" Charlie's response was always affirmative. He had no doubt that she did. In fact he communed with Marie all the time. Thus he carefully told the girls: "Just make sure that when you talk to her you think about her real hard. You can't think about anything else, either. And you have to be careful, real careful, never to lie to her. Whatever you say to her, it has to be true."

"If Mama's out there—you say she can be everywhere—what is she doing?"

This was a question that recurred a few times, to which Charlie responded, "I really don't know. Maybe she doesn't have to do anything. [Beat.] I suspect she's discovering things. Things we can't ever know about until we're with her."

"Things like why do people have to die?"

"Yup. That's what she's finding out, I think."

And sometimes came the question Charlie feared and needed: Did he want to be "discovering things" with their mama. He always answered affirmatively, tersely, and let it pass. They could never imagine how much he wanted that.

Two weeks after Marie's passing, about a week after Charlie had returned from Colombia, several people (led by Janette Overstreet) held a memorial ceremony for Marie. It was a simple outdoor affair on the north bank of the Colorado River near downtown Austin, at a spot where Charlie and Marie had walked or run together untold dozens of times. Except for possibly Jed, no one knew that the spot was only about fifty feet from where Charlie and Marie had married each other. At the service, Charlie could barely focus on anything that was said or read aloud or sung or played on instruments.

Afterwards Jed was able to talk to Charlie. "Thank God we've still got you," she said. "We need you, Charlie! Benny thinks he knows how *Goyem* think. He says that you think you're going to join her by dying as quickly as you can. 'Well,' he said, 'that's just *meshuga*. —Uh, that's Yiddish for something illusory or maybe delusory.— Y' know Benny's right on, Charlie. I mean, what do *we* know about what happens outside this life. You know?"

"Yeah, I know."

"So stick around. We need you, honey. Don't be 'perverse' as you like to say."

"Thanks" was all Charlie could respond because he was thinking about his dharma, which meant his being with Marie. If Marie did not share everything in his Life, then to Charlie nothing had value. Thus he faced some ineluctable problems.

*

Exactly a week after the memorial event for Marie, the day after Marie's sister Janette returned to West Texas, Wu Hsiu-fen arrived in Austin and presented herself at Charlie's house. Actually, she had secured Charlie's explicit concordance for her visit, and he had been apprised beforehand of the day and (more or less) the hour of her arrival.

"Do come. We have plenty of room," he had told her. He had seen no reason to say otherwise.

Yet from the moment of their reunion Charlie shunned regarding Hsiu-fen with any warmth. I believe she thought he was preoccupied by exigencies and, naturally, she would change that. To her credit she almost succeeded. After a week Charlie became more congenial to her; for instance he showed her singular parts of the city and some of its environs.

When Charlie was not closed off to everyone including her, Hsiu-fen knew that he liked to look at her, so she dressed accordingly. (Once Charlie even told her that she looked pretty; sometimes he was bemused, very briefly, by her liveliness and femininity.) The girls loved her presence, and I believe she began to love theirs. Felicitously, Hsiu-fen stepped into and filled the role of a much older, exotic sister. Even Marguerite and Jed and Benjamin took a liking to her after their initial responses of astonishment and relief. Their relief stemmed from a sense that perhaps Hsiu-fen's presence caused—or would cause—Charlie to find good reason for Living.

My role was to simply watch things unfold as they would. However, nothing really noteworthy happened while Hsiu-fen stayed at Charlie's house and endeavored to integrate herself there. Two weeks elapsed.

On a Friday night, fairly late, Hsiu-fen and Charlie actually talked to each other for the first time. By then Hsiu-fen was feeling frustrated and discouraged, so she had vigorously initiated and pressed their interaction.

Was Charlie pleased to have her living in his home and investigating degree programs at the University of Texas? —

Of course he was. And was she enjoying herself and being properly accommodated? —Yes she was. Good. Soon the weather in Central Texas would be intolerably hot. Already it was too warm.

Did Charlie have any plans, might he have a vision, for his life? —No, he could not say that he did. Would Charlie care to learn of Hsiu-fen's desires for her life? —Brief silence. A flurry of mundane distractions initiated by Charlie. Several moments were stretched into several more.

Finally Charlie spoke to Hsiu-fen as though he were confiding something hidden: "Suzi, I'm sorry that I'm so . . . abstracted." (He made two-handed gestures indicating mental diffusion.) "You see, for me this is like . . . foreign territory. My place is not here. I belong with Marie."

Hsiu-fen briefly gathered her thoughts before she responded: "But you are here. She's not here anymore!"

Silence for a while.

"Maybe," Hsiu-fen resumed, "someday you will belong with a person—a woman—who is here with you."

More silence. Then their exchange dissipated to prosaic fragments. Two days later they almost talked again, but they never did. After most of her third week at Charlie's house, Hsiu-fen announced: "I must go back to my job."

A day later, she left (tearfully) in a taxi cab toward which Charlie waved cordially but with little animus as it took her away. He had opted, explicitly, not to drive her to the airport. During the twenty-four hours before she left, Hsiu-fen had told Charlie and his daughters and Benjamin that she would return when she could, yet I was sure that she knew she would not be back.

For Wu Hsiu-fen, the whole episode was not one of sound and fury (and pain) signifying nothing. She simply recognized her failure to win Charlie's commitment to her, and I suspect that she began to doubt her worthiness. She probably felt pressure to minimize her losses. She still had her work and personal context, and both begged for her return.

My job precludes my making judgements about, say, Hsiu-fen's motives or ethics, and I abide by that. I will say that Hsiu-fen had regarded Marie with respect analogous to the honor due an opponent in one of your serious sports or in war. Marie would have understood this. Allow me to add that judgements about a person's ethics are best left to God. Does God, the Supreme Being, make those judgements? If you were God, would you bother?

Many, many times (several times each day), including the weeks Hsiu-fen was staying at his house, Charlie would recall an image of Marie and find himself uttering a prayer of gratitude—not to God but to the whole cosmos, to all of Eternity—and he felt sure his sentiment went directly home. *Thank You*, he would say. Thank You for granting that I honored her and gave her pleasure all the times I did. Thank you for granting that I made her heart glad! Thank You. Thank You. Thank You. Many times he had given her good reason to smile; this he knew. —*Good thing for my existence, then.*— He could tell himself this every day with surety. His Life therefore had been a success. He needed this conviction to sustain himself because he was haunted by Marie's words reaching across to him from early in their relationship and recurring over the years: "Remember," she had said, "it hurts me when we're separated." Sometimes she would add, "It's unnatural." Every time Charlie recalled hearing that he would say audibly, "That's putting it mildly!"

Now, given my experience and my function and my design, I could reasonably expect to recognize self-defeating behavior. And *you* might expect that I would, and you would be right. However, as I eventually learned, I can be fooled. Nor was I alone: Benjamin Ethan Berman, Jed's husband and Charlie's dear friend, a man irreproachably shrewd, induced Charlie to implicitly affirm Living one May evening a year after Marie died. The breakthrough step: he made Charlie admit to at least the potential desire to have sex with some of the beautiful women they saw downtown. But neither Benjamin nor I appreciated how well the desire for death can be dissembled.

*   *   *

July 29, 2001

Charlie's home phone rang in mid-afternoon, and although he had the bell muted and his message recorder engaged, he rolled off his bed from a fitful nap to answer it. As he lurched across the floor space to take up the receiver before the fourth ring he wondered why he was doing that, and simultaneously he knew: he needed relief, any kind of distraction, from a dream involving Marie. Her voice still sang in his mind as he blurted "hello" into the mouthpiece.

To Charlie's surprise, the voice on the other end didn't belong to a huckster (as Charlie and Marie referred to telemarketers), and it addressed him in familiar tones: "Hi, Hollie. This is Frank the Dago. I hope you remember me, but I'm not surprised if you don't."

Frank. Frank-With-The-Italian-Name that Charlie couldn't recall, although he soon remembered it sounded similar to "Jacuzzi," had been one of Charlie's favorite friends through most of high school. After graduation Frank had gone Ivy League, then to the U.S. State Department. This much Charlie recalled after Frank's salutation.

"I've heard about your loss a couple years ago," Frank said, "and, hell, I'm truly sorry."

Charlie tried to accept the commiseration with grace.

Then Frank asked, "In all earnest, how are you doing now?"

"I guess I'm okay. Sometimes the . . . dreams really get to me. Even now."

"Ah. Did I pick a bad time to call—or is this a very good time?"

"The latter."

"Good." Then Frank declared that perhaps he could offer a service to Charlie. "It might be outlandishly inappropriate," he said, "but, for all I know, it's exactly what the doctor would prescribe. That is, if you can find a doctor who knows about your past."

Charlie's internal antennae sprang erect. "I thought you'd gone with the State Department," he said.

"Oh, I had. I'm not with the Guv anymore."

"You're not . . . . Then who do you work for? I presume you're working."

"You've heard of E-Systems Corporation. I'm with them now. That's how I know something about what you used to do in your spare time. Certain DOD people requested that I contact you. They haven't got anything to offer you, but my company might."

"You know this phone might be tapped," Charlie said.

"Not anymore. Even if it were, that's okay." Then Frank asked if Charlie would like to take an expense-paid trip as a kind of diversion. It would not involve doing much, although it might be a bit tricky, and the compensation would be excellent for a four-day "errand." (Frank actually used that term.)

The proposition took Charlie aback, but Frank said, "It might help you distance yourself from things that are maybe too . . . *immediate*. You know what I mean?"

Charlie started to say, "We swore off doing errands; the last trip my wife took was strictly on her own." But he checked himself. Something was prompting him to investigate the offer, which dovetailed perfectly with a notion churning in his subconscious and emanating up.

"Where does this 'diversion' take me?" Charlie asked.

"Thailand. Does that sound good? Maybe we can stretch it to five days."

"I don't know if I can be gone that long."

"It's up to you."

Charlie found his mind dominated by a word: *Perfect*. Everything fit: Marie was gone. He and their past remained. Times were changing. Drastically. Governmental organizations were changing, reconstituted by technology. That's why E-Systems was handling key intelligence functions. For certain parties in the Defense Department, it was time to clear the slate. They had only to hang him outside the pale—and cut him loose. He might even find himself, anomalous and gasping his last breath, back in Cambodia! *Fin*, as Marie and Madame Picard would say. But if this turned out to be merely his paranoiac delusion, the trip would be worth his while monetarily. Charlie felt he was destined to accept Frank's offer, and so he did.

Several hours after he and Frank finished their interchange Charlie still felt satisfied that he would have regretted declining the errand to Thailand. Ah, he wondered, but might he not be enticing some terminal fate to befall him by going alone to Southeast Asia? Maybe, but that couldn't be substantiated, not yet. Besides, when Charlie tried to project his own oblivion, it felt good. *I can't help it if they nail me.* And Julia and Lisa and his son Brent: they were well provided for.

Come on! This was sick, Charlie thought. They (whoever "they" were) couldn't really "get" him, at least not easily. He had too much savvy and experience. Unless, of course, some gross accident happened to him . . . .

Under the aegis of E-Systems Corporation, six days later Charlie found himself in the Los Angeles International Airport, getting briefed by a young woman attired in black named Sally Shipway prior to his flight to . . . Shanghai International Airport, People's Republic of China. I'll be damned, Charlie uttered to himself when he discovered his destination was not Bangkok. By this time Charlie felt himself committed, with no option but to proceed. Again he contemplated his being set up to take a fall. Still, he knew this was unlikely, remembering that several years before, Eleanor Gilchrest (Yes! That was her name.) of E-Systems Corporation had arranged for him and Marie to do joint errands for the Defense Department, a course of events that had worked out very well. Still, times had definitely changed . . . .

When he arrived in Shanghai, Charlie successfully repudiated his mission on the grounds that he was there because of a bureaucratic bungle. Moreover, he had not agreed to go to China, nor would he have. (He had last been to that country with Marie; he refused to return without her.) If he couldn't go to Bangkok (and points nearby) as agreed upon and as he'd been instructed initially, he would go back home. And so he did, despite having been paid three thousand dollars in earnest money ("some pretty fair wages just for sitting around in airplanes," Frank commented two days later).

During some obscure instant, though, possibly occurring before he had even left Los Angeles for overseas, Charlie actuated a phenomenon of which he was entirely unaware: the fact that his existence was to include a stay in Shanghai had become electronic information, available in a flash to anyone who could access it. This development would have seemed innocuous to Charlie had he learned of it, and only one person on Earth would have considered the bit of information to be of any significance. Collaterally, that person happened to access it.

****

In Beijing, Lin Piao, now a sub-cabinet-level functionary on his way back up the hierarchy in the Commerce Ministry of the People's Republic—and coveting a position in Shanghai, his favorite city outside Hong Kong—perused a list of U.S. medical-equipment firms doing business in China. Names of company service representatives lately arrived in Shanghai from the U.S. came up on Lin's computer screen, and the name Grumbles, Hollis G. sprang off it.

City of origin? Los Angeles, California. However, Mr. Grumbles' home city came up as being . . . Austin, Texas! For Lin this knowledge was a catalyst.

Grumbles—a service representative? Maybe in some other millennium! —Never should he have been allowed to greet *this* millennium.— Lin needed no reminder that his existence was animated primarily by one desire: to avenge himself (and, yes, General Chang) on that cursed couple he had met at the Far Western Hotel in Singapore. He still kept, secreted in a desk drawer at home, notes on the information he'd extracted from Father Nobles. And now Charlie Grumbles was alive and (presumably) well, and still practicing his shameful Covert craft. . . in Lin's People's Republic!

Almost reflexively, Lin sent a coded Email message to an address in Hong Kong, where the message was relayed instantly to an address outside Taipei, Taiwan. The recipient, of course, was Colonel Chen, a man who considered himself true to his commitments. Essentially, Lin's transmission declared the time was at hand for Chen to act. Beyond the issue of honor, it would be worth Chen's while. They would meet in Hong Kong in three days.

*

September 1, 2001
Manila, Philippines

On furlough from the army in a foreign city he hated but found infinitely intriguing, Colonel Chen exited the Banco ng Pilipinas carrying more U.S. dollars than he had ever seen at one time, and that was only part of his fund. He was accompanied, one on each side, by two countrymen also on furlough from the army.

All three men carried black flight bags; all were well dressed, their sport coats and ties incongruous with the muggy ambience. (Chen, aged about fifteen years older than his companions, wore a bit more blue and gray than they.) Physically, the three looked equally fit.

They took a taxi to the Manila International Airport outside Quezon City. En route Chen explained logistics. He and his companions—who were actually his subordinates—spoke to each other in Minnan often interjected with English. They liked to practice using English, which two men would soon have cause to use exclusively.

"You will withdraw five thousand dollars each in what they call travelers' checks. You can do this in the Bank of America branch outside the Dallas-Fort Worth Airport." Chen added, "You have a joint account totaling twenty thousand dollars."

One of the men asked, "Why can't we withdraw ten thousand each?"

"You should not require it. Carrying so much money would be senseless. It's yours only if you need it for emergency."

The two men concurred. The Bank of America money was meant only to cover their expenses in the U.S. Their personal remuneration for carrying out the mission on which they were embarking had already been electronically transferred to their home bank accounts.

Chen was sparing no expense in accomplishing the objectives to which he was committed, although he had promised Lin Piao a scrupulous accounting of the 110,000 dollars entrusted to him. His men were paid twenty thousand dollars each, plus expenses. He would pay himself the same amount for directing and managing this operation, plus reimbursement for expenses such as the purchase of pistol silencers he had mailed piecemeal to an address (of an émigré software engineer) in Austin, Texas, and weapons he had already purchased and secured at the same address.

Before Chen saw his compatriots off on their trip he felt the need to render a final rubric. "Have good fortune and a pleasant sojourn," he told them. "Spare no speed in returning home, but make no unseemly haste."

One of the men responded in English, "Prices are high in Austin. We cannot afford to stay for weekend, unless we get bartending jobs!"

Chen feigned beleagueredness. He had been to their destination several years before. "That's why you go without me," he said. "On my salary, I would have to sleep in their jail."

They laughed ruefully, and soon Chen shook each man's hand and bowed to him, and he and they set off for different places.

****

September 3, 2001
Austin, Texas

Lisa and Julia would not be out of school for at least another hour, so Charlie had time to fill. Earlier this day he had consummated selling his and Marie's "ranch" (which he had refused to visit) jointly to one of his cousins and to a former business partner who had become a friend. ("At least it'll stay in the family," they all had said.) When Charlie had returned home he mowed the lawn in mid-day heat so it would look good to his daughters. Most of the mundane things he had to do were done.

Charlie feared and hated such times as this. He didn't feel animated to focus on anything consequential. He'd been able to sell the "ranch" only because he needed to be rid of it. But even if he kept himself busy he would unexpectedly hear Marie's voice—usually her last word would be about a specific subject—exactly as though she had just spoken to him from the next room. Naps were even more painful because dreams expressly involving Marie were always rife with immediacy. Sometimes he would recall his dreamed experiences as being utterly poignant even though, while they were happening, he *knew* he was dreaming.

But on the verge of waking from a nap, and during moments when his mind balanced on the cusp of wakefulness and sleep—those were Charlie's devastating times. From a soft mindlessness he would spring alert to Marie's voice saying very distinctly, "Time to get up, babe!" Other times, usually while seated in a chair and contemplating dozing off, he could feel—literally feel—his lips on her cheek or neck, or (*worse*) experience the two of them ardently kissing. Immediate but ersatz reality like that was reason for despair.

This afternoon Charlie was glad to occupy himself by taking a shower, and for once his mind caused him to experience something actually benign. As he dried himself with a towel, a skein of mental associations caused him to suddenly recall, of all the things available to flash on: televised images he had seen recently of Elvis Presley impersonators commemorating something in Las Vegas. The capper was the TV camera inside a transport plane watching perhaps eight impersonators simultaneously parachute out over a desert.

This recollection was too much to bear with a straight face. Charlie felt it coming, and it came: a laugh exploded and he couldn't contain it. After it happened he had to grin as the absurd images recurred in his mind.

"God-*damn*!" he said audibly, delightedly. He actually let himself titter.

As Charlie finished drying himself he realized that he hadn't smiled (other than pretending to smile for his daughters' benefit) since he could recall. And the laugh, definitely his first laugh in well over two years, caused him actual physical soreness. Dismay gripped him when he realized he hadn't shared the laugh with Marie, but he dispelled the pang.

Absurd, Charlie told himself, his head shaking. *Elvis impersonators*! Amazingly to Charlie, he'd been hearing about that phenomenon for over twenty years, ever since he'd returned stateside. And more amazing, he'd heard it was actually proliferating.

"Geezus, what next?" Charlie muttered and felt the corners of his lips twitching.

Naked and feeling dampness evaporating on his body, Charlie strode out the bathroom into his adjacent bedroom. Ah, *"The King"*! he thought in mid-stride and, loosening a tiny laugh, let himself recall the televised image of an especially outrageous Elvis impersonator.

Juxtaposed on that phantasm was Charlie's sight of two black-haired men in natty sport jackets standing near his bed looking at him. His head still wagging slightly from amusement and his face split by a grin, Charlie perceived the silencer on the end of the pistol pointed at his face and died without a thought, taking along a feeling uncomplicated and strong, much like the effect of a good sneeze. The unsigned letter from Shanghai informing Charlie that "the Angel of Revenge [was] on his way" and Charlie and his wife were going to pay dearly for having "spoiled a heroic vision six years ago in Singapore" arrived the next day. During a fit of grief, Jed pushed it into a pile of unopened mail, wrote "return to sender" on each item, and posted the lot.

*　　　　*　　　　*
*　　　　*　　　　*

CODA

This is not the end of our story by any means, if only because we've tried to hand Eternity—and you—a rose, and to a degree we've succeeded, although Charlie would agree that we've generated our share of absurdities as well. It's part of our lot as lesser gods, he would say, and that is axiomatic. Even Ariel can't evade the dictates of design.

Marie is saying that whenever we could, we lived on tiptoe, so to speak, from moment to moment to moment. Because we did that, reality has been enhanced. Our having completely vanished from Earth will never change that. We tell you this because you're designed for the same role we had.

Don't be too skeptical about the suprareality Charlie just mentioned even though you can't perceive or gauge it, for it's less unlikely, a lot less unlikely, than the existence of a beautiful planet encased in blue appearing in some little solar system at just the right distance from the sun, and then evolving actual life forms like people and birds and trees. If you hadn't experienced Life on Earth, you'd say, well, *maybe* such a phenomenon is possible—but only remotely. (*Very* remotely.) Most of reality simply doesn't compute.

Ah, yes. Relevant to those same topics we're supposed to tell you that Wu Hsiu-fen actually married Sam Wallaby and they located to the Boston area where she could do graduate work in a number of fields. Before he proposed marriage to Hsiu-fen, Sam visited Austin and left a red rose in our mail box. And Tatyana Platonov and her beloved Andrushka? They emigrated to Argentina and bought a small villa on the edge of Buenos Aires. Somehow they arrived there fairly well-to-do. You might as well believe this, for it's all true. You see, our source of information is unassailable.

Charlie and I want to tell you about how we are doing now, and we expect you will find this interesting:
The great serenity we're experiencing—it's really just a respite. Somewhere, we know, there is work for us to do, and we yearn to get on with it. Already we anticipate doing something that's ... thrilling! We don't know what it is yet, but it will be revealed.

*

*   *   *

Of course *I* am the "unassailable" source of information Charlie has referred to, and I get to conclude this because Marie and Charlie have said all they have to say.

478

As Marie has put it, some stories end very well. And she and Charlie would agree, with each other and with me, that no human story really ends; only our knowledge of it stops. Given my perspective, allow me to affirm this for you.

I want you to know something else: If I could have a Life anything like yours, even if I were convinced that no matter what I might do with it (and regardless of whom I might do it with), it would amount to absolutely nothing in the final schema of reality, I would be there with you right now anyway, with great gusto as Charlie might say. And if during your Lifetime that were to happen, and we—you and I—were to meet, I think you would recognize me, somehow, and I would be totally delighted.

*   *   *

ABOUT THE AUTHOR

Dennis Frank Tomas Maček, formerly a U.S. government operative, university English teacher, and air-conditioning technician, lives in Lincoln, Nebraska, with his wife Judith Kay Wilson, a retired professor of literacy. Both practice Zen Buddhism and are active politically to arrest climate change.

"I turned to A/C mechanics to gain freedom for me to write *A Rose from Charlie and Marie* and write screenplays. Marriage to my wife forms the foundation for my writing. We met at the University of Texas (in separate Ph. D. programs) in 1977. Judith is a master of many arts, including painting with watercolors, planting pollinators, and cooking pozole. She plans to learn yoga better. I am trying to learn to play guitar." --DFTM